CW00969815

GAIN-BASED DAMAGES

Gain-Based Damages

Contract, Tort, Equity
and Intellectual Property

JAMES EDELMAN

·HART·
PUBLISHING

OXFORD – PORTLAND OREGON
2002

Hart Publishing
Oxford and Portland, Oregon

Published in North America (US and Canada) by
Hart Publishing c/o
International Specialized Book Services
5804 NE Hassalo Street
Portland, Oregon
97213-3644
USA

Distributed in the Netherlands, Belgium and Luxembourg by
Intersentia, Churchillaan 108
B2900 Schoten
Antwerpen
Belgium

Hart Publishing is a specialist legal publisher based in Oxford, England.
To order further copies of this book or to request a list of other
publications please write to:

Hart Publishing, Salter's Boatyard, Folly Bridge,
Abingdon Road, Oxford OX1 4LB
Telephone: +44 (0)1865 245533 or Fax: +44 (0)1865 794882
e-mail: mail@hartpub.co.uk
WEBSITE: http//www.hartpub.co.uk

British Library Cataloguing in Publication Data
Data Available
ISBN 1 84113–334–5 (hardback)

Typeset by Hope Services (Abingdon) Ltd.
Printed and bound in Great Britain on acid-free paper by
T. J. International Ltd., Padstow, Cornwall

Preface

THIS BOOK IS the revised, updated and expanded version of a thesis completed as part of a doctorate at the University of Oxford written between 1998 and 2000. My doctoral studies were made possible through the generous support of the Rhodes Trust and I am indebted to the Trust and the Wardens during the period of my scholarship, Sir Anthony Kenny and Dr John Rowett, for their considerable financial and personal support and assistance.

I arrived at Oxford from the University of Western Australia having been briefly exposed to restitution and having, during my undergraduate studies, twice heard speeches from a visiting professor from Oxford, Professor Peter Birks. One of the themes in the second of these speeches was that restitution for wrongs was "behaving like a ship without a rudder". Different cases appeared to be going in entirely different directions. That lecture was the impetus for my desire to research and write on this area. Peter agreed to supervise the thesis and I had the dual benefit of a supervisor that never sleeps and is always available and always prepared to explain, discuss and particularly engage. I learned from Peter, and from his academic generosity, a great deal beyond the boundaries of my thesis.

Doctoral research is often a very solitary task. But rarely did I feel cast adrift into the enveloping sea of restitution and the waves of its many theories. Much of this was because of the kindness of many friends and the support of the academics at Oxford. Assistance came in many ways; from two very pro-active college supervisors, Colin Tapper and Katharine Grevling; support from my flatmates and close friends, Tom Rutledge, Danny Sriskandarajah and Liz Wall and Anya Emerson—who was there for me throughout; and from those friends and colleagues for their endless kindness in taking the time to discuss, debate, explain, assist, proof-read or comment: Chris Alexandrou, Georgia Bedworth, Adrian Briggs, Steven Elliott, Michael Izzo, Ben Kremer, Ewan McKendrick, Jonathon Moore, Dominic O'Sullivan, George Panagopoulos, Sarah Percy, Chris Savundra, Lionel Smith, Bill Swadling, Steve Watterson, Chris Withers and Sarah Worthington.

Although it is almost three years since I arrived in Oxford, this book has undergone a rapid evolutionary process. Much of the work on my doctoral thesis had been completed when the House of Lords delivered their decision in *Attorney-General* v. *Blake* which necessitated significant revisions. The *Blake* case is a watershed decision for English law which has entrenched the recognition of gain-based remedies for civil wrongs. The importance of that decision resonates throughout this book and especially in the chapter dealing with breach of contract. The book also incorporates numerous important decisions given after my doctorate was completed, including the important House of Lords decision on exemplary damages in *Kuddus* v. *Chief Constable of Leicestershire Constabulary*, and discussion of matters such as election and proprietary consequences of the analysis, which word limits did not permit in my thesis.

The book has also benefited tremendously from the powerful and searching analysis provided by my Qualifying Test assessors and final examiners, Mr Ed Peel, Professor Andrew Burrows and Dr Charles Mitchell, all of whom continued to correspond and discuss the thesis with me well after my exams were concluded.

It remains to express the great personal debt I owe to my family—Dinah, Ray, Talia, David, Lara and, most recently, Eva—for their constant love and support.

James Edelman
September 2001

Contents

Index of Authorities

Table of Abbreviations

TEXTS

J Beatson *Use and Abuse*	J Beatson *The Use and Abuse of Unjust Enrichment: Essays on the Law of Restitution* (Clarendon Press Oxford 1991)
P Birks *Future*	P Birks *Restitution—The Future* (The Federation Press Sydney 1992)
P Birks *Introduction*	P Birks *An Introduction to the Law of Restitution* (Revised edition Clarendon Press Oxford 1989)
P Birks (ed.) *Wrongs and Remedies*	P Birks (ed.) *Wrongs and Remedies in the Twenty-First Century* (Clarendon Press Oxford 1996)
A Burrows *The Law of Restitution*	A Burrows *The Law of Restitution* (Butterworths London 1993)
A Burrows *Remedies*	A Burrows *Remedies for Torts and Breach of Contract* (2nd edn. Butterworths London 1994)
R Chambers *Resulting Trusts*	R Chambers *Resulting Trusts* (Clarendon Press Oxford 1997)
W Cornish *Intellectual Property*	W Cornish *Intellectual Property* (4th edn. Sweet & Maxwell London 1999)
W Cornish et al *Restitution*	W R Cornish et al (eds) *Restitution: Past, Present & Future* (Hart Publishing Oxford 1998)
Goff and Jones	G Jones (ed.) *Goff and Jones on Restitution* (5th edn. Sweet & Maxwell London 1998)
Law Commission 1997	Law Commission *Aggravated, Exemplary and Restitutionary Damages* (Law Com No 247 1997)
Mason and Carter *Restitution*	K Mason, J Carter *Restitution Law in Australia* (Butterworths Sydney 1996)
Meagher, Gummow, Lehane *Equity*	R P Meagher, W M C Gummow, J R F Lehane *Equity Doctrines and Remedies* (3rd ed. Butterworths Sydney 1992)

Restatement on Restitution	American Law Institute *Restatement of the law of Restitution, Quasi-contracts and Constructive Trusts* (American Law Institute Washington 1937)
L Smith *Tracing*	L Smith *The Law of Tracing* (Oxford University Press Oxford 1997)
G Virgo *Restitution*	G Virgo *The Principles of the Law of Restitution* (Clarendon Press Oxford 1999)

COURTS

CA	Court of Appeal (Eng)
CABC	Court of Appeal of British Columbia (Can)
CA .. Cir	United States Circuit Court of Appeals (US)
CA Ken	Court of Appeal, Kentucky (US)
CANSW	Court of Appeal, New South Wales (Aust)
CANY	Court of Appeal New York (US)
CANZ	Court of Appeal of New Zealand (NZ)
DCNY	District Court New York (US)
FCA	Federal Court of Australia (Aust)
HCA	High Court of Australia (Aust)
HCI	High Court of Ireland (Ire)
HCNZ	High Court of New Zealand (NZ)
HCO	High Court of Ontario (Can)
HL	House of Lords (UK)
Man CA	Manitoba Court of Appeal (Can)
OCA	Court of Appeal of Ontario (Can)
PC	Privy Council (Cwth)
SCC	Supreme Court of Canada (Can)
SCCal	Supreme Court of California (US)
SCConn	Supreme Court of Connecticut (US)
SC K	Supreme Court of Kentucky (US)
SC Lou	Supreme Court of Louisiana (US)
SCM	Supreme Court of Massachusetts (US)
SCNH	Supreme Court of New Hampshire (US)
SCNS	Supreme Court of Nova Scotia (Can)
SCNSW	Supreme Court of New South Wales (Aust)

SCNY	Supreme Court of New York (US)
SC Okla	Supreme Court of Oklahoma (US)
SCQ	Supreme Court of Queensland (Aust)
SCSA	Supreme Court of South Australia (Aust)
SC Tex	Supreme Court of Texas (US)
SCUS	Supreme Court of the United States (US)
SCV	Supreme Court of Victoria (Aust)
SCW	Supreme Court of Washington (US)
SCWA	Supreme Court of Western Australia (Aust)

OTHER

BGB	German Civil Code: *Bürgerliches Gesetzbuch*
CUP	Cambridge University Press
OUP	Oxford University Press

Introduction

"WHEN AWARDING DAMAGES, the law does not adhere slavishly to the concept of compensation for financially measurable loss. When the circumstances require, damages are measured by reference to the benefit obtained by the wrongdoer."[1] So stated Lord Nicholls of Birkenhead in the leading speech in *Attorney General v. Blake*.

This book is an examination of two particular remedies given in response to wrongdoing, both of them gain-based—that is to say, measured by the gain or benefit to the defendant wrongdoer—rather than the loss to the claimant victim. It is argued that these two distinct measures are legitimate responses for torts, breach of contract, equitable wrongs and intellectual property wrongs. Further, the circumstances in which each of these remedies are available are rationalised and explained, providing a coherent framework within which this recognition of gain-based damages can operate.

The two monetary remedies for wrongdoing considered in this book are entitled "restitutionary damages" and "disgorgement damages". Restitutionary damages are a remedy which operates to reverse wrongful transfers of value from a claimant to a defendant. Disgorgement damages operate to strip a defendant of profit made by wrongful conduct. The crucial difference is that in the case of restitutionary damages the gain in question is that objective gain received by the defendant which has been wrongfully transferred from the claimant, while in the case of disgorgement damages the gain to be disgorged is that which has accrued to the defendant as a result of the wrong irrespective of whether there has been any transfer of value and not limited by any possible value transferred.

In proving the thesis that two forms of gain-based damages exist there are several hurdles that have to be overcome. The first is the view that remedies for wrongs can only be compensatory for loss and that a gain-based remedy for a wrong is therefore illegitimate. Closely related to this is the difficulty of using the word "damages" to describe remedies measured by gain rather than loss. The most convenient usage, and that advocated in this book, treats "damages" as any money remedy for a wrong and therefore tolerates "restitutionary damages" and "disgorgement damages". Chapter one confronts this issue immediately and examines, and rejects, the false view that the only money remedy available for wrongs is compensation. It is argued that the only way to define "damages" is as a money remedy for a wrong and that such money awards are not always concerned with compensation for loss. The false hegemony of

---

[1] *Attorney General v. Blake* [2001] 1 AC 268 (HL) 285.

compensation and the argument that it is co-terminous with "damages" are rejected by showing the legitimacy of exemplary damages as a remedy for wrongs, an award that is avowedly not concerned with compensation. Although this book focuses upon damages based upon gains to a defendant, and exemplary damages do not meet that definition, the study of exemplary damages is used in chapter one because there is no dispute that they are a form of "damages". Although there are some that argue that exemplary damages are not legitimate, their status and entrenched terminology as a form of "damages" is never disputed. By demonstrating the legitimacy of exemplary damages the exclusive link sometimes proposed between damages and compensation is broken.

The second hurdle to overcome is to establish that a body of causes of action can be collected together and classified as "wrongs". The conventional understanding of a wrong is confined to a common law tort, and torts are regarded as separate from otherwise similar events such as breaches of contract or conduct regarded as wrongful in equity. Chapter two argues that the category of wrongs spans both common law and equity and demonstrates how a wrong is to be identified. In many cases the process of distinguishing wrongs from other events, particularly unjust enrichments, is a very difficult task and involves consideration of the nature and operation of the event itself. In doing so, this chapter explains which events form part of the category of "wrongs" and will therefore be considered in later chapters.

The third hurdle lies in explaining the nature of these two different forms of gain-based damages; when and why they are awarded in response to wrongs. This question is confronted in chapter three and is the heart of the book and the core of its thesis. It explains the main thesis that there are two gain-based damages remedies available for wrongdoing. These awards are referred to as restitutionary damages and disgorgement damages. Chapter three also explains when each of these measures of damages are available and why and how difficult principles such as remoteness and causation and election between remedies, rarely considered in the context of gain-based damages, might operate.

The first of these two forms of gain-based damages, restitutionary damages, is explained as concerned with reversing wrongful transfers of value from a claimant to a defendant. Once a transfer of value is found to be wrongful a natural monetary response should be to reverse that transfer and restitutionary damages should be generally available. Restitutionary damages are measured by the objective value received by a defendant which has been transferred from the claimant's wealth. Restitutionary damages could therefore be said to focus upon an objective "enrichment" of a defendant and a requirement that the "enrichment" come "at the expense" of the claimant. These requirements are also two essential characteristics of an action in unjust enrichment. Thus there is a powerful parallel between restitutionary damages for wrongs and restitution for unjust enrichment. However, although it is now well established that an action for restitution is available to reverse illegitimate (but non-wrongful) transfers in unjust enrichment it is not yet as well accepted that a corresponding action for restitutionary damages exists where that transfer is *wrongful*. Chapter three establishes the theoretical grounding and explains how restitutionary damages do exist but are often concealed by obscure nomenclature. It explains the necessity of keeping restitutionary damages for wrongs and restitution for unjust enrichment distinct and separate.

The other gain-based damages remedy explained in chapter three is disgorgement damages. The remedy of disgorgement damages is explained as a remedy which operates to disgorge profits made by a wrongdoer as a result of a wrong. It is a remedy which operates, irrespective of any transfer of value, to provide deterrence where compensatory damages cannot adequately deter wrongdoing. This is in two circumstances. First, where a wrong is committed with a view to material gain and the profit made exceeds the compensation payable. In such a case it is only possible to deter such deliberate wrongdoing by showing that any profit made will be disgorged. Secondly, in cases of breach of fiduciary duty, even profit made by innocent commission of that wrong must be stripped as there is a need for such a high level of deterrence to protect the institution of trust inherent in the fiduciary relationship.

Two schools of argument oppose the recognition of a remedy entitled "disgorgement damages". The first lies in the view of many commentators that a single term should encompass both gain-based remedies of restitutionary damages and disgorgement damages. The second is the view that disgorgement damages is solely an equitable remedy and should simply be referred to as an "account of profits". Chapter three rejects both these views. In relation to the first view, it is shown that the two different remedies have entirely different rationales and great difficulty and confusion is created in the cases by the conflation of two different remedies under the same name. The second argument is rejected by showing that the "account of profits" is not the only remedy used by the law to perform this function of disgorging profits. The same function is performed by common law awards and sometimes simply referred to as "damages" or as "money had and received". As argued in chapter one, all such monetary remedies for wrongs should be referred to as "damages" and, given their common function, described by the epithet "disgorgement".

Chapters four, five, six and seven then deal with the application of the theory explained in the first three chapters. Each chapter considers a different group of wrongs and explains how restitutionary damages and disgorgement damages are awarded for those wrongs. Chapters four and five consider the main common law wrongs, torts and breach of contract respectively; chapter six considers the main equitable wrongs. The book concentrates on these non-statutory wrongs where the issues have been most clearly considered and does not deal generally with the application of the theory to the disparate body of statutory wrongs.[2] However, it is noted that where the statute does not provide any guidance as to

---

[2] Such as those breaches of European Community Law described as 'torts' or 'Eurotorts': *R v. Secretary of State for Transport ex parte Factortame (No 7)* [2001] 1 WLR 942.

the remedy which should be awarded the principles should be the same. Chapter seven does consider a group of wrongs, intellectual property wrongs, which historically spanned both common law and equity but are now generally governed by statute.

The final chapter, chapter eight, summarises the conclusions of the book and examines some of the issues that this analysis will help to resolve in the future. Most importantly, it shows that very difficult issues such as the availability of proprietary awards for wrongs can be more easily understood in the framework of an analysis which separates these gain-based damages remedies. In addition, issues of election between remedies, particularly between the two types of gain-based remedies and others can be far better understood with this analysis. It is well established that election between disgorgement damages and compensatory damages is required but the failure clearly to distinguish between restitutionary damages and disgorgement damages means that these issues have not been considered in the context of election between remedies including restitutionary damages.

Throughout this book a key principle constantly employed is that like events and responses should be treated alike.[3] This requires that language and nomenclature should not obscure the true nature of particular events or the law's response to them. This is the reason that the protean descriptions given to different awards which effect reversal of wrongful transfers are collected together as "restitutionary damages" and those descriptions given to awards which effect profit-stripping for wrongs are assimilated as "disgorgement damages". The converse to this principle is also true. Just as like responses should be treated alike, so too should different responses be treated differently. And this is the reason that this book insists upon separation of restitutionary damages and disgorgement damages.

---

[3] Professor Hart observed that although the difficult question of when cases are 'alike' and when they are 'different' is concealed by this simple statement, it is a fundamental requirement for a 'just' legal system: HLA Hart *The Concept of Law* (2nd edn. Clarendon Press, Oxford 1997) 159-167.

1

The Nature of "Damages"

INTRODUCTION

IN THE VAST majority of cases at common law in which damages are claimed, they are sought in order to redress loss which has been suffered. By redressing loss these awards aim to compensate the claimant and are often termed "compensatory damages". So common are compensatory damages at common law that compensation seems to some to be the sole purpose of common law damages awards. The supporters of this view argue that "where no loss has been suffered no substantial damages of any kind can be recovered".[1] In German law, it is the case that damages awards for wrongs do operate exclusively to compensate for loss.[2] However, this first chapter is devoted to demonstrating the falsity of this view in English common law and breaking the link between damages and compensation. Although common law damages are often concerned with compensating a claimant, they can (and do) have different goals. This chapter will show that "damages" means nothing more specific than a monetary award given for a wrong.[3]

Although this book is concerned with damages awards based upon gain, this chapter will defer discussion of these gain-based awards and, in order to demonstrate that damages awards can be based on principles other than compensating for loss, the focus will be upon a simpler, less contested and better known example. This is the remedy of exemplary damages: an award of damages which, it is universally acknowledged, is expressly not concerned with loss to a claimant. The primary purposes of exemplary damages are to punish a defendant and to create an example to deter the defendant and other potential defendants from similar conduct.

A discussion of exemplary damages might seem to be an odd starting point for a defence of gain-based awards for wrongs. But the reason for beginning in this way is that the single greatest obstacle to the acceptance of gain-based damages is the intuitively attractive, but false, notion that damages must be tied to

---

[1] *Stoke-on-Trent City Council v. W & J Wass Ltd* [1988] 1 WLR 1406 (CA) 1410 (Nourse LJ).

[2] §823 BGB; B S Markesinis *The German Law of Obligations: Vol II The Law of Torts: A Comparative Introduction* (3rd edn. Clarendon Press Oxford 1997) 12.

[3] This definition of damages has been adopted by various commentators: J Stapleton "A New Seascape for Obligations: Reclassification on the Basis of Measure of Damages" in P Birks (ed.) *The Classification of Obligations* (Oxford Clarendon Press 1997) 193, 193; P Birks *Future* 23; P Cane "Exceptional Measures of Damages: A Search for Principles" in P Birks (ed.) *Wrongs and Remedies* 300.

compensation. Exemplary damages have the following in common with gain-based damages: they are calculated other than by reference to the claimant's loss. For nearly 40 years English law has been attracted by, and has nearly succumbed to, the notion that exemplary damages are anomalous and should be eliminated for this very reason. A recent study by the Law Commission and a very recent decision of the House of Lords has restrained, perhaps even reversed, the English flirtation with this view. The rehabilitation of exemplary damages is the essential foundation for the recognition of the legitimacy and utility of other kinds of non-compensatory damages.

This chapter is divided into three sections. Section A, examines the arguments that damages should be equated with compensation for loss. Section B examines the specific application of these views in the context of exemplary damages. Section C demonstrates that the conclusion that exemplary damages are a legitimate form of non-compensatory damages necessitates recognition of other forms of non-compensatory damages.

A   Damages as compensation

1) Arguments that damages must be compensatory

One frequently encounters the view that awards of damages are only made to compensate a claimant for loss suffered. There are two classic judicial statements, which are often referred to in discussions concerning damages for torts and breach of contract. The first is Lord Blackburn's statement in the tort case of *Livingstone* v. *Rawyards Coal Company*:[4]

> "It is a general rule that, where any injury is to be compensated by damages, in settling the sum of money to be given for reparation of damages you should as nearly as possible get at that sum of money which will put the party who has been injured, or who has suffered, in the same position as he would have been in if he had not sustained the wrong for which he is now getting his compensation or reparation."

The second is Baron Parke's statement in the breach of contract case, *Robinson* v. *Harman*:[5]

> "The rule of the common law is, that where a party sustains a loss by reason of a breach of contract, he is, so far as money can do it, to be placed in the same situation, with respect to damages, as if the contract had been performed."

These statements have been referred to again and again, sometimes just as "general principle"[6] but, on other occasions, as a "fundamental principle"[7] or

---

[4] (1880) 5 App Cas 25 (HL) 39.

[5] (1848) 1 Ex 850, 855; 154 ER 363, 365.

[6] *British Transport Commission* v. *Gourley* [1956] AC 185 (HL) 197, 212.

[7] *British Westinghouse Electric and Manufacturing Co Ltd* v. *Underground Electric Railways Co of London Ltd* [1912] AC 673 (HL) 689; *Tai Hing Cotton Mill Ltd* v. *Kamsing Knitting Factory* [1979] AC 91 (PC) 104; *Ruxley Electronics and Construction Ltd* v. *Forsyth* [1996] AC 344 (HL) 355, 365–366; *Dodd Properties (Kent) Ltd* v. *Canterbury City Council* [1980] 1 WLR 433 (CA) 451.

even as an absolute rule, a "principle that is absolutely firm, and which must control all else."[8]

2) Counter-arguments

If it were correct, as an absolute proposition, that damages are only concerned with compensating for loss, *exemplary* damages or *nominal* damages could not exist. Neither are concerned to compensate a claimant for loss. The Law Commission, in its Consultation Paper on *Aggravated, Exemplary and Restitutionary Damages*,[9] observed that, at least empirically, claims that tort law is exclusively concerned with compensation are "simply false". The existence of exemplary damages especially, anomalous or not, in different forms for thousands of years[10] shows the express concern of the civil law with matters beyond compensation. Despite this, Dr McGregor begins his seminal treatise on damages with the statement that "[d]amages are pecuniary compensation".[11]

(a) Nominal Damages

Despite his opening statement, Dr McGregor does, in fact, devote a section of his book to "damages not based strictly on compensation",[12] in which he discusses exemplary and nominal damages. He begins by acknowledging the non-compensatory nature of nominal damages which have been described in the following manner:[13]

> "A technical phrase which means that you have negatived anything like real damage, but that you are affirming by your nominal damages that there is an infraction of a legal right, which, though it gives you no right to any real damages at all, yet gives you the right to the verdict or judgment because your legal right has been infringed."

Dr McGregor sought to resolve this apparent contradiction in an essay in which he argues that "nominal damages . . . are not really damages" and are unnecessary.[14] He argues that they are no longer needed as a "peg on which to hang costs" as costs are now in the court's discretion. A court can now give costs to a party that is not entitled to damages. He also argues that nominal damages are not needed by a court to assert that a right has been infringed since a court can make such an assertion by a declaration. However, whether needed or not, it is an empirical fact that nominal damages remain to serve these non-compensatory functions.

[8] *Skelton* v. *Collins* (1966) 115 CLR 94 (HCA) 128.
[9] Law Commission *Aggravated, Exemplary and Restitutionary Damages* (Consultation Paper 132 1993) 5.31.
[10] The earliest known case being in Babylonian Law in the Code of Hammurabi about 4000 years ago.
[11] H McGregor (ed.) *McGregor on Damages* (16th edn. Sweet & Maxwell London 1997) 1.
[12] *McGregor on Damages* above note 11 chapters 10, 11 and 12.
[13] *Owners of the Steamship "Mediana"* v. *Owners, Master and Crew of the Lightship "Comet"* [1900] AC 113 (HL) 116.
[14] H McGregor "Restitutionary Damages" in P Birks (ed.) *Wrongs and Remedies* 203, 203–204.

(b) *Exemplary damages*

Exemplary damages cannot be dismissed as perfunctorily. Even Dr McGregor accepts that exemplary damages are "damages". He argues, however, that they are an anomaly and rarely available. It will be seen below that Dr McGregor is not alone and that this debate as to the legitimacy of exemplary damages has occupied English courts in much detail. Other jurisdictions can be equally forceful. In *Fay* v. *Parker*,[15] for example, the Supreme Court of New Hampshire, setting aside part of a judgment that related to exemplary damages, described exemplary damages in the following manner:

> "a monstrous heresy . . . an unhealthy excrescence, deforming the symmetry of the body of the law . . . out of place, irregular, anomalous, exceptional, unjust, unscientific, not to say absurd and ridiculous when classed among civil remedies."

(c) *The "rule" in the Livingstone case*

A third counter-example illustrating the existence of non-compensatory damages is ironically the case of *Livingstone* v. *Rawyards Coal Company*[16] itself, a case which is usually understood or cited as fundamental to the "rule" that damages are compensatory. In fact, obiter dicta in all the speeches in the House of Lords in the *Livingstone* case support the existence of damages based on principles other than compensation for loss.

The *Livingstone* case was an appeal brought to the House of Lords from the First Division in Scotland. Both the appellant and respondent assumed that the coal under the appellant's property was reserved to the respondent. Acting upon this assumption the respondent mined under the appellant's land for coal. The appellant later realised that he had been mistaken and sued to recover the value of the profits that the respondent had reaped from his coal.

The claim was framed as one for compensatory damages for loss. The appellant argued that the loss suffered was the value of the coal and should be measured by the net profit from the sale of the coal by the respondents. The House of Lords held that the appellant could not have worked the land himself and that the only loss to the appellant was the lost ability to offer the right to mine the coal for a price and an element for damage done to the land.[17]

Although only compensatory damages were sought, all members of the House of Lords indicated that further damages might have been awarded in different circumstances. Each speech acknowledged that if there had been evidence of "bad faith or sinister intention"[18] the appellant could have recovered the market value of the coal, without even a deduction for the respondent's cost of working

---

[15] 53 NH 342 (SCNH 1873) 382 (Foster J).

[16] (1880) 5 App Cas 25 (HL).

[17] The size of the land was so small that the expense of sinking a pit to mine only that land would have been far greater than the value of the coal.

[18] *Livingstone* above note 16, 31 (Earl Cairns LC), 34 (Lord Hatherley), 39 (Lord Blackburn).

the coal. But due to the innocence of the respondent only a compensatory award was allowed. Compensatory damages were therefore awarded but it was recognised that they were not the only damages potentially available. The award of the market value of the coal, less the cost of removing the coal, is explained later in this book as an example of the non-compensatory award of disgorgement damages. It focuses upon the profit made by the defendant as a result of the wrong.[19] But the refusal to allow a deduction for the cost of working the coal adds to the award a punitive element. Lord Diplock has acknowledged that this is recognition of exemplary damages.[20] Even the *Livingstone* case confirms that damages awards need not be compensatory.

The House of Lords has also recently recognised, by a majority, in *Attorney General* v. *Blake*,[21] that the statement concerning compensation in the *Livingstone* case is only a "general principle". Lord Nicholls, in the leading speech[22] stated that "the common law, pragmatic as ever, has long recognised that there are many commonplace situations where a strict application of this [compensatory] principle would not do justice between the parties." At common law the award of exemplary damages has been the most prominent of these situations. The following section now considers exemplary damages, and argues that these damages awards are legitimate and that their existence demonstrates the fact that damages are not exclusively concerned with compensation for loss.

B Legitimacy of exemplary damages

1) Their purpose

Historically the award of exemplary damages was accompanied by numerous epithets. Courts have used words such as "wilful, wanton, high-handed, oppressive, malicious, outrageous"[23] to describe the fact that these damages respond to the manner in which the wrong has been committed by the defendant. They are not concerned with compensating the claimant for loss suffered and thus "are essentially different from ordinary damages . . . the object . . . is to punish and deter".[24]

The principal aims of an award of exemplary damages are illustrated by the debate surrounding the title which should be attributed to this form of damages.

---

[19] See ch. four, text accompanying note 163. Another non-compensatory award considered later in this book which might have been possible could have been an award of the fair market rate which could have been sought for the right to remove the coal. This damages award is explained as restitutionary damages.

[20] *Broome* v. *Cassell & Co* [1972] AC 1027 (HL) 1129.

[21] [2001] 1 AC 268 (HL) (Lord Nicholls, Lords Browne-Wilkinson, Goff and Steyn, Lord Hobhouse dissenting).

[22] *Blake* above note 20, 278.

[23] *Rookes* v. *Barnard* [1964] AC 1129 (HL) 1229 (Lord Devlin).

[24] *Rookes* above note 23, 1221.

Whilst in the United States and Canada, courts have settled on the term "punitive" damages, other jurisdictions such as Australia and New Zealand have preferred the English term "exemplary". The use of "punitive" highlights the punishment goal of punishing a defendant. "Exemplary" focuses upon example and deterring potential other defendants from this type of conduct.

The Law Commission has recommended a change to the term "punitive" as a more accurate and less confusing label.[25] The Law Commission preferred "punitive" damages arguing that whilst exemplary damages are concerned with retribution, deterrence, conveying of disapproval and, to a lesser extent, satisfaction for victims[26] each of these goals was an aspect of punishment. This approach views punishment as the "keynote"[27] goal of exemplary damages. On the other hand, the Irish Law Commission Consultation Paper[28] has tentatively recommended retention of the term "exemplary damages". The Irish Law Commission preferred the term "exemplary" as reflecting the wider social goal of deterrence despite punishment being the immediate aim. Lord Hailsham, in *Broome* v. *Cassell & Co*,[29] took a similar approach arguing that the main aim is deterrence, both general and specific, and punishment is incidental to this. He stated that the goal of exemplary damages was

> "[t]o teach the defendant and others that 'tort does not pay' by demonstrating what consequences the law inflicts rather than simply to make the defendant suffer an extra penalty for what he has done, although that does, of course, precisely describe its effect."

It seems difficult, however, to attribute a primary role to only punishment *or* deterrence. On the one hand, exemplary damages may be awarded in situations where the conduct is unlikely ever to be repeated and thus primarily for punishment and not deterrence. On the other hand, exemplary damages may also be awarded even when they can serve no punitive purpose. In *Lamb* v. *Cotogno*[30] the driver of a car had intentionally driven his vehicle whilst the claimant was clinging to the bonnet. The claimant had suffered serious injury when the defendant had braked sharply and caused the claimant to be propelled from the bonnet of the car. Exemplary damages were awarded and the claimant appealed to the High Court of Australia. The High Court was confronted with an argument that exemplary damages could not be awarded as the damages would have been paid by the claimant's insurer under the Motor Vehicles (Third Party Insurance) Act 1942 (NSW). The Court held that punishment of the offender was

---

[25] *Law Commission 1997* 4.1, 5.39.

[26] "Satisfaction" is a means to prevent a victim seeking revenge or self-help: W Holdsworth *A History of the English Law* (4th edn. Methuen London 1927) 43–45, 50–51; *Merest* v. *Harvey* (1814) 5 Taunt 442; 128 ER 761.

[27] *Daniels* v. *Thompson* [1998] 3 NZLR 22 (CANZ) 29.

[28] *A Law Reform Commission Consultation Paper on Aggravated, Exemplary and Restitutionary Damages* (Law Reform Commission Ireland 1998) 9.33.

[29] *Broome* above note 20, 1073.

[30] (1987) 164 CLR 1 (HCA).

not the only purpose of exemplary damages. In this case whilst an exemplary award may not punish the claimant, it would operate "to mark the court's condemnation of the defendant's behaviour"[31] and deter conduct of a similar nature which does not involve the use of a motor vehicle.

Although there is recognition of other roles for exemplary damages beyond deterrence and punishment, those other roles are now regarded as secondary. The earliest cases recognised exemplary damages as needed to assuage any urge for revenge and to appease the victim.[32] Although there is no longer as much need to discourage "duelling"[33] or self-help, the award still has a clear appeasement effect. But such considerations, when referred to now, are simply seen as "an aspect" of the award but of less force.[34]

2) *Their operation*

(a) *The categories test*

In *Rookes* v. *Barnard*,[35] the discussion of exemplary damages in the speech of Lord Devlin was accepted and adopted by the other Law Lords.[36] Although stating that punitive damages were "anomalous" in that "the object of damages in the usual sense of the word is to compensate",[37] Lord Devlin favoured retention of exemplary damages in three "categories". These categories were as follows:[38]

1 Oppressive, arbitrary or unconstitutional action by the servants of the government';
2 Where the defendant's conduct has been calculated by him to make a profit for himself which may well exceed the compensation payable to the plaintiff; and
3 Any case in which exemplary damages are expressly authorised by statute.

Even if a case fell within one of these categories, Lord Devlin stated that exemplary damages could only be awarded "if, but only if, the . . . compensation [awarded] . . . is inadequate to punish [the defendant] for his outrageous conduct".[39] Lord Devlin further referred to three considerations. The first was that the plaintiff must be the victim of the punishable behaviour. Second, the amount of the award should not be a greater penalty than if the conduct were criminal. Restraint should be exercised in making the award. Third, the "means of the parties" were said to be relevant to the assessment.

---

[31] *Lamb* v. *Cotogno* above note 30, 10.
[32] *Wilkes* v. *Wood* (1763) Lofft 1, 18; 98 ER 489, 498 (Pratt LCJ); *Merest* v. *Harvey* (1814) 5 Taunt 442, 443; 128 ER 761, 761 (Heath J).
[33] *Uren* v. *John Fairfax & Sons Pty Ltd* (1966) 117 CLR 118 (HCA) 148 (Windeyer J).
[34] *Lamb* v. *Cotogno* above note 30, 9.
[35] *Rookes* above note 23.
[36] *Rookes* above note 23, 1179 (Lord Reid), 1197 (Lord Evershed), 1203 (Lord Hodson), 1238 (Lord Pearce).
[37] *Rookes* above note 23, 1221.
[38] *Rookes* above note 23, 1226–1227.
[39] *Rookes* above note 23, 1227–1228.

(b) *The cause of action limitation*

Further restrictions upon exemplary damages were imposed by the decision of the Court of Appeal in *AB* v. *South-West Water Services Ltd.*[40] The Court of Appeal considered that the effect of the speeches in *Broome* v. *Cassell & Co*[41] and their consideration of the *Rookes* case was that exemplary damages were not only restricted to the categories Lord Devlin had mentioned. They were only available for torts in which exemplary damages had been awarded prior to the *Rookes* case in 1964. The Law Commission referred to this as the "cause of action" limitation considering it "rationally indefensible" to limit the availability of exemplary damages by reference to the existence of precedent prior to the arbitrary date of the decision in the *Rookes* case.[42]

The cause of action limitation was recently rejected by the House of Lords in *Kuddus* v. *Chief Constable of Leicestershire Constabulary.*[43] An action had been brought against the defendant Chief Constable seeking to hold him vicariously liable for misfeasance in public office allegedly committed by one of his constables in forging the claimant's signature on a statement withdrawing a complaint. The defendant sought to strike out that part of an action which sought exemplary damages on the basis that the tort of misfeasance in public office was not a tort which had been recognised prior to 1964. Lords Slynn, Mackay and Hutton considered that the decisions in the *Rookes* and *Broome* cases had not unequivocally laid down such a "cause of action" limitation and that such an irrational and arbitrary limitation should be rejected.[44] Lord Nicholls and Lord Scott disagreed and thought that those cases had laid down such a limitation and the Court of Appeal in the *AB* v. *South-West Water* case had thus applied the correct test. However, Lord Nicholls agreed that the cause of action limitation was irrational and illogical and should now be rejected.[45] Only Lord Scott, in dissent on this point, favoured a "pragmatic" version of the cause of action limitation. Lord Scott accepted that the cause of action limitation was irrational and did not depend on principle[46] but he would have preferred to maintain a limitation on exemplary damages such that they would remain unavailable for negligence, nuisance and strict liability torts as well as liability in tort for breach of statutory duty.[47]

---

[40] [1993] QB 507 (CA).
[41] *Broome* above note 20, 1073.
[42] *Law Commission 1997* 4.4, 5.49.
[43] [2001] 2 WLR 1789 (HL).
[44] *Kuddus* above note 43, 1796 (Lord Slynn) 1802 (Lord Mackay) 1815 (Lord Hutton).
[45] *Kuddus* above note 43, 1805, 1807.
[46] *Kuddus* above note 43, 1820.
[47] *Kuddus* above note 43, 1821.

3) *Answering objections*

(a) *The primacy objection*

(i) Polarised views

The first objection to exemplary damages is the reason for the focus upon these damages in this chapter. This objection is that damages are exclusively concerned with compensating for loss and thus the existence of exemplary damages, with their non-compensatory aims, cannot be legitimate.

In *Broome* v. *Cassell & Co Ltd*[48] this issue arose. The House of Lords were called upon to reconsider the basis for Lord Devlin's speech in *Rookes* v. *Barnard*. The *Broome* case involved a jury award of exemplary damages against the publishers and authors of a book that was libellous of a retired navy officer. The defendants had known and been told that passages in the book were libellous prior to publication but had proceeded nevertheless. The trial judge instructed the jury that an award of exemplary damages could be made separately from one of compensatory damages if the conduct fell within Lord Devlin's second limb in *Rookes* v. *Barnard*. The jury held that the conduct was calculated for gain and awarded £15,000 compensatory damages and £25,000 exemplary damages against the defendants. The Court of Appeal affirmed this ruling, as did the House of Lords.

Nothing about the *Broome* case would have been remarkable, and the case would not have reached the House of Lords, were it not for the fact that the Court of Appeal expressed the view that the categories test in *Rookes* v. *Barnard* was wrongly decided and *per incuriam* previous House of Lords decisions. The Court of Appeal directed lower courts not to follow this aspect of *Rookes* v. *Barnard* in future. The House of Lords, by majority, upheld the categories test in *Rookes* v. *Barnard* and were scathing of the approach taken by the Court of Appeal.[49] In the process of the discussion of exemplary damages, two Law Lords dealt with the objection to exemplary damages that they do not compensate for loss in detail and reached diametrically opposed conclusions.

Lord Reid, like Lord Devlin in the *Rookes* case, emphasised that exemplary damages were an "anomaly" in that they allowed a measure of damages which was not based upon compensation. Lord Reid argued that the "objections to allowing juries to go beyond compensatory damages are overwhelming".[50] He only retained exemplary damages out of respect for precedent, considering them too firmly embedded in the law:[51]

"the plaintiff, by being given more than on any view could be justified as compensation, was being given a pure and undeserved windfall at the expense of the defendant,

---

[48] [1972] AC 1027 (HL).

[49] *Broome* above note 48, 1054 (Lord Hailsham), 1092 (Lord Reid), 1107 (Viscount Dilhorne).

[50] *Broome* above note 48, 1087.

[51] *Broome* above note 48, 1086.

and that in so far as the defendant was being required to pay more than could possibly be regarded as compensation he was being subjected to pure punishment. . . I thought and still think that that is highly anomalous. It is confusing the function of the civil law which is to compensate with the function of the criminal law which is to inflict deterrent and punitive penalties."

Lord Wilberforce, however, took the opposite approach considering exemplary damages legitimate and useful:[52]

"It cannot be lightly taken for granted, even as a matter of theory, that the purpose of the law of tort is compensation, still less that it ought to be, an issue of large social import, or that there is something inappropriate, or illogical or anomalous (a question-begging word) in including a punitive element in civil damages, or, conversely, that the criminal law, rather than the civil law, is in these cases a better instrument for conveying social disapproval, or for redressing a wrong to the social fabric, or that damages in any case can be broken down into the two separate elements. As a matter of practice English law has not committed itself to any of these theories: it may have been wiser than it knew."

This division of views was noted by the Law Commission.[53] In considering whether exemplary damages should be abolished the Law Commission, in its Consultation Paper, stated that it would be "impossible to achieve a consensus. . . in the absence of agreement as to which of these perceptions is correct".[54] The conclusion reached, after detailed consultation, in its final report was that "it is coherent to pursue the aims of punishment (retribution, deterrence, disapproval) through the civil law".[55]

In *Kuddus v. Chief Constable of Leicestershire Constabulary*[56] the House of Lords revisited this issue. In raising the question whether the cause of action limitation should be maintained or rejected, all the Lords considered that the logical anterior question was whether exemplary damages were legitimate. If exemplary damages were illegitimate then, if they must be maintained because of respect for precedent, there would be a strong case for retaining the cause of action limitation, however illogical, to limit their availability. However, the parties to the case did not seek to argue that exemplary damages should be abolished or even to argue that they were an illegitimate form of damages. The parties agreed that exemplary damages were legitimate and the argument merely focussed upon whether the cause of action test proposed in the *Rookes* case commanded the support of a majority of the Law Lords in the *Broome* case. Nevertheless, all the Lords commented upon the anterior question of the legitimacy of exemplary damages.

---

[52] *Broome* above note 48, 1114.
[53] *Law Commission 1997* 5.16–5.18.
[54] *Law Commission 1997* 5.31.
[55] *Law Commission 1997* 5.22.
[56] *Kuddus* above note 43.

Three of the Lords did not express concluded opinions but were strongly in favour of exemplary damages and their legitimacy. Lord Slynn thought that "as the law now stands" the agreement of the parties that exemplary damages are legitimate was "well founded"[57] although he "did not consider it right to consider reopening the whole question" in that case.[58] Lord Mackay referred to the views of the Law Commission that exemplary damages should not be removed as "derived from a very full and careful consultation" and the "best indication. . .on the desirability of retaining the power to award exemplary damages".[59] Lord Hutton referred to decisions from his jurisdiction in Northern Ireland which led him to the conclusion that "exemplary damages serve a valuable purpose in restraining the arbitrary and outrageous use of executive power and in vindicating the strength of the law".[60]

Lord Nicholls did express a conclusive opinion. He expressly stated that exemplary damages were legitimate and "continue to discharge a role, perceived to be useful and valuable, in other common law jurisdictions" and he sided with Lord Wilberforce's powerful views in favour of exemplary damages.[61]

Only Lord Scott thought exemplary damages were illegitimate. Lord Scott sided with Lords Devlin and Reid and argued that the award of exemplary damages is an anomaly as it offended against the "fundamental principle of damages" which is to compensate for loss.[62] Ironically, as will be seen below, Lord Scott acknowledged the need for non-compensatory awards in cases where a defendant has committed a wrong with a view to material gain. However, Lord Scott considered that in such cases profit could be stripped by "restitutionary damages" (such an award described in this book as "disgorgement damages").[63] Lord Scott never explained why such "restitutionary damages", which also offend against the "fundamental principle of damages", should be legitimate but that exemplary damages should not.

In the result, the preponderance of modern authority now explicitly supports the legitimacy of exemplary damages, as a non-compensatory measure of damages. The conclusion can be supported in two further ways. First, indirect support by courts for the legitimacy of exemplary damages in recognition of the broad range of aims of tort law; aims which reach beyond compensation. Secondly, a powerful normative need can be shown for exemplary damages in order to avoid a breakdown of the rule of law. Each of these further supporting arguments is now explained.

[57] *Kuddus* above note 43, 1791.
[58] *Kuddus* above note 43, 1796.
[59] *Kuddus* above note 43, 1800, 1802.
[60] *Kuddus* above note 43, 1809, 1811.
[61] *Kuddus* above note 43, 1807.
[62] *Kuddus* above note 43, 1816.
[63] *Kuddus* above note 43, 1819.

(ii) The broad aims of tort law

At its base tort law is concerned with the normative role of regulating conduct.[64] In the process, it pursues a number of goals. Professor Glanville Williams identified four of these: appeasement, compensation, deterrence and justice.[65]

In *Smith New Court Securities Ltd* v. *Scrimgeour Vickers (Asset Management) Ltd*[66] Lord Steyn confronted a submission that the only purpose of the law of tort should be to compensate. Lord Steyn, in a passage which has been quoted by the Court of Appeal, stated that this is "far too narrow a view" and instead approved the broad view of Professor Glanville Williams.[67] In considering exemplary damages, the Court of Appeal in New Zealand have also made this point several times. For instance, in *Donselaar* v. *Donselaar*[68] Richardson J endorsed the comments of Lord Wilberforce adding that tort law

> "cannot be fitted neatly into a single compartment. In part this is because it serves various social purposes. It is not simply a compensation device or a loss distribution mechanism. It is a hybrid of private law and public interests, issues and concerns."

More recently, in *Daniels* v. *Thompson*[69] Thomas J referred to the functions of tort liability:

> "Compensation is the first and foremost function. But this function is not the sole or exclusive function. Other objectives such as deterrence, vindication, condemnation, education, the avoidance of abuses of power, appeasement of the victim and the symbolic impact of a decision as an expression of society's disapproval of certain conduct all have a role to play."

The reason why compensation is such a common remedy in tort is because it often achieves all of these goals. But as the Canadian Supreme Court have recently recognised, although compensatory damages are usually sufficient to deter wrongdoing, exemplary damages are needed when compensatory damages cannot so deter.[70]

(iii) Need for non-compensatory damages

This second category from *Rookes* v. *Barnard*—where a tort is committed with a view to material gain—is the broadest. In discussing the second category, Lord Devlin explained the need for it:[71]

> "Where a defendant with a cynical disregard for a plaintiff's rights has calculated that the money to be made out of his wrongdoing will probably exceed the damages at risk, it is

---

[64] P Cane *The Anatomy of Tort Law* (Hart Publishing Oxford 1997) 5.

[65] G Williams "The Aims of the Law of Tort" (1951) 4 CLP 137; See also American Law Institute *Restatement (Second) of the Law Torts* (American Law Institute Minnesota 1979) §901.

[66] [1997] AC 254 (HL).

[67] *Smith New Court* above note 66, 280. See *Standard Chartered Bank* v. *Pakistan National Shipping Corporation (No 4)* [2000] 3 WLR 1692 (CA) 1724.

[68] *Donselaar* v. *Donselaar* [1982] 1 NZLR 81 (CANZ) 90.

[69] *Daniels* v. *Thompson* [1998] 3 NZLR 22 (CANZ) 68.

[70] *Royal Bank of Canada* v. *W Got & Associates Electric Ltd* (2000) 178 DLR (4th) 385 (SCC) 394–395.

[71] *Rookes* v. *Barnard* [1964] AC 1129 (HL) 1227.

necessary for the law to show that it cannot be broken with impunity. This category is not confined to moneymaking in the strict sense. It extends to cases in which the defendant is seeking to gain at the expense of the plaintiff some object—perhaps some property which he covets—which either he could not obtain at all or could not obtain except at a price greater than he wants to put down. Exemplary damages can properly be awarded whenever it is necessary to teach a wrongdoer that tort does not pay."

This category of exemplary damages has been described as a "blunt instrument to prevent unjust enrichment"[72] and a "broad axe".[73] The instrument is blunt, or the axe broad, because exemplary damages are at large. They might not strip the precise amount of profit made; the award could be less or more.

As chapter three explains,[74] the "sharp" axe to strip such profits is an award of "disgorgement damages" which is an award requiring disgorgement of the precise amount by which profit has been made from the wrong. This is not to say that exemplary damages are obsolete because of the concurrent existence of disgorgement damages in these cases. It might be necessary to deter a wrong committed for the purpose of gain even though no profit eventuates.[75] Or a greater award and stronger deterrent might be needed beyond simply stripping a defendant's profits. As Lord Diplock noted in *Broome* v. *Cassell & Co:*[76]

"to restrict the damages recoverable to the actual gain made by a defendant, if it exceeded the loss to the plaintiff, would leave a defendant contemplating an unlawful act with the certainty that he had nothing to lose to balance against the chance that the plaintiff might never sue him or, if he did, might fail in the hazards of litigation."

Further, modern recognition of the existence of this sharper profit stripping award (disgorgement damages) prompted Lord Nicholls in the *Kuddus* case to suggest that the second category of exemplary damages could perhaps be expanded to deter all instances of outrageous conduct even without a motive for material gain.[77]

Whether the award is framed in the traditional language of exemplary damages or in terms of the sharper award, stripping only profits (disgorgement damages), in instances where a wrong has been committed with a view to material gain it is clear that an award of damages which goes beyond compensation is required. The fact that Lord Devlin created the second category of damages was explicit recognition of this. Without such a non-compensatory award, which operates *at least* to strip a defendant of profits made, the law cannot adequately protect the rights it purports to confer. For otherwise it allows a defendant to "hurt somebody because he thinks he may well gain by doing so even allowing for the risk that he may be made to pay damages".[78] To allow a wrongdoer to

---

[72] *Broome* above note 48, 1130.
[73] *Whitfeld* v. *De Lauret & Co Ltd* (1920) 29 CLR 71 (HCA) 82.
[74] See ch. three, text accompanying note 116.
[75] *Law Commission* 1997 4.17.
[76] *Broome* above note 48, 1130.
[77] *Kuddus* v. *Chief Constable of Leicestershire Constabulary* [2001] 2 WLR 1789 (HL) 1807.
[78] *Broome* above note 48, 1094 (Lord Morris).

"escape payment of damages on the theory that the registrant suffered no loss [and to] impose on the infringer nothing more serious than an injunction when he is caught is a tacit invitation to other infringement".[79] Even Lord Scott who, in the *Kuddus* case, would have been receptive to a submission that exemplary damages should be abolished, acknowledged that in cases of the second category from the *Rookes* case damages are available "in many tort actions" to extract the profit made by the wrongdoer.[80]

The most abhorrent of examples that can be given of the need for exemplary damages to deter wrongdoing in such instances can be seen in the famous case of *Grimshaw* v. *Ford Motor Company*.[81] That case concerned Ford, a car manufacturer, which made a financial decision to locate the fuel tank of the Ford Pinto in a position that was supposedly more economical. Management knew, from crash tests, that this positioning created a significant risk of death or injury from fire. The occupants of one of these Ford Pintos were involved in a collision which, because of the position of the fuel tank, resulted in the car catching fire. Mrs Gray, the driver, was killed and 13 year old Richard Grimshaw suffered severe burns and injuries. The case was primarily brought at common law on the basis of negligence.[82] A significant award of exemplary damages was made.[83] But if the law were truly only concerned with compensating for loss, it would permit the Ford Motor Company to make such a decision and gain, despite the deaths of customers. In the words of the Ontario High Court, "the law would say to the rich and powerful, 'Do what you like, you will only have to make good the plaintiff's actual financial loss, which compared to your budget is negligible' ".[84] This was what Lord Nicholls meant when, in the *Kuddus* case, he stated that:[85]

> "On occasion conscious wrongdoing by a defendant is so outrageous, his disregard of the plaintiff's rights so contumelious, that something more is needed to show that the law will not tolerate such behaviour. Without an award of exemplary damages, justice will not have been done"

(b) *Other objections*

(i) Punishment is the role of criminal law

In 1962 Professor Street marshalled the arguments for and against exemplary damages.[86] Many of these now "well-known"[87] arguments are directed towards showing that punishment should be the province only of the criminal law

---

[79] *Admiral Corp* v. *Price Vacuum Stores* 141 F Supp 796 (1956 ED Pa) 802.

[80] *Kuddus* above note 77 at 1819. Although describing those damages as "restitutionary damages" instead of "disgorgement damages".

[81] 174 Cal Rptr 348 (1981 CA 4th District Cal).

[82] A strict products liability claim was also brought.

[83] Quantum reduced to $3.5 million on further appeal *Ford Motor Company* v. *Grimshaw* 119 Cal App 3d (1983) 757, 819.

[84] *Natel* v. *Parisien* (1981) 18 CCLT 89 (HCO) (punitive damages for breach of a lease); *Brown* v. *Waterloo Regional Board of Commissioners of Police* (1982) 37 OR (2d) 277 (HCO) 292–293.

[85] *Kuddus* above note 77, 1806.

[86] H Street *Principles of the Law of Damages* (Sweet and Maxwell London 1962) 34.

[87] *Broome* above note 48, 1114 (Lord Reid).

because the civil law is said to have insufficient protection for the defendant: a defendant is denied the criminal burden of proof, there is effectively no appeal against sentence, no clear definition of the offence or penalty for which the defendant is liable and no right to have the penalty imposed by a judge.[88]

The additional safeguards of the criminal law, however, can be justified on the basis that the criminal law creates an offence against the state. Offences against the State carry with them a different stigma and the punishment consequences, such as imprisonment, are more severe. As a result greater evidential protection is required for the defendant. As the Law Commission have noted, once the difference in consequence is noted, objections based upon lesser safeguards "fall away".[89]

Further, where criminal punishment has already been awarded by the State then exemplary damages will usually be inappropriate. This was an important aspect of the reasoning of the majority in *Daniels* v. *Thompson*.[90] The plaintiffs in four cases, heard jointly by the New Zealand Court of Appeal, sought exemplary damages arising from sexual offences where a defendant had been found guilty (and in one case, acquitted) of some of those offences by a criminal court. A majority of the New Zealand Court of Appeal[91] accepted that proceedings for punitive damages should be stayed where criminal proceedings had been commenced or were likely to be commenced in respect of the same acts.[92] The basis of the Court's reasoning was that "the need to punish has already been met through the court system . . . the foundation of [exemplary damages] has been removed".[93] This conforms to the principle of the common law, embodied in many criminal statutes as well as constitutions, that no person shall be punished twice for the same cause; *nemo bis vexari pro eadem causa*.[94]

However, even the dissenting view, according exemplary damages a potential role even where criminal punishment has been imposed, suggests that the criminal punishment is a powerful factor to be considered in the making of any additional exemplary award. Thomas J, in dissent in the *Daniels* case, preferred the rule proposed by the Law Commission[95] and Ontario Law Reform Commission[96] that a criminal conviction should simply be one of the elements to be taken into account. The approach of Thomas J is also consistent with that of the High Court of Australia in *Lamb* v. *Cotogno*[97] in which the Court

---

[88] Ontario Law Reform Commission "Report on Exemplary Damages" (Ontario Law Reform Commission 1991) 19.

[89] *Law Commission 1997* 5.23.

[90] *Daniels* above note 69.

[91] Richardson P, Gault, Henry and Keith JJ; Thomas J dissenting.

[92] A separate argument of whether s. 26(2) of the New Zealand Bill of Rights Act 1990 acted as a bar to such actions, by prohibiting double jeopardy, was rejected on construction of the provision.

[93] *Daniels* above note 69, 49.

[94] This maxim has been described as "lying at the very foundation of human rights and privileges- a law of nature, and of obvious common sense and common justice': *Fay* v. *Parker* 53 NH 342 (1873 SCNH) 389.

[95] *Law Commission 1997* 5.116–5.117.

[96] Ontario Law Reform Commission above note 88 Recommendation 5(2).

[97] *Lamb* above note 30.

awarded exemplary damages despite the fact that the appellant had pleaded guilty to criminal charges arising out of the same facts.[98] Both the majority and minority approaches in the *Daniels* case have in common the fact that once it is accepted that the common law has goals beyond compensation, which include punishment, then care must be taken to consider other areas of the law where those goals also operate.

(ii) Encouragement of litigation, uncertainty of quantum and ineffective deterrents

Three additional objections are that exemplary damages encourage litigation, that they are too discretionary or uncertain and that they do not effectively deter wrongdoing. Each of these objections was rejected by the Law Commission as untenable. None of these arguments are particularly compelling and they can be disposed of briefly.

First, as the Law Commission explained, the combined facts that exemplary damages should continue to be moderate and exceptional, the high cost of litigation, the prospect of costs orders and the ability of courts to strike out plainly bad cases would all be powerful impediments against excessive litigation.[99]

Secondly, whilst it is true that awards of exemplary damages are uncertain, the judicial (or statutory) development of these damages (such as introducing "guideline judgments" and lists of factors suggested by the Law Commission[100]) will reduce this uncertainty. In cases of exemplary damages which fall within Lord Devlin's second category this objection also loses significant force. For in these cases the amount of profit expected from the wrong is a strong guideline as to the size of the exemplary damages award.

The final argument is the opposite objection to uncertainty. It is that a "moderate" and "predictable" award of exemplary damages is an ineffective deterrent. As the Law Commission states, the assumption seems to be that predictability allows defendants to engage in cost-benefit analyses to determine if the exemplary damages (in addition to any compensatory damages) exceed the benefit from the wrongdoing.[101] Lord Devlin's second category of exemplary damages is again a compelling example of why this reasoning is wrong. The very operation of the second category is to ensure that these cost-benefit analyses result in the conclusion that the wrongdoing is not worthwhile. If the exemplary damages award is based upon (and will probably exceed) the profits made from such calculated wrongdoing then it is apparent that such potential wrongdoers should come to the conclusion that it will not be profitable to engage in such activity. Cases, such as Ford's construction of the Pinto will only serve to illustrate the danger of leaving the exemplary award out of such an equation.

---

[98] See also the United States: American Law Institute *Restatement (Second) of the Law Torts* (1979 American Law Institute Minnesota) §908, Comment a.

[99] *Law Commission 1997* 5.30.

[100] *Law Commission 1997* 5.32.

[101] *Law Commission 1997* 5.36.

(iii) "Windfall"

This objection to exemplary damages coincides with an objection to disgorgement damages awards discussed later in this book, an award which operates to disgorge profits. The argument is that "if it is conceded that the law of torts ought to achieve certain public ends such as punishment, the state should receive any fine; why should the plaintiff get a windfall?"[102]

The windfall is that amount to which it is said the claimant "can have no possible claim"[103] because, absent the wrong, the claimant would never have received that benefit. But "windfall" is a dangerous word. It asserts ab initio that the claimant does not deserve what he recovers. But that assertion is the very matter under debate. The claimant has suffered a wrong. He deserves whatever solace the law chooses to give. The decision as to the award is made by the law.[104] The claimant merely "shakes the tree to obtain the fruit of justice".[105] As Lord Diplock put it in *Broome* v. *Cassell & Co*[106] "he can only profit from the windfall if the wind was blowing his way".

C Beyond exemplary damages

Exemplary damages are the most obvious and extreme form of damages which are unconcerned with a plaintiff's loss and therefore their legitimacy demonstrates that damages awards based upon factors other than compensation for loss cannot be automatically excluded.

It has been contended above that not only are exemplary damages now conclusively accepted into the law but that there is a powerful justification for them in cases of deliberate wrongdoing for profit. The remaining chapters of this book focus upon two other forms of non-compensatory damages which are less commonly recognised than exemplary damages. This chapter has, however, shown that there can be no prima facie objection to these forms of damages on the basis that they do not operate to compensate for loss.

One form of gain-based damages discussed in this book can operate in the same circumstances as the second limb of exemplary damages. One basis for the award of this remedy, described as disgorgement damages, is to strip profits made as a result of deliberate wrongdoing for the purpose of gain. Courts constantly emphasise that the award of only the profit made does not aim to punish, in the sense that it only operates to strip gain made from the wrong and does not leave a defendant any worse off. As a result disgorgement damages are not subject to all the objections to exemplary damages such as indeterminacy. Once

---

[102] Street above note 86.

[103] *Walker* v. *Sheldon* 10 NY 2d 401 (1961 SCNY) 409.

[104] E Weinrib "Restitutionary Damages as Corrective Justice" (2000) 1 Theoretical Inquiries in Law 1.

[105] G Pipe "Exemplary Damages After Camelford" (1994) 57 MLR 91, 97.

[106] *Broome* above note 48, 1126.

it is recognised that the non-compensatory award of exemplary damages is legitimate, then there cannot be any objection to gain-based damages awards such as disgorgement damages, which are subject to fewer objections, solely on the basis that they do not operate to compensate for loss. The availability of this profit-stripping award in the common law has recently been explicitly accepted by the House of Lords in *Attorney General* v. *Blake*[107] (although not described as disgorgement damages) as a remedy for a breach of contract (an area where exemplary damages have traditionally been considered unavailable). In the course of the leading speech, Lord Nicholls rejected the notion that damages must always be awarded to compensate for loss. His Lordship stated that "when awarding damages, the law does not adhere slavishly to the concept of compensation for financially measurable loss. When the circumstances require, damages are measured by reference to the benefit obtained by the wrongdoer".[108] The rest of this book therefore assumes the legitimacy of such gain-based damages and, in separating out the two forms of gain-based damages, explains when each are available, and the basis for each award.

CONCLUSION

This chapter has used the award of exemplary damages to demonstrate that compensation for loss is not and should not be the exclusive concern of common law damages. The common law has clearly accepted the existence of non-compensatory damages in the form of exemplary damages.[109] Exemplary damages are not an anomaly that should be abolished. There are powerful and compelling reasons for them in particular cases. Although there are indeed some objections to exemplary damages, these are not overwhelming and do not overcome the need for exemplary damages. They have a coherent role and their recognition and acceptance in English law is legitimated by history and utility. That is, they are useful and their usefulness has been recognised by the practice of courts for centuries.

Once the tie between damages and compensation is broken, the fact that a claimant recovers more than the loss he has suffered need no longer seem a "windfall". It has been shown that the word "windfall" tacitly asserts the propriety of the restriction to compensation and the anomalous nature of all other measures. Non-compensatory damages are not anomalous. Exemplary damages are just one example of this.

The terminological lesson of this chapter is therefore that the word "damages" can only mean money awards which respond to wrongs. "Compensatory damages" are clearly tied to the claimant's loss but "damages", unqualified, are

[107] *Attorney General* v. *Blake* [2001] 1 AC 268 (HL).
[108] *Blake* above note 107, 285.
[109] *Redrow Homes Ltd* v. *Betts Brothers Plc* [1999] 1 AC 197 (HL) 207 (Lord Jauncey) 209 (Lord Clyde).

not tied to any particular measure. The law already uses different epithets to describe the different types of damages. In addition to compensatory damages, exemplary damages and nominal damages are widely recognised. This book uses descriptive epithets to differentiate two additional forms of non-compensatory damages which, especially in the common law, are not as clearly recognised as exemplary damages. It will use the labels restitutionary damages and disgorgement damages.

2

The Category of Civil Wrongs

INTRODUCTION

T HIS CHAPTER IS an examination of the intensely difficult question
of whether a given cause of action is a wrong. It will be seen that although
the key to identifying a given cause of action as a wrong is proof that remedial
consequences flow from its characterisation as a breach of duty, such proof is
sometimes elusive. One important indicator is whether the cause of action in
question can give rise to a right to exemplary damages or, more commonly,
compensatory damages. But that test, while usually sufficient, cannot be necessary, for it is not impossible for a wrong to give rise only to other remedies.[1]
More importantly, the availability of compensation might not have historically
been considered for a particular cause of action, and a court might in the future
allow compensation for that cause of action. These are cases in which it is
extremely difficult to tell whether the cause of action is a wrong or not. In these
cases the only approach to determining whether a cause of action is a wrong is
to examine the nature and operation of that action historically to determine
whether the remedial effect is produced by a breach of duty.

This chapter is divided into two sections. Section A explains that wrongs are
not confined to the common law. It argues that the category of wrongs must
encompass conduct regarded as wrongful by equity, although it also explains
why criminal wrongs are not considered in this book. Section B advances the
definition of a wrong as a cause of action the remedial consequences of which
flow from its characterisation as a breach of duty. Unfortunately the availability of awards which might reveal this characterisation (such as compensatory
damages and exemplary damages) has not always been considered. This section
shows how an examination of the nature of these actions often reveals that such
remedies should not be available because the action is not one for a breach of
duty but an action in unjust enrichment. However, many of these actions in
unjust enrichment are capable of being characterised as breaches of duty. This
section explains why they need not be so characterised. A claimant who relies
upon an action in its character as a cause of action in unjust enrichment is choos-
ing not to rely upon it as a wrong. The possibilities for this kind of alternative
analysis are more common than has been thought.

---

[1] P Atiyah "Personal Injuries in the Twenty First Century: Thinking the Unthinkable" in P Birks
(ed.) *Wrongs and Remedies* 1. Even the availability of compensation might not be conclusive as it
is not impossible for events which are *not* wrongs to give rise to compensation: S Stoljar "Unjust

A Wrongs at common law and in equity

1) *The meaning of "tort"*

The starting point for determining the nature of a wrong must be that category of the common law known as torts. "Tort" is simply the French word for "wrong". Tort is a well established and accepted category of the law which is taken to mean non-contractual common law wrongs. However, explaining the basis for this category of "tort" is notoriously difficult. The primary reason for this difficulty lies in the exclusion of conduct regarded as wrongful in equity as well as common law. This section argues that the way out of this difficulty is to use a generic category, "wrongs", to bring together all causes of action, either legal or equitable, which involve breaches of duty.

The opening sentence of the 17th edition of *Clerk & Lindsell on Tort*[2] concedes that "[n]o entirely satisfactory definition of a tort can be offered". Similarly, the opening sentence of *Winfield & Jolowicz on Tort*[3] states that "[n]umerous attempts have been made to define "a tort" or "tortious liability", with varying degrees of lack of success." The difficulty arises from the fact that no coherent definition of a tort can be advanced which excludes equitable wrongs. Both texts cite Professor Winfield's classic definition that "tortious liability arises from breach of a duty primarily fixed by the law; such a duty is towards persons generally and its breach can be redressed by an action for unliquidated damages".[4] But even this definition, it may be noted, does not exclude equitable wrongs.

(a) *Equitable torts*

As Professor Winfield notes, all torts share the fact that they are breaches of duty. But there are many equitable causes of action that are also breaches of duty. Breach of trust is one common example. Professor Winfield attempts to exclude the cause of action in equity for breach of trust in two ways. First, by arguing that equity does not deal in unliquidated damages and secondly, that the law of trusts should be regarded as a separate development "within the province of Equity".[5]

(i) Winfield's first argument

Professor Winfield's first proposition, that equity does not deal in unliquidated damages, is simply incorrect. Such awards have been available in equity since the Middle Ages with the earliest statute, in the reign of Richard II, explicitly

Enrichment and Unjust Sacrifice" (1987) 50 MLR 603; G Muir "Unjust Sacrifice and the Officious Intervener" in P Finn *Essays on Restitution* (Law Book Company Sydney 1990) 297.

  [2] M Brazier (Gen ed.) *Clerk & Lindsell on Torts* (17th edn. Sweet & Maxwell London 1995) 1.
  [3] WVH Rogers (ed.) *Winfield & Jolowicz on Tort* (15th edn. Sweet & Maxwell London 1998) 1.
  [4] P Winfield *The Province of the Law of Tort* (CUP Cambridge 1931) 32.
  [5] Winfield above note 4, 113–115.

enabling the Chancellor to award damages.[6] In his compiled Chancery precedents from 1559–1646, Tothill listed 11 cases in the courts of Chancery where "damages" were awarded to compensate for loss.[7]

The notion that equity does not deal in unliquidated compensatory damages took root because the courts of Chancery developed different language and different procedures to describe and give effect to awards which were, in reality, compensatory damages. For example, the award against a trustee of an "account" for "wilful default" was a method commonly used to effect compensatory damages. The bill for an account for wilful default involved an inquiry into receipts and disbursements of a trustee to determine whether the trustee should be charged for any loss to the trust. It required instances of wrongdoing and encompassed both deliberate and careless breaches of trust.[8] It was "analogous to proceedings at law"[9] in that at law a mortgagee or executor was also required to account for any receipts they had failed to make as a result of their own negligence.[10] In *Re Salmon*[11] a trustee had made an authorised investment of the trust property but without due care. The Court of Appeal held that in an action for wilful default the trustee was liable to make good the deficiency. Explaining this action in modern terms, Ipp J, in the Supreme Court of Western Australia in *Permanent Building Society* v. *Wheeler*[12] noted that the duty of a trustee to exercise reasonable care ran parallel to common law duties of care (such as negligence).

In other instances different awards were made so that a compensatory award was unnecessary. The award of the "*common* account" also involved an inquiry as to whether the trustee should be charged with any deficiency in the trust. But the common account, which resembled the later nineteenth century description of "restitution to the trust estate" did not require any pleading of fault or loss. The "common account" merely required that the defendant be called upon to account for any deficiency in the trust.[13] The award of a common account was

---

[6] 17 Ric II c 6 (1393). For the history of the medieval jurisdiction of Chancery awards of damages until the mid-nineteenth century reforms see PM McDermott, "Jurisdiction of the Court of Chancery to Awards Damages" (1992) 108 LQR 652.

[7] Tothill (1559–1646) 51–52; 21 ER 121.

[8] JH Stannard "Wilful Default" [1979] Conv 345; *Re Chapman, Cocks* v. *Chapman* [1896] 2 Ch 763; *Armitage* v. *Nurse* [1998] Ch 241 (CA) 252 (Millett LJ) "A trustee is said to be accountable on the footing of wilful default when he is accountable not only for money which he has in fact received but also for money which he could with reasonable diligence have received. It is sufficient that the trustee has been guilty of a want of ordinary prudence."

[9] *Ex Parte Bax* (1751) 2 Ves Sen 388; 28 ER 248.

[10] *Bulstrode* v. *Bradley* (1747) 3 Atk 582; 26 ER 1136; *Re Salmon* (1889) 42 Ch D 351, 369.

[11] (1889) 42 Ch D 351.

[12] (1994) 14 ACSR 109 (SCWA)157.

[13] *Partington* v. *Reynolds* (1858) 4 Drew 253, 255–256; 62 ER 98 "There are two different modes of accounting . . . and accordingly there are two different forms of decree in use to compel him to account . . . They proceed on totally distinct grounds. The one supposes no misconduct [common account]; the other is entirely grounded in misconduct." (Kindersley V-C). See also TH Haddan *Outlines of the Administrative Jurisdiction of the Court of Chancery* (W Maxwell London 1862) 229–242; S Elliott 'Compensation Claims Against Trustees' (D.Phil Thesis University of Oxford 2001).

simply based upon the fact that the trustee held office as trustee and was liable for the property. It involved an account of the property actually received and what had become of it.[14] Although the award often resulted in the same quantum as a compensatory award its overt concern was "perfection" of the trust property. Questions of loss were irrelevant. As a result, a common misconception, ignoring the existence of an account for wilful default, was that because the common account was not compensatory, courts of equity "never entertained a suit for damages . . . It was [always] a suit for the restitution of the actual money or the thing or the value of the thing".[15]

In cases of actual fraud such as fraudulent misrepresentation, courts of equity were prepared to acknowledge that awards made were equivalent to unliquidated compensatory damages.[16] In these cases courts of common law and chancery courts had concurrent jurisdiction.[17] Although there was some conflict between different tests at common law and in equity it was accepted that it was no objection to an action for fraudulent misrepresentation in equity that the same cause of action arose at common law, "for in cases of fraud. . . the court of equity has a concurrent jurisdiction with the common law".[18]

Peek v. *Gurney*[19] was a case brought as a bill in Equity to recover compensation for loss suffered due to deliberate misstatements made in a company prospectus. In an appeal to the House of Lords, Lord Chelmsford stated that the loss could be recovered in equity just as it could be recovered at common law. The action failed as the claimants had not received the prospectus from the defendant company directors as a subscriber but only later as a subsequent purchaser of shares on the market. However, speaking of the nature of the action, Lord Chelmsford stated:[20]

> "It is a suit instituted to recover damages from the respondents for the injury the Appellant has sustained by having been deceived and misled . . . It is precisely analogous to the common law action for deceit. There can be no doubt that Equity exercises a concurrent jurisdiction in cases of this description, and the same principles applicable to them must prevail both at Law and in Equity."

---

[14] *Read's Case* (1603) 5 Co 33b, 34a; 77 ER 103; *Pybus* v. *Smith* (1790) 1 Ves 189, 193; 30 ER 294.

[15] *Re Collie; ex p Adamson* (1878) 8 Ch D 807 (CA) 819 (James, Bagallay LJJ). See also *Bartlett* v. *Barclays Bank Trust Co Ltd (No 2)* [1980] Ch 515, 543; *Re Dawson* [1966] 2 NSWR 211.

[16] *Schroeder* v. *Mendl* (1877) 37 LT 452 (CA) 454. See also cases where compensation for loss to a claimant also seeking specific performance of a contract of sale: *Todd* v. *Gee* (1810) 17 Ves Jun 274; 34 ER 106; *Phelps* v. *Prothero* (1855) 7 De G M & G 722; 44 ER 280.

[17] "Where there is a claim for damages on the ground of fraud. . . it is immaterial whether it is framed or considered as an action in tort or a claim for equitable relief": L A Sheridan *Fraud in Equity* (Pitman and Sons London 1956) 36; *Canson Enterprises Ltd* v. *Boughton & Co* (1991) 85 DLR (4th) 129 (SCC) 141.

[18] *Colt* v. *Woollaston* (1723) 2 PW 154, 156; 24 ER 679, 680; *Metropolitan Bank* v. *Heiron* (1880) 5 Ex D 319 (CA) 343; *Boston Deep Sea Fishing & Ice Co* v. *Ansell* (1888) 39 Ch D 389 (CA) 367–368.

[19] (1873) LR 6 HL 377 (HL).

[20] *Peek* v. *Gurney* above note 19, 390, 393; *Ramshire* v. *Bolton* (1869) 8 LR Eq 294; *Slim* v. *Croucher* (1860) 1 De G F & J 518, 524; 45 ER 462, 465 (Lord Campbell LC).

Aside from its concurrent jurisdiction in fraud cases, modern recognition that equity made awards of compensation in its exclusive jurisdiction did not occur in the House of Lords until 1914 in *Nocton* v. *Lord Ashburton*.[21] In that case, the Court of Appeal had held that a solicitor, Nocton, had been fraudulent in obtaining a release of security held by his client, Lord Ashburton, over property in which Nocton had a personal interest. The Court of Appeal awarded compensatory damages for deceit at common law. In the House of Lords, their Lordships held that the conduct did not amount to deceit but did amount to the equitable wrong of breach of fiduciary duty. Although stating that the award in equity was not called compensatory damages, Viscount Haldane LC, in the leading speech, acknowledged that it was practically the same:[22]

> "Courts of Equity had jurisdiction to direct accounts to be taken, and in proper cases to order the solicitor to replace the property improperly acquired from the client, or to make compensation if he had lost it by acting in breach of a duty."

This point has now been iterated and reiterated[23] and references to this award of compensation in equity for breach of fiduciary duty have even been used as a basis to extend liability for compensatory damages at common law for the tort of negligence.[24] Although the modern tendency is to call the equitable compensatory award "equitable compensation" rather than "compensatory damages" both are money awards designed to compensate for loss caused by a wrong and the different labels are a "difference without a distinction".[25] As Lord Nicholls acknowledged, giving the advice of the Privy Council in *Tang Man Sit* v. *Capacious Investments Ltd*:[26]

> "In the present case nothing turns on the historic distinction between damages, awarded by common law courts, and compensation, a monetary remedy awarded by the Court of Chancery for breach of equitable obligations. It will be convenient therefore to use the nomenclature of damages which has been adopted throughout this case."

---

[21] [1914] AC 932 (HL); I Davidson "The Equitable Remedy of Compensation" (1982) 13 MULR 349. In fact, in 1902 the Court of Appeal had made such an award for loss caused by a breach of fiduciary duty and Vaughan Williams LJ had stated in that "I am clear that there is a remedy in the shape of damages": *Re Leeds and Hanley Theatres of Varieties Ltd* [1902] 2 Ch D 809, 825.

[22] *Nocton* v. *Lord Ashburton* above note 21, 965.

[23] *Target Holdings Ltd* v. *Redferns (a firm)* [1996] 1 AC 421 (HL) 434; *Bristol and West Building Society* v. *Mothew* [1998] Ch 1 (CA) 17; *Aquaculture Corporation* v. *New Zealand Green Mussel Co Ltd* [1990] 3 NZLR 299 (CANZ) 301 (Cooke P); C Rickett "Equitable Compensation: The Giant Stirs" (1996) 112 LQR 27.

[24] *White* v. *Jones* [1995] 2 AC 207 (HL) 270–274, 285–286; *Henderson* v. *Merrett Syndicates Ltd* [1995] 2 AC 145 (HL) 179, 204–205. See also *Hedley Byrne & Co Ltd* v. *Heller & Partners Ltd* [1964] AC 465 (HL).

[25] *Day* v. *Mead* [1987] 2 NZLR 443 (CANZ) 451; *Canson Enterprises Ltd* v. *Boughton & Co* (1991) 85 DLR (4th) 129 (SCC) 145–146.

[26] [1996] AC 514 (PC) 520. Recently the Court of Appeal also referred interchangeably to "damages" and "equitable compensation" for a breach of fiduciary duty: *United Pan-Europe Communications NV* v. *Deutsche Bank AG* [2000] 2 BCLC 461(CA). See also Mason and Carter *Restitution* 681.

(ii) Winfield's second argument

Professor Winfield's second argument for excluding breach of trust or other equitable wrongs from tort was finally rejected by the editors of the current (18th) edition of *Clerk & Lindsell*.[27] It is the purely historical reason that "all matters relating to trust fall within the province of the Chancery Division".[28] As Professor Birks has pointed out, such a distinction comes at the expense of rational principle and could lead to like wrongs being treated differently simply because they were born in different courts.[29] Recognising this weakness, the editors of *Clerk & Lindsell* now include the equitable wrongs of breach of fiduciary duty and breach of confidence in their tort text with the weak disclaimer that "strictly speaking, they cannot be regarded as torts".[30] And unlike the previous edition which began by enunciating the difficulty of defining a tort, the eighteenth edition begins by quoting from Professor Birks that "[t]orts are civil wrongs".[31]

Modern courts are also slowly recognising this need for a common category of wrongdoing spanning common law and equity. For instance, some legislation makes reference only to consequences flowing from a "wrong" or "wrongful act". Courts have accepted that equitable causes of action for breach of confidence[32] or dishonest assistance[33] fall within this definition.

In *Dubai Aluminium Co Ltd* v. *Salaam*[34] a partner of a firm had engaged in a number of sham transactions which resulted in transfers of large sums of money from the claimant corporation. The corporation brought an action for compensatory damages against all the partners. The issue was whether the cause of action in equity for the wrong of "knowing assistance" could be a "wrongful act or omission" within the terms of the Partnership Act 1890, s10 in order to make the other partners liable. Rix J, following an earlier judgment of Millett J in *Agip (Africa) Ltd* v. *Jackson*,[35] held that a knowing assistance claim in equity fell within the section. The Court of Appeal upheld this finding and Aldous LJ focussed upon the meaning of the word "tort":[36]

"the word 'tort' deriving from the Latin *tortus* meaning twisted or wrong, has become limited to encompass certain civil wrongs, but unless there are compelling reasons to

---

[27] A Dugdale (General ed.) *Clerk & Lindsell on Torts* (18th edn. Sweet & Maxwell 2000) 8.

[28] See also JD Davies "Restitution and Equitable Wrongs" in FD Rose (ed.) *Consensus ad Idem, Essays in Honour of Guenter Trietel* (Lloyds London 1996) 158, 176.

[29] P Birks "The Concept of a Civil Wrong" in D Owen (ed.) *Philosophical Foundations of Tort Law* (Clarendon Press Oxford 1995) 31, 35.

[30] *Clerk & Lindsell on Torts* above note 27, 8.

[31] *Clerk & Lindsell on Torts* above note 27, 1.

[32] *Talbot* v. *General Television Corporation Pty Ltd* [1980] VR 224 (SCV).

[33] *Dubai Aluminium Co Ltd* v. *Salaam* [1999] 1 Lloyds Rep 415.

[34] [1999] 1 Lloyds Rep 415.

[35] [1991] 1 Ch 265, 296.

[36] *Dubai Aluminium Co Ltd* v. *Salaam* [2001] QB 113 (CA) 140–141. Although the Latin adjective *tortus* (from *torqueo*) means "curved, bent or twisted" it seems never to have been used in Latin of "wrong" or "error", which is a French metaphorical development from "bent" or "twisted": P Glare (ed.) *Oxford Latin Dictionary* (Clarendon Press Oxford 1985) 1952.

the contrary, it would not be right to confine the words 'wrongful acts' to such acts as are regarded as tortious."

Exactly the same recognition of equitable wrongs, as part of a common category of civil wrongs, was also recently made by Judge Mann QC in *Casio Computer Co Ltd* v. *Sayo*,[37] in a judgment upheld by the Court of Appeal.[38] In that case the question was whether a claim for knowing assistance fell within Article 5(3) of the Brussels Convention on Jurisdiction and Enforcement of Judgments in Civil and Commercial Matters 1968. That article provides that "A person domiciled in a Contracting State may, in another Contracting State, be sued . . . in matters relating to tort, delict or quasi-delict, in the courts for the place where the harmful event occurred." One question was whether a claim for knowing assistance fell within the meaning of "tort, delict or quasi-delict". Judge Mann QC held that it did stating that "even though the English law of tort is not operating . . . one can see parallels. A wrong is being committed and loss can be said to be caused or at least contributed to".[39] In the Court of Appeal this reasoning was upheld and knowing assistance was referred to in the leading judgment by Tuckey LJ as an "equitable wrong".

A final example of a move toward recognition of a common category of wrongdoing is the way in which common law torts have influenced the development of equitable wrongs in the award of exemplary damages for equitable wrongs.[40] Traditionally exemplary damages have not been awarded for equitable wrongs, only for torts. The question of their availability for equitable wrongs arose in the New Zealand case of *Aquaculture Corporation* v. *New Zealand Green Mussel Co Ltd*.[41] The New Zealand Green Mussel Company had used information confidentially provided to one of its executives by Aquaculture Corporation. The use of this information enabled the New Zealand Green Mussel Company to manufacture and market a therapeutic drug and possible remedy for arthritis. The New Zealand trial judge, Prichard J, considered that Aquaculture had suffered a loss of $1.5 million but did not make that award as he considered that compensatory damages were not available in equity. Instead he awarded $100,000 in exemplary damages.[42] The Court of Appeal overturned the finding that compensatory damages were unavailable and awarded $1.5 million in compensatory damages. Although exemplary damages were not seen as

---

[37] (2001) 98 LSG 45.

[38] *Casio* v. *Sayo* [2001] EWCA Civ 661 (CA).

[39] *Casio* above note 37, 47. See also *Douglas* v. *Hello! Ltd* [2001] 2 WLR 992 (CA) 1024, Sedley LJ calling breach of confidence a 'tort'.

[40] See also the suggestions that the same approach should be taken to issues of causation and remoteness when assessing equitable compensation for breach of an equitable duty as that approach at common law: *Bristol and West Building Society* v. *Mothew* [1998] Ch 1 (CA) 17; *Seager* v. *Copydex Ltd* [1967] 1 WLR 923 (CA). Cf. *Target Holdings Ltd* v. *Redferns (a firm)* [1996] 1 AC 421 (HL) 434.

[41] *Aquaculture Corporation* above note 23, 301 (Cooke P); *Cook* v. *Evatt (No 2)* [1992] 1 NZLR 676 (HCNZ) (breach of fiduciary duty).

[42] *New Zealand Green Mussel Co Ltd* v. *Aquaculture Corporation* (1986) 1 NZIPR 667 (HCNZ).

necessary the court agreed that exemplary damages can be awarded if the compensatory award is inadequate. Canadian Courts have also allowed exemplary damages for equitable wrongs[43] and, in its Report on *Aggravated, Exemplary and Restitutionary Damages*,[44] the Law Commission recommended that English law follow these cases in providing for the availability of exemplary damages for equitable wrongs. Central to this recommendation was the Law Commission's definition of a wrong which included conduct regarded as wrongful in equity as well as that regarded as tortious at common law.

Although equitable wrongs are treated in a separate chapter in this book, this is simply a division of convenience reflecting the historical concerns in different areas of the law of wrongs. The fact that there is no meaningful distinction between the classes of equitable wrongs and common law wrongs is stressed throughout this book. Indeed, chapter seven considers "intellectual property wrongs" which straddle both common law and equity.

2) Civil wrongs and criminal wrongs

Although the literature in relation to civil remedies (including gain-based damages) for criminal wrongs has grown,[45] this issue is not examined in this book. The wrong in these cases is different from those considered in this book since it is committed against the State. In addition, there are powerful arguments against allowing the civil law a complementary role to the criminal law.

One argument already recognised by the courts is that the civil law has no role in prescribing damages where the legislature has developed its own scheme for punishment of these wrongs.[46] Moreover, no case has recognised that the civil law can have a role in such instances. The related argument that a cause of action can arise in tort based upon a criminal prohibition has been rejected by the House of Lords.[47]

B   The nature of a wrong

1) Conduct relied upon as a breach of duty

The common element shared by wrongs is that they are a breach of duty.[48] However, the fact that a cause of action is *capable* of being characterised as a

[43] *Norberg* v. *Wynrib* (1992) 92 DLR (4th) 440 (SCC) 505–507; *McDonald Estate* v. *Martin* [1995] CCL 1142 (Man CA); *Gerula* v. *Flores* [1995] CCL 8583 (OCA).

[44] *Law Commission 1997* 5.54, 5.55.

[45] G Virgo *Restitution* ch. 19; *Goff and Jones* ch. 38.

[46] *Chief Constable of Leicestershire* v. *M* [1989] 1 WLR 20, 23; *Halifax Building Society* v. *Thomas* [1996] Ch 217 (CA) 229, 230.

[47] *Lonrho Ltd* v. *Shell Petroleum Co Ltd (No 2)* [1981] 3 WLR 33 (HL).

[48] In *Stubbings* v. *Webb* [1993] AC 498 (HL) the House of Lords accepted that a breach of duty was the basis of a tort but held that the phrase in the Limitation Act 1939 was restricted to certain non-intentional torts because of its juxtaposition in a sentence with negligence and nuisance.

breach of duty is not sufficient to establish a wrong. It is necessary to determine that the remedy granted responds to the cause of action in its character as a breach of duty, so that it can be known that this is the characterisation adopted by the law.

The first stage of inquiry, identifying a breach of duty, is not difficult. The difficulty arises in determining whether the law, in granting a remedy, is relying upon the facts in their character as a breach of duty or is relying upon some other characterisation of the facts. It is a matter of everyday observation that the same set of facts can give rise to different causes of action.

This section considers how a wrong may be identified. Since the principal alternative is unjust enrichment, the first task is to explain what is meant by the category of unjust enrichment and why that category should be considered independent from the category of wrongs. It will then be seen that an indicator that a cause of action is a wrong is the availability of exemplary or compensatory damages, remedies which are unavailable for actions in unjust enrichment but which demonstrate characterisation of the cause of action as a breach of duty. However, the lack of an award of compensation historically should not be taken as conclusive proof that a cause of action is *not* a wrong. As a result, this section examines the nature and basis of many of the causes of action for which compensatory damages have not been awarded historically and shows why the best characterisation of most of them, given their historical operation, is that they are not wrongs but actions in unjust enrichment. This section concludes by examining causes of action for which compensation has not been historically awarded but which, of their nature, are wrongs and acknowledges the possibility that even where a cause of action should be characterised as an action in unjust enrichment, a new concurrent wrong might be recognised by the courts or Parliament. It also explains that there are some causes of action which are extremely difficult, if not impossible, to classify. The cause of action for unconscionable transactions is one of these. In such cases it is necessary for courts to decide, in the future, which characterisation of the particular event should be preferred.

2) Distinguishing wrongs from other events

(a) *Unjust enrichment*

(i) The archetypal action in unjust enrichment

The archetypal action in unjust enrichment is an action for restitution of a mistaken payment. An insurance company mistakenly pays out a policy to the defendant believing it to be valid. The insurance company has a right to repayment of that money from the defendant.[49] This is now accepted to be an action in unjust enrichment. As early as 1948 Lord Wright recognised that "any civilised system of law is bound to provide remedies for cases of what has been

---

[49] *Kelly* v. *Solari* (1841) 9 M & W 54; 152 ER 24.

called unjust enrichment . . . Payment under a mistake of fact is only one head of this category of the law".[50] The House of Lords has recently emphasised that a cause of action seeking recovery of a mistaken payment is not "founded upon any wrong by the third party . . . It is founded simply on the fact that . . . as we say nowadays, for the third party to retain the money would result in his unjust enrichment at the expense of the owner of the money".[51] Unjust enrichment is firmly established as a category of the law unconcerned with wrongdoing.[52]

Although it is now clear that a mistaken payment is not a wrong but an action in unjust enrichment, an attempt might have been made to characterise this cause of action as a breach of a duty to repay the money in order to suggest that the cause of action is a wrong.[53] This characterisation would be on the basis that the action is based upon a duty not to accept mistaken payments. This would, however, be an extraordinary duty. It is recognised that the cause of action begins to run from the time of receipt of the money not the time of the recipient's knowledge of the mistake.[54] Characterisation of the receipt of a mistaken payment as a breach of duty would mean that a passive, even ignorant, recipient has a duty at the time of the receipt to prevent a mistaken payment. But this might be an impossible duty to fulfil as the money might have been paid into the recipient's account without his knowledge. Even instances of the strict liability tort of conversion (or "wrongful interference with goods") require some positive act of interference with the defendant's property.[55] Professor Weinrib's remarks on strict liability are apposite in the instance of a purely passive receipt such as a mistaken payment:[56]

> "In judging an action by its effects, strict liability treats the defendant's agency as an incoherent normative phenomenon. . .the act turns out to be wrongful—and therefore impermissible—because of the effect that completes the action. The agent is conceded a capacity for purposiveness that, when the harm occurs, turns out to have been morally incapable of being exercised and therefore to have been no capacity at all."

---

[50] *Fibrosa Spolka Akcyjna* v. *Fairbairn Lawson Combe Barbour Ltd* [1943] AC 32 (HL) 61.

[51] *Lipkin Gorman* v. *Karpnale Ltd* [1991] 2 AC 548 (HL) 572; *Fibrosa Spolka Akcyjna* v. *Fairbairn Lawson Combe Barbour Ltd* above note 50.

[52] *Woolwich Equitable Building Society* v. *Inland Revenue Commissioners* [1993] AC 70 (HL) 197; *Westdeutsche Landesbank Girozentrale* v. *Islington LBC* [1996] AC 669 (HL) 710; *Kleinwort Benson* v. *Glasgow CC* [1997] 3 WLR 923 (CA) 931, 947; *Banque Financière de la Cité* v. *Parc (Battersea) Ltd* [1998] 2 WLR 475 (HL); *Kleinwort Benson* v. *Lincoln CC* [1999] 2 AC 349 (HL) 408.

[53] PA Butler 'Viewing Restitution at the Level of a Secondary Remedial Obligation (1990) 16 Uni Q Law J 27, 33–34.

[54] *Baker* v. *Courage & Co* [1910] 1 KB 56; *Kleinwort Benson* v. *Lincoln City Council* [1999] 2 AC 349 (HL) 359 (Lord Browne-Wilkinson), 386 (Lord Goff), 409 (Lord Hope); *David Securities Pty Ltd* v. *Commonwealth Bank of Australia Ltd* (1992) 175 CLR 353 (HCA).

[55] Torts (Interference with Goods) Act 1977 s. 1. In fact the strict-liability wrong of conversion developed because of the absence of any generalised primary right in the common law, akin to the Roman *vindicatio*: D Ibbetson *An Historical Introduction to the Law of Obligations* (OUP Oxford 1999).

[56] E Weinrib *The Idea of Private Law* (Harvard Univ Press Mass 1995) 181–182.

(ii) The unjust enrichment inquiry

It is now accepted that as an independent category of rights and obligations four elements must be considered for actions in unjust enrichment:[57] the defendant must be enriched; that enrichment must be unjust; the enrichment must come at the expense of the claimant; and a court should consider if any defences apply. Two points should be noted.

The first is in relation to the inquiry whether the enrichment is unjust. It is not enough for courts to refer simply to an action as one in "unjust enrichment". As Lord Goff stated in *Lipkin Gorman* v. *Karpnale Ltd,*[58] "even though the underlying principle of recovery is the principle of unjust enrichment, nevertheless, when recovery is denied, it is denied on the basis of legal principle." An "unjust factor" or "reason for restitution" must be given.[59]

The second point relates to the requirement that the enrichment is "at the expense of " the claimant.[60] This insists that the enrichment should be "by subtraction from" the claimant.[61] As Morritt LJ has stated, this requires that "the immediate source of the unjust enrichment must be the plaintiff".[62] In the House of Lords in *Banque Financière de la Cité* v. *Parc (Battersea) Ltd,*[63] Lord Clyde makes this point forcefully (although loosely using the word "loss" instead of "transfer"):[64]

"The principle [of unjust enrichment] requires at least that the plaintiff should have sustained a loss through the provision of something for the benefit of some other person with no intention of making a gift, that the defendant should have received some form of enrichment, and that the enrichment has come about because of the loss."

The Supreme Court of Canada is equally explicit and has made this point on a number of occasions.[65] In *Citadel General Assurance Co* v. *Lloyds Bank Canada,*[66] La Forest J, delivering the judgment of himself, Gonthier, Cory, McLachlin, Iacobucci and Major JJ made the same point although avoiding the use of the word "loss":

[57] P Birks *Introduction* 21. See *Banque Financière de la Cité* v. *Parc (Battersea) Ltd* [1999] 1 AC 221 (HL) 227 (Lord Steyn) 234 (Lord Hoffmann, with whom Lord Griffiths, Steyn, Clyde and Hutton agreed generally); *Portman Building Society* v. *Hamlyn Taylor Neck* [1998] 4 All ER 202 (CA) 206.
[58] *Lipkin Gorman* above note 51, 578.
[59] "The approach of the common law is to look for an unjust factor": *Kleinwort Benson* v. *Lincoln City Council* above note 52, 409 (Lord Hope).
[60] This phrase seems to have originated in an article by Professor Ames: J B Ames "The History of Assumpsit" (1888) 2 Harv L R 1. *Kleinwort Benson* v. *Birmingham City Council* [1996] 3 WLR 1139 (CA) 1157.
[61] P Birks *Introduction* 23.
[62] *Kleinwort Benson* v. *Birmingham City Council* above note 60,1156.
[63] *Banque Financière* above note 52, 237.
[64] As will be noted in ch. three a financial "loss" is not required-merely a transfer of value from the claimant. Lord Clyde's reference to "loss" is best viewed in this broader sense of "subtraction" or "transfer" not requiring a financial minus to the defendant.
[65] *LAC Minerals Ltd* v. *International Corona Resources Ltd* [1989] 2 SCR 574 (SCC)669; *Air Canada* v. *British Columbia* [1989] 1 SCR 1161 (SCC) 1202–1203. *Regional Municipality of Peel* v. *Canada* (1992) 98 DLR (4th) 140 (SCC) 154–155;
[66] [1997] 3 SCR 805 (SCC) 824. See also similar statements in Australia in *Hill* v. *Van Erp* (1997) 188 CLR 159 (HCA) 226–227 (Gummow J).

"A claim for unjust enrichment, is concerned with giving back to someone something that has been taken from them (a restitutionary proprietary award) or its equivalent value (a personal restitutionary award) . . . [the function] is to ensure that when a plaintiff has been deprived of wealth that is either in his possession or would have accrued for his benefit, it is restored to him. The measure of restitutionary recovery is the gain the defendant made at the plaintiff's expense."

In this book, the term "restitution" is used to describe this measure. The use of this term is explained in greater detail in chapter three. It is enough, at this point, to note that "restitution" is used to refer to the reversal of a transfer of value from a claimant to a defendant. It will be seen that this is a narrower use of the word than that which is usually advocated by commentators.

(iii) Two meanings of unjust enrichment

The law of unjust enrichment and the law of wrongdoing should be seen as completely independent. The law of wrongdoing is concerned with providing remedies for causes of action which rely upon breaches of duty. The law of unjust enrichment is concerned with various *non-wrongful* causes of action which operate only to reverse transfers of wealth (obtained by subtraction) from a claimant to a defendant. This approach means that any award of restitution as a response to a wrong is part of the law of wrongs. The principle of reversing "unjust enrichment" has no part to play.

Commentators are divided on whether this approach is the best method for organising the law. Difficulty arises because the remedy of restitution can occur for a wrong as well as for an unjust enrichment. An alternative view is that a principle of unjust enrichment underlies all cases in which the remedy of restitution is awarded. This view is supported by Goff and Jones,[67] Professors Maddaugh and McCamus,[68] Professor Tettenborn,[69] President Mason and Professor Carter,[70] the United States *Restatement of Restitution*[71] and the reporter of the new *Restatement*, Professor Kull.[72] This alternative view can be labelled the "quadrationist" view because it argues that restitution and unjust enrichment "quadrate".[73] It has been expounded in detail most recently by Professor Burrows.[74]

Advocating this alternative view, Professor Burrows argues that the category of wrongs has not traditionally been regarded as wholly independent from the

---

[67] A Burrows *The Law of Restitution* ch. 14, "Unjust Enrichment by Wrongdoing"; *Goff and Jones* 709; G McMeel *The Modern Law of Restitution* (Blackstone Press London 2000) 307.

[68] PD Maddaugh and JD McCamus *The Law of Restitution* (Canada Law Book Co Ontario 1990) 35.

[69] A Tettenborn "Misnomer—A Response to Professor Birks" in W Cornish et al *Restitution* 31.

[70] Mason and Carter *Restitution* 56–57.

[71] *Restatement of Restitution*, 14–15. This position is maintained in the discussion draft for the second Restatement: American Law Institute *Restatement of the Law of Restitution and Unjust Enrichment: Discussion Draft* (American Law Institute Philadelphia 2000) 6–7.

[72] A Kull "Rationalising Restitution" (1995) 83 Cal L Rev 1191.

[73] P Birks "Unjust Enrichment and Wrongful Enrichment" (2001) 79 Texas Law Rev 1767, 1769.

[74] A Burrows "Quadrating Restitution and Unjust Enrichment: A Matter of Principle" [2000] RLR 257.

category of unjust enrichment. He also argues that there is no incoherence in a classification which collates cases in which restitution is awarded for non-wrongful unjust enrichments with cases in which restitution is awarded for a wrong. He argues that all such cases in which restitution is awarded can be seen as based upon a common principle of unjust enrichment.

Professor Birks' work, *Introduction to the Law of Restitution,* equivocates on this point.[75] Professor Birks acknowledges the two possibilities diagramatically. The first, and the view this book prefers, is to regard wrongdoing and unjust enrichment as independent categories. Restitution can be a response to an unjust enrichment. Restitution can also be an independent response to a wrong. Professor Birks demonstrates this in a diagram with the event on the horizontal axis and response on the vertical axis:[76]

	Wrongs	Unjust Enrichments
Restitution	✔	✔
Compensation	✔	X
Punishment/ Example	✔	X

The contrary, quadrationist view is that awards of restitution for wrongdoing should be grouped with awards of restitution based upon unjust enrichment rather than with awards based upon wrongs. Unjust enrichment then is a category divided in two: unjust enrichment by wrongdoing (or "dependent" unjust enrichment) and unjust enrichment by subtraction (or "autonomous" unjust enrichment). This was diagrammatically represented by Professor Birks as follows:[77]

	Wrongs	Unjust Enrichment By Wrongs	Unjust Enrichment by Subtraction
Restitution	X	✔	✔
Compensation	✔	X	X
Punishment/ Example	✔	X	X

Professor Birks now explicitly supports the first model[78] and others take a similar position.[79]

[75] P Birks *Introduction* 42–44.

[76] In the diagrams which follow the events and responses are abbreviated to focus upon the categories of wrongs and unjust enrichment. One response included by Professor Birks which is omitted, but discussed in detail in ch. 5, is "perfection" or "performance".

[77] P Birks *Introduction* 42.

[78] P Birks "Misnomer" in W Cornish et al *Restitution* 1.

[79] G Virgo *Restitution* 445–448; R Grantham and C Rickett *Enrichment and Restitution in New Zealand* (Hart Publishing Oxford 2000) 471.

The first model, or narrow view, which considers unjust enrichment as a separate and independent category from wrongdoing, should be preferred for two reasons. The first is the conceptual confusion which otherwise results. The second is the importance of appreciating that the wrong is the basis of the cause of action.

Although the position adopted by the judiciary, with a lax use of the word "unjust enrichment" appears to be the quadrationist view, there are significant problems with this approach, which can only lead to confusion.[80] All the judicial references to the principle of unjust enrichment in the context of the law of wrongs have been made in circumstances where the remedy is one which is operating to strip a defendant of profit made from the wrong[81] (although there have also been judicial references to a category of "unjust enrichment by wrongdoing").[82] The confusion caused by this view is that it suggests a commonality between these awards which operate to strip a claimant of profits made from the wrong and awards of restitution for (non-wrongful or autonomous) actions in unjust enrichment by treating them as both based on a common principle of unjust enrichment. There is no such commonality.

Awards designed to strip a defendant of profits do not exist in the law of unjust enrichment. It will be shown in detail in chapter three that this type of profit-stripping award should not even be referred to as restitution as it is an entirely different remedy based upon an entirely different premise. The term "restitution" should be used only to refer to awards that operate to reverse transfers of value. In cases of awards which operate to strip profits, the term "disgorgement" should be used. The "principle" behind such an award is not unjust enrichment but deterrence of wrongdoing. The result can be represented by a diagram similar to the one above:

	Wrongs	Unjust Enrichments
Restitution	✔	✔
Disgorgement	✔	X
Compensation	✔	X
Punishment/Example	✔	X

A profits-based disgorgement award is not available in an action for non-wrongful unjust enrichment because unjust enrichment is not concerned with deterring breaches of duty. Deterrence cannot be relevant to the many

---

[80] J Edelman "Unjust Enrichment, Restitution and Wrongs" (2001) 79 Tex Law Rev 1869.

[81] *My Kinda Town* v. *Soll* [1982] FSR 147, 156; *Westdeutsche Landesbank* v. *Islington LBC* [1996] AC 669 (HL) 723; *Dart Industries Inc* v. *Décor Corp Pty Ltd* (1993) 179 CLR 101 (HCA) 111, 123; *Potton Ltd* v. *Yorkclose Ltd* [1990] FSR 11; *Attorney General* v. *Guardian Newspapers (No 2)* [1990] 1 AC 109 (HL) 266; *Reading* v. *The King* [1948] 2 KB 268, 275; *LAC Minerals Ltd* v. *International Corona Resources Ltd* [1989] 2 SCR 574 (SCC); *Sheldon* v. *Metro-Goldwyn Pictures Corp* 309 US 390 (1940) (SCUS) 399; *Canadian Aero Service* v. *O'Malley* (1973) 40 DLR (3d) 371 (SCC) 392.

[82] *Banque Financière de la Cité* v. *Parc (Battersea) Ltd* above note 52, 226 (Lord Steyn); *Portman Building Society* above note 57, 206 (Millett LJ).

strict liability actions in unjust enrichment such as mistaken payments. Just as it is meaningless to suggest that a passive recipient of a mistaken payment is under a duty not to receive it, it would also be meaningless to suggest that the same recipient should be deterred from the initial passive receipt.

The fact that profits-based disgorgement awards are not possible in autonomous unjust enrichment is demonstrated in the "at the expense of" requirement of a transfer of value from the claimant.[83] The profit made by the defendant is a different measure from the value transferred from the claimant. Although the two awards might coincide where profits are stripped in their character as the *traceable substitute* of value transferred from a claimant, if these cases are part of the law of unjust enrichment it is clear that they are not concerned with stripping profits *qua* profits.[84] The term "unjust enrichment" should never be used to describe a deliberate profit-stripping deterrent measure.

The confusion deriving from the use of the term unjust enrichment in the law of wrongs to describe awards of disgorgement (or profit-stripping) based upon deterrence can be seen by contrasting two United States decisions. The first is the decision of the 10th Circuit of the United States Court of Appeals in *Beck and Others* v. *Northern Natural Gas Company*.[85] Chapter four discusses this case in more detail but it can be briefly outlined here. The Northern Natural Gas company committed an innocent trespass by storing excess gas under the claimants' properties. The additional profits made as a result of the storage were around $12 million. The reasonable rental rate for the storage, however, was around $2 million. The claimants appealed from an award of the reasonable rental rate seeking an award of the profits from the wrong of trespass, describing the additional profits as "unjust enrichment", arising from the trespass. The court held that the "unjust enrichment" did not allow disgorgement of profits not subtracted from the claimants. The profits conferred upon Northern Natural Gas had not come "from" (or, at the expense of) the claimants.[86] The reason why "unjust enrichment" could not provide recovery of the profits in this case was because they could only be reached by a profit-stripping deterrent remedy. Unjust enrichment is concerned with reversing transferred enrichment.[87]

---

[83] In ch. three it is explained that a "transfer" in the law of unjust enrichment, just as in the law of wrongs, includes situations which are not intended by the transferor or even known to him and which result in no loss to him: P Birks "At the Expense of the Claimant: Direct and Indirect Enrichment in English Law" (2000) Oxford U Comparative L Forum 1 at ouclf.iuscomp.org.

[84] In these cases the claimant reverses a transfer by tracing the "property into its product" for this "involves a decision by the owner of the original property to assert his title to the product in place of his original property": *Lipkin Gorman* v. *Karpnale Ltd* above note 51, 573; *Trustee of the Property of Jones* v. *Jones* [1997] Ch 159 (CA) 169. See ch. 3, text accompanying note 259–264.

[85] *Beck and Others* v. *Northern Natural Gas Company* 170 F 3d 1018 (1999 10th Cir CA).

[86] "the landowners offered nothing to show that the profits earned by Northern could reasonably be considered a benefit conferred upon Northern by *them*": *Beck* above note 85, 1024. See J Edelman "Claims to Profits in Actions for Trespass" (2000) 116 LQR 18.

[87] Nor could the profits be reached even in unjust enrichment by "tracing" the value transferred into the profits for, as the law currently stands, the process of tracing involves transactional links not causal links: L Smith "Restitution: The Heart of Corrective Justice" (2001) 79 Texas Law Rev 2115, 2162.

However, in the United States, Kentucky Court of Appeal case of *Edwards* v. *Lee's Administrators*, the term "unjust enrichment", was used confusingly in this "disgorgement" sense to allow the stripping of profits.[88] Edwards had built a hotel on his land and attracted numerous tourists to visit a cave that lay beneath his land. However a third of the cave lay beneath Lee's land. The court accepted that in knowingly allowing the tourists underneath Lee's land, Edwards had committed the wrong of trespass. Stites J held that the award should be the profit from the wrongdoing (a third of the net profits) because of what he referred to as the "unjust enrichment".[89] Although Stites J thought that the reasonable rental value was the same as the actual profit made from the trespass[90] he explained that cases involving profit-stripping share the "philosophy of all these decisions . . . that a wrongdoer shall not be permitted to make a profit from his own wrong".[91]

The preferable view is that these disgorgement awards are not part of the law of unjust enrichment which is not concerned with such explicit deterrence but concerned with reversing transferred enrichment. The Court of Appeal has stated that where profits "do not represent property . . . lost, [the claimant] cannot rely on the principle of subtractive unjust enrichment".[92] For the same reason, the High Court of Australia has recently rejected any role for the principle of unjust enrichment in a case concerned with profit-stripping because the account of profits does not focus upon any transfer from (described as "detriment to") the claimant:[93]

> "it has been suggested that the liability of the fiduciary to account for a profit made in breach of the fiduciary duty should be determined by reference to the concept of unjust enrichment . . . But the authorities in Australia and England deny that the liability of a fiduciary to account depends upon detriment to the plaintiff."

The Supreme Court of Canada have taken the same approach in relation to a proprietary award operating to disgorge a profit, holding that such an award cannot be part of the law of unjust enrichment because it does not depend "on 'enrichment' of the defendant and corresponding 'deprivation' of the plaintiff."[94] And, in the House of Lords, Lord Goff has stated that to "restore the parties to the position they were in before they entered the transaction . . . is, of course, the function of the law of restitution".[95]

---

[88]   *Edwards* v. *Lee's Administrators* 96 SW 2d 1028 (1936 CA Ken).

[89]   *Edwards* v. *Lee's Administrators* above note 88, 1032.

[90]   *Edwards* v. *Lee's Administrators* above note 88, 1031.

[91]   *Edwards* v. *Lee's Administrators* above note 88, 1032.

[92]   *Halifax Building Society* v. *Thomas* [1996] Ch 217 (CA) 224 (Peter Gibson LJ); *Macmillan Inc* v. *Bishopsgate Investment Trust Plc (No 3)* [1995] 1 WLR 978, 988 (Millett J); *Hill* v. *Van Erp* (1997) 188 CLR 159 (HCA) 226 (Gummow J).

[93]   *Warman International Ltd* v. *Dwyer* (1995) 182 CLR 544 (HCA) 557.

[94]   *Korkontzilas* v. *Soulos* [1997] 2 SCR 217 (SCC) 227. See also at 240 "While cases often involve both a wrongful act and an unjust enrichment, constructive trusts may be imposed on either ground: where there is a wrongful act but no unjust enrichment and corresponding deprivation; or where there is an unconscionable unjust enrichment in the absence of a wrongful act". See also ch. eight, Conclusion, text accompanying note 118.

[95]   *Westdeutsche Landesbank Girozentrale* v. *Islington LBC* [1996] AC 669 (HL) 681.

It is true that there are awards made in the law of wrongs which *do* operate to reverse transfers in the same manner as transfers are reversed for actions in non-wrongful unjust enrichment. These are awards which effect "restitution" as the term is used in this book. But there has been no judicial recognition of these cases as based on the principle of unjust enrichment and there is a further reason why these restitutionary remedies, like those disgorgement remedies, should be considered part of the law of wrongs rather than based on a common principle of "unjust enrichment". This is the importance of recognising the wrong as the basis of the cause of action. Separate treatment of wrongs and actions in unjust enrichment draws attention to the fact that there are often two different causes of action concurrently available and which can lead to different results.

Considering a shared principle of unjust enrichment as the basis for restitutionary damages for a wrong encourages the view that the two actions are really a single action in non-wrongful unjust enrichment.[96] This view can only be easily dispelled by emphasising that in one case the cause of action is based on the wrong and, in the other, on the non-wrongful unjust enrichment. This is most clearly done by accepting that wrongs which allow the response of restitutionary damages are part of the law of wrongs and actions in non-wrongful unjust enrichment which allow the response of restitution are part of the law of unjust enrichment.

This point is again emphasised in chapter three where it is noted that the actions, because they are based upon different elements, can lead to different results, although they may share an available response of reversing transfers. Examples considered in chapter three where differences could arise are in the availability of defences, awards of interest, limitation periods, choice of law rules and, most importantly, instances in which an action for restitutionary damages for a wrong exists but where there is no corresponding action for non-wrongful unjust enrichment. Indeed, in the context of determining the jurisdiction in which an action can be brought in private international law, courts now adopt a distinction between actions in "unjust enrichment" and actions in "tort" (which, as noted above, includes actions for equitable wrongs).[97]

(b) *Other causes of action*

Although the principal competitor is unjust enrichment, a cause of action for a wrong can also encounter other competitors. For, aside from actions in unjust

---

[96] J Beatson *Use and Abuse* ch. 8; D Friedmann "Restitution of Benefits Obtained Through the Appropriation of Property or the Commission of a Wrong" (1980) 80 Col LR 504; D Friedmann "Restitution for Wrongs: The Basis for Liability" in W Cornish et al *Restitution* ch. 9; S Worthington "Reconsidering Disgorgement for Wrongs" (1999) 62 MLR 218; Mr Jaffey also adopts the view that transfers are not reversed in the law of wrongs but instead of relying upon a principle of unjust enrichment he suggests that they are a type of "simulated or imputed contract" or "inferred contract": P Jaffey *The Nature and Scope of Restitution* (Hart Publishing Oxford 2000) 364–365; P Jaffey "Disgorgement for Breach of Contract" [2000] RLR 578, 585.

[97] *Kalfelis v. Bankhaus Schröder, Münchmeyer, Hengst and Co* [1998] ECR 5565 (ECJ); *Kleinwort Benson Ltd v. Glasgow City Council* [1999] 1 AC 153 (HL) 188, 196 (Lord Hutton).

enrichment, there are a number of other causes of action which are not wrongs. Numerous difficult questions arise as to how these actions should be categorised: rights to recover a reward for salvage, the right to recover income tax and judgment debts.[98] Another action for which classification is difficult is a general right of restitution based upon "vindication of a claimant proprietary rights".[99] If such an action exists[100] it is based solely and directly on the existence of proprietary rights in the claimant and not upon any breach of duty by the defendant.[101]

There are numerous more very difficult questions aside from classification that arise in relation to such non-wrongful acts. However, these questions are not part of this chapter nor of this book. This chapter is only devoted to examination of the scope of the law of wrongs.

3) Identifying wrongs

(a) A breach of duty

The difficulty in identifying a wrong lies in ascertaining when a remedy is given for a breach of duty and when it is not. Some cases are not difficult. As discussed above, torts are collected together on the basis that they are all causes of action which give remedies due to the fact that they are breaches of duty. On the other hand, although a mistaken payment might (with great difficulty) be characterised as a breach of a duty not to receive mistaken payments,[102] it was shown that the House of Lords has acknowledged that a mistaken payment is not a breach of duty—a characterisation which would have been extraordinarily difficult to make—but an action in unjust enrichment. Other cases are more difficult, particularly because the notion of a breach of duty (as breaches of fiduciary duty in chapter six show) is independent of any requirement of fault.

Problems arise because, where a cause of action is *capable* of being characterised as a breach of duty, it is difficult to know conclusively whether the cause of action relies upon a characterisation of the facts as a breach of duty in awarding the remedy. A conclusive indicator is whether exemplary damages are available. It only makes sense to impose punishment or deterrence for events which are breaches of duty. Another powerful indicator is whether compensatory damages are available when loss is suffered.[103] Professor MacCormick has

---

[98]   P Birks "Rights, Wrongs and Remedies" (2000) 20 OJLS 1, 28.

[99]   G Virgo *Restitution* 593; R Grantham and C Rickett *Enrichment and Restitution in New Zealand* (Hart Publishing Oxford 2000) 38.

[100]   Support for these views can be seen in various speeches in the House of Lords in *Foskett* v. *McKeown* [2001] 1 AC 102 (HL) 108, 115, 129, which recently stated that a claim based upon tracing property in equity was not a claim in unjust enrichment but a claim to vindicate a property right.

[101]   G Virgo *Restitution* 593; R Grantham and C Rickett *Enrichment and Restitution in New Zealand* above note 79, 38; L Smith "Unjust Enrichment, Property and the Structure of Trusts" (2000) 116 LQR 412, 421–425.

[102]   PA Butler "Viewing Restitution at the Level of a Secondary Remedial Obligation" (1990) 16 Uni Q Law Journ 27.

[103]   A Burrows *The Law of Restitution* 378.

observed that compensation, as reparation for harm, flows logically from a characterisation of an event as a breach of duty.[104] Unjust enrichment does not allow compensation as a response because an action in unjust enrichment is solely concerned with reversing illegitimate transfers: "it cannot explain any other measure of response".[105]

But the converse is not true. The *absence* of exemplary damages or the *absence* of compensatory damages does not mean that a cause of action is not a wrong. The most pertinent example of this is an innocent breach of copyright, discussed in detail in chapter seven. For such an innocent breach the only remedy that the legislation provides is *not* available is compensatory damages (and presumably also exemplary damages).[106] Even more extreme disgorgement remedies are available. Professor Atiyah has also argued that compensatory damages should be abolished in cases of personal injury.[107] But this would not strip negligence of its character as a wrong.

In *United States* v. *Burke*,[108] the question before the United States Supreme Court was whether back-pay awards under a statute for unlawful discrimination under the Civil Rights Act 1964 (US) were "tort-like" and therefore exempt from income tax. Blackmun J (joined in the majority by Rehnquist CJ, White, Stevens and Kennedy JJ) held that they were not. The majority's reasoning relied upon the fact that compensatory damages were not available. Quoting from *Salmond on the Law of Torts*,[109] the majority stated that "an action for damages is an essential characteristic of every true tort".[110]

Although the majority relied upon the absence of compensatory damages, and although this is a strong indicator, it cannot be determinative of the fact that a cause of action is not a wrong. Even if compensatory damages have not been awarded historically, a claimant may bring an action seeking compensatory damages where they have never previously been allowed *or* refused.[111] It would be a circular argument if a court refused compensatory damages because the cause of action is not a wrong if the unavailability of compensatory damages is the determinative test for whether the cause of action is a wrong.

Courts must decide conclusively, as they have in cases of mistaken payments, that the conduct does not amount to a breach of duty. In making that decision the *nature* and *basis* of the cause of action must be examined to determine

---

[104] N MacCormick "The Obligation of Reparation" in N MacCormick (ed.) *Legal Right and Social Democracy* (Clarendon Press Oxford 1982) 190, 221.

[105] P Birks "The Concept of a Civil Wrong" in D Owen (ed.) *Philosophical Foundations of Tort Law* (Clarendon Press Oxford 1995).

[106] Copyright Act 1988 s. 97(1).

[107] P Atiyah "Personal Injuries in the Twenty First Century: Thinking the Unthinkable" in P Birks (ed.) *Wrongs and Remedies* 1.

[108] 112 S Ct 1867; 504 US 229 (1992 SCUS).

[109] R Heuston *Salmond on the Law of Torts* (12th edn. Sweet & Maxwell London 1957) 9. See also R Heuston and R Buckley *Salmond on the Law of Torts* (21st edn. Sweet & Maxwell London 1996) 13.

[110] *United States* v. *Burke* above note 108, 236.

[111] *Boustany* v. *Piggott* (1995) 69 P & CR 298 (PC); *Mahoney* v. *Purnell* [1996] 3 All ER 61.

whether the remedies for the cause of action depend upon its characterisation as a breach of duty. This was why the minority (O'Connor and Thomas JJ) in *United States* v. *Burke* thought that the duties created by the Civil Rights Act were "tort-like" in nature. They criticised the approach of the majority as "focussing upon remedies", stating that this "misapprehends the nature of the inquiry." The inquiry "whether Title VII suits are based on the same sort of rights as a tort claim must be answered with reference to the nature of the statute".[112]

As a result of the indicia of wrongdoing, being the availability of exemplary damages or compensatory damages a list of non-statutory wrongs must include (1) torts; (2) equitable wrongs of breach of confidence, breach of fiduciary duty (including breaches of trust), actual fraud (including fraudulent misrepresentation) and knowing participation in a breach of fiduciary duty (the latter of which is discussed in detail below); (3) infringements of intellectual property (including passing off, trademark, patent, design and copyright infringement); and (4) breach of contract and the action for breach of promise referred to as "estoppel".

However, because the historical absence of compensatory damages does not necessarily exclude the possibility that a cause of action is a wrong, it is necessary to explain why a number of causes of action should be excluded from the category by examining the nature of those actions. This is particularly so given that there are suggestions that these actions *are* wrongs or should allow compensatory damages. An examination of the nature of many of the causes of action below suggests that they are best regarded as unjust enrichments and not wrongs, although significantly there are some wrongs which should be recognised although compensation has historically not been given (or sought). Further, it is noted that in many of these cases, there is nothing to prevent a court considering that the facts may also be seen as a breach of duty and awarding compensatory damages for its breach. In this manner new wrongs may be formulated and the penultimate part of this section explains and considers such wrongs. The final discussion in this section explains that there are some causes of action where compensation has historically been absent which, of their nature, are extremely difficult, if not impossible to classify. Courts must decide whether to prefer a characterisation of these actions as a breach of duty and because of this nature to award compensatory damages in future actions where they are sought.

(b) *Unjust enrichments where no contract is involved*

It has already been shown that the law, entirely sensibly, regards a mistaken payment as an action in unjust enrichment and not a wrong.[113] One way of examining the nature of particular causes of action is to compare them to

---

[112] *United States* v. *Burke* above note 108, 251
[113] See text above accompanying notes 49–56.

the action for restitution of a mistaken payment. By viewing these actions as comparable to a mistaken payment, it is argued that, in awarding restitution, they do not respond to a possible characterisation of the facts as a breach of duty. Several actions in unjust enrichment are now examined, actions which some commentators have suggested are best seen as wrongs.

(i) Ignorance

Ignorance is an "unjust factor" which is yet to be explicitly recognised in any judicial decision. It is suggested that an action for ignorance arises where the property of a claimant is transferred from her when she is totally ignorant of the transfer. Professor Birks argues that the existence of a cause of action for ignorance should follow a fortiori from the existence of a cause of action for a mistaken payment.[114] He argues that if a claimant can recover when she makes a payment mistakenly, recovery should certainly be possible when the payment occurs in total ignorance.[115] Such a characterisation makes it apparent that, like a mistaken payment, ignorance is not a wrong.

There has, however, been much controversy over the nature of the action for ignorance. It has been argued that non-passage of property prevents enrichment and, therefore, any cause of action.[116] It has also been argued that in cases which involve non-wrongful interference with a claimant's proprietary right, the action is not one for ignorance but an action for non-wrongful interference with property[117] or an action for vindication of a proprietary right.[118]

(ii) Undue influence

Undue influence is an equitable cause of action. It allows recovery of value transferred to a party in a position of influence and as a consequence of that influence. Such "undue" influence can be demonstrated in two ways. A claimant can raise a presumption of undue influence in instances of suspicious transfers. Alternatively, a claimant can prove that the defendant exerted undue influence on the claimant to enter into the transaction.[119]

A presumption of undue influence can be raised in two ways. In cases which arise from a particular relationship, undue influence is automatically presumed upon demonstration of that relationship and a suspicious transfer: there is a

---

[114] P Birks *Introduction* 141.

[115] *Neate* v. *Harding* (1851) 6 Exch 349; 155 ER 577; *Moffat* v. *Kazana* [1968] 3 All ER 271. The same is, of course, true of a case of not true ignorance but "powerlessness": P Birks *Introduction* 174.

[116] W J Swadling "A Claim in Restitution" [1996] LMCLQ 63; E Bant " 'Ignorance' as a Ground of Restitution—Can it survive?" [1998] LMCLQ 18.

[117] Professor Jones points to remarks in the speech of Lord Goff in *Lipkin Gorman* suggesting that the basis of the action in that case was in unjust enrichment and was based upon the plaintiff's (traceable) proprietary right *Goff and Jones* 175–177. See also L Smith "Unjust Enrichment, Property and the Structure of Trusts" (2000) 116 LQR 412, 421–425.

[118] *Foskett* v. *McKeown* above note 100, 108, 115, 129; R Grantham and C Rickett "Property and Unjust Enrichment: Categorical Truths or Unnecessary Complexity?" [1997] NZLR 668, 684–685; G Virgo *Restitution* 656–673; L Smith "Restitution: The Heart of Corrective Justice" (2001) 79 Texas Law Rev 2115, 2163.

[119] *Barclays Bank Plc* v. *O'Brien* [1994] 1 AC 180 (HL) 189. *Royal Bank of Scotland plc* v. *Etridge (No2)* [2001] 3 WLR 1021 (HL) 1030–1034 .

presumption that a doctor exercised undue influence over a patient,[120] a solicitor over a client,[121] a parent over a child,[122] or a spiritual adviser over a follower.[123] Alternatively, a presumption can be raised if it can be shown that the relationship was such that the claimant had placed confidence and trust in the defendant to such an extent that the claimant was excessively dependent upon the defendant. Then it is unnecessary to show that the suspicious (or disadvantageous) transaction was the product of undue influence. In the absence of a presumption, it is necessary to show that undue influence was actively exercised to induce the contested transaction.

One view is that undue influence is a wrong. In *Barclays Bank plc* v. *O'Brien*,[124] Lord Browne-Wilkinson, on numerous occasions, referred to undue influence, duress and misrepresentation as "wrongs". Lord Millett once argued that undue influence is a species of breach of fiduciary duty, concerned with the manner in which consent is obtained.[125] If Lord Millett's suggestions are accepted, undue influence will be a wrong consisting of a breach of a defendant's duty not to "exploit the influence which he may have over another".[126] Although compensatory damages have traditionally not been available for undue influence, if undue influence is seen to be a wrong there is no reason why they should not be. Indeed, in *Mahoney* v. *Purnell*,[127] May J has already suggested that compensatory damages (equitable compensation) should be available for the wrong of undue influence.[128]

The contrary view is that undue influence is an action in unjust enrichment and that the transaction is reversed not because of any breach of duty by the defendant but because of a significant impairment of the autonomy of the weaker party.[129] In actions for undue influence it is not necessary that the undue influence come *from the defendant*. Where the undue influence does not come from the defendant the focus must be upon the vitiation of the claimant's consent and not upon any wrongful conduct by the defendant. For example, in *Bridgeman* v. *Green*,[130] the undue influence of a gentleman's butler led to him making payments to the butler, the butler's wife and the butler's brother. The Court held as follows: [131]

---

[120]   *Mitchell* v. *Homfray* (1881) 8 QBD 587.

[121]   *Wright* v. *Carter* [1903] 1 Ch 27.

[122]   *Lancashire Loans* v. *Black* [1934] 1 KB 380.

[123]   *Allcard* v. *Skinner* (1887) 36 Ch D 145.

[124]   *Barclays Bank Plc* v. *O'Brien* above note 119, 189, 191, 194, 195, 197, 198, 199. See also *Etridge (No 2)* above note 119, 1030, 1040, 1041, 1050, 1056.

[125]   P Millett "Equity's Place in the Law of Commerce" (1998) 114 LQR 214, 219.

[126]   P Millett above note 125, 219. See also *Etridge (No 2)* above note 119, 1029, 1034.

[127]   [1996] 3 All ER 61.

[128]   JD Heydon "Equitable Compensation for Undue Influence" (1997) 113 LQR 8. Cf P Birks "Unjust Factors and Wrongs" [1997] RLR 76 who argues that the award would have been one of pecuniary rescission. In the result it did not matter as a fiduciary relationship was found to exist.

[129]   P Birks and NY Chin "On the Nature of Undue Influence" in J Beatson and D Friedmann (eds) *Good Faith and Fault in Contract Law* (Clarendon Press Oxford 1995) 69; *Etridge (No 2)* above note 119, 1071 (Lord Scott).

[130]   (1757) Wilm 58; 97 ER 22.

[131]   *Bridgeman* v. *Green* above note 130, 64–65; 25.

"there is no pretence that [the butler's] brother, or his wife, was party to any imposition, or had due or undue influence over the plaintiff; but does it follow from thence, that they must keep the money? No: whoever receives it, must take it tainted and infected with the undue influence and imposition of the person procuring the gift, and protect it against the equity of the person imposed upon. Let the hand receiving it be ever so chaste, yet if it comes through a polluted channel, the obligation of restitution will follow it."

This principle, that a transfer to a wholly innocent defendant can be set aside because of undue influence by a third party, has subsequently been applied on numerous occasions.[132] In such cases, it can be seen that the defendant is in the same position as the recipient of a mistaken payment: the defendant is a completely passive recipient of the payment. The court looks to "the quality of the consent or assent of the weaker party" and not to the behaviour of the recipient.[133] Perhaps for this reason Lord Millett has now observed judicially that actions for duress or undue influence merely operate to vitiate a transaction or contract, "there is no "obligation" not to exercise undue influence in order to persuade a party to enter into a contract";[134] in other words there is no duty not to unduly influence another.

Because of the necessity of characterising undue influence as an unjust enrichment action in three party cases, and the fact that the same logic applies in two party cases, undue influence is an action in unjust enrichment and not a wrong. However it will be noted at the conclusion of this section that it is possible that the approach originally suggested by Lord Millett might also be accepted in the two party case. This would introduce a new wrong which, in two party cases, would exist concurrently with the unjust enrichment action for undue influence.

(iii) Duress

Duress is the cause of action at common law that reverses transfers of money or property which are made as a result of illegitimate pressure. In *Universe Tankships Inc of Monrovia* v. *International Transport Workers' Federation*,[135] a workers' union "blacked" the claimants' ships which did not hold a union-approved certificate. This meant that the ships were unable to depart from the English port. The claimants, fearing disastrous commercial consequences, acceded to the demands of the union and made payments to the crew members of additional back pay and a payment to the union's welfare fund. The

---

[132] *Wright* v. *Carter* [1903] 1 Ch 27; *Bullock* v. *Lloyds Bank Ltd* [1955] Ch 317; *Bester* v. *Perpetual Trustee Co Ltd* [1970] 3 NSWR 30 (SCNSW); *Smith* v. *Kay* (1859) 7 HLC 759; *Liles* v. *Terry* [1895] QB 679; *Goddard* v. *Carlisle* (1821) 9 Price 169; 147 ER 57; *Cooke* v. *Lamotte* (1851) 15 Beav 234; 51 ER 527; *Huguenin* v. *Baseley* (1807) 14 Ves 273; 33 ER 526; *Bainbrigge* v. *Browne* (1881) 18 Ch D 188; *Barron* v. *Willis* [1900] 2 Ch 121; *Morley* v. *Loughnan* [1893] 1 Ch 736.

[133] *Commercial Bank of Australia* v. *Amadio* (1983) 151 CLR 447 (HCA) 474 (Deane J); *Hodgkinson* v. *Simms* [1994] 3 SCR 377 (SCC) 379.

[134] *Agnew* v. *Länsförsäkringsbolagens* [2001] 1 AC 223 (HL) 264.

[135] *Universe Tankships Inc of Monrovia* v. *International Transport Workers' Federation* [1983] 1 AC 366 (HL).

claimants sought restitution of the payments made, although they later dropped the claim for the back pay payments. This was because legislation had been held to legitimate such demands.[136]

The House of Lords held that the payments to the welfare fund were recoverable as they had been made as a result of duress. Lord Diplock explained the basis of the recovery:[137]

> "The rationale is that his apparent consent was induced by the pressure exercised upon him by that other party which the law does not regard as legitimate, with the consequence that the consent is treated in law as revocable unless approbated either expressly or by implication after the illegitimate pressure has ceased to operate on his mind. It is a rationale similar to that which underlies the avoidability of contracts entered into under colour of office, or under undue influence or in consequence of threats of physical duress."

The basis for the action for duress is, therefore, the defective consent of the claimant rather than any breach of duty by the defendant. In the same way as undue influence, duress should be an available cause of action in a three party situation. Indeed, duress is, in many cases, indistinguishable from actual undue influence. Once it is accepted that pressure in duress cases need not be tortious or unlawful generally as long as it is "illegitimate",[138] it is very difficult to draw a line between cases of "undue" pressure amounting to actual undue influence and cases of pressure amounting to duress.[139] Thus, in a case in which X coerces Y to make a payment to Z, Y can bring the action for duress against Z to recover the money. Although there are no cases specifically on this point,[140] Goff and Jones argue that this result should follow by analogy with the cases of money paid by mistake to a third party.[141] An innocent recipient of money paid under compulsion should be in no better position than an innocent recipient of money paid under mistake.

As a result, compensatory damages should be unavailable and duress should be considered as an action in unjust enrichment. Lord Diplock made clear that this was the effect of his understanding of the nature of duress. In another passage in the *Universe Tankships* case, quoted by Lord Goff in the leading speech in *The Evia Luck*,[142] Lord Diplock stated that it is necessary to identify a tort separate from the unjust enrichment action for duress in order to recover compensatory damages:[143]

---

[136] *NWL Ltd* v. *Woods* [1979] 1 WLR 1294 (HL).

[137] *Universe Tankships* above note 135, 384.

[138] *Barton* v. *Armstrong* [1976] AC 104 (PC) 121 (Lords Simon and Wilberforce dissenting only on the application of the facts); *Universe Tankships* above note 135, (Lord Scarman); *Dimskal Shipping Co* v. *ITF* [1992] 2 AC 152 (HL) 169 (Lord Goff).

[139] P Birks *Introduction* 184; *Etridge (No 2)* above note 119, 1029.

[140] *Universe Tankships* would have been such a case if the action against the *crew* for return of the additional back pay (induced by the duress of the union) had not been dropped. Similarly, in a later case with very similar facts an action against the crew failed only because they had not been joined as parties: *Dimskal Shipping Co* v. *International Transport Workers' Federation* [1992] 2 AC 152 (HL) 163.

[141] *Goff and Jones* 308.

[142] *Dimskal Shipping Co* above note 140, 166; *Universe Tankships* above note 135, 385.

[143] *Dimskal Shipping Co* above note 140, 169.

"the use of economic duress to induce another person to part with property or money is not a tort per se; the form that the duress takes may, or may not, be tortious. The remedy to which economic duress gives rise is not an action for damages but an action for restitution of property or money extracted under such duress and the avoidance of any contract that had been induced by it. Where the particular form taken by the duress used is itself a tort, the restitutionary remedy for money had and received by the defendant to the plaintiff's use is one which the plaintiff is entitled to pursue as an alternative remedy to an action for damages in tort."

In the case of duress, this tort is most likely to be the tort of intimidation (which can operate in a two-party context as well as a three-party context).[144]

(iv) Innocent misrepresentation

Before 1889, the elements of the cause of action for misrepresentation, both at common law and in equity, were uncertain. It was clear that in some circumstances a false statement which had been relied upon and which caused loss could make the mis-representor liable for compensatory damages. The uncertainty concerned the degree of fault that had to accompany the making of a false statement. It seemed that "fraud" was necessary in order for compensatory damages to be awarded. Common law and equity appeared to take different approaches. Some decisions suggested that "fraud" in equity was satisfied by the making of a statement, however innocently, without reasonable grounds. Fraud at common law, however, required knowledge of the falsity of a statement or recklessness as to its truth by the representor.

In *Slim* v. *Croucher*,[145] the defendant had misrepresented information to a lender about a borrower's entitlement to be granted a lease. This led the lender to make a loan to a borrower. It turned out that the borrower was not entitled to the lease as the defendant had leased it to someone else. The defendant claimed that he had simply forgotten. The case was brought in equity before the Lord Chancellor and the lender sought an award from the defendant to make good the loss.

Lord Campbell LC was confronted with an objection that "this is a demand for damages" although the representation "was not a wilful misrepresentation".[146] The Lord Chancellor, regarding it as a case of concurrent jurisdiction at common law and equity arising from fraudulent misrepresentation,[147] stated that the element of fraud was satisfied because a "person makes a misrepresentation as to what he ought to have known, and what he did at one time know, although he alleges that at the particular time he had made the representation he had forgotten it".[148]

---

[144] *Godwin* v. *Uzoigwe* (1993) 23 Family Law 65 (CA); *Rookes* v. *Barnard* [1964] AC 1129 (HL) 1205 (Lord Devlin); *Dusik* v. *Newton* (1985) 62 BCLR 1 (BCCA) 39; *Central Canadian Potash Co* v. *Govt of Saskatchewan* [1979] 1 SCR 42 (SCC) 87.

[145] (1860) 1 De G F & J 518, 524; 45 ER 462, 465.

[146] *Slim* above note 145, 524; 465; *Burrowes* v. *Lock* (1805) 10 Ves 470, 475; 32 ER 927, 929.

[147] *Slim* above note 145, 523; 464.

[148] *Slim* above note 145.

At common law the requirements to prove a fraudulent misrepresentation were more stringent. In *Pasley* v. *Freeman*,[149] the defendant represented to the claimant that a third party's credit was good. The defendant knew that it was not. The defendant was held liable for compensatory damages. The judgment of Buller J in *Pasley* v. *Freeman*,[150] was based on the fact that the statement was known by the defendant to be false. The common law position became entrenched that an action for fraudulent misrepresentation required knowledge of the untruth or recklessness as to the truth of a statement.[151]

Although there were attempts to differentiate cases such as *Slim* v. *Croucher* on the grounds that they were cases of compensatory damages in lieu of making good a representation,[152] there was a real conflict in the authorities. Cases such as *Slim* v. *Croucher* were known as cases of a damages liability for "innocent mistake".[153] Further, Lord Eldon LC, in *Evans* v. *Bicknell*,[154] had been of the opinion that common law cases of fraudulent misrepresentation such as *Pasley* v. *Freeman*[155] were better heard in a court of equity than a court of law. At the very least, he acknowledged that there was a concurrent jurisdiction.

This conflict came before the House of Lords in 1889 pursuant to a common law action for fraudulent misrepresentation in *Derry* v. *Peek*.[156] In that case, counsel before the House of Lords referred to cases such as *Slim* v. *Croucher* and *Evans* v. *Bicknell* and argued that making an untrue statement without reasonable grounds was sufficient to amount to deceit.[157] The House of Lords disagreed. Each of the speeches considered the question of what the representor's duty might be. Each stated that there was no duty to speak the truth. In the words of Lord Bramwell, the duty is to speak "*what is believed* to be the truth":[158] "that there is "a right to have true statements only made," I cannot agree, and I think it would be much regretted if there was any such right. Mercantile men. . . would indeed cry out".[159] Lord Herschell spoke to similar effect:

> "For if there be a right to have true statements only made, this will render liable to an action those who make untrue statements, however innocently. This cannot be meant. I think it must be intended to make the statement of the right correspond with that of the alleged duty."[160]

---

[149] (1789) 3 TR 51; 100 ER 450.

[150] *Pasley* v. *Freeman* above note 149.

[151] *Bree* v. *Holbech* (1781) 2 Doug 654, 656; 99 ER 415, 416; *Glamorganshire Iron & Coal Co* v. *Irvine* (1866) 4 F & F 947; 176 ER 861; *Westfield* v. *Davidson* (1887) 3 TLR 362.

[152] *Peek* v. *Gurney* (1873) LR 6 HL 377 (HL) 390.

[153] *Ramshire* v. *Bolton* (1869) 8 LR Eq 294, 301 (Sir Richard Malins VC).

[154] (1801) 6 Ves Jun 174, 183; 31 ER 998, 1002; *Slim* v. *Croucher* (1860) 1 De G F & J 518, 524; 45 ER 462, 464.

[155] (1789) 3 TR 51; 100 ER 450.

[156] (1889) 14 App Cas 337 (HL).

[157] *Derry* v. *Peek* above note 156.

[158] *Derry* v. *Peek* above note 156, 351.

[159] *Derry* v. *Peek* above note 156, 350.

[160] *Derry* v. *Peek* above note 156, 362.

The House of Lords therefore held that the duty was simply to make only statements which the representor "honestly believe[d] . . . to be a true and fair representation of the facts." As this duty had not been infringed, no damages were awarded.[161]

Following *Derry* v. *Peek*, the rules as to what was fraudulent at common law and in equity became uniform. Neither equity nor common law allowed an action for compensatory damages for misrepresentation where that misrepresentation was innocent even if it were made without reasonable grounds.[162] However, it will be seen below that any misrepresentation, even a reasonable one, was still held to allow rescission of a contract. Given the decisive conclusion that such innocent statements do not amount to a breach of a duty, this response of reversing a bargain, which does not focus upon fault, should be explained as an action in unjust enrichment. This point is explained in more detail below.[163]

Despite the fact that an innocent misrepresentation is an action in unjust enrichment there is nothing to prevent an innocent misrepresentation also being actionable as a wrong as it seemed to be in equity before *Derry* v. *Peek*.[164] It will be seen below that legislation has moved the law to that position.

(c) *Unjust enrichment actions when a contract is involved*

(i) The role of fault

The unjust enrichment actions above were considered and explained in the context of transactions which were not bargains. In a bargaining situation the law's position is slightly different. Even though the consent of the contracting claimant might be impaired (as a result of a misrepresentation, undue influence, duress, non-disclosure) the transaction will not usually be reversed. In a bargaining situation it is not enough that the consent of one party is impaired. To allow bargains to be reversed simply on the basis of impaired consent would too greatly upset the security of receipts and bargains. In *Riverlate Properties Ltd* v. *Paul*,[165] Russell LJ explained this as follows:

> "If a man may be said to have been fortunate in obtaining a property at a bargain price, or on terms that make it a good bargain, because the other party unknown to him has made a miscalculation or other mistake, some high-minded men might consider it appropriate that he should agree to a fresh bargain. . .But if equity were to enforce the views of those high-minded men, we have no doubt that it would run counter to the attitudes of much of the greater part of ordinary mankind (not least the world of commerce)."

The compromise reached by the law has been to allow a contract to be reversed or avoided where the vitiation of the claimant's consent can "in some

---

[161] *Derry* v. *Peek* above note 156, 376 (Lord Herschell).
[162] *Low* v. *Bouverie* [1891] 3 Ch 82; *Elkington & Co* v. *Hurter* [1892] 2 Ch 452; *Gilchester Properties Ltd* v. *Comm* [1948] 1 All ER 493.
[163] Below, text accompanying notes 167–191.
[164] Above, text accompanying notes 145–148.
[165] [1975] Ch 133 (CA) 141.

way be laid at [the defendant's] door".[166] This is consistent with the protection of the security of receipts since, in a bargaining situation, a defendant runs the risk of impairing a claimant's consent by *his own action* but does not take the risk of impairment of the claimant's consent by third parties or by the claimant's own mistake. In this way, the requirement that the defendant induces the mistake of the claimant can be explained without an analysis which relies upon a breach of duty. An examination of the nature of the actions we have been investigating in a bargaining context explains why this is the best analysis and why the basis of the cause of action remains unchanged.

(ii) Innocent misrepresentations

In *Redgrave* v. *Hurd*,[167] the defendant had agreed to purchase the claimant's house as part of an agreement that the defendant join the claimant in the claimant's partnership prior to the claimant's retirement. The defendant refused to carry out the agreement and the claimant sought specific performance of it. The defendant counter-claimed, seeking rescission of the contract relying upon misrepresentations made by the claimant.

Difficulty arose because the defendant did not plead that the claimant knew of the falsity of the statements. The Court of Appeal held that, as a result, compensatory damages could not be awarded demonstrating a refusal to characterise the action as a breach of duty. However, rescission of the contract was still allowed for this "innocent misrepresentation". Although Jessel MR remarked that this was a "doctrine in equity settled beyond controversy",[168] it appears that this was the first case explicitly to recognise such a jurisdiction.[169] Nevertheless, the principle is now well established that, "however free the defendant might have been from any intention to deceive he was not allowed (in equity) to retain what he had obtained from a plaintiff by a material misstatement on which the latter was entitled to rely as being true".[170]

Some of the comments in *Redgrave* v. *Hurd* tend to distract from the fact that innocent misrepresentation is a cause of action in unjust enrichment. Jessel MR explained the action as based on a notion of ex-post unconscientiousness: [171]

> "A man is not allowed to get a benefit from a statement which he now admits to be false or because it is unconscientious to allow a man, having obtained a beneficial contract by a statement which he now knows to be false [to] insist upon keeping that contract."

[166] J Cartwright "Taking Stock of O'Brien" [1999] RLR 1, 5.

[167] (1881) 20 Ch D 1 (CA).

[168] *Redgrave* v. *Hurd* above note 167, 13.

[169] Meagher, Gummow, Lehane *Equity* 354.

[170] *Nocton* v. *Lord Ashburton* above note 21, 955 (Lord Haldane LC). See *Adam* v. *Newbigging* (1888) 13 App Cas 308 (HL); *Boyd and Forrest* v. *Glasgow SW Railway Co* (1915) SC 20 (HL); *Abram Steamship Co* v. *Westville Shipping Co* [1923] AC 733 (HL); *MacKenzie* v. *Royal Bank of Canada* [1934] AC 468 (PC) 475; *Senanayake* v. *Cheng* [1965] 3 All ER 296 (PC); *A H McDonald & Co Ltd* v. *Wells* (1931) 45 CLR 506 (HCA).

[171] *Redgrave* v. *Hurd* above note 167, 12–13.

This reference to unconscientiousness should not distract from the fact that innocent misrepresentation is a cause of action in unjust enrichment for an induced mistake. The requirement that the defendant induce the mistake does not make the cause of action into a wrong but is necessary to preserve the security of receipts and reflect the risks inherent in the bargain.

Even apart from the *refusal* to award compensatory damages, three reasons can be given why this is the case. First, the fact that the claimant later discovers the statement to be untrue is wholly irrelevant to the cause of action. Like the mistaken payment, the cause of action is complete at the time the innocent misrepresentation is made (inducing the claimant's mistake).

In *Leaf* v. *International Galleries*,[172] the claimant had purchased a painting following a misrepresentation that the painting was a Constable. The action for innocent misrepresentation was held to be barred by *laches* because five years had passed and the claimant had not taken action. Yet neither the defendant misrepresentor nor the claimant knew of the misrepresentation for most of this period. Nonetheless, the cause of action was held to have arisen and then lapsed. The fact that the defendant "now knows" the statement to be false is wholly irrelevant as the cause of action arises at the time it is made.

The second reason why an innocent misrepresentation operating to rescind a contract should be seen as a cause of action in unjust enrichment is, as Lord Herschell stated in *Derry* v. *Peek*,[173] because rescission is allowed, "however honestly it may have been made, however free from blame the person who made it" and despite the fact that there is no "right to have true statements only made".[174] As Lord Wright later stated,[175] "a case of innocent misrepresentation may be regarded rather as one of misfortune than as one of moral obliquity. There is no deceit or intention to defraud." The Law Lords in *Derry* v. *Peek* were scathing of contrary suggestions made by Jessel MR in another case in the same year as *Redgrave* v. *Hurd*.[176] In criticising Jessel MR's contrary suggestions, Lord Bramwell, in *Derry* v. *Peek*,[177] ventured so far as to remark that "[Sir George Jessel's] knowledge of actions of deceit was small, if any."

A third reason can be seen where relief is sought in three-party situations where the misrepresentation was not made by the defendant. In *Barclays Bank Plc* v. *O'Brien*,[178] Mrs O'Brien had given a guarantee to Barclays Bank as a result of a misrepresentation by her husband. Although the misrepresentation did not come from the defendant, the bank, the House of Lords held that the guarantee could be rescinded.

In the leading speech, Lord Browne-Wilkinson acknowledged the tension between the need to give relief when the claimant's consent had been impaired

[172] [1950] 2 KB 86 (CA).
[173] *Derry* v. *Peek* above note 156, 359.
[174] *Derry* v. *Peek* above note 156, 350.
[175] *Spence* v. *Crawford* [1939] 3 All ER 271 (HL) 288.
[176] *Smith* v. *Chadwick* (1881) 20 Ch D 27 (HL) 44, 67.
[177] *Derry* v. *Peek* above note 156, 347.
[178] [1994] 1 AC 180 (HL)

(and protect the matrimonial home) and the need to protect the security of receipts in bargains (and not to reduce the flow of loan capital by making institutions unwilling to accept security).[179] This tension was to be resolved by a requirement that where the misrepresentation did not come from the defendant bank, the bank must have constructive notice of the misrepresentation.[180]

A number of factors combined to amount to this constructive notice. The first was the fact that the bank had notice of a relationship of trust and confidence. This notice was of "the underlying risk of one cohabitee exploiting the emotional involvement and trust of the other".[181] The second reason was the fact that a transaction was not to the co-habitee's financial benefit. In such cases, there is a "substantial risk" in transactions of that kind that the cohabitee does not come to the transaction with a free mind.[182] Both of these factors were necessary for a finding that the bank had constructive notice of a misrepresentation. Thus, in another case based on similar facts, heard with the *O'Brien* case, the opposite result was reached because the transaction, a loan, was equally to the benefit of the wife.[183]

These requirements for relief from a misrepresentation made by a third party, established in the *O'Brien* case, have now been clarified by the House of Lords in *Barclays Bank Plc* v. *Boulter*[184] where it was concluded that the burden of showing constructive knowledge lay on the claimant.[185] The burden then shifts to the bank to show that it took reasonable steps to ensure the "consent was properly obtained".[186] Although in *Barclays Bank Plc* v. *O'Brien*[187] Lord Browne-Wilkinson had referred on numerous occasions to undue influence and misrepresentation as wrongs, Lord Hoffmann, in the leading speech in *Barclays Bank* v. *Boulter*,[188] specifically avoided reference to these causes of action as wrongs and referred to them as "vitiating circumstances".

In Australia this reasoning has been carried to its logical conclusion. There need not be any conduct from a third party at all if what is in issue is the state of mind of the defendant and the bank's constructive notice of that state of mind. The High Court of Australia in *Garcia* v. *National Australia Bank Ltd*[189] accepted that the constructive notice need not be of any conduct of the third party, simply constructive notice of a *mistake* is sufficient. Such constructive

---

[179] *Barclays Bank Plc* v. *O'Brien* above note 178, 188.
[180] Which is the logical extension of cases where the *actual* knowledge of the defendant allowed the reversal of the transaction: *Talbot* v. *Von Boris* [1911] 1 KB 854 (CA) 863; *Kesarmal* v. *NKV Valliappa Chettiar* [1954] 1 WLR 380 (duress); *Lancashire Loans Ltd* v. *Black* [1934] 1 KB 380 (undue influence); *Etridge (No 2)* above note 119, 1072.
[181] *Barclays Bank Plc* v. *O'Brien* above note 178, 198.
[182] *Barclays Bank Plc* v. *O'Brien* above note 178, 196.
[183] *CIBC Mortgages Plc* v. *Pitt* [1994] 1 AC 200 (HL).
[184] [1999] 1 WLR 1919 (HL).
[185] *Barclays Bank Plc* v. *Boulter* above note 184, 1925.
[186] *Barclays Bank Plc* v. *Boulter* above note 184, 1925.
[187] *O'Brien and Etridge (No 2)* above note 124.
[188] *Barclays Bank Ltd* v. *Boulter* above note 184, 1925 citing *Bainbrigge* v. *Browne* above note 132, 197. See also *Etridge (No 2)* above note 119, 1071 (Lord Scott).
[189] (1998) 194 CLR 395 (HCA)

knowledge will exist in instances in which a mistaken party enters into a transaction with the bank and receives no benefit but which benefits another with whom they have a relationship of close trust and confidence and where no sufficient explanation has been provided by the bank. The nature of the action in such cases is clearly the mistake of the claimant.[190] Indeed the High Court acknowledged, and referred to authority which recognised, that if no bargain were involved (as in a gift by deed) then a contract might be set aside because of the mistake of the claimant without any constructive knowledge by the defendant.[191]

(iii) Non-disclosure

The cause of action for non-disclosure is an action for rescission of a contract where one party has not disclosed all relevant information. Although there is usually no duty of disclosure when entering into a contract, in certain contracts of "utmost good faith", both parties are under duties of disclosure. In *Pan Atlantic Insurance Co Ltd* v. *Pine Top Insurance Co Ltd*,[192] the House of Lords held that non-disclosure in such situations allows rescission of the contract if it has "in fact induce[d] the making of the contract (in the sense in which that expression is used in the general law of misrepresentation)".[193] In these cases, non-disclosure might be characterised as a wrongful breach of a duty of disclosure. Alternatively, it might be an unjust enrichment, characterised as the law giving relief for mistake where the defendant in this particular and special type of contract bears the risk of any mistake caused by his non-disclosure.

The latter interpretation was clearly established in *Banque Keyser SA* v. *Skandia (UK) Insurance Ltd*.[194] In that case, a syndicate of the claimant banks had arranged for insurance cover from the defendant insurance companies in relation to a number of loans. The agent for the banks had acted fraudulently which had resulted in loans being made prematurely. The insurance companies were aware of this fraud but did not disclose it and continued to insure the loans. It was questioned whether this non-disclosure could render the insurance companies liable for compensatory damages.

The trial judge, Steyn J considered the situation before him to be "novel".[195] He was unaware of any previous claim for compensatory damages for non-disclosure.

---

[190] S Gardner "Wives' Guarantees of their Husbands' Debts" (1999) 115 LQR 1,5; E Stone "Infants, Lunatics and Married Women: Equitable Protection in Garcia v National Australia Bank" (1999) 62 MLR 604, 608.

[191] *Bank of Victoria Ltd* v. *Mueller* [1925] VLR 642. See *Garcia* above note 189. See also the same result in similar English cases concerning mistakes made in deeds of gift: *Gibbon* v. *Mitchell* [1990] 3 All ER 338; *Walker* v. *Armstrong* (1856) 8 De GM & G 531; 44 ER 495; *Walton* v. *Peirson* [1922] 2 Ch 509; *Meadows* v. *Meadows* (1853) 16 Beav 401; 51 ER 833; *Ellis* v. *Ellis* (1909) 26 TLR 166; *Phillipson* v. *Kerry* (1863) 11 WR 1034.

[192] [1995] 1 AC 501 (HL). Rejecting *Container Transport International Inc* v. *Oceanus Mutual Underwriting Association (Bermuda) Ltd* [1984] 1 Lloyds Rep 476 (CA); *Highlands Insurance Co Ltd* v. *Continental Insurance Co Ltd* [1987] 1 Lloyd's Rep 109.

[193] *Pan Atlantic Insurance Co Ltd* v. *Pine Top Insurance Co Ltd* above note 192, 618 (Lord Mustill).

[194] *Banque Keyser SA* v. *Skandia (UK) Insurance Ltd* [1990] 1 QB 665.

[195] *Banque Keyser SA* v. *Skandia (UK) Insurance Ltd* above note 194, 706.

However, Steyn J began from the position that the non-disclosure was a "breach of the duty of the utmost good faith".[196] Although there is no *general* duty of disclosure, even of facts which a party is "morally bound" to disclose,[197] Steyn J thought that non-disclosure in insurance contracts was a breach of a particular duty. With this assumption, Steyn J awarded compensatory damages for the breach.

The Court of Appeal disagreed. Examining the *nature* of the principle of disclosure, Slade LJ, delivering the judgment of the court, concluded that it was not a wrong and *therefore* could not result in compensatory damages.[198] The Court of Appeal held that the jurisdiction to rescind for non-disclosure is the same as that for innocent misrepresentation, duress and undue influence. They stated that, "since duress and undue influence as such give rise to no claim for damages, we see no reason in principle why non-disclosure as such should do so".[199]

The Court of Appeal considered that if compensatory damages were to be given for a non-disclosure then, effectively, a wrong of absolute liability would be created. The Court held that "it would not be right for this court by way of judicial legislation to create a new tort, effectively of absolute liability, which could expose either party to an insurance contract to a claim for substantial damages in the absence of blameworthy conduct".[200] On appeal to the House of Lords, the decision of the Court of Appeal was upheld, although on different grounds. However, Lord Templeman expressed agreement obiter dicta with the Court of Appeal that breach of a duty of disclosure does not sound in damages.[201] Lord Jauncey also appeared to consider it necessary for damages that there is "the necessary proximity to give rise to a duty of care . . . to establish negligence".[202] This view was recently endorsed by Lord Hobhouse in *Manifest Shipping Co Ltd* v. *Uni-Polaris Shipping Co Ltd*.[203] In a speech with which Lords Steyn and Hoffmann concurred, Lord Hobhouse stated that the decision of the Court of Appeal in the *Banque Keyser* case had "finally and authoritatively" concluded the question of the availability of compensatory damages for breach of a duty of disclosure and that the obligation does not arise from any contractual duty of disclosure but from a "principle of law"[204] which allows adjustment of the parties' financial positions "under the law of restitution".[205]

---

[196] *Banque Keyser SA* v. *Skandia (UK) Insurance Ltd* above note 194 , 705.
[197] *Peek* v. *Gurney* (1873) LR 6 HL 377 (HL) 390 (Lord Chelmsford).
[198] *Banque Keyser SA* v. *Skandia (UK) Insurance Ltd* above note 194 (CA), 780.
[199] *Banque Keyser SA* v. *Skandia (UK) Insurance Ltd* above note 194 (CA) 780.
[200] *Banque Keyser SA* v. *Skandia (UK) Insurance Ltd* above note 194 (CA) 781.
[201] *Banque Keyser SA* v. *Skandia (UK) Insurance Ltd* above note 194 (HL) 280.
[202] *Banque Keyser SA* v. *Skandia (UK) Insurance Ltd* above note 194 (HL) 282.
[203] *Manifest Shipping Co Ltd* v. *Uni-Polaris Shipping Co Ltd* [2001] 2 WLR 170 (HL). See also *Agnew* v. *Länsförsäkringsbolagens* [2001] 1 AC 223 (HL) 264 (Lord Millett).
[204] *Manifest Shipping Co Ltd* above note 203, 185.
[205] *Manifest Shipping Co Ltd* above note 203, 187.

(d) *Wrongs without historical awards of compensation*

The lack of necessity of the "availability of compensation" question as a test for whether a particular event is a wrong means that the list of wrongs is not closed. Compensation could, in future, be awarded for causes of action for which compensation has historically not been considered, and wrongs therefore recognised, in three ways.

First, some causes of action for which compensatory damages have been historically unavailable are, of their nature, wrongs. Even without compensatory awards such causes of action are wrongs. The most obvious of these is the action for innocent copyright infringement considered in chapter seven. Another example considered below is the cause of action which arises where a defendant has dishonestly received property in breach of trust. Although compensation has historically not been awarded in such an action, it should be regarded as part of a broader equitable wrong and it is treated as such in this book.

A second manner in which a cause of action might be recognised as a wrong although historically there had been no award of compensation for it, is if courts create a novel or new wrong. The point was made earlier (and is further explained below) that, the facts of cases in which unjust enrichments have traditionally operated might also be open to new characterisation allowing an alternative analysis of the action as a wrong.

Finally, there are cases that, of their nature, are extremely difficult to classify. In such cases it is necessary for courts to decide, as they did in the case of non-disclosure, whether the action is based upon a breach of duty and therefore should give rise to compensatory damages or not. The most obvious example of this is the equitable cause of action for unconscionable transactions, an action considered by many academic commentators to be an action in unjust enrichment but which could easily be characterised as a wrong. Indeed, examination of the nature of that action by courts seems now increasingly to suggest that it is becoming regarded as an equitable wrong.

(i) Wrongs that exist without compensation

The most obvious of these cases, mentioned above and discussed in detail in chapter seven, is the cause of action for breach of copyright where the breach is not wilful. In that case it will be seen that legislation has prevented judicial recognition of a claim for compensatory damages. But the action is the same action as for the wrong of breach of copyright committed wilfully.

A more difficult case is the equitable wrong of dishonest receipt of property in breach of trust which is discussed in detail in chapter six. There, it is explained that the wrong is best seen as subsumed within a broader wrong of dishonest participation in a breach of fiduciary duty. Lord Nicholls was the first to observe that the difficulty surrounding the extent of knowledge required for "knowing receipt" is partly a product of the conflation of two different claims:

a strict liability receipt-based claim in unjust enrichment (based on receipt of the claimant's equitable property) and a wrongs-based claim for "dishonest receipt". The latter should merge with the well-recognised equitable wrong of dishonest assistance in a breach of fiduciary duty[206] for "receipt of property is incidental, in the sense that it is merely the form which the dishonest participation takes".[207]

However, it has been argued that an action for knowing or dishonest receipt of property in breach of fiduciary duty cannot be a wrong because it does not give rise to compensation.[208] But it is not merely logic that compels the conclusion that, as a wrong, dishonest receipt should be treated in the same way as dishonest assistance. There is also strong support in the cases for the view of dishonest receipt as a wrong.

In *Carl Zeiss Stiftung* v. *Herbert Smith & Co (No 2)*,[209] the claimants were an East German company called the Carl Zeiss Stiftung Foundation. Litigation had been commenced by Carl Zeiss against a West German company of the identical name for passing off. In this litigation the West German company were represented by the law firm Herbert Smith. The West German company sued Herbert Smith claiming that all moneys received from the defendants (including fees, costs, disbursements) were the property of the claimant as the solicitors had knowingly received all payments from the company with knowledge it was being paid in breach of trust.

In the Court of Appeal, the claim failed because there was held to be insufficient knowledge of the existence of a trust; its existence involved very complicated issues of law.[210] Like the other members of the Court of Appeal,[211] Edmund-Davies LJ considered the claim as one for a wrong, treating the "touchstone" of knowing receipt as dishonesty, or at least a "want of probity"[212] which he held was necessary to establish a "wrongful act".[213]

Additional support for viewing knowing (dishonest) receipt of property in breach of fiduciary duty as a wrong can be seen in the first instance decision of Rix J in *Dubai Aluminium Co Ltd* v. *Salaam*.[214] On a point of which the Court of Appeal assumed the correctness, Rix J considered that the partners of Mr Amhurst (the partner that had assisted in unlawfully transferring money from the claimant company) were vicariously liable for both the equitable wrongs of knowing receipt and knowing assistance. It is beyond doubt that Rix J considered knowing receipt

---

[206] *Royal Brunei Airlines* v. *Tan* [1995] 2 AC 378 (PC).

[207] Lord Nicholls "Knowing Receipt: The Need for a New Landmark" in W Cornish et al *Restitution* 244.

[208] A Burrows *The Law of Restitution* 155–156.

[209] [1969] 2 Ch 276 (CA).

[210] *Carl Zeiss Stiftung* above note 209, 293 (Danckwerts LJ) 297 (Sachs LJ).

[211] *Carl Zeiss Stiftung* above note 209, 290–291 (Danckwerts LJ) 298 (Sachs LJ).

[212] The same analysis as Lord Nicholls drew from the authorities in knowing assistance cases in the *Tan* case: *Royal Brunei Airlines* v. *Tan* [1995] 2 AC 378 (PC).

[213] *Carl Zeiss Stiftung* above note 209, 304.

[214] [1999] 1 Lloyds Rep 415.

as a wrong as he held that it fell within the definition of "any wrongful act or omission" within the terms of the Partnership Act 1890, section 10.[215]

Viewed in this way, as a breach of duty, there is no reason why compensation should *not* be available for a cause of action involving dishonest receipt. Indeed, in the United States it *has* been held to be available. In *Re Rothko*[216] an expressionist painter died leaving, as his principal asset, 798 paintings of tremendous value. The executors of the estate in conduct described as "manifestly wrongful and indeed shocking"[217] sold the paintings within three weeks, at a gross undervalue, to related corporations, "MAG" and "MNY". The New York Court of Appeals affirmed the findings of the courts below that MAG and MNY were chargeable with notice of the executors' breach of duty as they had knowingly participated in the violation of the executors' fiduciary duty.[218] However the corporations had since (in violation of an injunction) disposed of some of the paintings, again at an undervalue.

The recipient corporations were held liable for compensatory damages, which the Court of Appeals called "appreciation damages" measured, in the same manner as the tort of deceit,[219] by the value of the paintings at the time of the judgment rather than the value of the paintings at the time of the dishonest receipt. The Court of Appeals held that the enhanced measure of compensatory damages was necessary to put the beneficiaries in the position they would have been in had the breach (sale) not occurred.[220]

(ii) Creating new wrongs

Although an examination of many of the above causes of action reveals that they are not wrongs and should be seen as causes of action in unjust enrichment, it might be that upon an alternative characterisation they could *become* wrongs as well through the creation of new, parallel causes of action. A court could create such a new wrong by an alternative characterisation of the facts as a breach of duty. For instance, as we have seen, if Lord Millett's extra-judicial suggestions are accepted undue influence may also become a wrong of "undue exploitation" consisting of a breach of duty not to "exploit the influence which he may have over another".[221] Lusina Ho has argued for the existence of such a wrong, although in more limited circumstances than its counterpart in unjust enrichment.[222]

---

[215] The Court of Appeal did not consider this point: *Dubai Aluminium Co Ltd* v. *Salaam* [2001] QB 113 (CA).

[216] 43 NY 2d 305 (1977 CANY).

[217] *Re Rothko* above note 216, 314.

[218] *Re Rothko* above note 216, 316.

[219] *Smith New Court Ltd* v. *Scrimgeour Vickers* [1997] AC 254 (HL).

[220] *Re Rothko* above note 216, 321.

[221] P Millett "Equity's Place in the Law of Commerce" (1998) 114 LQR 214, 219.

[222] L Ho "Undue Influence and Equitable Compensation" in P Birks and F Rose *Restitution and Equity (Vol 1): Resulting Trusts and Equitable Compensation* (LLP London 2000) 193. This view was criticised in R Chambers "Resulting Trusts and Equitable Compensation" (2001) 15 TLI 2, 11–12.

A wrong which forms the counterpart to duress offers another example. In *Universe Tankships* v. *International Transport Workers Federation*,[223] despite the comments of Lord Diplock, Lord Scarman argued that "duress, if proved, not only renders voidable a transaction into which a person has entered under its compulsion but is actionable as a tort, if it causes damage or loss".[224] The existence and recognition of such tortious compulsion (which would be a tort of two-party intimidation)[225] again should not distract from the existence of the unjust enrichment of duress.

Another example is the wrong of innocent (but unreasonable) misrepresentations inducing entry into a contract. Three years after the *Hedley Byrne* case, section 2(1) of the *Misrepresentation Act* 1967 introduced liability for compensatory damages for innocent misrepresentations which induced a contract, accompanied by a defence if the representor could prove that he had reasonable grounds to believe, and did believe, that the statement was true. The legislation establishes a duty to make only reasonable statements in contractual negotiations and declares that damages are to be assessed as if the statement had been made fraudulently, an approach which has been deemed the "fraud fiction".[226]

The position now, in relation to statements which induce entry into a contract, is that an innocent misstatement inducing entry into a contract might be an action in unjust enrichment of mistake (allowing rescission of a contract) or a wrong of innocent misrepresentation (subject to a defence that the representor had reasonable grounds to believe, and did believe, that the statement was true). As an unjust factor the action does not focus upon any degree of fault in the making of the representation. It simply requires that the representation be false and therefore that the claimant be mistaken. But as a wrong, liability exists in misrepresentations innocently inducing a contract (where the defendant cannot show that the statement was reasonable) as well as misrepresentations made negligently or fraudulently.

(iii) Where classification is impossible
Another manner in which wrongs might be recognised arises in actions which, of their nature, cannot be conclusively classified so might be classified by courts as wrongs. The most likely candidate for recognition as a wrong in this manner is the action in equity for unconscionably inducing entry into a transaction.

The jurisdiction to set aside such unconscionably induced transactions originated in a jurisdiction to relieve against harsh bargains made with expectant heirs or the poor and ignorant.[227] This cause of action requires that the defendant "take advantage" of a claimant's "special disadvantage" resulting in a transaction

---

[223] *Universe Tankships Inc of Monrovia* v. *International Transport Workers' Federation* [1983] 1 AC 366 (HL).
[224] *Universe Tankships* above note 223, 400. However, this view was expressly rejected by Lord Diplock: *Universe Tankships* above note 223, 385.
[225] See note 144 above.
[226] G Treitel *The Law of Contract* (10th edn. Sweet & Maxwell London 1999) 324.
[227] *Fry* v. *Lane* (1888) 40 Ch D 312.

that is not "fair, just and reasonable." The cause of action to reverse unconscionable transactions therefore "looks to the conduct of the stronger party in
attempting to enforce, or retain the benefit of, a dealing with a person under a special disability."[228] Although Lord Selborne described this jurisdiction as the old-
est head of equity,[229] and although the action has flourished in the Antipodes,[230]
it has remained relatively dormant in England until very recently.[231]

Many commentators focus on the "special disadvantage" as the basis of the
action and argue that unconscionable transactions are a cause of action in
unjust enrichment.[232] The difficulty with this approach is that the special disadvantage or weakness of the claimant by itself is never sufficient for relief. Fault
on the part of the defendant is always required and the modern action for
unconscionable transactions seems to focus more upon the defendant's fault
than upon the claimant's impairment. In *Louth* v. *Diprose*,[233] the claimant was
infatuated with the defendant who was largely indifferent to him. He purchased
a house for her after she took advantage of his lovesickness by manufacturing
an atmosphere of crisis and by making suicide threats. The transaction was
reversed.[234] Lovesickness by itself is a very weak ground for vitiated intention.
Moreover, in many unconscionable transaction cases, as in the *Louth* case, no
bargain is involved so the fault of the defendant cannot be seen as a requirement
to protect the security of bargained-for receipts.

Quoting from an extra-judicial article by Sir Anthony Mason,[235] the High
Court of Australia in *Bridgewater* v. *Leahy*[236] stated that although "it is the
actual or presumed impairment of the judgement of the weaker party that is the
critical element in the grant of relief on the ground of undue influence" an action
based upon unconscionable conduct is different because it "focuses more on the
unconscientious conduct of the defendant."[237] In that case the only "special disadvantage" relevant to any potential impairment of the claimant's was his
"enormous affection" and "complete trust" in his nephew for whom he forgave

---

[228] *Commercial Bank of Australia Ltd* v. *Amadio* (1983) 151 CLR 447 (HCA) 474; *Louth* v.
Diprose (1992) 175 CLR 621 (HCA) 627.

[229] *Earl of Aylesford* v. *Morris* (1873) 8 LR Ch 484, 489.

[230] *Hart* v. *O'Connor* [1985] AC 1000 (PC); *Blomley* v. *Ryan* (1956) 99 CLR 362 (HCA);
Commercial Bank of Australia v. *Amadio* above note 228; *Louth* v. *Diprose* above note 228, 638;
Bridgewater v. *Leahy* (1998) 194 CLR 387 (HCA).

[231] *Credit Lyonnais Bank Nederland NV* v. *Burch* [1997] 1 All ER 144 (CA); *Boustany* v. *Piggott*
(1995) 69 P & CR 298 (PC); *Portman Building Society* v. *Dusangh* [2000] Lloyds Rep Bank 197 (CA).

[232] G Virgo *Restitution* 286–297; P Birks *Introduction* 204–208; A Burrows *The Law of
Restitution* 203–204; D Capper "Undue Influence and Unconscionability: A Rationalisation" (1998)
114 LQR 479; R Chambers *Resulting Trusts* 137–138.

[233] *Louth* v. *Diprose* above note 228, 638.

[234] Although the Full Court of the Supreme Court would have preferred to award a monetary
restitutionary remedy reversing the transaction they allowed the trial judge's award of a trust and
the High Court dismissed an appeal: See *Louth* v. *Diprose* (1990) 54 SASR 438 (SCSA) 449.

[235] A Mason "The Impact of Equitable Doctrine on the Law of Contract" (1998) 27 Anglo-
American Law Review 1, 6–8.

[236] (1998) 194 CLR 457 (HCA) 478.

[237] *Bridgewater* above note 236, 478.

a substantial debt.[238] In *Harry* v. *Kreutziger*,[239] Lambert JA stated "that single question is whether the transaction, seen as a whole, is sufficiently divergent from community standards of commercial morality that it should be rescinded."

Nevertheless, compensatory damages have historically been unavailable for unconscionable transactions. One explanation might be that the doctrine is an action in unjust enrichment and the "unjust factor is the shabby behaviour of the defendant".[240] But it is difficult to see how this cause of action in unjust enrichment can be based primarily, perhaps exclusively, upon the fault of the defendant without relying upon any characterisation of the facts as a breach of duty. Further, by focussing upon the behaviour of the defendant the cause of action for an unconscionable transaction is different from other actions in unjust enrichment such as duress or undue influence because a transaction with an innocent defendant procured by the unconscionability of a third party cannot be set aside. The wrong focuses upon the fault of the defendant, not the state of mind of the claimant. The Court of Appeal has thus referred to unconscionable transactions as "moral fraud".[241]

The effect of this analysis means that an award of compensatory damages might, in the future, be possible in an action for such unconscionable transactions. Indeed, Lord Templeman in the Privy Council,[242] has suggested that compensatory damages (equitable compensation) are available for an unconscionable transaction[243] and, in Australia, there is clear authority that compensatory damages are available for unconscionable transactions either as a supplementary legislative remedy once the action is made out[244] or independently in the form of equitable compensation.[245] Once this recognition is effected the equitable cause of action for unconscionable transactions will undoubtedly no longer be regarded as an unjust enrichment and properly be considered a wrong.

CONCLUSION

This chapter proposed a model of a civil wrong. A civil wrong is a cause of action to which the law responds with a remedy because it is a breach of duty. Other non-wrongful causes of action, especially actions in unjust enrichment, can often be characterised as breaches of duty but are not wrongs because the remedy is not dependent upon such characterisation.

---

[238] *Bridgewater* above note 236, 492.

[239] [1979] 95 DLR (3d) 231 (CABC) 241.

[240] P Birks "The Role of Fault in the Law of Unjust Enrichment" in W Swadling and G Jones (eds) *The Search for Principle—Essays in Honour of Lord Goff of Chieveley* (OUP Oxford 1999) 235, 268.

[241] Recently see the unconscionable bargain case of *Portman Building Society* v. *Dusangh* [2000] Lloyds Rep Bank 197 (CA) 202, 206.

[242] *Boustany* v. *Piggott* above note 231.

[243] Although in that case the Rent Restriction Act 1973 of Antigua was held to make the case an inappropriate one for compensation.

[244] Trade Practices Act 1974 (Cwth) s. 51AA, s. 87 (1A).

[245] *Harrison & Anor* v. *Schipp* [2001] NSWCA 13 (CANSW).

A problem arises because a single set of facts can give rise to different causes of action. The difficulty arises in determining whether, where it is possible to characterise a cause of action as based upon a breach of duty, the law is actually responding to that breach of duty in the provision of a remedy. It was shown that one test is the availability of exemplary damages or compensatory damages. In situations in which compensatory damages have historically been unavailable, this is an indicator that the cause of action might not be a wrong. However, the historic absence of compensatory damages is not conclusive. Attention must be given to the nature of the cause of action to determine whether the law is treating it as a breach of duty.

This chapter examined the nature of a number of causes of action for which the availability of compensatory damages has never been tested. It showed that even when those causes of action are characterised as actions in unjust enrichment, it is not impossible for a court or Parliament to create new wrongs including by an alternative characterisation of these actions in unjust enrichment as causes of action based upon a breach of duty.

Following this approach, it will be seen in the next four chapters that those non-statutory causes of action which conclusively rely upon a breach of duty and should, of their nature, be considered as wrongs are (1) torts, (2) breach of contract and the action for breach of a promise which is referred to as an estoppel, (3) equitable wrongs of breach of confidence, breach of fiduciary duty (including breaches of trust), knowing participation in a breach of fiduciary duty and actual fraud (usually fraudulent misrepresentation). In addition, because of their origins at both common law and in equity, and because most statutes dealing with infringements of intellectual property (including passing off, trademark, patent, design and copyright infringement) have left the remedies to the common law or equity, intellectual property wrongs are included in this book. These four groups of wrongs form, respectively, chapters four, five, six and seven of this book.

3

Two Measures of Gain-based Damages

T HE LEGITIMACY OF damages which are not based upon loss was justified in
chapter one. The category of civil wrongs was explained in chapter two. This
chapter introduces the terminology and operation of gain-based damages for civil
wrongs. It also sets out the central proposition underpinning the remainder of this
book, which is that there are two distinct measures of gain-based damages, too
often run together.

The term "restitutionary damages" has sometimes been used, particularly by
academic commentators, as a unitary term to describe gain-based damages for
wrongs. But great confusion still surrounds these awards. Both the circumstances in which such gain-based damages will be made and their measure are
very uncertain. Once gain-based damages are divided into two different categories this confusion can be overcome. In the simplest terms the distinction
drawn by this chapter is between awards which operate to reverse a wrongful
transfer of value (restitutionary damages) and those which operate to
disgorge profits which have accrued to a defendant from a wrong (disgorgement
damages).

This chapter shows that by separating these two different measures of damages it is simple to explain both when gain-based awards should be available
for wrongdoing and the measure of such awards. It is unsurprising that with
the common treatment of these two types of award alike as "restitutionary
damages" so many different theories have been proposed to explain when
these "restitutionary damages" should be awarded but that no theory has been
generally accepted.[1] The use of two different terms paves the way for a
straightforward and principled approach.

In order to demonstrate this, this chapter is divided into four sections. Section
A, considers the two different awards and explains the way they are measured.
Section B then explains how the two different measures are based upon differ-
ent rationales. It shows how confusion and error result when decisions do not

---

[1] For example J Beatson *Use and Abuse* 15–17, 206–244; P Birks *Introduction* 313; I Jackman
"Restitution for Wrongs" [1989] CLJ 302; D Friedmann "Restitution of Benefits Obtained Through
the Appropriation of Property or the Commission of a Wrong" (1980) 80 Col LR 504; *Goff and
Jones* 709–814.

differentiate between the two types of gain-based damages for wrongdoing, including confusion in the law of unjust enrichment manifest in speeches in the House of Lords in *Westdeutsche Landesbank Girozentrale v. Islington LBC*.[2] Section C distinguishes these two measures of gain-based damages from other awards with which they are often confused. In particular, it focuses upon distinguishing compensatory damages for wrongs and restitution for unjust enrichment. The final section, Section D, considers future issues that will require resolution once these two types of gain-based damages are both recognised. Primarily these are issues of causation and remoteness of damages which have not been much considered in relation to gain-based damages.

A Restitutionary damages and disgorgement damages

1) Restitutionary damages

(a) Definition

In the context of the law of wrongs, this book uses the term "restitutionary damages" to refer to a monetary award which reverses a transfer of value. It is an award which gives back value transferred from a claimant to a defendant as a result of a defendant's wrong and is almost always measured by the objective gain received by the defendant. A simple example can be given. A defendant wrongfully takes £100 of a claimant's money. Ignoring any loss suffered, the claimant may seek to bring an action for restitutionary damages to reverse the wrongful transfer of the £100. This type of action might be pleaded as "money had and received" for the wrong[3] but it will be referred to in this book as restitutionary damages for the wrong. It reverses the transfer and, in the words of Lord Goff, aims to "restore the parties to the position they were in before they entered the transaction . . . [this] is, of course, the function of the law of restitution".[4]

In cases where the wrongful transfer involves money, the transfer of value might sometimes be equivalent to the loss suffered. But the restitutionary damages award is not concerned with financial loss and opens other possibilities which will be seen below, such as subjective devaluation of the award.[5] Thus, even in cases where the quantum of compensatory and restitutionary damages might be the same, it has been recognised that it is important to keep the two awards distinct.[6]

---

[2] [1996] AC 669 (HL).
[3] *United Australia Ltd* v. *Barclays Bank Ltd* [1941] AC 1 (HL).
[4] *Westdeutsche* above note 2, 681.
[5] *BP Exploration Co (Libya) Ltd* v. *Hunt (No 2)* [1979] 1 WLR 783, 799 (Robert Goff J); F Rose "Interest" in P Birks and F Rose (eds) *Lessons of the Swaps Litigation* (LLP London 2000) 291, 308.
[6] "In many cases, however, the two approaches would result in the same measure of damages. Where this is the case, it is particularly important that the court should be careful to express its award in terms of compensatory damages. It should not leave it open to the interpretation that it has awarded damages on a restitutionary basis": *Freeman* v. *Niroomand* (1996) 52 Con LR 116 (CA) (Millett LJ). See also *Porter* v. *Magill* [2000] 2 WLR 1420 (CA) 1497 "restitutionary damages, as a term of art, must however be sharply distinguished from compensatory damages" (Robert Walker LJ).

In fact, even in the simple example above, the financial loss to the claimant might not coincide with the gain transferred to the defendant. As will be seen below, the objective value where money is wrongfully transferred is the £100 as well as the value of its use (in market terms, compound interest). The quantum of any loss to the claimant (perhaps the claimant would never have invested the money or would have lost it) is irrelevant. The defendant has had the benefit of the money as well as its use which are both objectively valued. Section C of this chapter explains in detail why the awards of compensatory damages and restitutionary damages must be kept distinct. For present purposes it is enough to note that the restitutionary damages award focuses only upon the objective value transferred to the defendant and not upon any financial loss. Even where the two awards result in the same quantum it is important to keep them distinct.

Restitutionary damages are not confined to cases where the transfer is of money. They may also be awarded in instances where non-monetary benefits are wrongfully transferred. For instance, consider a situation where a tenant wrongfully remains on the landlord's premises committing the wrong of trespass to land.[7] Value, in the form of the use of the landlord's premises, has been transferred to the trespassing tenant. Restitutionary damages could be sought by the landlord to reverse that wrongful transfer of value, measured in the form of the fair market value for the wrongful use of the land gained by the defendant during the appropriate period.

Once again, the reference to a transfer of value does not mean that the claimant must have a *financial* loss to match the transfer of value. In the example of the trespassing tenant, the landlord may not have been able to lease the premises to anyone. This transfer of value has been described as a subtraction from the claimant's *dominium*[8] rather than from his financial wealth. In other words, the generation of value has come from the assets of the claimant even though the claimant may not have suffered any financial loss.

It might be objected that where the transfer is of the *use* of money or the *use* of property there is only a transfer from the claimant in the metaphysical sense that the defendant has utilised the valuable opportunity inherent in the claimant's asset. But the word "transfer" is still used in this book as it directs attention to the fact that the objective value received by the defendant must come *from* the claimant. As explained in chapter two, it is the same requirement as the "at the expense of" element in unjust enrichment; a requirement which is also described by some as necessitating a "transfer" from the claimant.[9] Professor Friedmann has described this as a requirement of an "appropriation".[10]

---

[7] *Swordheath Properties Ltd* v. *Tabet* [1979] 1 WLR 285. See also Mason and Carter *Restitution* 651.

[8] J Beatson *Use and Abuse* 232.

[9] L Smith *Tracing* 29; R Grantham & C Rickett *Enrichment and Restitution in New Zealand* (Hart Publishing Oxford 2000) 5, 470.

[10] D Friedmann "Restitution of Benefits Obtained Through the Appropriation of Property to the Commission of a Wrong" (1980) 80 Col LR 504.

Professor Birks describes the same requirement in the law of unjust enrichment in the following terms:[11]

> "Where D sells C's goods, D is enriched by the price received. Can it be said to be at C's expense in a non-wrong [unjust enrichment] sense—in the 'from' sense? The answer is that it can if the courts are willing to accept that the earning opportunities inherent in an asset are all attributed to the owner of that asset. If they are, then it follows that 'from my property' is equivalent to 'from me'."

Some commentators, such as Professor Burrows and Mr Virgo, prefer to represent this "from" or "subtraction" element in the law of unjust enrichment as a requirement that the defendant suffer some "loss".[12] However, in actions in unjust enrichment based upon the unjust factor of "ignorance"[13] where the enrichment of the defendant is the *use* of a bicycle or a horse it is very difficult, if not impossible, to point to a "loss" on the part of the claimant.[14] Indeed, after introducing this requirement of a "loss", Mr Virgo immediately concedes that it does not mean that the restitutionary award cannot exceed the amount of the "loss":[15]

> "it does not follow that the defendant is liable to make restitution only to the extent that the claimant has suffered a loss. This is because the function of the requirement that the benefit was obtained at the plaintiff's expense is simply to show that there is a causal link between the plaintiff's loss of an enrichment and the defendant's gain."

Precisely the same analysis applies to restitutionary damages in the law of wrongs. The restitutionary award need not correlate with financial loss suffered because the use of the claimant's property might not result in any financial loss to the claimant. Rather than strain the meaning of the word "loss" this book prefers to refer to subtractions (either monetary or non-monetary) from the claimant or the claimant's *dominium* as "transfers".[16]

(b) The awards which are restitutionary damages

Restitutionary damages are therefore not damages which operate to compensate for loss suffered by a claimant, but damages which reverse wrongful transfers of wealth from a claimant by subtracting the objective benefit received by the defendant. Historically, money awards which reverse transfers have been referred to with numerous different labels. All the different manners in which money awards were given to reverse wrongful transfers should be treated in common as restitutionary damages. These different awards will be explained in

---

[11] P Birks "Unjust Enrichment and Wrongful Enrichment" (2001) 79 Texas Law Rev 1767, 1785.

[12] A Burrows *The Law of Restitution* 19; G Virgo *Restitution* 105.

[13] P Birks *Introduction* 146.

[14] "Against what loss do you want to be restored? I restore the horse. There is no loss. The horse is none the worse; it is better for the exercise.": *Watson Laidlaw & Co Ltd* v. *Pott Cassells & Williamson* (1914) 31 RPC 104 (HL) 119.

[15] G Virgo *Restitution* 105.

[16] See also R Chambers *Resulting Trusts* 97–98.

detail throughout this book. It is enough at this point simply to note all the different historical means and terms used for restitutionary damages.

Historically restitutionary damages awards were made under a number of different names: wayleaves, common counts of *indebitatus assumpsit*[17] (as well as *quantum meruit* and *quantum valebant* awards),[18] mesne profits, reasonable royalties, monetary awards made in the context of rescission, damages in lieu of injunctions or specific performance or even awards simply labelled "damages" and assessed according to a "user principle". Each of these awards, when made for wrongs, operated to reverse wrongful transactions.[19]

Even these individual awards themselves are sometimes described in a number of different ways. One award which this book focuses upon in chapter six is monetary awards which effect rescission.[20] This money remedy effecting rescission has itself been referred to in a number of different ways. In some cases of rescission for fraud the common money count of "money had and received" was used to effect the reversal of the transaction,[21] Professor Birks has used the term "pecuniary rescission" to describe these monetary awards of rescission in the law of unjust enrichment,[22] the Supreme Court of Canada has referred to such awards as "the monetary equivalent of a rescissionary remedy",[23] the United States Supreme Court has described monetary rescission awards for wrongs as "rescissory damages"[24] and the Misrepresentation Act 1967 uses the term "damages in lieu of rescission".[25] This book treats all these labels for monetary rescission in the same way as all the other awards which reverse wrongful transfers of value. All are referred to as restitutionary damages, a term which, it will be seen, has gained much recognition in courts although is often not used in a sufficiently precise sense.[26]

---

[17] E Lawes *Practical Treatise on Pleading in Assumpsit* (W Reed London 1810) 418–503.

[18] From the mid-19th century these forms were pleaded as *indebitatus assumpsit*: JH Baker "The History of Quasi-Contract in English Law" in WR Cornish et al. *Restitution* 37, 41.

[19] Although the count of money had and received in *indebitatus assumpsit* was also used in the 20th century as disgorgement damages. Below note 43.

[20] The more common method of effecting rescission, by proprietary remedies, is discussed in chapter 8.

[21] *Clarke* v. *Dickson* (1858) El Bl & El 148; 120 ER 463.

[22] P Birks "Unjust Factors and Wrongs: Pecuniary Rescission for Undue Influence" [1997] RLR 76.

[23] *Hodgkinson* v. *Simms* [1994] 3 SCR 377 (SCC) 384, also referring to this approach as "restitutionary": [1994] 3 SCR 377 (SCC) 383.

[24] *Randall* v. *Loftsgaarden* 478 US 647 (1986 SCUS) 657.

[25] S. 2(2).

[26] See use of this term, for example, in *Daly* v. *Hubner* (High Court 9 July 2001) (Etherton J); *Freeman* v. *Niroomand* (1996) 52 Con LR 116 (CA) (Millett LJ); *Porter* v. *Magill* [2000] 2 WLR 1420 (CA) 1497 (Robert Walker LJ); *Gondal* v. *Dillon Newsagents Ltd* [2001] RLR 221 ; *Attorney General* v. *Blake* [1998] Ch 439 (CA) 457–459; *Jaggard* v. *Sawyer* [1995] 1 WLR 269 (CA) 281 (Bingham MR); *Kuddus* v. *Chief Constable of Leicestershire Constabulary* [2001] 2 WLR 1789 (HL) 1819 (Lord Scott); *Alfred McAlpine Construction Ltd* v. *Panatown Ltd* [2001] 1 AC 518 (HL) 588 (Lord Millett). As will be seen below, in the *Blake* case, Lord Nicholls insisted upon calling a profit-stripping award given for the breach of contract an "account of profits" because he considered the use of the only other term proffered during the hearing, restitutionary damages, an "unhappy expression" in a case of profit disgorgement; *Attorney General* v. *Blake* [2001] 1 AC 268 (HL) 284.

(c) Measuring restitutionary damages

In reversing a transfer of value, restitutionary damages focus upon the fact that value has been transferred from a claimant and that value is measured as the objective receipt by the defendant. An example seen in chapter two was the case of *Beck and Others* v. *Northern Natural Gas Company*.[27] It will be recalled that the storage of gas under the claimants' properties, committing the tort of trespass, transferred value from the claimants, being the value of the right to store gas under the claimants' property, the value of the "use" of the property. The objective value transferred was the reasonable market rate for the storage of gas under the defendants' properties.

As noted in chapter two, this objective measure of value transferred to a defendant is an almost perfect parallel to the measure of value transferred, or enrichment, to a defendant in the law of unjust enrichment. In this book, the phrase "value transferred" is preferred to the term "enrichment at the expense of" to differentiate cases of restitutionary damages for a wrong from restitution for unjust enrichment. More importantly it is also preferred because the term "enrichment" is a narrower term which, some have argued, does not encompass pure services. "Value" or "benefit" in the law of wrongs covers both and the notion of transfer merely requires that there be a *receipt* of the benefit. Thus, in a case where the defendant committed trespass by ejecting the claimant from leased premises, restitutionary damages were allowed by the Court of Appeal for the benefit of the lease received by the defendant. However the award did not include the value of a reversionary lease of which the claimant was also deprived because the defendants never received the benefit of that reversionary lease.[28]

In the law of unjust enrichment, where these issues of "enrichment at the expense of the claimant" have recently been much discussed by commentators, there are two key areas of difficulty which have been identified in determining the enrichment to the defendant from the value transferred. The first, which was considered briefly in chapter two, arises where the value transferred is property and the property has been substituted for a more valuable item. Courts have allowed claims to restitution of the (greater) value of the substitute in the defendant's hands.[29] For a claim in unjust enrichment, the "at the expense of" element in this claim might be explained on the basis that the claim for restitution of the greater value is itself generated by another unjust enrichment action (for "ignorance"),[30] or simply on the basis that the property rights have "persisted" into the

---

[27]   170 F 3d 1018 (1999 10th Cir CA).

[28]   *Gondal* v. *Dillon Newsagents Ltd* [2001] RLR 221 . See also A Burrows *The Law of Restitution* 8–9; G Virgo *Restitution* 59–60.

[29]   *Trustee of the Property of Jones* v. *Jones* [1997] Ch 159 (CA) 169; *Foskett* v. *McKeown* [2001] 1 AC 102 (HL).

[30]   P Birks "Property, Unjust Enrichment and Tracing" [2001] CLP (forthcoming).

transfer.[31] This same result, when it occurs in the law of wrongs, is explained below in terms of remoteness of damages;[32] the later substitution is not too remote from the initial transfer and can itself be regarded as a wrongful interference with property.[33]

A second area of difficulty is where the objective value to the defendant is different from the (subjective) value that the defendant places upon the transferred benefit. The question is whether the defendant should be entitled to resile from the objective market measure by what Professor Birks entitled "subjective devaluation".[34] Professor Birks distilled from cases in the law of unjust enrichment a principle that a defendant will be regarded as enriched, and the benefit measured objectively (by the objective value transferred) where that defendant has been incontrovertibly benefited (as in the case where the transfer is of money, has been realised in money[35] or would be regarded by any reasonably man as objectively beneficial[36]), or where the defendant requested or freely accepted (with an opportunity to reject) the benefit.[37] In other circumstances, "subjective devaluation" of the objective value of the benefit transferred to its value to the defendant might be possible.

Where a wrong has been committed it should be extremely difficult for a defendant to argue that the benefit transferred is worth less to him than its objective value. Indeed, in all the different awards given historically which effected restitutionary damages, English law never allowed devaluation from an objective measure of benefit. This might be justified because a defendant wrongdoer could be regarded as having, by his wrong, "reprehensibly sought out" the benefit (even if the wrong was not committed wilfully) so that he cannot later argue that it is worth less to him than if it had been properly obtained at an objective rate.[38] Nevertheless in two decisions of the Court of Appeal in 1993, it was accepted that a lower subjective measure could, exceptionally, be used. In those cases, trespasses were committed in circumstances in which the defendants had "no practical ability" or choice but to commit the trespass. The measure of transferred benefit was therefore not the market rate for the use but the (lower) necessary expenses saved by the defendants which represented the *subjective* value to them of the trespass.[39]

---

[31] G Virgo *Restitution* 591; R Grantham & C Rickett *Enrichment and Restitution in New Zealand* (Hart Publishing Oxford 2000) 34. Professor Smith argues that the vindication requires the existence of the asset *at the time of litigation* rather than at the time of receipt of the transferred enrichment: L Smith "Restitution: The Heart of Corrective Justice" (2001) 79 Texas Law Rev 2115, 2163–2174.

[32] See below, text accompanying notes 259–263.

[33] Torts (Interference with Goods) Act 1977 s. 1.

[34] P Birks *Introduction* 109. Mr Virgo suggests that the onus of subjective devaluation is for the defendant to establish: G Virgo *Restitution* 61–62.

[35] Professor Jones suggests it it enough that the benefit merely be *realisable*: *Goff and Jones* 23.

[36] *Monks* v. *Poynice Pty Ltd* (1987) 11 ACLR 637 (SCNSW) 640.

[37] P Birks *Introduction* 109–132. See also *Goff and Jones* 26.

[38] A Burrows *The Law of Restitution* 13–14.

[39] *Ministry of Defence* v. *Ashman* [1993] 2 EGLR 102 (CA) 106; *Ministry of Defence* v. *Thompson* [1993] 2 EGLR 107 (CA).

2) *Disgorgement damages*

(a) *Definition*

There is another gain-based remedy that may be sought for a wrong. In this case, the gain from the wrong is not measured by what might have been transferred from the claimant. Instead, the measure of the gain ignores whether or not any transfer has occurred and is measured by the actual profit accruing to the defendant from the wrong.

Whether a transfer of value occurs or not is irrelevant. There might be no transfer of value. The value might be generated from a third party or through the defendant's own skill and initiative. For example, consider the case where a defendant trustee wrongfully uses information obtained while acting in a fiduciary capacity and makes a personal profit. The amount of the profit might be primarily the result of the defendant's skill and experience. The defendant's actions might exploit an opportunity which the claimant could never have acquired or even be to the *benefit* of the claimant, enhancing the claimant's wealth *as well as* the defendant's.[40] But when disgorgement damages are available this gain must be given up. Alternatively, there might be a transfer of value but disgorgement damages, focusing upon the actual profit made by the defendant rather than the objective value received from the claimant, can lead to a very different measure as is explained below. This book adopts the term "disgorgement", to differentiate these damages, based on actual profits made by a defendant, from those that respond to a transfer of value from the claimant.

(b) *The awards which are disgorgement damages*

The most common form which disgorgement damages have taken is the account of profits. The account of profits is an award made in equity which has the express purpose "to determine as accurately as possible the true measure of the profit or benefit obtained"[41] by the defendant from the wrong. In a recent article Mr Doyle and Mr Wright, noting that such a profit-stripping remedy does not require a subtraction "at the expense of" the claimant, have nevertheless argued that this profit-stripping remedy need not have any different nomenclature from the term "account of profits".[42] However, there is a powerful reason why the account of profits remedy should be subsumed within the broader label "disgorgement damages". This is because precisely the same profit-stripping remedy is available at common law. Awards of money had and received for

---

[40] *Boardman v. Phipps* [1967] 2 AC 46 (HL); *Canadian Aero Service v. O"Malley* (1973) 40 DLR (3d) 371 (SCC) 383–384; *Industrial Development Consultants Ltd v. Cooley* [1972] 2 All ER 162; *Furs Ltd v. Tomkies* (1936) 54 CLR 583 (HCA).

[41] *Warman International Ltd v. Dwyer* (1995) 182 CLR 544 (HCA) 558; *In re Jarvis* [1958] 1 WLR 815, 820.

[42] S Doyle and D Wright "Restitutionary Damages—The Unnecessary Remedy?" (2001) 25 Melb Uni LR 1.

wrongs at common law sometimes performed this identical profit-stripping operation[43] and, as Lord Nicholls recognised in *Attorney General* v. *Blake*,[44] so too did other awards at common law, their nature disguised by unqualified references to "damages" which effected "an account of profit realised. . .in respect of wrongs attended with profit to the wrongdoer".[45] These awards of "damages" allowed disgorgement of profits at common law because "this Court never allows a man to make a profit by a wrong".[46] In fact, an award of an account of profits itself has even been described by the Canadian Supreme Court as an award of "damages".[47]

Although neither money had and received nor the account of profits has traditionally operated to disgorge *non-monetary* profits made by a defendant, such non-monetary gains made by wrongdoers should not be treated any differently from monetary profits. There are many older cases, particularly concerning the wilful removal of coal, discussed in chapter four, in which the award of "damages" at common law[48] or an "account" in equity[49] operated to disgorge the full market value of the coal removed[50] rather than limiting the award to the lower restitutionary market value for the (transferred) right to remove it (even if the removal was innocent). Indeed, Millett J has recognised that an account of profits should cover a situation where profits were made by the design of houses in breach of copyright, although those profits were "unrealised" (in money) by the sale of the houses.[51]

(c) *Measuring disgorgement damages*

One of the most difficult issues in measuring disgorgement damages involves determining whether the profit accruing to the defendant should be measured by expense saved or by actual profit made. The latter measure has been the one preferred by the courts subject to causation and remoteness considerations explained below. The two measures can be compared in several situations.

(i) Where profit is made and no expense saved

In a case in which only profit is made and no expense saved the two measures do not conflict. For instance, consider a case such as *Reading* v. *Attorney General*.[52] In that case an army sergeant took bribes to wear his uniform sitting

[43] *Reading* v. *Attorney General* [1951] AC 507 (HL) 513, 515–516, 517; *Mahesan S/O Thambiah* v. *Malaysian Government Officers Co-Operative Housing Society* [1979] AC 374 (PC) 376; *Armagas Ltd* v. *Mundogas SA* [1986] AC 717 (CA) 742–743 (Robert Goff LJ); decision aff'd [1986] 1 AC 717 (HL); *Federal Sugar Refining Co* v. *US Sugar Equalization Board Inc* (1920) 268 F 575 (DCNY).

[44] [2001] 1 AC 268 (HL) 284.

[45] *Powell* v. *Aiken* (1858) 4 K & J 343, 351; 70 ER 144, 147.

[46] *Jegon* v. *Vivian* (1871) LR 6 Ch App 742, 762.

[47] *Canadian Aero Service* v. *O'Malley* (1973) 40 DLR (3d) 371 (SCC) 392.

[48] *Morgan* v. *Powell* (1842) 3 QB 278; 114 ER 513.

[49] *Phillips* v. *Homfray* (1871) 6 Ch App 770.

[50] Which could only be the *profit* from the trespass and not a restitutionary award because the coal is not a chattel whilst in the land: *Jegon* v. *Vivian* (1871) LR 6 Ch App 742.

[51] *Potton Ltd* v. *Yorkclose Ltd* [1990] FSR 11 18.

[52] [1951] AC 507 (HL).

in the front of lorries illegally containing alcohol, so that they passed border checkpoints without being searched. The Crown seized the bribes and Reading brought an action to recover them. The House of Lords held that Reading was not entitled to recover the bribes as he was liable to account to the Crown for the profits made. Yet Reading did not "save any expense" in any real sense. The activity was entirely wrongful and could not have been committed, with more expense, without wrongdoing.

(ii) Where no profit is made but expense is saved

On the other hand, expense might be saved by a defendant wrongdoer in circumstances in which no real profit is made. A defendant contracts to provide an enhanced delivery service for a mail order business but in fact provides only the basic service.[53] No profit might be made on the contract but significant expense might be saved. Although courts have been very reluctant to give substantial awards in these cases, Finn J has argued extra-judicially that "the courts should mirror the liability they are prepared to impose where actual profits have been made".[54] However, in the leading speech in the House of Lords in *Attorney General* v. *Blake*,[55] Lord Nicholls has recently affirmed that this notion of expense saved does "not fall within the concept of an account of profits as ordinarily understood." Lord Nicholls was instead concerned to develop compensatory damages to cover a situation where a service is not fully provided rather than rely upon disgorgement damages.[56]

The exclusion of this "mirror" of liability from disgorgement damages might be justified on the basis that deterrence of wrongdoing is not required where the defendant incurs a loss. It is argued below that the purpose of disgorgement damages is deterrence of wrongdoing and it might be argued that wrongdoers only need to be deterred from making profits not incurring losses. However, it is possible that a defendant might commit a wrong with a view to *reducing* a loss. But courts are reluctant to deter this type of wrongdoing. In *Co-operative Insurance Society Ltd* v. *Argyll Stores (Holdings) Ltd*[57] Lord Hoffmann, in the leading speech, stated that "it cannot be in the public interest for the courts to require someone to carry on business at a loss if there is any plausible alternative by which the other party can be given compensation." Economic arguments are also advanced to support this approach.[58] Further, by focussing only upon actual profits made the remedy of disgorgement damages is kept clearer and more certain and deterrence might be achieved in these situations through exemplary damages.[59]

---

[53] *White Arrow Express Ltd* v. *Lamey's Distribution Ltd* [1995] CLC 1251 (CA) where substantial damages were refused. H Beale "Damages for Poor Service" (1996) 112 LQR 205.

[54] P Finn *Fiduciary Obligations* (Law Book Co Sydney 1977) 129.

[55] *Blake* above note 44, 286.

[56] Although such damages can only be seen as based on loss of contractual "performance" rather than financial loss: See *Alfred McAlpine Construction Ltd* v. *Panatown Ltd* [2001] 1 AC 518 (HL) and ch. 5 further.

[57] [1998] AC 1 (HL) 15.

[58] RA Posner *Economic Analysis of Law* (5th edn. Aspen New York 1998) 132–133.

[59] *Law Commission* 1997 4.18.

(iii) Where profit is made and expense is saved

Where the two measures *are* in competition is in cases of value transferred where profit is made. Consider an example. A defendant wrongfully uses a claimant's confidential information in manufacturing a carpet grip.[60] The defendant makes a significant profit. What is the gain accruing to the defendant as a result of the wrong? Is it the expense saved from not having to employ a consultant or not having to purchase the information? Or is it the actual profit made from the sale of the carpet grip less an allowance for the skill and effort of the defendant?

If the measure were expense saved then the disgorgement damages award would often coincide with the measure of restitutionary damages in cases where value is transferred because in those cases the value transferred is usually the expense saved.[61] The market value of expense saved or value transferred might be the cost of employing a consultant or if the information is particularly special the market price would be "much higher . . . the price which a willing buyer desirous of obtaining it would pay for it".[62] This measure might also coincide with the loss suffered unless the defendant was not in the business of selling that sort of information or would have sold it at a lower price.[63] However, courts have not accepted "expense saved" as a measure of disgorgement damages and have preferred the profit measure subject to allowances.[64]

An example of the rejection of the expense saved method of assessing disgorgement damages in favour of a method which examined the actual profit made occurred recently. In *Celanese International Corpn v. BP Chemicals Ltd*,[65] the defendant used a product in breach of the claimant's patent in two separate manufacturing processes, each producing acetic acid, at the same site. The two processes were effectively separate businesses and regarded by the trial judge as such. The wrongful use of the claimant's patented method by the defendant allowed a more efficient method of production and the claimant sought disgorgement damages (in the form of an account of profits). One of the businesses made a large loss, although there were significant savings from the wrongful use of the patent. However Laddie J affirmed the principle above that disgorgement damages did not extend to expense saved where no profit had been made.

The other business made significant profits. The defendant argued that the same profits could have been made by using another non-infringing method of production; therefore little expense had been saved and disgorgement damages should be nominal. Laddie J followed a number of authorities[66] and rejected the

---

[60] *Seager v. Copydex Ltd (No 2)* [1969] 1 WLR 809 (CA).

[61] However, there are instances where the expense saved is less than the value transferred: *Ministry of Defence v. Ashman* [1993] 2 EGLR 102 (CA); *Ministry of Defence v. Thompson* [1993] 2 EGLR (CA) 107; *London & Brighton Railway Co v. Watson* (1879) 4 CPD 118, 119.

[62] *Seager v. Copydex (No 2)* above note 60, 813.

[63] *Cadbury Schweppes Inc v. FBI Foods Ltd* [1999] SCR 142 (SCC).

[64] In some cases however the two measures will be the same, such as where the additional profit *is the very expense saved*.

[65] [1999] RPC 203. See also *Cala Homes Ltd v. Alfred McAlpine Ltd* [1996] FSR 36, 44.

[66] *Potton Ltd v. Yorkclose Ltd* [1990] FSR 11; *Peter Pan Manufacturing Corporation v. Corsets Silhouette Ltd* [1964] 1 WLR 96 ; *Siddell v. Vickers* (1888) 16 RPC 416.

expense saved method which he referred to as the "incremental approach". He gave several reasons. First, the expense saved method might depend on fortu-itous circumstances and would not operate to deter wrongdoing:

> "quite independently and at the same time, some other inventor invents another new process for making the same product but does not patent it so that the infringer could have made the same product in a non-infringing way. The fact is that he did not do so. The profits he made were made by use of the patented invention and he should account for them."

Secondly, he argued that the claimant cannot increase the award which focuses upon gain accruing to a defendant by saying that the defendant could and should have generated higher profits. Therefore, the defendant should not be able to reduce the award by arguing that the profits could have been made in another non-wrongful manner so that no expense was saved. This is also con-sonant with a well-established principle that a person whose unlawful act brings about an evidential difficulty will have that difficulty resolved against her.[67]

There is another reason which can be added to those given by Laddie J. This is the enormous difficulty in estimating the expense saved if the alternative method of making the profit were adopted. Economists refer to this cost as the "opportunity cost". Determining the opportunity cost to the wrongdoer involves an extraordinarily difficult calculation of an amount peculiarly within the knowledge of the wrongdoer.[68] This concern was expressed by McHugh J in *Dart Industries Inc v. Décor Corp Pty Ltd*:[69]

> "In a litigious world of unlimited time and resources, the best approach for determin-ing the profit derived from the infringement might be to estimate the profit of the prod-uct after allowing a proportion of the overheads and then deduct the opportunity cost of producing the infringing product. This would show the true gain of the infringer from producing or distributing the infringing product instead of the next best alterna-tive . . . But to adopt any of these methods would make an often complex subject more complex than it already is . . . the person taking the accounts would have to *estimate* one or more of the following figures: the gross revenue from the alternative, the direct costs of the alternative and the proportion of overhead attributable to the alternative."

(d) *Choice of the term "disgorgement damages"*

As explained above, the term "disgorgement damages" is preferred in this book because it encompasses awards other than an account of profits which perform the same operation. As was seen above, sometimes this award was effected sim-ply by referring to damages (without any descriptive epithet). On other occa-sions disgorgement was effected by the award of money had and received.

---

[67] For numerous illustrations of this principle in relation to a wrongdoer who prevents accurate valuation of property, or confusion in accounting, or in mixing funds at law or in equity see L Smith *Tracing* 77–78.

[68] EA Farnsworth "Your Loss or My Gain? The Dilemma of the Disgorgement Principle in Breach of Contract" (1985) 94 Yale LJ 1339, 1391.

[69] (1993) 179 CLR 101 (HCA) 398. See also *Siddell* v. *Vickers* (1892) 9 RPC 152 (CA), 163 (Lindley LJ).

The use of this term is not unknown to courts. The Supreme Court of Canada has referred to an account of profits as "disgorgement"[70] and in *Attorney General* v. *Blake*[71] Lord Steyn refrained from using the term "account of profits" and referred to "disgorgement of profits". Lord Diplock has also used disgorgement to refer to the effect of money had and received when that award operated to strip profits[72] and the Court of Appeal have recently referred to an account of profits, a (proprietary) constructive trust and "disgorgement" interchangeably.[73]

On the other hand, in *Watson* v. *Holliday*[74] Kay J held that an account of profits was not an award of damages. The claim for an account of profits was brought against a defendant for breach of patent. Because the defendant was bankrupt the claimant had to prove his claim in the bankruptcy. But section 31 of the Bankruptcy Act 1869 excluded from proof in the bankruptcy "demands in the nature of unliquidated damages arising otherwise than by reason of a contract". Kay J held that an account of profits was not excluded because it was not "damages".[75] This view should be rejected. The award of money had and received, which Kay J recognised can operate in exactly the same manner as an account of profits,[76] has been recognised in the United States as an award of damages when given for a wrong. In *Hart* v. *E P Dutton & Co Inc*,[77] the claimant sued the publisher of a book for libel for holding him out as a traitor during World War II. Hart sued for the profits the publisher had made through the sale of the book as money had and received. The problem was that an action for damages for libel was subject to a one year limitation period which had expired. Hart argued that the action for money had and received, to strip the defendant of the profits, was not an action for damages. The action failed. One reason for this was that the limitation period could not be avoided. The New York Supreme Court stated:

> "whatever the plaintiff may call the action . . . in the absence of any statute or common law authority, it must be considered as an action for damages . . . In applying the statute of limitations the Court should look for the reality and the essence of the action and not its mere name."[78]

This is the preferable view. As explained in chapter one, since the term "damages" cannot mean anything more than a money award for a wrong, the term

---

[70] *Hodgkinson* v. *Simms* above note 23, 383; *Cadbury Schweppes Inc* v. *FBI* above note 63, 155.

[71] [2001] 1 AC 268 (HL) 291, 292.

[72] *Mahesan S/O Thambiah* v. *Malaysian Government Officers Co-Operative Housing Society* [1979] AC 374 (PC) 376.

[73] *United Pan-Europe Communications NV* v. *Deutsche Bank AG* [2000] 2 BCLC 461(CA).

[74] (1882) 20 Ch D 780, 784.

[75] *Watson* v. *Holliday* above note 74.

[76] In *Watson* Kay J followed Lord Westbury LC from *Neilson* v. *Betts* (1871) LR 5 HL 1, 22 and stated that the account is like an equitable claim for money had and received.

[77] 93 NYS (2d) 871 (1949 DCNY).

[78] *Hart* v. *Dutton* above note 77, 878; Affirmed *Hart* v. *E P Dutton & Co Inc* 98 NYS (2d) 773 (1950) (SCNY App).

"disgorgement damages" is used in this book. Indeed, in the leading speech in *Attorney General* v. *Blake*[79] Lord Nicholls accepted that "damages" could be awarded based upon the profit a defendant had made from wrongdoing[80] but he insisted upon calling the profit-stripping award given for the breach of contract an "account of profits" because he considered the use of the only other term proffered during the hearing, restitutionary damages, an "unhappy expression" in a case of profit disgorgement.[81] The epithet "disgorgement" is a way to cut through these difficulties.

3) Other uses of "disgorgement" and "restitution"

(a) Disgorgement as a single term for all gain-based damages

Professor Lionel Smith was amongst the first commentators to discuss the term "disgorgement" in detail as a word which describes gain-based damages awards for wrongs.[82] Other commentators have followed Professor Smith's lead and adopted the term "disgorgement" to refer to all gain-based awards for wrongs.[83]

However Professor Smith, like many of the other commentators that follow him, uses the term disgorgement in a different sense from that used in this book. Professor Smith uses the term "disgorgement" as a single term to refer to all gain-based damages for wrongdoing.[84] This approach has the benefit of clearly distinguishing between categories of unjust enrichment and wrongdoing. The approach Professor Smith advocates suggests a single gain-based response of disgorgement for wrongs and a single gain-based response of restitution for unjust enrichment. For this reason, Professor Birks has argued that "[t]he attraction of Dr Smith's terminology is that, universally adopted, it would go far towards restoring and securing the quadration between autonomous unjust enrichment and restitution".[85]

In contrast, this book uses the term disgorgement damages to refer only to cases in which the measure of the defendant's gain focuses on the actual value or profit which accrues to the defendant from the wrong. Some commentators, akin to the approach in this book, (notably Professors Cane and Watts) have favoured acceptance of the term disgorgement damages whilst still preserving a

---

[79] *Blake* above note 71, 278–280; *Kuddus* v. *Chief Constable of Leicestershire Constabulary* [2001] 2 WLR 1789 (HL) 1803.

[80] *Blake* above note 71.

[81] *Blake* above note 71, 284. See also Mason and Carter *Restitution* 606.

[82] L Smith "The Province of the Law of Restitution" (1992) 71 CBR 672, 686.

[83] R Grantham & C Rickett *Enrichment and Restitution in New Zealand* (Hart Publishing Oxford 2000) 471; P Cane "Exceptional Measures of Damages" in P Birks (ed.) *Wrongs and Remedies* 302; S Worthington "Reconsidering Disgorgement for Wrongs" (1999) 62 MLR 218; P Cane *Tort Law and Economic Interests* (2nd edn. Clarendon Press Oxford 1996) 299; N Andrews "Civil Disgorgement of Wrongdoers' Gains: The Temptation to do Justice" in W Cornish et al. *Restitution*, 155; P Jaffey "Restitutionary Damages and Disgorgement" [1994] RLR 30; P Jaffey *The Nature and Scope of Restitution* (Hart Publishing Oxford 2000) 364–365.

[84] L Smith *Tracing* 297.

[85] P Birks "Misnomer" in W Cornish et al *Restitution* 12–13.

distinct role for restitutionary damages in cases involving transfers of value. However both have still used disgorgement in slightly different senses. Professor Cane uses the term disgorgement damages to include some cases which focus on the objective value of the benefit transferred.[86] Such cases focussing upon the gain arising from a transfer from the claimant, and operating to reverse that gain are restitutionary damages. Professor Watts is careful to maintain a distinction between the two approaches[87] although he considers disgorgement damages only in the context of an account of profits.[88] As explained above, and shown throughout chapters four to seven, disgorgement damages have been effected in several different ways at common law as well as in equity.

(b) *Restitutionary damages as a single term for all gain-based damages*

A more broadly accepted alternative is that of Professor Birks. His approach, followed by numerous others, uses the term "restitutionary damages", in the same manner as Professor Smith uses "disgorgement", to refer to all gain-based damages for wrongdoing.[89]

Professor Birks has recently acknowledged that awards of gain-based damages exist in the law of wrongs which do not focus upon reversing any wrongful transfer from the claimant.[90] Although initially sceptical as to whether a different name is needed for these damages,[91] Professor Birks has recently acknowledged that these disgorgement awards are "quite different measures" from those which reverse transfers of value.[92] The following section is devoted to showing that without a bifurcated approach which explicitly recognises two different measures, it is difficult to appreciate when each gain-based award for wrongdoing is available and the measure of the awards. Confusion in the courts is demonstrated from this very conflation.

---

[86] P Cane *Tort Law and Economic Interests* (2nd edn. Clarendon Press Oxford 1996) 299.

[87] The "aim [of restitution is] one of ensuring that transfers of assets or at least the value inherent in them occur only with the untainted consent of the owner or rightful possessor . . . On this basis restitution has no desire to strip unearned gain": P Watts "Property and Unjust Enrichment: Cognate Conservators" [1998] NZLR 151, 162.

[88] P Watts "Property and Unjust Enrichment: Cognate Conservators" [1998] NZLR 151, 156; P Watts "Restitutionary Damages for Trespass" (1996) 112 LQR 39, 41.

[89] P Birks *Introduction* 313; A Burrows *The Law of Restitution* 376; *Law Commission 1997*; G McMeel *The Modern Law of Restitution* (Blackstone Press London 2000) 327; I Jackman "Restitution for Wrongs" [1989] CLJ 302; *Attorney General* v. *Blake* [1998] Ch 439 (CA) 457–459; *Jaggard* v. *Sawyer* [1995] 1 WLR 269 (CA) 281 (Bingham MR). Others prefer simply using the term "restitution" avoiding the word damages: *Goff and Jones* 709 "restitutionary claims against wrongdoers"; G Virgo *Restitution* 443.

[90] Professor Birks refers to awards which operate to reverse transfers as "giving back" and those which operate to strip profit from a wrongdoer as "giving up": P Birks "Misnomer" in W Cornish et al. *Restitution* 13.

[91] P Birks "The Law of Restitution at the End of an Epoch" (1999) 28(1) UWAL Rev 13, 22.

[92] P Birks "Unjust Enrichment and Wrongful Enrichment" (2001) 79 Texas Law Rev 1767, 1774.

B The need to distinguish restitutionary damages and disgorgement damages

The need to differentiate between restitutionary damages and disgorgement damages arises primarily because each of these gain-based awards is based upon a different set of principles. As such they can result in awards of different amounts. Restitutionary damages might be available when disgorgement damages are not and vice versa.

The greatest need for both terms arises when the two damages awards are concurrently available. In these circumstances without two terms to describe the different gain-based awards for wrongdoing it is very difficult to know which award should be used and therefore what the appropriate measure is for the award of damages. The lack of two distinct terms is also a significant reason for the absence of an accepted theory which can explain why courts award gain-based damages in a particular case at all. This is because if two different measures of damages with different rationales are conflated then no theory can satisfactorily explain when each award will be made and why.

To explain how these difficulties arise in practice it is necessary to consider the different principles motivating the award of restitutionary and disgorgement damages respectively, and then to demonstrate the confusion evident as a result of the predominant unitary use of the term "restitutionary damages" to describe both types of award.

1) Different rationales and availability

(a) *Restitutionary damages*

The rationale for awarding restitutionary damages for a wrong is that because the transfer was procured by the defendant's wrong the law should not recognise the validity of the transfer of the money or benefit transferred and should reverse the transfer from the claimant to the defendant.

Professor Fuller and Mr Perdue considered the nature of what they described as the "restitution interest" in damages more than 60 years ago and argued that the restitution interest presents a claim to legitimacy twice as strong as that of damages assessed by reference to loss caused by reliance upon the wrong:[93]

> "If, following Aristotle, we regard the purpose of justice as the maintenance of an equilibrium of goods among members of society, the restitution interest presents twice as strong a claim to judicial intervention as the reliance interest, since if A not only causes B to lose one unit but appropriates that unit to himself, the resulting discrepancy between A and B is not one unit but two."

Although Professor Fuller and Mr Perdue were considering the case of a direct subtraction from the claimant's wealth (and therefore a financial loss) and

---

[93] LL Fuller and WR Perdue "The Reliance Interest in Contract Damages" (1936) 46 Yale LJ 52, 56.

corresponding accretion to the defendant's wealth, there should not be any difference where the defendant appropriates value in the form of a subtraction of non-monetary benefits from the claimant's *dominium*. For instance, if a defendant wrongfully uses a claimant's dock to store its pontoon then the value that the defendant has gained from that wrongful storage should be paid to the claimant.[94] The value of the storage came from using the claimant's property. There was a transfer of value deriving from the claimant's *dominium*. As the act of storage was wrongful, restitutionary damages should operate to reverse the wrongful transfer.

This book argues that restitutionary damages should in theory always be available for wrongs. If conduct is deemed a wrong, the law should always be prepared to reverse a transfer of value that is the result of that conduct. To do otherwise would be to legitimate the wrong. As Lord Shaw said of restitutionary damages in *Watson, Laidlaw and Co Ltd* v. *Pott, Cassels and Williamson*,[95] "unless such abstraction or invasion were to be sanctioned by law, the law ought to yield a recompense."

(b) *Disgorgement damages*

Disgorgement damages are more difficult to justify than either compensatory damages or restitutionary damages because the measure of the gain is not made according to what has been transferred or subtracted from the claimant. Instead, the claimant ignores whether a transfer has occurred or not and requires the defendant to disgorge any profit from the wrong.

Courts often make the award of disgorgement damages by invoking the maxim *commodum ex iniuria sua nemo habere debet*: "a man shall not be allowed to profit from his own wrong." The maxim has been acknowledged to be "in very general terms".[96] Professor Dworkin has noted that "rules" such as this are not really rules at all but just vague guidelines: "it is as if a zoologist had proved that fish are not mammals, and then concluded that they are really only plants".[97] A competing principle might be the reluctance to make a claimant better off as a result of the award than he was prior to the wrong.[98] As Glidewell LJ stated in *Halifax Building Society* v. *Thomas*:[99]

"The proposition that a wrongdoer should not be allowed to profit from his wrongs has an obvious attraction. The further proposition, that the victim or intended victim of the wrongdoing, who has in any event suffered no loss, is entitled to retain or recover the amount of profit is less obviously persuasive."

---

[94] *Penarth Dock Engineering Co Ltd* v. *Pounds* [1963] 1 Lloyds Rep 359.

[95] (1914) 31 RPC 104 (HL) 119.

[96] *Attorney General* v. *Guardian Newspapers (No 2)* [1990] 1 AC 109 (HL) 286 (Lord Goff); Mason and Carter *Restitution* 598–599.

[97] R Dworkin *Taking Rights Seriously* (Duckworth London 1978) 39.

[98] Compare compensatory damages, which have been justified in making a defendant worse off because of the strength of the harm principle (avoid harming others): P Cane *The Anatomy of Tort Law* (Hart Publishing Oxford 1997) 113.

[99] [1996] Ch 217 (CA) 229.

Restitutionary damages, which serve the dual purpose of aiming to restore both the claimant and the defendant to their respective positions before the wrong occurred, are therefore easier to justify than disgorgement damages which focus only upon restoring the defendant to his previous position by stripping him of value from the wrong. The question is what rationale can be advanced to justify a damages award which allows a claimant a profit that he might not otherwise have made and which might not have been generated as a result of his wealth. Although various theories have been advanced for the basis of disgorgement damages in the context of the award of an account of profits it is argued that the best approach is to regard disgorgement damages as based upon notions of deterrence of wrongdoing.

(i) The rationale is not compensation

One theory is that when disgorgement damages were given in equity, as an account of profits, this was simply equity's method of compensating a claimant for loss.[100] The basis for this "peculiar measure" in equity was said to be because "a court of equity . . . is not content with an action for damages; for it is nearly impossible to know the extent of the damage."[101] There are two reasons why this approach must be rejected.

First, it will be seen throughout this book that the account of profits remained available even where it was apparent that no loss whatsoever had been suffered. As explained above the wrong might even *benefit* the claimant.[102] It is entirely fictitious to irrebuttably presume that a loss has been suffered in order to justify an account of profits.

Secondly, the common law often encountered similar difficulties in assessing compensatory damages but recognised that the fact that they "cannot be assessed with certainty does not relieve the wrongdoer of the necessity of paying damages".[103] The explicit modern recognition by courts that compensatory damages are available in equity must destroy the compensatory rationale for the account of profits.[104] Lord Nicholls, speaking for a majority of the House of Lords, has stated that "whether this justification for ordering an account of profits holds good factually in every case must be doubtful".[105]

---

[100] *Colbeam Palmer Ltd* v. *Stock Affiliates Pty Ltd* (1968) 122 CLR 25 (HCA) 33, quoting from *Ashburner's Principles of Equity:* D Brown *Ashburner's Principles of Equity* (2nd edn. Butterworths London 1933) 40.

[101] *Hogg* v. *Kirby* (1803) 8 Ves 215, 223; 32 ER 336, 339.

[102] See above text accompanying note 40.

[103] *Chaplin* v. *Hicks* [1911] 2 KB 786, 792 (Williams LJ); *Owners of the Steamship "Mediana"* v. *Owners, Master and Crew of the Lightship "Comet"* [1900] AC 113 (HL) 116–117.

[104] *Nocton* v. *Lord Ashburton* [1914] AC 932 (HL) 956; *Target Holdings Ltd* v. *Redferns (a firm)* [1996] 1 AC 421 (HL) 434; *Bristol and West Building Society* v. *Mothew* [1998] Ch 1 (CA) 17; *Aquaculture Corporation* v. *New Zealand Green Mussel Co Ltd* [1990] 3 NZLR 299 (CANZ) 301 (Cooke P). See further ch. two text accompanying notes 6–26.

[105] *Attorney General* v. *Blake* [2001] 1 AC 268 (HL) 280.

(ii) The rationale is not that the defendant acted on behalf of the claimant

A second explanation is that by seeking disgorgement damages the claimant adopts the defendant's acts as his own.[106] This rationale is entirely fictional. For example, the Crown in *Reading* v. *Attorney General*,[107] would never purport to adopt or ratify the defendant's bribes. This adoption theory has sensibly been described as "dubious"[108] and was rejected more than 100 years ago by the United States Supreme Court.[109]

(iii) The rationale is deterrence

The basis for disgorgement damages, it is argued, is the need to ensure deterrence of wrongdoing. Preventing a defendant from profiting from a wrong ensures that both the defendant (in future cases), and others that might be in a similar position, are deterred from committing that type of wrong where profit might be a motive or encouragement.

This rationale is most evident in the case where profits are stripped from a defendant under the second limb of exemplary damages in *Rookes* v. *Barnard*.[110] The stripping of profit in that case is explicitly acknowledged to be for the purposes of punishment and deterrence. But the award of disgorgement damages, unlike exemplary damages, is limited to the amount of the profit. Courts constantly stress that the goal of an account of profits is not to punish.[111] In one sense, all damages awards "punish" a defendant by making a subtraction from that defendant's net wealth.[112] But in this case the excesses of a purely penal approach are controlled by a limiting principle. The damages are limited to the amount the defendant has gained from the wrong. This should not be understood as suggesting that the award has no penal effect but simply that the penal effect does not control the *measure* of the award. The measure of the award is dictated by the minimum amount necessary to make the wrong unprofitable. It is based on the need to deter wrongdoing and provides a monetary remedy which effects deterrence in circumstances in which a greater level of deterrence is required than compensatory damages can produce.

(iv) When deterrence is required: compensation inadequate

For many wrongs the award of compensatory damages will be sufficient to satisfy the need for deterrence. The Supreme Court of Canada recently recognised,

---

[106] *Neilson* v. *Betts* (1871) LR 5 HL 1 (HL) 22 (Lord Westbury); *De Vitre* v. *Betts* (1873) LR 6 HL 319 (HL); *Sutherland* v. *Caxton* [1936] Ch 323, 336; *Watson* v. *Holliday* (1882) 20 Ch D 780, 784.

[107] [1951] AC 507 (HL).

[108] WR Cornish *Intellectual Property* (4th ed. Sweet & Maxwell London 1999) 77.

[109] *Tilghman* v. *Proctor* 125 US 664 (1887) (SCUS) 668: "A substitute for legal damages" (Gray J for the Court). See also *Cala Homes* above note 65.

[110] [1964] AC 1129 (HL) 1226–1227 (Lord Devlin).

[111] *Vyse* v. *Foster* (1872) LR 8 Ch App 309, 333; *McCarey* v. *Associated Newspapers* [1965] 2 QB 86 (CA) 107; *Potton Ltd* v. *Yorkclose Ltd* [1990] FSR 11, 15; *My Kinda Town* v. *Soll* [1982] FSR 147 155; *Westdeutsche Landesbank Girozentrale* v. *Islington LBC* [1996] AC 669 (HL) 723; *Dart Industries Inc* v. *Décor Corp Pty Ltd* (1993) 179 CLR 101 (HCA) 111; *Warman International Ltd* v. *Dwyer* (1995) 182 CLR 544 (HCA) 557.

[112] *Roginsky* v. *Richardson-Merrell Inc* 378 F 2d 832 (2nd Cir 1967) 841 (Friendly J).

in the context of making an award of exemplary damages, that "as a rule, deterrence can be achieved through the award of compensatory damages and refusal to grant exemplary damages is not condonation of the violation of the rule of law".[113] However, there are two circumstances in which compensatory damages are insufficient to deter wrongdoing and disgorgement damages are required to provide adequate protection of rights.

The first is the instance of wrongs committed deliberately and cynically. This was explained by Lord Morris in *Broome* v. *Cassell & Co*,[114] considering the second limb or basis for exemplary damages:

> "where someone faces up to the possibility of having to pay damages for doing something which may be held to have been wrong but where nevertheless he deliberately carried out his plan because he thinks it will work out satisfactorily for him. He is prepared to hurt somebody because he thinks he may well gain by doing so even allowing for the risk that he may be made to pay damages."[115]

This same deterrence might be achieved by exemplary damages under Lord Devlin's second limb. But it might also be achieved by disgorgement damages which, as seen in chapter one, are a sharper and less objectionable tool in such instances as they are not subject to objections such as indeterminacy.[116] Lord Nicholls recognised this in *Kuddus* v. *Chief Constable of Leicestershire Constabulary*[117] and it led him to suggest that if the second category of exemplary damages were so confined, the sharper disgorgement damages might replace it entirely. He therefore suggested that it is perhaps time to expand that category to punish all instances of outrageous conduct even without a profit motive. This would mean that deterrence of cynical wrongdoing could be effected by disgorgement damages and other deliberate wrongdoing, for reasons entirely independent of material gain, could be deterred and punished with exemplary damages.

In making the award of exemplary damages under the second limb of *Rookes* v. *Barnard*,[118] judges have emphasised that it is sufficient that the defendant has sought to gain from the breach *generally*. Lord Hailsham explained in the *Broome* case that the requirements are (i) knowledge or a reckless disregard for the legality of the action being taken and (ii) a decision to carry on that conduct because the prospects of material advantage outweigh the prospects of material loss.[119]

---

[113] *Royal Bank of Canada* v. *W Got & Associates Electric Ltd* (2000) 178 DLR 385 (SCC) 394–395.
[114] [1972] AC 1027 (HL) 1095.
[115] *Rookes* v. *Barnard* [1964] AC 1129 (HL) 1094.
[116] See for instance the powerful objections of O'Connor J in *Pacific Mutual Life Insurance Co* v. *Haslip* 111 S Ct 1032 (1991 SCUS) 1066–1067. In the United States there is also a move towards the punitive award being capped at the defendant's profit made: *Douglass* v. *Hustler Magazine Inc* 769 F 2d 1128 (1985 CA 7th Circuit).
[117] [2001] 2 WLR 1789 (HL) 1807
[118] *Rookes* above note 115.
[119] *Broome* v. *Cassell & Co* [1972] AC 1027 (HL) 1079.

The rules applicable under this limb of exemplary damages should also apply to disgorgement damages so that they are available to strip profit where a wrongdoer has "acted in the hope or expectation of material gain".[120] These cases of disgorgement damages, used to strip profit from wrongs committed deliberately or recklessly for gain will be referred to in this book, as cases of "cynical breach".[121] Cynical breach should be interpreted widely and any conception of material gain should be sufficient. Indeed, once it is shown that a wrong has been deliberately committed, in circumstances in which the defendant profited, it is likely to be very difficult for a defendant to prove that material gain was not the object of the wrong.

There is one other case in which the law recognises a need for deterrence even though the defendant's breach has not been deliberate or reckless and calculated for gain. This is where there are institutions which require such a degree of protection that the prospect of gain for even inadvertent wrongdoing should be removed and potential defendants should be put on their guard. One institution which has been recognised as deserving this protection is the relationship of extreme trust and confidence or "fiduciary relationship". Fiduciaries are liable to disgorge any profits made[122] in breach of their duties, however innocently, because of this need for protection or prophylaxis to "express the policy of the law in holding fiduciaries to their duty".[123]

Another institution has sometimes been treated in the same manner as the fiduciary institution and awards of disgorgement damages given even for innocent breaches: this is the institution of property.[124] The award of disgorgement damages for innocent infringements of property rights has, however, been limited to some instances of intellectual property wrongs. Chapter seven will show how these awards were justified on the basis of either a fiction of fraud or a fiction that the disgorgement damages were compensation. For the reasons above, both of these rationales should be rejected. However, there is nothing in the "institution" of property that can justify or support these instances in which disgorgement damages have been awarded for innocent infringement of property rights.

First, the high degree of institutional protection afforded to fiduciary relationships can be justified as necessary to place the fiduciary on constant alert even to the possibility of innocent breach. Such vigil is necessary in relationships characterised by vulnerability and susceptibility to abuse. In comparison, the possibility of an innocent commission of a property wrong is not something against which a vigil can be maintained. The existence of property rights is not

---

[120] *John* v. *Mirror Group Newspapers Ltd* [1997] QB 586, 618–619.

[121] Adopting the term used by Lord Devlin in *Rookes* v. *Barnard* above note 115, 1227; P Birks *Introduction* 327; J Beatson *Use and Abuse* 16.

[122] *Regal (Hastings) Ltd* v. *Gulliver* [1967] 2 AC 134 (HL); *Boardman* v. *Phipps* [1967] 2 AC 46 (HL); "an acknowledgement of the . . . need to compel obedience . . . to norms of exemplary behaviour": *Canadian Aero Service* v. *O'Malley* (1973) 40 DLR (3d) 371 (SCC) 384.

[123] *Maguire* v. *Makaronis* (1996) 188 CLR 449 (HCA) 468.

[124] IM Jackman "Restitution for Wrongs" [1989] CLJ 302.

as obvious to a defendant as the existence of a relationship of trust and confidence or the vulnerability of the claimant. An innocent recipient of property, no matter how alert, often has no means to determine whether rights are held in the property by some unseen future claimant. Indeed, sometimes the existence of those rights depends upon very fine issues.[125] There is also great difficulty in determining what is meant by "property" and which rights therefore should incur this high degree of institutional protection. For instance, even defamation has been regarded as analogous to a property right.[126]

(c) *The rationales compared*

The difference between restitutionary damages and disgorgement damages in terms of theory therefore is apparent. Whilst awards of restitutionary damages are primarily concerned with corrective justice and reversing transfers between the parties, disgorgement damages are concerned with broader notions of deterrence. Restitutionary damages therefore should generally be available but disgorgement damages should only be available where there is an additional interest that compels an award to strip a defendant of every gain made from the wrong. That additional interest in cases of disgorgement damages is a need for additional deterrence of wrongdoing and historically this interest has been recognised in relationships of close trust and confidence and in instances of wrongs committed cynically, that is, deliberately or recklessly with a view to gain.

2) *When both remedies are concurrently available*

As a result of their different rationales and different availability in some instances restitutionary damages might be available and disgorgement damages might not or vice versa. For instance, in a fiduciary might make a personal profit without any transfer from the claimant; only disgorgement damages, the value accruing to the defendant from the wrong, will then be available. An illustration of this is the case of *Boardman* v. *Phipps*[127] discussed in chapter six. In brief, the appellants while acting as fiduciaries (agents for a trustee) acquired information and used that information to make a significant profit through the purchase of shares in a company. A majority of the House of Lords held that the information was not the property of the trust to which they owed fiduciary duties. Nor was there any possibility that the trust would have acquired further shares in that company.[128] Indeed, the trust *benefited* from the increase in value of the shares from the appellants' acquisition. Although there was therefore no transfer of value from the trust, the appellants were held liable for disgorgement damages to disgorge the profits made from the purchase of the shares.

---

[125] *Cundy* v. *Lindsay* (1878) 3 AC 459 (HL); *Ingram* v. *Little* [1961] 1 QB 31 (CA); *Lewis* v. *Averay* [1972] QB 198 (CA).

[126] *De Crespigny* v. *Wellesley* (1829) 5 Bing 392, 406; 130 ER 1112, 1118 (Best CJ).

[127] [1967] 2 AC 46 (HL).

[128] *Boardman* v. *Phipps* above note 122, 119 (Lord Upjohn).

Alternatively, facts might arise in which only restitutionary damages are available because although no actual profit is made, significant value is *transferred* as a result of a wrong. In *Inverugie Investments Ltd* v. *Hackett*[129] the defendants were the owners and reversioners of a large hotel and the claimant was a long-term lessee of 30 apartments within the hotel complex. The defendants cynically committed the tort of trespass by ejecting the claimant from the apartments and taking over the apartments for over 15 years. The trespass proved foolish and over the 15 year trespass period the hotel ran at a loss. The defendant only had an occupancy rate of 35–40 per cent. As a result disgorgement damages would have been nominal as there was no profit to disgorge.[130] However, the Privy Council made an award of restitutionary damages calculated on the market value of the price of hire of the 30 apartments (the market value being the market price less expenses and ground rent). These restitutionary damages amounted to more than two million dollars. As Rigby LJ stated over a century ago in *Whitwham* v. *Westminster Brymbo Coal and Coke Co*,[131] "in fact it is a matter of indifference whether the defendants made a profit or loss out of the transaction."

Although in some cases only one measure of gain-based damages might be available, in many cases both measures will be available. Suppose the hotel in the *Inverugie* case were run by the defendants at a large profit and at a rate exceeding the market hire price of the apartments. Perhaps the profit from the cynical trespass was $10 million. Chapter four explains and considers a number of cases in which disgorgement damages of such profits from cynical trespass have been available. Whether a claimant will prefer restitutionary damages or disgorgement damages will depend solely on the amount of actual gain made by the defendant as a result of the wrong (disgorgement damages) compared to the market value of the use transferred (restitutionary damages).[132]

3) Confusion without the use of two terms

Two cases in which gain-based awards have been made are now examined. In each the confusion results from the failure to differentiate between restitutionary damages and disgorgement damages. These two cases are given by way of simple example. In the conclusions to this book the most obvious example of where confusion will arise in the future without the use of the two terms is illustrated. This is in cases of election. Confusion is likely where courts are required to tell when a claimant should elect between two remedies which are described by the same name. In this book's conclusions, this possibility for confusion is also shown by reference to the Privy Council decision of *Tang Man Sit* v. *Capacious Investments Ltd*.[133]

---

[129] [1995] 1 WLR 713 (PC).
[130] *Inverugie Investments Ltd* above note 129, 715.
[131] [1896] 2 Ch 538 (CA).
[132] P Watts "Restitutionary Damages for Trespass" (1996) 112 LQR 39, 41.
[133] [1996] AC 514 (PC). See ch. eight, conclusions, text accompanying note 6–14.

(a) *Awards of compound interest*

The first example of confusion relates to the award of compound interest and points up confusion that has arisen in the House of Lords. Compound interest might be sought for a wrong as a measure of restitutionary damages or as a measure of restitution for an action in unjust enrichment. For example, suppose X fraudulently misappropriates £1,000 of Y's money. Y should be entitled to seek restitutionary damages to reflect the value of what has been transferred from him or her. This is the £1,000 *plus the value of its use*.[134] In commercial terms, the value of the use of money is measured in compound interest at market rates.[135]

Alternatively, what is sometimes labelled "compound interest" might also be an award of disgorgement damages. Suppose X had cleverly invested the £1,000 earning profit at a rate higher than the market interest rates. That higher profit earned might be sought as disgorgement damages. This disgorgement award, confusingly also entitled "compound interest" is well established as an award which is made in cases of fraud or other equitable wrongs to ensure that a defendant disgorges all profit for which he should account.[136] It operates to disgorge the amount of interest the defendant has *actually made* or, if it can be safely presumed that commercial use has been made of the money, the amount which the defendant can be presumed to have made.[137]

There can therefore be very significant differences between the restitutionary damages award and the disgorgement damages award in relation to this compound interest component. For example if the market rate of interest was five per cent (compounded annually), but the fraudster X, through skill and experience, had invested at a rate of nine per cent (also compounded annually) the disgorgement damages award (nine per cent annual compounding) would be higher than the restitutionary damages award (five per cent annual compounding).

---

[134] *Kuwait Oil Tanker Co SAK* v. *Al Bader* [2000] 2 All ER (Comm) 271 (CA); J Edelman "Claims to Compound Interest Part II: Extending Compound Interest claims for Wrongdoing" (2000) 28 ABLR 115; F Rose "Interest" in P Birks and F Rose (eds) *Lessons of the Swaps Litigation* above note 5, 291, 309, 313 noting that this principle also should apply in cases of restitution of payments made after a judgment is reversed.

[135] *Maguire* v. *Makaronis* above note 123, 476–477.

[136] *Attorney General* v. *Alford* (1855) 4 De G M & G 843, 851;43 ER 737, 741; *Burdick* v. *Garrick* (1870) LR 5 Ch App 233, 241; *Vyse* v. *Foster* (1872) LR 8 Ch App 309, 333; *Penny* v. *Avison* (1856) 3 Jur (New Ser) 62, 62; *Wallersteiner* v. *Moir (No 2)* [1975] 1 QB 373 (CA) 388, 406; *Westdeutsche Landesbank Girozentrale* v. *Islington LBC* [1996] AC 669 (HL) 693; *National Bank of New Zealand Ltd* v. *Development Finance Corporation of New Zealand Ltd* [1990] 3 NZLR 257 (CANZ) 263; *Southern Cross Commodities Pty Ltd (In Liq)* v. *Ewing* (1987) 91 FLR 271 (FCA) 272, 298; *Belmont Finance Corporation Ltd* v. *Williams Furniture Ltd (No 2)* [1980] 1 All ER 393 (CA) 419.

[137] *General Communications Ltd* v. *Development Finance Corporation of New Zealand Ltd* [1990] 3 NZLR 406 (CANZ) 436; *National Bank of New Zealand Ltd* v. *Development Finance Corporation of New Zealand* [1990] 3 NZLR 257 (CANZ) 263.

The problem that arises is that both restitutionary damages and disgorgement damages are being referred to by a single term "compound interest". The confusion is vividly apparent in the decision of the House of Lords in *Westdeutsche Landesbank Girozentrale* v. *Islington LBC*,[138] although arising in the context of unjust enrichment (where disgorgement should never be available) rather than wrongdoing.

The *Westdeutsche* case involved an interest rate swap contract which had been entered into between a local authority and a bank. The swap transaction involved the bank making an up-front lump sum payment to a local authority which represented (discounted) fixed interest payments on a notional capital sum that would have been made over a period of time. In exchange, the local authority made a number of payments of interest at the market rate on the same notional sum. The practical effect of this was to enable the local authority to borrow money uninhibited by statutory controls. However, these contracts were *ultra vires* the power of the local authority and void.[139] The trial judge and Court of Appeal held that the transaction should be reversed and the bank was entitled to restitution of the money it had paid up front, less the payments made by the local council. Much academic dispute has ensued over the "unjust factor" or basis for the remedy of restitution for unjust enrichment in the *Westdeutsche* case, however the sole issue before the House of Lords was whether the bank was entitled to compound interest on the money for which restitution was made.[140]

In the course of their speeches, no member of the House of Lords differentiated between the two measures. A majority of the House rejected the claim holding that only fraud or breach of fiduciary duty[141] could support an equitable award of "compound interest". Equity could not allow any claim for compound interest beyond these situations because legislative provisions in relation to interest had closed the door for future common law or equitable development.[142] It was assumed in all the majority speeches that the claim for compound interest to perfect the award of restitution for unjust enrichment in the *Westdeutsche* case was the same as the compound interest awards which operated to disgorge profits wrongfully made.

The problem and confusion arose in the speeches of the minority, Lords Goff and Woolf, both of whom would have allowed a claim to compound interest. In parts of his speech Lord Goff seemed to consider compound interest in the restitutionary sense. Lord Goff referred to the fact that the council had had the

---

[138] *Westdeutsche* above note 136.

[139] *Hazell* v. *Hammersmith & Fulham London Borough Council* [1992] 2 AC 1 (HL).

[140] Lords Goff and Browne-Wilkinson thought it was probably failure of consideration and Lord Woolf simply referred to it as a claim in "unjust enrichment": [1996] AC 669 (HL) 683 (Lord Goff) 710 (Lord Browne-Wilkinson) 723 (Lord Woolf).

[141] The House of Lords was unanimous in rejecting a submission by the bank that the local authority received the money as a resulting trustee and was therefore liable to disgorge any compound interest profit: [1996] AC 669 (HL) 689, 709, 718, 720, 738. In any event, even some commentators who would support a finding of a resulting trust in such a case argue that a resulting trustee in these circumstances would not be under fiduciary duties: R Chambers *Resulting Trusts* 216–218.

[142] *Westdeutsche* above note 136, 717, 718, 740–741.

"use of the bank's money"[143] and that "there is no reason why the bank should be denied a complete remedy".[144] This type of award focuses upon the need to reverse completely the transfer due to unjust enrichment by awarding the claimant bank the full value of what has been transferred: a complete remedy. This is the money plus the market value of its use. Unfortunately, Lord Goff justified the recognition of such a restitutionary award of compound interest by "expanding its recognition"[145] from the cases in the law of wrongs in which profits were disgorged for fraud or breach of fiduciary duty:[146]

> "The seed is there but the growth has hitherto been confined within a small area. That growth should now be permitted to spread naturally elsewhere within this newly recognised branch of the law. No genetic engineering is required."

Other parts of Lord Goff's speech also support this view of compound interest as a disgorging measure. Lord Goff stated that the award of compound interest arose because "the council can properly be said to have profited from the bank's money so as to make an award of compound interest appropriate".[147]

Lord Woolf also argued for the extension of this measure of compound interest from the disgorgement damages cases of compound interest in the law of wrongs. He referred to *Burdick* v. *Garrick*,[148] stating:

> "[Compound interest] is the making of the award not as a punishment but to disgorge a profit made or presumed to have been made of a sum of money which should not have been made. Here this was because the contract was void as being ultra vires. There would be no difference of principle if the contract was void for mistake."[149]

On the other hand Lord Woolf also sometimes justified the recognition of compound interest in terms which suggested he was contemplating a restitutionary damages measure. He spoke of "the court's ability to grant full restitution"[150] and approved of the statement by Hobhouse J that the award should "reflect the actual value of money"[151] and that there is no reason to "deny the plaintiff a complete remedy".[152]

As Lords Goff and Woolf were in the minority, resolution of the method by which the compound interest would have been calculated will never be required. The danger of their reasoning though is that it could have admitted a disgorgement remedy into the law of unjust enrichment. As chapter two explained, such disgorgement remedies have properly never been part of unjust

---

[143] *Westdeutsche* above note 136, 698.
[144] *Westdeutsche* above note 136, 691.
[145] *Westdeutsche* above note 136, 693.
[146] *Westdeutsche* above note 136, 697. Also at 693 "whether the jurisdiction . . . may be permitted to expand . . . elsewhere within that rubric of the law [of restitution]".
[147] *Westdeutsche* above note 136, 698.
[148] *Burdick* v. *Garrick* above note 136.
[149] *Westdeutsche* above note 136, 723.
[150] *Westdeutsche* above note 136, 720.
[151] *Westdeutsche* above note 136, 719.
[152] *Westdeutsche* above note 136, 720.

enrichment and should have no place in that branch of the law. Further, even if the basis of the claim in the *Westdeutsche* case had been for a wrong (so that both the restitutionary damages measure of compound interest and the disgorgement damages measure would be available) the different measures could have led to very different results. One could readily imagine situations in which the council had invested the borrowed money in trade or commerce and made a profit which was either far more or far less than the market rate of interest measure (restitutionary damages).

On the facts of the *Westdeutsche* case itself there could have been a significant difference between the two measures. Although the council did save the expense of not having to borrow money elsewhere, counsel for the local authority acknowledged that there was no evidence that the council had used the money in trade or commerce.[153] There was therefore no evidence that the local authority had actually *profited* from the saved expense. If this were found to be the case the restitutionary damages measure would have been considerably greater than the disgorgement damages measure. In any event, the disgorgement measure should not even have been countenanced as the *Westdeutsche* case concerned a cause of action in *unjust enrichment*.

(b) *Gain-based damages for breach of contract*

The second example is the Israeli Supreme Court case of *Adras* v. *Harlow & Jones Gmbh*.[154] Adras had agreed to purchase steel from Harlow. After delivery of some of the steel, and before the remainder was due, the Yom Kippur war broke out and steel prices rose. In breach of contract[155] Harlow sold the remaining steel to a third party for a significantly higher price. However, by the time delivery was due steel prices had fallen to the pre-war rates so the claimant could purchase the steel elsewhere without suffering any loss.

The claimant sought the difference between the contract price of DM 570 per ton and the "market price" at the time of the breach of contract of DM 900 a ton. This claim was for restitutionary damages. It refers to the value transferred by the wrong. At the time of the breach of contract the claimant's contractual right to the delivery of the steel was worth the net market value of DM 330. By converting or wrongfully selling the steel the defendant wrongfully transferred the value of those rights from the claimant to itself.

However, as an alternative to this measure, the claimant claimed the difference between the contract price and the price for *which Harlow sold the steel*, DM 804.70. This is the measure of the actual monetary gain as a result of the wrong rather than of the value of the rights transferred. The disgorgement damages award was only DM 234.70 per ton compared to the restitutionary damages measure of DM 330.

---

[153] *Westdeutsche* above note 136, 674–675.

[154] (1988) 42(1) PD 221 (Hebrew); [1995] RLR 235(English).

[155] It is not necessary to consider the difficult issue of whether there was really any breach; it suffices to assume the decision was correct on this aspect.

A majority of the Supreme Court thought that a gain-based remedy was appropriate. However the majority conflated the two measures and, as a result awarded the wrong amount.[156] The problem was that the majority awarded the disgorgement damages measure but their reasoning supported the higher restitutionary damages measure. Nor was there any discussion as to why the higher restitutionary damages award was not appropriate.

The majority was comprised of S Levin, Barak and Bach JJ (Ben Porath V-P and D Levin J dissented). The problem arose because in considering the award for the breach of contract all the judgments referred to both gain-based measures of damages as "restitution". In conflating the two awards the result was that the lower disgorgement damages award was given whilst the higher restitutionary damages award should have also been available.

Barak J reached this conclusion on the basis that contractual rights should be "protected interests" in the same way as a property right and that the law should allow a benefit which comes from the claimant to be restored.[157] Conflating these restitutionary damages (reversing transfers) and disgorgement damages into the single term "restitution", Barak J then slipped into discussion of deterrence and the need to encourage people to keep their promises by stripping them of profits and approved the award of disgorgement damages.[158]

S Levin J recognised that there were two different measures of "restitution" being described by the same name. One measure operates to reverse a transfer, to "put the parties back in the position they occupied prior to the contract";[159] while the other "is meant to act as a deterrent to breach".[160] This approach would have neatly recognised both restitutionary damages and disgorgement damages. However, S Levin J thought that the former measure could only apply outside contract in an "extra-contractual" claim and the latter measure could only apply for the breach of contract.[161] The former, "extra-contractual" claim is what English lawyers would consider a claim in unjust enrichment for failure of consideration. Again, the use of the single term "restitution" to describe both responses confused S Levin J into considering that only one response could be possible when considering the breach of contract as a wrong.

Bach J agreed with the reasoning of both Barak J and S Levin J and awarded disgorgement damages again explaining the award as one of deterrence.[162]

---

[156] The judgments also took the approach, rejected in ch. 2, of regarding the gain-based remedies for breach of contract as part of "unjust enrichment" rather than part of the law of wrongs. The relevant Unjust Enrichment Law however was worded in such a way as to encompass gain-based responses within the law of wrongs and the law of (non-wrongful) unjust enrichment. See diagram accompanying note 77, ch. 2.

[157] *Adras* above note 154, 269–270.

[158] *Adras* above note 154, 272.

[159] *Adras* above note 154, 243.

[160] *Adras* above note 154, 241.

[161] The former measure therefore required termination of the contract whilst the latter did not: *Adras* above note 154, 243.

[162] *Adras* above note 154, 276.

As a result of the conflation of these two awards the lower disgorgement damages award was made when the higher restitutionary damages award should have been available.

The problem in English contract law is not as acute. Although, as will be seen in chapter five, both restitutionary damages and disgorgement damages for a breach of contract have been recognised, the recent House of Lords decision in *Attorney General* v. *Blake*[163] refused to conflate these two awards. Lord Nicholls in the leading speech preferred the term "account of profits" instead of "the unhappy expression 'restitutionary damages' " to describe an award of disgorgement damages.[164] In the other majority speech, Lord Steyn referred to the award as "disgorgement of profits".[165]

C Distinguishing gain-based damages from other awards

1) *Restitutionary damages and restitution*

As discussed in chapter two, a law of unjust enrichment exists independently of any wrongdoing and has been recognised as such in English law. However, in many cases of wrongdoing there exists a corresponding action for unjust enrichment. The same set of facts might give rise to an action for unjust enrichment or an action for a wrong.

An example of the concurrent operation of the two actions on the same set of facts can illustrate this point. In the case of property transferred by deceit or fraudulent misrepresentation, the fraudulent misrepresentation is also an induced mistake in the mind of the defendant. An action in unjust enrichment seeking restitution for mistake arises from the same set of facts as an action for restitutionary damages for the wrong of deceit. This possibility of dual analysis is what Professor Birks has termed "alternative analysis".[166] In the old forms of action courts rarely specified whether the action relied upon the wrong or not and many cases, such as the example above,[167] can now be analysed as actions for restitutionary damages for a wrong or restitution for unjust enrichment.

The response of restitution, reversing a transfer as a result of unjust enrichment, therefore operates in an identical manner to restitutionary damages which reverse transfers as a result of wrongs. Because of this overlap, there have been suggestions that all the cases of what have been called restitutionary damages in this book are not cases of wrongdoing at all but are unjust enrichments.

---

[163] [2001] 1 AC 268 (HL).
[164] *Blake* above note 163, 284.
[165] *Blake* above note 163, 291, 292.
[166] P Birks *Introduction* 314–315.
[167] *Madden* v. *Kempster* (1807) 1 Camp 12; 170 ER 859.

Professors Beatson and Friedmann argue that although in some cases it might appear that courts are relying upon the wrong, the response of reversing the transfer is really independent of any wrongdoing and part of the law of unjust enrichment.[168] As Professor Beatson argues "the restitutionary claim is not generated by the breach of duty. It is generated by a receipt attributable to the plaintiff's property [or] . . . not conferred officiously".[169]

Dr Worthington and Mr Jaffey have recently followed this theme with a slight variation. Although they argue that transfers are only reversed in the law of unjust enrichment, they acknowledge that the remedy of profit stripping (disgorgement damages) is a different remedy and does operate in the law of wrongs.[170]

Six reasons can be given as to why the remedies of restitution for unjust enrichment and restitutionary damages for a wrong should be kept separate and why the remedy of restitutionary damages for wrongs should not be assimilated into the law of unjust enrichment. The first is the general reason that the argument misconceives the operation of concurrent liability. The other five reasons are specific reasons, explaining how different results can arise if, on one set of facts, a claimant seeks to bring an action for restitutionary damages for a wrong rather than for restitution for unjust enrichment.

(i) Concurrent liability

The overlapping actions for wrongdoing and for unjust enrichment contain different elements. For instance, consider the overlapping claims for mistake (a mistaken payment) and deceit. The action for mistake does not depend upon any intention or conduct of the payee. The payee may be wholly innocent.[171] On the other hand, deceit, although inducing a mistake, requires proof that the payee defendant made representations knowing them to be false, or being reckless as to their truth.[172]

The first reason why restitutionary damages for wrongs should not be assimilated into restitution for unjust enrichment is because it is not apparent why one body of law, operating upon different principles, should give way to the other. In *Henderson v. Merrett Syndicates Ltd*[173] Lord Goff considered arguments that development of tort liability might circumvent contractual rules of privity. He dismissed such arguments on the basis that there is nothing wrong with concurrent liability:

---

[168] J Beatson *Use and Abuse* ch. 8; D Friedmann "Restitution of Benefits Obtained Through the Appropriation of Property or the Commission of a Wrong" (1980) 80 Col LR 804; D Friedmann "Restitution for Wrongs: The Basis for Liability" in W Cornish et al. *Restitution* ch. 9.

[169] J Beatson *Use and Abuse* 208.

[170] S Worthington "Reconsidering Disgorgement for Wrongs" (1999) 62 MLR 218; P Jaffey *The Nature and Scope of Restitution* (Hart Publishing Oxford 2000) 364–365. Mr Jaffey, however, regards "unjust enrichment" as a category which should be replaced with inferred contracts and vitiated transfers.

[171] *Kelly v. Solari* (1841) 9 M & W 54; 152 ER 24.

[172] *Derry v. Peek* (1889) 14 App Cas 337 (HL).

[173] [1995] 2 AC 145 (HL) 193–194; *Hill v. Van Erp* (1998) 188 CLR 159 (HCA) 231 (Gummow J).

"there is no sound basis for a rule which automatically restricts the claimant to either a tortious or a contractual remedy . . . I do not find it objectionable that the claimant may be entitled to take advantage of the remedy which is most advantageous to him."

(ii) Alternative analysis might not be possible

A number of cases can be given where the response of restitutionary damages was given for a wrong but the facts would not have allowed a corresponding action for restitution for unjust enrichment.

The gain-based *indebitatus assumpsit* count of money had and received was one method by which courts reversed transfers. Money had and received is discussed further in chapter four, but it is sufficient to note at this point that it was a remedy which was explicitly not based upon any loss to the claimant. In cases involving a transfer to an infant money had and received was only available to reverse the transfer where the infant had committed a wrong. In *Bristow* v. *Eastman*[174] an infant had embezzled money and Lord Kenyon held that the money could only be recovered because the "substance" of the action was a wrong which was either fraud or trover (conversion).[175]

Another case of restitutionary damages for which alternative analysis in unjust enrichment is not possible is *Moses* v. *Macferlan*.[176] Macferlan had obtained an indorsement by Moses on promissory notes in return for an undertaking that Macferlan would not sue Moses, as endorser on the notes. But, ignoring his promise, Macferlan sued Moses and recovered the money in a Court of Conscience. Moses later sued Macferlan to recover the money paid as money had and received. Moses succeeded. As an unjust enrichment the restitution of the payment could only be explained on the ground of compulsion. But to suggest that a payment pursuant to a legal process could be overturned on the basis of compulsion would be contrary to the rule of *res judicata*. The decision of Lord Mansfield requiring restitution of the payment was criticised on this basis in later cases.[177]

Professor Birks has pointed out that this case is explicable but only on the basis that it is a case of restitutionary damages for a breach of contract.[178] Indeed Lord Mansfield acknowledged that the earlier decision of the Court of Conscience was correct: the action by Moses "admits the commissioners did right".[179] It is apparent that Lord Mansfield was considering that the breach of contract was the reason for recovery when he referred to the admission that "unquestionably an action might be brought on the agreement" as a decisive answer to any objection that the judgment was *res judicata*.[180]

---

[174] (1794) 1 Esp 172; 170 ER 317.

[175] *Bristow* v. *Eastman* above note 174, 173; 317.

[176] (1760) 2 Burr 1005; 97 ER 676.

[177] *Phillips* v. *Hunter* (1795) 2 H. Bl 414; *Marriot* v. *Hampton* (1797) 7 TR 269; 101 ER 969.

[178] P Birks "Restitutionary Damages for Breach of Contract: *Snepp* and the fusion of law and equity" [1987] LMCLQ 421, 429–430. See also Anon "Moses v. Macferlan—Is it Sound Law" (1915) 24 Yale LJ 246, 249–250 and J P Dawson *Unjust Enrichment* (Little Brown & Co Boston 1951) 11.

[179] *Moses* v. *Macferlan* above note 176, 1009; 678. The decision of the Court of Conscience was predicated on a lack of jurisdiction to hear oral evidence as to the collateral promise: see the explanation of Lord Kenyon in *Marriot* v. *Hampton* (1797) 7 TR 269.

[180] *Moses* v. *Macferlan* above note 176, 1010; 679.

(iii) Availability of different defences

The most obvious defence which might not apply where restitutionary damages are sought for a wrong but which does apply for alternative analysis in unjust enrichment is the defence of change of position.

Lord Goff has suggested that the change of position defence, available generally in cases of unjust enrichment, might not be available to a wrongdoer.[181] The United States *Restatement of Restitution* takes this position.[182] Although there has been no evidence that English law, since the reception of the defence in 1991,[183] is prepared to extend it to a wrongdoer, some commentators have suggested that change of position might, or even should, be introduced into the law of wrongs.[184] It is suggested here that such a development might not be desirable.

Consider a case in which £1,000 of cotton is innocently converted by a purchaser who buys the cotton thinking the vendor has valid title. The purchaser honestly believes that the vendor has properly obtained the cotton and there is no indication otherwise. In reliance, the purchaser changes his position by paying £1,000. In fact, the vendor has no title to the cotton. In a claim for compensatory damages in such a case the defence of change of position has been refused because people "deal with the property in chattels or exercise acts of ownership over them at their own peril".[185] This is a long-standing principle of English law.[186]

In the above discussion of the rationale for restitutionary damages it was seen that the rationale behind restitutionary damages might even be more compelling than the rationale for compensation for the wrong. The need for corrective justice suggests that wrongful transfers should not be sanctioned by the law and should always be reversed. It is difficult to see why a defendant should be able to resist this logic with a defence of change of position to an action for restitutionary damages for conversion whilst such a defence is not available where compensatory damages are sought for conversion.

Further, in the leading House of Lords decision on restitutionary damages for conversion, admittedly prior to the recognition of the defence of change of position, restitutionary damages were awarded despite an obvious change of position. The case is discussed in detail in chapter four but the facts can be briefly

---

[181] *Lipkin Gorman* v. *Karpnale Ltd* [1991] 2 AC 548 (HL) 580.

[182] *Restatement of Restitution* s. 141(2).

[183] *Lipkin Gorman* v. *Karpnale Ltd* [1991] 2 AC 548 (HL).

[184] A Burrows "Quadrating Restitution and Unjust Enrichment: A Matter of Principle" [2000] RLR 257, 265–266; C Harpum, "Knowing Receipt: the Need for a New Landmark: Some Reflections" in W Cornish et al *Restitution* 250; P Hellwege "The Scope of Application of Change of Position in the Law of Unjust Enrichment: A Comparative Study" [1999] RLR 92, 96–100; G Virgo "What is the Law of Restitution About" in W Cornish et al. *Restitution* 321; G Virgo *Restitution* 727; *Goff and Jones* 826.

[185] *Fowler* v. *Hollins* (1872) LR 7 QB 616, 639 (Cleasy B). See W Swadling "Some Lessons from the Law of Torts" in P Birks (ed.) *The Frontiers of Liability* (Vol 1 OUP Oxford 1994) 41, 47 citing also the Law Reform Commission for the proposition that "questions of fault were irrelevant in actions for conversion."

[186] *Cundy* v. *Lindsay* above note 125; *Ingram* v. *Little* above note 125.

outlined to illustrate this point. In *United Australia Ltd* v. *Barclays Bank Ltd*[187] a cheque payable to United Australia was fraudulently indorsed by the secretary of United Australia to a company, MFG. MFG presented the cheque to their bankers, Barclays Bank, who credited MFG's account. After MFG went into liquidation, United Australia sued Barclays Bank seeking restitutionary damages (money had and received) for conversion as well as compensatory damages for conversion and negligence. The action for money had and received succeeded despite the change of position by Barclays Bank.

In cases like the *United Australia* case, assuming that a corresponding action to the wrong of conversion exists in unjust enrichment,[188] the response of restitution for the unjust enrichment will yield a different result to restitutionary damages for the wrong if change of position is not an available defence in the law of wrongs.

(iv) Different principles of private international law

Another way in which the value of the awards might differ is in the application of different principles of choice of law for the purposes of private international law. There is a strong argument that the law applicable to unjust enrichment actions is the law of the place of the enrichment.[189] As restitutionary damages cases are based upon the wrong, restitutionary damages for wrongdoing should be governed by the law of the place of the wrong[190] and the unjust enrichment cases will be governed by the place of the enrichment.

(v) Different limitation periods

An example of the different limitation periods that might arise for restitutionary damages for a wrong compared with restitution for an unjust enrichment can be seen in *Chesworth* v. *Farrar*.[191] In that case, a deceased's estate included an antique shop which contained goods of the claimant. The executors of the estate lost many of the goods and sold others. Two claims were brought against the executor. The first was a claim for loss suffered due to the executor's failure to take care of the claimant's goods under a contract of bailment. The second was a claim for money had and received for the proceeds from the sale of the goods.

---

[187] [1941] AC 1 (HL).

[188] See ch. 2, text accompanying note 115–118.

[189] *El Ajou* v. *Dollar Land Holdings Plc* [1993] 3 All ER 717, 736 (Millett J); *Chase Manhattan Bank NA Israel-British Bank (London) Ltd* [1981] Ch 105; *Re Jogia (A Bankrupt)* [1988] 1 WLR 484; *Macmillian Inc* v. *Bishopsgate Investment Trust Plc (No 3)* [1996] 1 WLR 387 (CA) , 408 (Auld LJ accepting that at the moment there is a "tendency" to accept this proposition which is endorsed in *Dicey & Morris*: L Collins (Gen Ed) *Dicey and Morris on Conflict of Laws* (Sweet & Maxwell London 2000) 1485. Mr Briggs, however, has notes that this case law is "extraordinarily unsatisfactory": A Briggs "From Complexity to Anticlimax: Restitution and Choice of Law" [1996] RLR 88, 91. However he suggests adoption of the place of enrichment as a rebuttable presumption in cases of unjust enrichment where there is no prior relationship between the parties. A Briggs *Conflict of Laws* (OUP Oxford 2001). Cf G Panagopoulos *Restitution in Private International Law* (Hart Publishing Oxford 2000).

[190] L Collins (Gen Ed.) *Dicey and Morris* above note 189, 1498–1499, 1501–1502.

[191] [1967] 1 QB 407.

The problem was that the limitation period for an action for a wrong against an executor was very short and had expired.[192] In relation to the claim for breach of a duty of bailment, Edmund Davies J held that the claim was one in respect of a cause of action in tort and was barred by the expiry of the limitation period.[193]

However, in relation to the claim for the proceeds from sale, Edmund Davies J held that this action for money had and received was not "an action in tort".[194] He quoted from Lord Wright[195] that "[s]uch remedies . . . fall within a third category of the common law [separate from contract or tort] which has been called quasi-contract or restitution".[196] It would seem that the best explanation or "vindicating property rights", the *Chesworth* case is that it was a cause of action for "ignorance", as considered in chapter two. The claim in unjust enrichment succeeded where the claim in tort failed.

On the other hand, in a United States case, again where money had and received was sought for the proceeds of sale of the claimant's goods, the claimant based the claim for money had and received upon the wrong of conversion. Accepting that the "gist of the action" was the wrong of conversion the Second Circuit Court of Appeals held that the limitation period for the wrong of conversion applied.[197]

This type of reasoning might be criticised on the basis that the "same mischief would arise" whether the action is one for an unjust enrichment or a tort[198] and the dual characterisation allows the policy of the statute to be avoided by bringing the action in unjust enrichment.[199] But the question must be asked whether the policy of the statute really is the same in cases of unjust enrichment. Where it is not the breach of duty upon which reliance is placed but an unjust enrichment at the expense of the claimant then it might be that the policy of the act is different.[200] The very short limitation period in that case originated from an ancient rule that the estate of a deceased was not liable for any wrong of the deceased person. But this rule was only ever applicable to torts.[201] It might not

---

[192] Law Reform (Miscellaneous Provisions) Act 1934 s1(3).

[193] *Chesworth* v. *Farrar* above note 191.

[194] *Chesworth* v. *Farrar* above note 191, 417.

[195] *Fibrosa Spolka Akcyjna* v. *Fairbairn Lawson Combe Barbour Ltd* [1943] AC 32 (HL) 61.

[196] Although at one point in his judgment he makes the suggestion that the basis of the action is the *tort of conversion* this is best seen as a reference to the fact that the ingredients of the tort of conversion are the same as the action in unjust enrichment: "[I]t is a *sine qua non* . . . to establish that a tort has been committed": *Chesworth* v. *Farrar* above note 191, 417. For this explanation in a different context see V House "Unjust Enrichment: The Applicable Statute of Limitations"(1950) 35 Corn L Q 797, 805.

[197] *Loughman* v. *Town of Pelham* 126 F (2d) 714 (2nd Circ 1942) 719.

[198] *Waterhouse* v. *Keen* (1825) 4 B & C 200, 214; 107 ER 1033, 1038.

[199] *Beaman* v. *ARTS Ltd* [1948] 2 All ER 89, 92–93.

[200] F Rose "Lapse of Time: Limitation" in P Birks and F Rose (eds) *Lessons of the Swaps Litigation* above note 5, 348, 355, 357.

[201] *Sollars* v. *Lawrence* (1743) Willes 413, 421; 125 ER 1243, 1247 (Willes CJ); W Swadling "The Myth of *Phillips* v. *Homfray*" in W Swadling and G Jones (eds) *The Search for Principle: Essays in Honour of Lord Goff of Chieveley* (OUP Oxford 1999) 277, 288.

be illogical for a different limitation period to apply to an action which requires different elements, such as proof of enrichment.

(vi) Different awards of interest
Another difference arises between restitution for an unjust enrichment and restitutionary damages for a wrong because of the need to prove enrichment in the case of an unjust enrichment and not in the case of a wrong. Awards of interest generally run from the date of accrual of the cause of action.[202] The fact that the enrichment might arise at a different time from when the wrong is committed means that the cause of action for a wrong might arise at a different time from the cause of action for an unjust enrichment. Thus, for exactly the same reason that limitation periods might be different for wrongs and unjust enrichments the award of interest might also be different.

2) *Distinguishing restitutionary damages and compensatory damages*

(a) *The overreach of compensatory damages*
Another area of confusion is between awards of compensatory damages and those of restitutionary damages. Some commentators and courts have tried to justify awards of restitutionary damages as damages for a "lost opportunity to bargain".[203] The argument is that although the claimant has not suffered any actual financial loss in some cases of restitutionary damages, these awards, which effect a transfer of value, are not based upon objective gain transferred to the defendant but should still be viewed as compensatory by assuming that the claimant lost an opportunity to bargain with the defendant. Thus, on this view, all restitutionary damages awards are really awards of compensatory damages.

This approach, explaining awards of restitutionary damages as compensatory, assumes that such a bargain would have resulted in the defendant agreeing to pay the claimant the reasonable value or market price for the value transferred and therefore that is the financial loss suffered by the claimant. The argument is that the market value is a *presumption* of the value that would have been achieved in a bargain with the claimant.[204] A number of commentators have rightly rejected this approach as a fiction.[205] It can be shown to be fictitious in three ways. This is because the market value is used as the measure of damages where the claimant would clearly have sought and obtained more than market value; where the claimant would have obtained less than market value; and where the claimant would never have bargained at all.

---

[202] *Westdeutsche Landesbank Girozentrale* v. *Islington LBC* [1996] AC 669 (HL) 717.

[203] RJ Sharpe and SM Waddams "Damages for lost opportunity to bargain" (1982) 2 OJLS 290. See *Tito* v. *Waddell (No 2)* [1977] Ch 106, 335; *Jaggard* v. *Sawyer* [1995] 1 WLR 269 (CA); *Gafford* v. *Graham* (1998) 76 P & CR 18.

[204] RJ Sharpe and SM Waddams "Damages for lost opportunity to bargain" (1982) 2 OJLS 290, 296.

[205] P Birks "Profits of Breach of Contract" (1993) 109 LQR 518; A Burrows *The Law of Restitution* 393; Mason and Carter *Restitution* 604, 700.

(i) Where the claimant would have obtained more than market value

First, consider a case such as *Jaggard v. Sawyer*.[206] In that case, the defendant, in breach of restrictive covenant built a driveway that trespassed on the claimant's land. An injunction could have been awarded for the trespass but was refused for policy reasons.[207] Instead both the trial judge and the Court of Appeal awarded a sum of damages in lieu of an injunction under Lord Cairns' Act.[208] The damages awarded were the price that a reasonable claimant would have charged to relax the covenant. This is an award of restitutionary damages. It focuses on reversing the value of the non-monetary benefit (the use of the driveway).

However, the two substantial judgments in the Court of Appeal explained the award as one of a loss of a bargaining opportunity. Sir Thomas Bingham MR rejected comments by Steyn LJ in *Surrey County Council* v. *Bredero Homes Ltd*[209] that "the object of the award . . . was not to compensate the plaintiff for financial injury, but to deprive the defendants of an unjustly acquired gain." Instead, the Master of the Rolls approved remarks of Megarry V-C in *Tito* v. *Waddell (No 2)* that:[210]

> "the plaintiff has suffered a loss in that the defendant has taken without paying for it something for which the plaintiff could have required payment, namely, the right to do the act. The court therefore makes the defendant pay what he ought to have paid the plaintiff, for that is what the plaintiff has lost."

Millett LJ took a similar approach viewing the reasonable award as one of compensation.[211] However, the fiction of this approach is immediately apparent by referring to the manner in which the Master of the Rolls assessed the damages. He stated that[212] although "a plaintiff should not be treated as eager to sell, which he very probably is not . . . the court will not value the right at the ransom price which a very reluctant plaintiff might put on it." The same reasoning was employed in a similar case where the claimants could have sought an injunction to prevent the defendant from trespassing over their road to reach his house.[213] Although all the evidence showed that the price that would have been sought and probably paid for relaxing the covenant was £6,000, Graham J made an award of the reasonable market value of the right of £2,000[214] stating that the claimants "must be treated as being willing to accept a fair price".[215]

If the damages were truly compensatory and concerned with what the claimant has lost then that ransom price *should* be the amount by which they are assessed. But the "presumption" of market price cannot be rebutted.

[206] *Jaggard v. Sawyer* above note 203.
[207] The main reason being that it was the only means of access to the defendant's house.
[208] Chancery Amendment Act 1858, now s. 50 Supreme Court Act 1981.
[209] [1993] 1 WLR 1361 (CA) 1369.
[210] *Jaggard v. Sawyer* above note 203, 282; *Tito v. Waddell (No 2)* [1977] Ch 106, 335.
[211] *Jaggard v. Sawyer* above note 203, 290, 292.
[212] *Jaggard v. Sawyer* above note 203, 282–283.
[213] *Bracewell* v. *Appleby* [1975] Ch 408.
[214] *Bracewell* above note 213, 420.
[215] *Bracewell* above note 213, 419.

(ii) Where the claimant would have obtained less than the market value
The second reason is that, just as the damages are not increased to reflect the claimant's true loss, so too the damages are not reduced in cases where the claimant's loss is less. The case of *Inverugie Investments Ltd* v. *Hackett*[216] was considered above as an example of restitutionary damages. The Privy Council did not allow a reduction in the award where *in fact* occupancy rates for the period of trespass were so low that the defendant would probably have made a loss itself operating the hotel, or only obtained a low rate for leasing the hotel to the defendants.

(iii) Where no bargain would ever have been made
The final reason why the "loss of bargaining opportunity" approach is fictitious is because there might be cases in which no bargain would ever have been struck. *Wrotham Park Estate Co* v. *Parkside Homes*[217] is a fine example of this. In that case a restitutionary damages award was given when the defendants, in deliberate contravention of a restrictive covenant prohibiting development, developed land and sold homes on it making profits of £50,000. Brightman J awarded what he regarded as compensatory damages of £2,500 in lieu of an injunction under the equivalent of Lord Cairns' Act.[218] The Wrotham Park Estate Company were deprived of a valuable right (to prohibit development). The value of that right, transferred to the defendant, was assessed at £2,500. Brightman J determined this value as a "sum of money as might reasonably have been demanded by the plaintiffs from [the defendant] as a quid pro quo for releasing the covenant".[219] The award cannot be compensatory for two reasons. First, the claimants' land had suffered no loss of amenity. Secondly, there was an express finding that the claimants would never have consented to such a relaxation.[220] The claimants could not be said to have lost any opportunity to bargain that they would never have exercised. In chapter four it will be seen that this exact reasoning was applied by the Court of Appeal in *Gondal* v. *Dillon Newsagents Ltd*[221] in which a compensatory damages award was refused in favour of an award of restitutionary damages because the compensatory award could only have been nominal.[222]

(iv) Rejecting the fiction of lost opportunity to bargain
Five years after *Jaggard* v. *Sawyer*, Millett LJ changed his mind. As a party to the joint judgment of the Court of Appeal in *Attorney General* v. *Blake*[223] he

---

[216] [1995] 1 WLR 713 (PC).

[217] [1974] 1 WLR 798.

[218] Chancery Amendment Act 1858, now s. 50 Supreme Court Act 1981. As Lord Wilberforce observed in *Johnson* v. *Agnew* [1980] AC 367(HL) 400, damages under Lord Cairns' Act are awarded on the same basis as damages at common law.

[219] *Wrotham Park* above note 217, 815.

[220] *Wrotham Park* above note 217, 815.

[221] [2001] RLR 221.

[222] See ch. 4, text accompanying note 95–101; J Edelman "The Compensation Strait-Jacket and the Lost Opportunity to Bargain Fiction" [2001] RLR 104.

[223] [1998] Ch 439 (CA).

acknowledged that instead of relying upon presumptions and fictions of loss "it would surely be preferable, as well as simpler and more open, to award restitutionary damages".[224] The same approach was taken by Lord Nicholls in the same case in the leading speech in the House of Lords, stating that:[225]

> "these awards cannot be regarded as conforming to the strictly compensatory measure of damage for the injured person's loss unless loss is given a strained and artificial meaning. The reality is that the injured person's rights were invaded but, in financial terms, he suffered no loss."

Unfortunately, referring to *Jaggard* v. *Sawyer* and cases under Lord Cairns' Act, Lord Nicholls stated that the analysis of these cases as compensatory damages for the loss of a bargaining opportunity was correct. This was despite acknowledging that even in these very cases the measure of damages is "assessed by reference to the benefits likely to be obtained in the future by the defendant".[226] In dissent in the *Blake* case, Lord Hobhouse regarded all awards of restitutionary damages as compensatory damages for loss of an opportunity to bargain.[227] So although the death knell has sounded for the lost opportunity to bargain fiction there are still some remaining remnants. Perhaps these references could have been avoided in the *Blake* case if the decision of the Court of Appeal in *Gondal* v. *Dillon Newsagents Ltd*[228] had been discussed. Unfortunately that decision remained unreported until December 2001.

(b) *The overreach of restitutionary damages*

The opposite confusion sometimes exists when *compensatory* damages are given for equitable wrongs. Courts of equity sometimes use the word "restitution" to describe awards of equitable compensation which are really compensatory damages.[229] In these cases the use of the word "restitution" is used in a compensatory sense of restoring a *person to a condition* rather than its proper sense of restoring a thing or its value to a person. This book only uses the term compensatory damages to refer to this process of restoring a person to a condition (whether in equity or at common law) and the term restitutionary damages to refer to the process of restoring a thing or its value wrongfully taken from a person.[230]

---

[224] *Attorney General* v. *Blake* (CA) above note 223, 458.

[225] *Attorney General* v. *Blake* [2001] 1 AC 268 (HL) 279.

[226] *Blake* above note 225, 281.

[227] *Blake* above note 225, 298.

[228] *Gondal* above note 221.

[229] *Canson Enterprises Ltd* v. *Boughton & Co* (1991) 85 DLR (4th) 129 (SCC); *Swindle* v. *Harrison* [1997] 4 All ER 705 (CA); *Target Holdings Ltd* v. *Redferns (a firm)* [1996] AC 421 (HL) 434. See G Virgo *Restitution* 449; C Rickett "Equitable Compensation: The Giant Stirs" (1996) 112 LQR 27, 28; A Tettenborn "Misnomer—A Response to Professor Birks" in W Cornish et al. *Restitution* 31, 31.

[230] This distinction between "restitution of a person to a proper state" and "restitution of a thing to a person" was made in S Elliott "Restitutionary Compensatory Damages for a Breach of Fiduciary Duty" [1997] RLR 135, 142.

D Remoteness and causation of gain-based damages

Because of the infancy of gain-based damages and the fact that these forms of damages have, historically, been hidden in other forms of language, issues of causation, remoteness of damages and election are still relatively unexplored.

Courts are slowly recognising that in considering gain-based damages these issues do arise. In relation to issues of remoteness of damages for instance, in *Celanese International Corpn* v. *BP Chemicals Ltd*,[231] Laddie J recognised that an award of disgorgement damages needs to consider issues of causation and remoteness. Laddie J, quoting from a Canadian case,[232] stated that "just as in a reference on a claim for damages issues of fact relating to causality and remoteness may properly be explored, so may they be likewise on an accounting of profits." In *Hodgkinson* v. *Simms*[233] both the majority and the minority of the Supreme Court of Canada in considering restitutionary damages for a breach of fiduciary duty acknowledged that the remoteness principles of compensatory damages at common law could also be used in cases where disgorgement damages were calculated. This is unsurprising once it is considered that the only difference between compensatory damages and disgorgement damages is that the former aim to put the claimant in the position as if the wrong had not occurred and the latter aim to put the defendant in that position.[234]

1) Causation

(a) Restitutionary damages

A difficulty of causation in restitutionary damages arises in a situation where a transfer is procured as a result of a wrong but *some part* of the transfer was not a result of the wrong, and would have occurred in any event. To what extent should the transaction be reversed in such circumstances?

This issue has a direct parallel to the consideration given by courts to "rescission on terms" and "partial rescission".[235] In instances where rescission for a wrong is being effected by money the issue as to whether the money payment should be made so that the transaction can be completely reversed is this question of the extent to which the wrong caused the payment.

In *Barclays Bank* v. *O'Brien*[236] the Court of Appeal held that a security, procured by an innocent misrepresentation of a third party that the security was

---

[231] [1999] RPC 203, 219.

[232] *Imperial Oil* v. *Lubrizol* [1996] 71 CPR (3d) 26, 30. See also *Frank Music Corp* v. *Metro-Goldwyn Mayer Inc* 886 F 2d 1545 (1989 9th Cir CA) 1553.

[233] [1994] 3 SCR 377 (SCC) 383–384, 387–388.

[234] P Cane *The Anatomy of Tort Law* (Hart Publishing Oxford 1997) 112; Mason and Carter *Restitution* 605.

[235] Although the two concepts are quite distinct (rescission on terms could involve for instance an entirely new contract): *Solle* v. *Butcher* [1950] 1 KB 671; *Grist* v. *Bailey* [1967] Ch 532.

[236] [1993] QB 109 (CA).

limited to £60,000, should be set aside. However the Court of Appeal held that the *entirety* of the security was not to be set aside. It required that the £60,000 to which the claimant thought the security was limited, be paid to the bank. The House of Lords dismissed the appeal without comment on this aspect of the case, although holding that the rescission arose on a different basis. Partial rescission in this manner has been allowed in several cases[237] but rejected in others.[238] Although the *O'Brien* case was not one of a wrong,[239] the same approach would be applied if it had been a fraudulent misrepresentation or other wrong by the bank which caused the transfer. The explanation in terms of causation is that the transfer caused by the misrepresentation was that value in excess of £60,000. That is then the value which is to be reversed.[240]

(b) *Disgorgement damages*

Courts encounter two difficult issues in assessing causation in relation to awards which effect disgorgement damages. The first is what to do where only part of the profits arise from the wrong. The second is the method of stripping profits from the wrong where there are multiple claimants.

(i) Where only part of the profits are derived from the wrong

In order to ensure that only the gain due to the wrongdoing is stripped from the wrongdoer it is necessary that disgorgement damages identify those profits which are not attributable to the wrong. The difficulty arises in a process of apportioning the gain, made where part of the activity is non-infringing. In such cases the court must do its best to split the profits between infringing and non-infringing parts.

An example is *Potton Ltd* v. *Yorkclose Ltd.*[241] In that case the defendant had designed several houses in infringement of the claimant's copyright. Millett J held that the profit from the breach of copyright which would be realised by the sale of the 14 houses which infringed the claimant's copyright was to be disgorged to the claimant. However, it was necessary to exclude any part of the profits from the sale which were not attributable to the wrong. Millett J stated that the disgorgement damages should not include any profit which resulted independently from the wrong; landscaping, any increase in value of the houses during the interval between the completion of the infringing building works and the sale, profits due to advertising or marketing and additional work done.[242]

In other cases, part of the contribution to the profit might be the "skill, efforts, property and resources of the [wrongdoer], the capital he has introduced

---

[237] *Bank Melli Iran* v. *Samadi-Rad* (High Court 9 February 1994) (Robert Walker QC).

[238] *Allied Irish Banks Plc* v. *Byrne* (High Court 1 February 1994) (Ferris J); *TSB Bank Ltd* v. *Camfield* [1995] 1 WLR 430 (CA).

[239] See ch. 2, text accompanying note 178–188.

[240] Another way of expressing this same conclusion is to consider it as a requirement of "counter-restitution of the plaintiff's subjectively devalued receipt": M Chen-Wishart "Unjust Factors and the Restitutionary Response" (2000) 20 OJLS 557, 568–576.

[241] [1990] FSR 11.

[242] *Potton* above note 241, 16, 18

and the risks he has taken so long as they are not risks to which the principal's property has been exposed".[243] In these cases the account of profits always allowed an innocent wrongdoer an "allowance" for this skill and effort[244] and the same allowance has been effected in cases where profits are stripped at common law (and labelled "damages"[245] or "money had and received"[246]). It has been noted that the denial of this allowance where the wrong is deliberate[247] is, in effect, a punitive measure additional to the disgorgement damages.[248]

(ii) Wrongs to multiple potential claimants

Related to this first causation issue of disgorgement damages is the problem where only part of the profits have been made from the wrong to a single claimant although all the profits were made by wrongful conduct.

Consider, for example, *Grimshaw* v. *Ford Motor Company*.[249] In that case the additional profit from the deliberate failure to take safety precautions was $15.30 per car. It seems clear that a disgorgement damages award is appropriate but the problem is how to apportion that award across a number of claimants. The wrong to each individual claimant only caused a profit of $15.30.

A more difficult instance cited by Goff and Jones[250] is a case of a factory that, committing the wrong of nuisance, pollutes a number of landowners' properties. The measure of disgorgement damages is the profits generated by the product which used the polluting method. The difficulty is in determining the proportions in which the profits should be distributed to the claimants.

These difficulties in apportionment were a reason why the Court of Appeal suggested that exemplary damages in such cases should not be available.[251] Goff and Jones take the same approach.[252] However, other cases have suggested that if exemplary damages are to be awarded for a wrong affecting two or more claimants, those damages should simply be divided amongst the claimants.[253]

---

[243] *Warman International Ltd* v. *Dwyer* (1995) 182 CLR 544 (HCA) 561.

[244] *Boardman* v. *Phipps* [1967] 2 AC 46 (HL) 127; The cases in which a fiduciary engaging in conscious wrongdoing is refused an allowance are examples of an additional punitive or exemplary award in addition to the disgorgement damages award.

[245] *Jegon* v. *Vivian* (1871) LR 6 Ch App 742.

[246] C Needham "Recovering the Profits of Bribery" (1979) 95 LQR 536, 552–553. Cf *Mahesan S/O Thambiah* v. *Malaysian Government Officers Co-Operative Housing Society* [1979] AC 374 (PC).

[247] This point was made in consideration of the *Livingstone* case, ch. 1 text accompanying note 16. See also American Law Institute *Restatement (Third) of Restitution and Unjust Enrichment* (2000) §3; *Restatement of Restitution* §203 comment a. See also *Edwards* v. *Lee's Administrators* 96 SW 2d 1028 (1936 CAKen) affirming an order of the Supreme Court of Kentucky which subtracted from the "damages" (measured by the profit made) all cash expenses in making the profit except labour costs: See *Edwards* v. *Simms* 232 Ky 791 (1929 SCK).

[248] D Friedmann "Restitution for Wrongs: The Measure of Recovery" [2001] Texas Law Rev 1879, 1889. See also *Sheldon* v. *Metro-Goldwyn Pictures Corp* 309 US 390 (1940 SCUS) 397).

[249] 174 Cl Rptr 348 (1981 SCCal). Text, ch. 1 accompanying note 81.

[250] *Goff and Jones* 785–786.

[251] *AB* v. *South West Water Services Ltd* [1993] QB 507 (CA).

[252] *Goff and Jones* 787.

[253] *Riches* v. *News Group Newspapers Ltd* [1986] QB 256.

The Law Commission preferred the latter approach as the most principled.[254] It is clearly the most simple and certain.

The problem of division of the proceeds could be satisfactorily answered by allowing a class action claim for disgorgement damages: "Where it is not economically feasible to obtain relief within the traditional framework of a multiplicity of small individual suits for damages, aggrieved persons may be without any effective redress unless they may employ the class-action device".[255] Individual claimants should, in addition, be entitled to pursue separate claims for restitutionary damages, subject to disallowance to avoid double recovery.[256]

In the case of later claimants a "first past the post" approach has been proposed by the Law Commission.[257] Another alternative is a system where the court makes a "Group Litigation Order" and a single case proceeds as a representative test claim for all listed parties in the group (including parties which can later be added).[258]

2) Remoteness of damages

(a) Restitutionary damages

The remoteness difficulty for restitutionary damages arises in a situation where a transfer is procured as a result of a wrong but where the property is then sold at a price higher than the market value. Can a claimant argue that the value transferred is not the value of the initial transfer but that in reversing the transfer, the subsequent transfer (sale) must also be taken into account? In other words, in order to properly reverse the transfer should later transfers also be taken into account? The answer is that they can provided that the property of the later transfer can be traced from the property of the initial transfer.

Consider the following example. X commits the wrong (tort) of conversion by taking Y's goods which are valued at £100. X sells the goods for £200, a price significantly above the market value at the time of the conversion (perhaps even a price above the market value at the time of sale). Could Y argue that in order to reverse the value transferred it is possible to take into account subsequent transfers which can be traced from the initial transfer? In other words, can Y argue that the value transferred was not merely the £100 but, by tracing the further transfer of the goods, the later value received of £200?

---

[254] *Law Commission 1997* 3.80.

[255] *Deposit Guaranty National Bank* v. *Roper* 445 US 326 (1980 SCUS) 338–339. See Civil Procedure Rules (UK) Rules 19.10–19.15 as amended by the Civil Procedure (Amendment) Rules 2000 (S.I. 2000 No. 221 2 May 2000).

[256] Class actions for restitutionary damages are not necessary as there is no essential deterrent policy behind those damages. Nor might they be feasible given the different considerations for each individual claimant: *Rhone-Poulenc Rorer Inc* 51 F 3d 1293 (1995 7th Cir CA). See further ch. 8.

[257] *Law Commission 1997* 5.162.

[258] Civil Procedure Rules (UK) Rules 19.10–19.15 as amended by the Civil Procedure (Amendment) Rules 2000 (S.I. 2000 No. 221 2 May 2000).

In the old forms of action, courts allowed such higher claims as "money had and received".[259] These are cases of restitutionary damages where the award is calculated on the basis that the subsequent transfer is not too remote from the initial transfer so as to be taken into account when the transaction is reversed. Indeed, the later transfer and sale is also wrongful (and historically was regarded as an independent wrong)[260] and tracing into the proceeds of the later transfer simply operates as a remoteness link demonstrating this later value as also wrongfully transferred.

In the context of reversing transferred gains in other areas of the law, not concerning wrongs, the House of Lords have reached precisely the same conclusion that, provided a transactional link can be shown through tracing, the later transfer can also be reversed.[261] These cases, which Professors Birks and Burrows have argued are cases of restitution for unjust enrichment,[262] and which others have argued are cases of restitution to vindicate proprietary rights,[263] demonstrate awards of restitution identical to these cases of restitutionary damages for events other than wrongs.

In cases in which the sale of property is also an intentional cynical wrong disgorgement damages might reach the same result in stripping the claimant of the profit from sale as the profit derived from the wrong (although the profits could still be greater than the restitutionary damages award).[264] But, just as it is important not to mistake the same restitutionary award in the law of unjust enrichment for a disgorgement award, it is also essential that, in the law of wrongs, in cases of non-cynical or innocent wrongdoing, these awards be recognised as restitutionary damages in the law of wrongs and not disgorgement damages.

---

[259] *Lightly* v. *Clouston* (1808) 1 Taunt 112; 127 ER 774; *Lamine* v. *Dorell* (1701) 2 Ld Ray 1216; 92 ER 303; *Oughton* v. *Seppings* (1830) 1 B and Ad 241; 109 ER 776; *King* v. *Leith* (1787) 2 TR 141, 145; 100 ER 78, 78–79; *Parker* v. *Norton* (1796) 6 TR 695, 700; 101 ER 779, 779–780; *Feltham* v. *Terry* (1772) Lofft 207, 208; 98 ER 613, 613.

[260] JW Salmond "Observations on Trover and Conversion" (1907) 21 LQR 43,46–47; JB Ames "History of Trover" (1898) 11 Harv Law Rev 374.

[261] *Trustee of the Property of Jones* v. *Jones* [1997] Ch 159 (CA); *Foskett* v. *McKeown* [2001] 1 AC 102 (HL). Cf *Restatement of Restitution* §155, Illustration 2, 610–611. The words "non-wrongful" are used instead of unjust enrichment because the House of Lords in the *Foskett* case preferred to base their analysis upon "property" rather than upon "unjust enrichment".

[262] Professor Birks asserts that the later transfer is an independent unjust enrichment action of "ignorance"; a parallel to the later sale as an independent wrong: P Birks "Property, Unjust Enrichment and Tracing" [2001] CLP (forthcoming). Professor Burrows also suggests the possibility of alternative analysis of the wrongs cases which involve subsequent transfers as cases of unjust enrichment: A Burrows *The Law of Restitution* 58–59, 384.

[263] G Virgo *Restitution* 591; R Grantham & C Rickett *Enrichment and Restitution in New Zealand* (Hart Publishing Oxford 2000) 34. Professor Smith now makes a similar argument but, more elaborately, he notes that the vindication requires the existence of the asset *at the time of litigation* rather than at the time of receipt: L Smith "Restitution: The Heart of Corrective Justice" (2001) 79 Texas Law Rev 2115, 2163–2174.

[264] Although disgorgement damages could exceed this amount if profits had been made from the use of the goods prior to the sale which exceed the market value of the use of those goods.

(b) *Disgorgement damages*

Suppose X obtains £200 by committing a wrong against Y. X then invests that £200 in shares which become worth £10,000. X sells the shares and uses the £10,000 to purchase a house which is now worth £100,000. If disgorgement damages are available, can the disgorgement damages reach the £10,000 or the £100,000 or are they limited to an award of the initial gain to the defendant from the wrong of £200?

Professor Birks suggests that anything after the "first non-subtractive receipt" is too remote.[265] But, as Professor Burrows suggests, to limit an award to the amount of an initial gain would be "an essentially arbitrary restriction".[266] Although in a sense any test for remoteness of damages is arbitrary, perhaps a good starting point would be the developed tests for remoteness in other areas. The test in tort for example[267] is whether the loss is reasonably foreseeable.[268]

In the case of an innocent wrongdoer who is to be stripped of profits (such as an innocent fiduciary) this remoteness test of "reasonable foreseeability of that kind of profit" would seem to be appropriate. A case which did import such a remoteness rule to disgorgement damages from rules governing loss at common law was *Frank Music Corp* v. *Metro-Goldwyn Mayer Inc.*[269] In that case, the defendant hotel, in breach of copyright, had included a segment from the defendant's musical in its revue. The segment comprised 12 per cent of the running time of the revue. Subject to a 25 per cent allowance for the defendant's contribution the 9th Circuit Court of Appeals held that the claimant was entitled to 12 per cent of the profits from the revue (being a total of 9 per cent). However, the claimants argued that they were also entitled to a share of the profits of the hotel and its gaming operations on the basis that the revue also enticed people to the hotels and thus led to increased profits in those other indirect areas. Further, the claimants sought a share of additional "downsteam corporate benefits" received by the hotel's parent corporation. In considering these claims to additional profits the 9th Circuit held that the first set of indirect profits could be recovered but not the second. The Court stated that the test should be the same as that at common law:[270]

---

[265] P Birks *Introduction* 351.

[266] A Burrows *The Law of Restitution* 412.

[267] Suggestions that a single test for breach of contract should also be one of reasonable foreseeability have been rejected : *Koufos* v. *Czarnikow Ltd* [1969] 1 AC 350 (HL) 389, 424. Cf *Banque Bruxelles* v. *Eagle Star* [1995] 2 All ER 769 (CA) 841 (Sir Thomas Bingham MR suggesting that "the essence of the test is the same"). However there is no clear enunciation of the test in contract or how much stricter it is than that in tort: A Burrows *Remedies for Torts and Breach of Contract* (2nd edn. Butterworths London 1994) 40–57. Lord Denning has suggested that the test is one of "serious possibility": but his Lordship confined this to cases of lost profit, suggesting that in cases of physical damage the tort standard of "reasonable foreseeability" should apply: *Parsons* v. *Uttley Ingham* [1978] 1 All ER 525.

[268] *Hughes* v. *Lord Advocate* [1963] AC 837 (HL); *Jolley* v. *Sutton LBC* [2000] 1 WLR 1082 (HL).

[269] 886 F 2d 1545 (1989 9th Cir CA).

[270] *Frank Music* above note 269, 1553.

"The question of whether specific profits were made from an infringement is similar to that of proximate cause in the tort context: just as there comes a point beyond which effects cannot legally be attributed to an initial tortious action, so too there comes a point beyond which an infringer's profits from its enterprises as a whole, cannot legally be attributed to a particular act of infringement."

More recently, in *CMS Dolphin Ltd* v. *Simonet*,[271] Lawrence Collins J held that a director was liable for the profits from breaches of fiduciary duty in diverting business contracts to his new company before his contract had concluded with the previous company. He held that such disgorgement damages should include the remoter profits made from those profits provided there is a "reasonable connection":

"[O]ther contracts might not have been won, or profits made on [the initial profit from the diverted contracts], without (e.g.) the opportunity or cash flow benefit which flowed from contracts unlawfully obtained. There must, however, be some reasonable connection between the breach of duty and the profits for which the fiduciary is accountable."

But what of the case where the initial gain resulted from a deliberate cynical wrong? In such a case, acceptance that the basis of disgorgement damages is deterrence should perhaps provide a powerful reason for preventing a defendant from retaining any gain from a deliberate, cynical wrong whether it is the second subtractive receipt or not even reasonably foreseeable. The only issue in such cases of deliberate, cynical wrongful conduct should usually be for the claimant to show that the £200 wrongful gain directly caused the £100,000 profit.[272] Indeed, where compensatory damages are sought against an intentional tortfeasor, the "reasonable foreseeability" test for remoteness is not applied.[273] It is said that "the intention to injure the plaintiff . . . disposes of any question of remoteness of damages".[274] If a claimant's direct loss is never too remote when the defendant's wrong was intentional, then likewise a defendant's direct *gain* (whether it is the first or a subsequent non-subtractive gain) should never be too remote when the wrong was intentional.

Attorney General for Hong Kong v. *Reid*[275] exemplifies this issue. There, a corrupt prosecutor had received bribes to obstruct prosecutions. He had invested some of those bribes in properties in New Zealand which appreciated in value.[276] The question before the Privy Council was whether the Crown, as the employer of the corrupt Hong Kong Attorney General, had a *proprietary*

---

[271] (High Court 23 May 2001).

[272] This is broader than the inquiry which suggests that the link is one of tracing: L Smith *Tracing* 30–31.

[273] *Doyle* v. *Olby (Ironmongers) Ltd* [1969] 2 QB 158 (CA); *Smith New Court* v. *Scrimgeour Vickers (Asset Management) Ltd* [1997] AC 254 (HL) ; W Rogers *Winfield & Jolowicz on Tort* (Sweet & Maxwell London 1998) 363.

[274] *Quinn* v. *Leatham* [1901] AC 495 (HL) 537 (Lord Lindley).

[275] [1994] 1 AC 324 (PC).

[276] Only one of the three properties were registered in his name but the Privy Council proceeded on the assumption that the other two were held on trust for him.

right in the properties so that a caveat could be lodged. A personal remedy to account to the Crown for the profits from the use of the property was therefore not sought because the litigation focussed upon the caveat. Although a personal remedy seeking the value of the land would be a second non-subtractive receipt, on the principles of remoteness for intentional wrongs it could have been disgorged as a profit directly caused by the intentional breach of fiduciary duty.

Lord Templeman, delivering the advice of the Privy Council, adopted this very reasoning, but to reach the conclusion that a *proprietary* remedy was available. Just as deterrence requires the broader remoteness test for compensatory damages in cases of intentional tortious wrongdoing, Lord Templeman accepted that "the false fiduciary will receive a benefit from his breach of duty unless he is accountable not only for the original amount or value of the bribe but also for the increased value of the property representing the bribe." Lord Templeman considered it necessary to strip the fiduciary of "any surplus in excess of the initial amount of the bribe because he is not allowed by any means to make a profit out of a breach of duty".[277]

The reason why Lord Templeman thought that the increased value could be disgorged only with a proprietary remedy was because, approving extra-judicial statements by Sir Peter Millett,[278] he considered that the personal award was limited to the first receipt.[279]

The result has been criticised on the basis that there is no reason why a proprietary award (which can operate to prejudice creditors) is necessary and surely the less extreme personal remedy of disgorgement damages should serve the same purpose.[280] Indeed in a decision of the Court of Appeal, which was disapproved by Lord Templeman, Lindley LJ had refused to give a proprietary remedy over the initial bribe because this confounds "ownership with obligation".[281] As the profits were directly made from the receipt of the bribe it should, with an understanding of rules of remoteness for disgorgement damages, be possible to strip the profits with the personal disgorgement damages award. Indeed Lord Millett has now acknowledged that once it is accepted that Reid is under an obligation to pay over or account for the initial bribe "no one disputes that, if the obligation exists, it carries with it the duty to pay over or account for any profits made by the use of the money".[282] The cases discussed above, concerning dis-

---

[277] *Attorney General for Hong Kong* v. *Reid* above note 275, 331.
[278] P Millett "Bribes and Secret Commissions" [1993] RLR 7.
[279] P Millett above note 278, 17.
[280] *Fyffes Group Ltd* v. *Templeman* [2000] 2 Lloyds Rep 643, 688; P Birks "Property in the Profits of Wrongdoing" (1994) 24 UWAL Rev 8, 12; L Smith *Tracing* 21; W Swadling "Property and Unjust Enrichment" in JW Harris (ed.), *Property Problems: From Genes to Pension Funds* (Kluwer Law International London 1997) 130, 142; R Goode "Ownership and Obligation in Commercial Transactions" (1987) 103 LQR 433, 442–445; P Birks "Obligations and Property in Equity: *Lister* v. *Stubbs* in the limelight" [1993] LMCLQ 30; D Crilley "A Case of Proprietary Overkill" [1994] RLR 57.
[281] *Lister & Co* v. *Stubbs* (1890) 45 Ch D 1 (CA) 15 (Lindley LJ).
[282] *Trustee of the Property of Jones* v. *Jones* [1997] Ch 159 (CA) 167.

gorgement awards of compound interest, effect this very disgorgement of remoter profits with a personal award.[283]

CONCLUSION

This chapter has sought to argue that a coherent view of gain-based awards in the law is now possible. The first step of this process, advocated in chapter one, was the recognition that damages for wrongdoing need not be based upon loss to a claimant. The second step is the recognition, advocated by this chapter, of the existence of two different types of gain-based awards for wrongdoing. The remainder of this book demonstrates that these different gain-based damages occur throughout the law of wrongs and are consistently applied as would be expected by their rationale. Restitutionary damages are invariably available to reverse a wrongful transfer whether the wrong was committed innocently or not. Disgorgement damages are available to deter wrongdoing but only where a wrong is committed cynically or, in cases of breach of fiduciary duty, where the institution of trust and confidence requires additional protection by stripping even innocent wrongdoers of profits made.

Without the use of two different terms, signifying the fact that the different awards have different rationales, confusion will result. With two terms the answers can be principled and consistent. Emperor Joseph II told Mozart that he used too many notes.[284] Yet without these notes the picture is chaotic. Different labels are required for different gain-based remedies for wrongdoing, premised upon different principles. Without different labels there can only be remedial chaos. It is time to recognise that disgorgement damages and restitutionary damages are distinct phenomena and to develop approaches to gain-based damages consonant with the different philosophy of each.

---

[283] Above text accompanying notes 134–153
[284] P Shaffer *Amadeus: A Drama* (S French New York 1981).

4

Torts

INTRODUCTION

T HIS CHAPTER IS concerned with application of the theory of gain-based damages, developed in the first three chapters, to the disparate body of common law wrongs known as torts. It is not possible nor, for the purposes of this book, necessary to examine all of the many torts. Instead, a number of torts are examined in order to illustrate, consistent with this book's central thesis, the general availability of restitutionary damages for torts and the availability of disgorgement damages for torts committed cynically.

The first section of this chapter considers restitutionary damages for torts and, consistent with the rationale explained in chapter three, shows that these damages, reversing the transfer of value that results from the tort, are generally available. This general availability can only be appreciated once all the different labels used to effect the reversal of a transfer of value for a tort are considered together. In the final part of this section perceived barriers to restitutionary damages for torts are considered and rejected.

The second section focuses upon disgorgement damages and shows them to be available in circumstances of cynical, wilful commission of wrongs. Like restitutionary damages, disgorgement damages are shown to be given effect by the use of a number of different labels, all of which have the common goal of stripping profits from the defendant and perceived barriers to disgorgement damages are also examined and rejected.

A Restitutionary damages

This consideration of restitutionary damages for torts is divided into four parts. The first considers all the forms that restitutionary damages have taken for torts and explains the commonality of these different awards. It shows that, considered together, these awards reflect a willingness of the law to reverse any transfer made pursuant to a tort. It will be seen that restitutionary damages have been awarded for numerous torts including trespass, conversion, detinue (and the statutory equivalent of those two torts), deceit, interference with contractual relations and nuisance. The second part examines one of the more confusing aspects of the history of restitutionary damages. In many cases in which restitutionary damages are awarded for torts courts have stated that the tort was "waived". This part advocates abandoning this confusing phrase which has caused significant confusion. The third part examines six progressive modern cases which have explicitly recognised restitutionary damages and the final part shows how several cases which have traditionally been regarded as cases refusing restitutionary damages are not the obstacles it is sometimes suggested they are.

1) Different labels

A number of different labels were used historically to effect a reversal of a tortious transfer of value. A commonality between these gain-based awards was not recognised. These awards included the forms of action in *indebitatus assumpsit*,[1] awards of mesne profits and wayleaves and awards of "damages in lieu of injunctions or specific performance" under Lord Cairns' Act.[2]

In the early nineteenth century, in a formulaic system based upon procedure, it was the form of action that mattered rather than the classification of the cause of action or the nature of the response. In examining these differently labelled awards of restitutionary damages, modern cases will often be used as examples, to show that courts are unfortunately still using this ancient terminology to effect awards which all operate as restitutionary damages.

(a) *Wayleaves*

In numerous cases, dating from the mid-nineteenth century, awards of what was referred to as a "wayleave" were made.[3] Wayleave awards were concerned with the value transferred to a defendant from the use of the claimant's land. Although sometimes referred to as "compensation",[4] these awards were not concerned with any loss suffered.

In *Whitwham* v. *Westminster Brymbo Coal and Coke Co*,[5] the defendant had caused damage to the claimant's land by dumping waste upon it from the defendant's colliery. The Court of Appeal held that the claimant was entitled to compensation for the damage caused to the land as well as an additional wayleave award for the "value transferred"; the market value of the *use* of the land. Lindley LJ emphasised that the focus was not upon the loss which had been suffered by the claimant. He stated that "on what principle of justice can it be said that these defendants are to use the plaintiffs" land for years for their own purposes, and to pay nothing for it, in addition to the injury they have done".[6]

---

[1] Money had and received, money paid, money lent and advanced, money promised, goods sold and delivered and work and labour. From the mid-19th century forms of action for the fair value of goods and services (*quantum valebant* and *quantum meruit*) were pleaded as *indebitatus assumpsit*: JH Baker "The History of Quasi-Contract in English Law" in W Cornish et al *Restitution* 37, 41.

[2] Chancery Amendment Act 1858, now s. 50 Supreme Court Act 1981.

[3] *Hilton* v. *Woods* (1867) LR 4 Eq 432, 441; *Powell* v. *Aiken* (1858) 4 K & J 343; 70 ER 144; *Phillips* v. *Homfray* (1883) 24 Ch D 439 (CA); *Martin* v. *Porter* (1839) 5 M & W 351; 151 ER 149; *Jegon* v. *Vivian* (1871) LR 6 Ch App 742.

[4] *Phillips* v. *Homfray* (1871) LR 6 Ch App 770, 781.

[5] [1896] 2 Ch 538 (CA).

[6] *Whitwham* above note 5, 542.

(b) *Mesne profits*

The award of mesne profits was "simply [restitutionary] damages for a trespass against a tenant who holds over at the end of a tenancy."[7] The award of mesne profits differed from a wayleave because mesne profits were given in cases in which there was an occupation of the land rather than just a use of it. It is clear that cases of mesne profits cannot be seen as compensatory for any loss suffered without the use of a fiction that loss is irrebuttably presumed. It is constantly stated that "there is no need for the landlord to show that he could or would have let the premises to someone else at the material time."[8] Yet the view sometimes persists that these cases are instances of compensatory damages.

The Court of Appeal decision in *Ministry of Defence* v. *Ashman*[9] is discussed below[10] for the explicit recognition by two of the three judges that these awards of mesne profits are awards of "restitution" for trespass (more properly "restitutionary damages"). However, in that case Lloyd LJ, although agreeing in the order, would have preferred to analyse cases of mesne profits as compensatory, yet "special cases where the plaintiff can apparently recover more than his loss".[11] In *Inverugie Investments Ltd* v. *Hackett*,[12] as Lord Lloyd, he retreated somewhat from this view. That case was considered in chapter three as an illustration of the difference between restitutionary damages and disgorgement damages. The claim was for mesne profits to reflect the wrongful (trespass) use of apartments in the claimants' hotel over a 15 year period by the defendant. In delivering the advice of the Privy Council Lord Lloyd stated: [13]

> "The trespasser may not have derived any actual benefit from the use of the property. But under the user principle [the defendant] is obliged to pay a reasonable rent for the use which he has enjoyed. The principle need not be characterised as exclusively compensatory, or exclusively restitutionary, it combines elements of both."

The reason why Lord Lloyd refused to characterise the award as exclusively restitutionary was because, he noted, the actual profit to the defendant is irrelevant. However, once it is recognised that actual profit is a disgorgement award then there is no obstacle to recognition of this award of mesne profits as exclusively restitutionary. Indeed the perceived element of "compensation" is simply a confusion arising from the fact that there must be a transfer *from* or *at the*

[7] *Ministry of Defence* v. *Ashman* [1993] 2 EGLR 102 (CA) 105 (Lloyd LJ); *Elliott* v. *Boynton* [1924] 1 Ch 236, 250.

[8] *Dean and Chapter of the Cathedral of Christ Canterbury* v. *Whitbread Plc* [1995] 1 EGLR 82, 85; *Swordheath Properties Ltd* v. *Tabet* [1979] 1 WLR 285 (CA) 288;

[9] [1993] 2 EGLR 102 (CA).

[10] See text below accompanying note 90.

[11] *Ministry of Defence* v. *Ashman* [1993] 2 EGLR 102 (CA).

[12] [1995] 1 WLR 713 (PC). See also *LJP Investments Ltd* v. *Howard Chia Investments Pty Ltd* (1990) 24 NSWLR 499 (SCNSW); C Mitchell "Mesne Profits and Restitutionary Damages" [1995] LMCLQ 343.

[13] *Inverugie* above note 12, 718.

expense of the claimant. Something must be transferred from the claimant although the claimant need not suffer any financial loss.

(c) *"Damages"*

Another means of awarding restitutionary damages was to describe the award simply as "damages". The true nature of many damages awards as restitutionary was often hidden and justified as compensatory damages by use of fictions.[14] This process of disguising restitutionary damages awards as "damages" also occurred in equity with awards of "damages" under Lord Cairns' Act[15] (in lieu of specific performance or an injunction). The basis for assessing the award of "damages" under Lord Cairns' Act is the same as at common law.[16]

Many of the cases awarding restitutionary damages in the late nineteenth century concerned the unlawful removal of coal under the land of the claimant. Whether the remedy was sought for trespass at common law (and described simply as "damages") or in equity (as "damages under Lord Cairns' Act") the award was commonly made to reverse the value transferred by the trespass rather than to compensate for financial loss. The value transferred was the market value of the use of the land; the right of removal of the coal at "the same rate as if the mines had been purchased by the defendants at the fair market value".[17] These restitutionary damages were available even where the coal was removed innocently.[18] As Sir Richard Malins V-C stated in *Hilton* v. *Woods*,[19] even "if . . . the Defendant . . . acted fairly and honestly in the full belief that he had a right to do what he did, [the jury] might give the fair value of the coals as if the coal field had been purchased from the Plaintiff."

The judges in these cases usually referred to this award of restitutionary damages simply as "damages" although sometimes they were referred to as compensatory damages.[20] The difficulty is compounded because some modern cases also refer to these awards as compensatory damages.[21] *Bracewell* v. *Appleby*[22] was instanced in chapter three as an example of this use of the fiction of compensation to explain an award of restitutionary damages.[23] The defendant was in the advanced stages of building a house to which access was only possible by

[14] See ch. 3 text accompanying notes 203–228 .

[15] Chancery Amendment Act (21&22 Vict c27).

[16] *Jegon* v. *Vivian* above note 3, 762; *Johnson* v. *Agnew* [1980] AC 367 (HL).

[17] *Jegon* v. *Vivian* above note 3, 762; *Hilton* v. *Woods* above note 3, 441; *Wood* v. *Morewood* (1841) 3 QB 440,441; 114 ER 575, 576.

[18] It will be noted below that in cases of wilful or cynical breach courts would award disgorgement damages of the entire profits made- as the value of the coal "when gotten".

[19] *Hilton* v. *Woods* above note 3, 441.

[20] *Phillips* v. *Homfray* above note 3, 780 (Lord Hatherley LC); *Jegon* v. *Vivian* above note 3, 762 (Lord Hatherley LC).

[21] *Swordheath Properties Ltd* v. *Tabet* [1979] 1 WLR 285 (CA) 288; *Yakamia Dairy Pty Ltd* v. *Wood* [1976] WAR 57 (SCWA) 61; *Attorney General* v. *Blake* [2001] 1 AC 268 (HL) 278 (Lord Nicholls stating that the damages are "compensation for the wrong done to the plaintiff . . . measured by a different yardstick.").

[22] [1975] Ch 408.

[23] Ch. 3, text accompanying note 213–215

trespassing on the claimants' land. Because the claimants had delayed seeking an injunction to restrain the defendant from building until the house was in its advanced stages an injunction was refused. However, damages were awarded under Lord Cairns' Act for the trespasses and future trespass to reverse the transfer of value and were assessed as "equivalent to a proper and fair price which would be payable for the acquisition of the right of way in question".[24]

In the *Bracewell* case, Graham J justified his reference to "compensating" the claimants on the basis that the claimants had lost an opportunity to bargain and he made an award of the reasonable market value of the right of £2,000.[25] The fiction of this approach is that, despite acknowledging that the price which, in reality would have been agreed for relaxing the covenant was £6,000 (hence the *true* value of the bargain lost), Graham J stated that the claimants "must be treated as being willing to accept a fair price".[26] Chapter three explained how this "lost opportunity to bargain" approach has now been rejected.[27]

Other modern cases simply refer to the award of restitutionary damages as "damages" sometimes even recognising that these "damages" are not really compensatory.[28] In *Carr-Saunders* v. *Dick McNeil Associates Ltd*[29] the claimant had acquired prescriptive rights to the use of light on the second floor of his premises. That right was conferred pursuant to statute.[30] The defendant had built two additional storeys on his premises which interfered with and restricted the claimant's access to light. The claimant sought damages in lieu of a mandatory injunction requiring the defendant's additional storeys to be pulled down. Referring to *Bracewell* v. *Appleby*,[31] Millett J recognised that the award differed from "compensation for the loss of the actual legal right".[32] He held that it should be calculated so as to restore to the claimant the value transferred of a licence[33] to use "not only his direct light, but also sky visibility, a pleasant view of the brickwork and a sloping roof, sunlight and so on".[34]

The same unqualified use of the word "damages" was made recently in *Costello* v. *Chief Constable of Derbyshire Constabulary*.[35] In that case the police, under section 19 of the Criminal Evidence Act 1984, had confiscated a car from the appellant which they suspected of having been stolen. The Court of Appeal held that the Act only permitted the police a temporary right to retain

[24] *Bracewell* above note 22, 419.
[25] *Bracewell* above note 22, 420.
[26] *Bracewell* above note 22, 419–420.
[27] Ch. 3, text accompanying notes 203–228.
[28] *Roberts* v. *Rodney District Council* (2 Feb 2001 High Court Auckland) Barker J stating that wrongful use damages are an anomalous measure which assumes that the plaintiff has incurred loss.
[29] [1986] 1 WLR 922.
[30] Prescriptive Act 1832 s. 3.
[31] *Bracewell* above note 22.
[32] *Carr-Saunders* above note 29, 931.
[33] He referred, in addition to the *Bracewell* case, to another case in which the reasonable value of rights transferred had been awarded where no loss had been suffered: *Wrotham Park Estate Co Ltd* v. *Parkside Homes Ltd* [1974] 1 WLR 798.
[34] *Carr-Saunders* above note 29, 931–932. See Mason and Carter *Restitution* 647.
[35] [2001] 1 WLR 1437 (CA).

the car for specified purposes and vested no title in them. Accordingly, their retention of the car deprived the appellant of his possessory title and he was entitled to an order for the delivery up of the car. However, the retention of the car had also transferred the right to its *use* from the appellant to the police. Recognising this, in a single sentence at the end of the leading judgment, Lightman J simply stated that the appellant was also entitled to "damages for the wrongful failure to deliver it up".[36]

Another example, considering the same issue in more detail, is a case concerning the legislation which "abolished" the tort of detinue in favour of a broad statutory wrong of "wrongful interference with goods".[37] That legislation refers to money remedies for the statutory wrong simply as "damages". In a modern case under the statute, restitutionary damages were awarded in the same manner as prior to the statute.[38] In *Hillesden Securities Ltd* v. *Ryjak Ltd*[39] the claimant was a finance company which owned a Rolls Royce motor vehicle. The vehicle was leased by the previous owner from the finance company and the lessee purported to sell it to the defendant. The defendant admitted that the sale was wholly ineffective but disputed any liability to pay damages for the value transferred from having had the use of the vehicle subsequent to the ineffectual sale. Parker J held that the word "damages" in the legislation was broad enough to include an award of the full market hire of the Rolls Royce during the whole period of detention.

2) *Indebitatus assumpsit*

(a) *The form of action*

Indebitatus assumpsit was a species of *assumpsit* which encompassed several common forms of pleading. The forms of pleading in *indebitatus assumpsit* alleged that the defendant, being indebted for a sum of money (*indebitatus*), promised to pay the sum of the debt and had failed to pay.[40] Alongside *indebitatus assumpsit* were similar pleadings for the value of services performed and for the fair value of goods (*quantum meruit* and *quantum valebant* respectively) which were pleaded as *indebitatus assumpsit* from the mid-nineteenth century.[41] There was no explanation in the form of pleading as to how the debt or liability for the fair value of the goods or services arose. One circumstance in which *indebitatus assumpsit* was used was as a pleading for a debt created by a genuine contract. Another, and of key relevance to this chapter, is that *indebitatus assumpsit* was also used to reverse transfers which had occurred pursuant to

---

[36] *Costello* above note 35, 1452.

[37] Torts (Interference with Goods) Act 1977, s. 3(2)(c).

[38] See *Strand Electric and Engineering Co Ltd* v. *Brisford Entertainments Ltd* [1952] 2 QB 246 discussed below, text accompanying notes 84–87.

[39] [1983] 2 All ER 184.

[40] E Lawes *Practical Treatise on Pleading in Assumpsit* (W Reed London 1810) 418–503.

[41] JH Baker "The History of Quasi-Contract in English Law" in W Cornish et al. *Restitution* 37, 41.

torts where no contractual debt existed at all. Many of these awards were restitutionary damages for torts.

(b) *"Implied contract"*

Between 1673 and 1705 it became common for *indebitatus assumpsit* counts to be used in circumstances where a promise to pay was completely fictitious.[42] This fiction later led to the actions brought in this manner becoming known as *quasi-contract* (duplicating the Roman *quasi ex contractu*) and later as "implied contract". The action was "like" a contract because of the fictitious promise to pay although in reality there was no separate promise.

Indebitatus assumpsit was pleaded in a number of "common counts" which alleged a fictitious promise used by courts to describe this "implied contract".[43] Each of these counts could be pleaded in circumstances of tortious wrongdoing. A common example is the count of money had and received. The pleading of an action for money had and received, borrowed from the writ of account against a receiver,[44] alleged that the defendant "had and received money to the use of" the claimant and[45]

> "Not regarding his said several promises and undertakings, but conniving and fraudulently intending craftily and subtilly to deceive and defraud [the plaintiff] hath not yet paid the said several sums of money or any part thereof . . . [and] hath hitherto wholly refused and still refuses."

The true basis of the claim was thus hidden by such simple pleadings that were said to be based upon "implied contract". Even in cases in which it was apparent that the true basis of the claim was a tort, courts insisted upon the implied contract analysis. In *Foster* v. *Stewart*[46] Lord Ellenborough CJ stated that:

> "though it has been truly said that those decisions are founded upon the principle that the money belongs in natural justice and equity to the plaintiff, yet in order to obtain that justice, the law raises a promise to the plaintiff as if the money were received to his use, which in reality was received by a tortious act."

The fiction can be seen in *Lamine* v. *Dorrell*.[47] The defendant claimed a right to administration of the claimant's estate and sold debentures which the claimant had owned. The administration was set aside and the claimant, on behalf of the estate, sought recovery of the proceeds from the wrongful sale of

---

[42] *City of London* v. *Goree* (1677) 2 Levinz 174; *Aris* v. *Stukely* (1678) 2 Mod 260; 86 ER 1060; *Shuttleworth* v. *Garnett* (1688) 3 Mod 240; 87 ER 156; AH Chaytor and WJ Whittaker (eds) FW Maitland *The Forms of Action at Common Law* (CUP Cambridge 1965) 70; D Ibbetson "Sixteenth Century Contract Law: *Slade's Case* in Context" (1984) 4 OJLS 295.

[43] D Ibbetson *A Historical Introduction to the Law of Obligations* (OUP Oxford 1999) 148.

[44] JH Baker *An Introduction to English Legal History* (3rd edn. Butterworths London 1990) 419.

[45] HJ Stephen *A treatise on the principles of pleading in civil actions* (4th edn. Saunders and Benning London 1838) 312.

[46] (1814) 3 M & S 191, 200; 105 ER 582, 585.

[47] (1701) 2 Ld Ray 1216, 1216; 92 ER 303, 303.

debentures in *indebitatus assumpsit* on the count of money had and received. The court held that the proceeds received could be recovered by the claimant and all the judges acknowledged that the basis for the action was effectively trover (conversion) of the debentures and proceeds (and therefore not with any implied contract or consent to the administration and sale). But judges were accustomed to describing such torts as actions upon an implied contract. Powell J acknowledged the difficulty of implied contract stating that "when the act that is done is in its nature tortious it is hard to turn that into a contract . . . [but the law] has been carried thus far already."

This count of money had and received usually arose to reverse a transfer of money from the claimant to him. As apparent from the pleading it was expressly concerned with the receipt of a benefit or gain by the defendant. But although money had and received operated to reverse a transfer,[48] the form of the action did not reveal whether the cause of action was for a wrong or an unjust enrichment. Even when courts explained the basis for the action it was commonly said to be on the basis of the implied contract fiction. Some cases admitted reliance upon the tort, as was seen in the *Lamine* case. *Holt* v. *Ely*[49] is another example. There, the claimant was the trustee of a fund from which certain bills of exchange were to be paid. The defendant fraudulently represented that he held such a bill and the claimant paid money to the defendant. The court held that the claimant was entitled to bring an action for money had and received to recover the value of the money paid to the defendant because of the fraud.

Instances in which courts admitted to reliance upon the tort included claims for fraud and deceit,[50] for the value of work and labour transferred to another by committing the tort of "seduction" (which was the precursor to the modern tort of interference with contractual relations),[51] for the value of goods "sold and delivered" committing the tort of conversion[52] and in cases of trespass.[53] However, in some cases the court would simply refer to "implied contract" and it was not obvious whether the basis of the action was unjust enrichment or a tort.[54]

---

[48] In the 20th century, however, divorced from its pleading requirements, money had and received was sometimes used to effect disgorgement damages. See ch. 3, text accompanying note 43 and J Edelman "Money Had and Received: Modern Pleading of an Old Count" [2000] RLR 547.

[49] (1853) 1 E&B 794, 799; 118 ER 634, 636. See also *Clarke* v. *Dickson* (1858) El Bl & El 148; 120 ER 463 where it was accepted obiter dicta that money had and received was a means to recover the value of money paid under a fraudulent transaction (contract) which was to be reversed through rescission.

[50] *Holt* v. *Ely* above note 49; *Russell* v. *Bell* (1842) 10 M & W 340, 352; 152 ER 500; *Hill* v. *Perrott* (1810) 3 Taunt 274; 128 ER 109; *Bristow* v. *Eastman* (1794) 1 Esp 172, 173; 170 ER 317, 317.

[51] *Lightly* v. *Clouston* (1808) 3 Taunt 112; 127 ER 774; *Foster* v. *Stewart* (1814) 3 M & S 191; 105 ER 582.

[52] *Russell* v. *Bell* (1842) 10 M & W 340, 352; 152 ER 500, 506.

[53] *London & Brighton Railway Co* v. *Watson* (1879) 4 CPD 118, 119.

[54] *Madden* v. *Kempster* (1807) 1 Camp 12; 170 ER 859.

(c) *Waiver of tort*

In cases in which courts did not refer to a possible existing tort in awarding one of the counts in *indebitatus assumpsit* the basis for the reversal might have been an existing tort or it might have been an action in unjust enrichment. The "implied contract" fiction disguised which of these characterisations was relied upon and further confusion resulted from a related fiction known as "waiver of tort".

(i) The fictions

As noted, in the sixteenth century the *indebitatus assumpsit* forms of action were extended by use of the fiction of "implied contract".[55] The term "waiver of tort" arose in these situations in which a tort had been committed but the cause of action was thought to arise by "implying a contract". Thus, when a claimant brought an action in *indebitatus assumpsit* to reverse a wrongful sale of his goods, he was said to "dispense with the wrong and suppose the sale made by his consent".[56]

The reason for the fiction arose because a claimant might have brought an action seeking a remedy for the tort as well as an action for the "implied contract".[57] The availability of both of these actions on the same set of facts appeared to be inconsistent. One was based upon the wrong and the other upon the fiction of implied consent. By relying upon an implied contract the claimant was said to acknowledge that the acts were done by "implied" consent and not by wrong. It was therefore thought that the action in implied contract only arose where there had been a judgment of "not guilty" for the tort[58] or if the tort had been "waived".

Although the "implied contract" was a fiction, it survived any heavy judicial criticism until 60 years ago.[59] Following a trend of academic writing,[60] the House of Lords, in *United Australia Ltd* v. *Barclays Bank Ltd*,[61] abandoned the fiction of implied contract and recognised that the claim in *indebitatus assumpsit* to reverse the transfer in that case was based upon a tort.[62] The fiction of implied contract has now been conclusively rejected.[63]

---

[55] JH Baker "The History of Quasi-Contract in English Law" in W Cornish et al. *Restitution* 37, 40.

[56] *Lamine* v. *Dorell* (1701) 2 Ld Ray 1216; 92 ER 303.

[57] *Lamine* above note 56, 1217; 304 (Holt CJ); *Birch* v. *Wright* (1786) 1 TR 378; 99 ER 1148, 387.

[58] *Buckland* v. *Johnson* (1854) 15 CB 145; 139 ER 375.

[59] P Birks, G McLeod "The Implied Contract Theory of Quasi-Contract: Civilian Opinion Current in the Century Before Blackstone" (1986) 6(1) OJLS 46.

[60] Lord Wright "*Sinclair* v. *Brougham*" [1938] CLJ 305; RM Jackson *The History of Quasi-Contract* (CUP Cambridge 1936); HC Gutteridge, RJA David "The Doctrine of Unjustified Enrichment" [1934] CLJ 204; W Friedmann "The Principle of Unjust Enrichment in English Law" (1938) 16 Can Bar Rev 243, 365; P Winfield *Province of the Law of Tort* (CUP Cambridge 1931) 116–189.

[61] [1941] AC 1 (HL).

[62] *Halifax Building Society* v. *Thomas* [1996] Ch 217 (CA) 227.

[63] *Lipkin Gorman* v. *Karpnale Ltd* [1991] 2 AC 548 (HL); *Westdeutsche Landesbank Girozentrale* v. *Islington LBC* [1996] AC 669 (HL).

The effect of abandoning the implied contract fiction should have also led to the abandonment of the term "waiver of tort". The reasoning that the tort was "waived" where a claimant recovered upon a fictitious "implied contract" (as the "implied consent" would, by virtue of the fiction, negate the wrong) could no longer apply if the implied contract fiction was rejected. But the term "waiver of tort" is still used. And it is not merely a problem of nomenclature. Difficulties arise because there are now at least three possible (and non-fictitious) meanings of "waiver of tort".

The first possible meaning is that the tort is genuinely forgiven. These cases are rare and are confined to agency law where the principle of extinctive ratification allows a principal to truly "waive" a tort and ratify the agents wrongful conduct.[64] The second meaning is that the remedy elected by the claimant is restitutionary damages rather than compensatory damages for the tort and the third meaning of "waiver of tort" is to signify that the claimant does not rely upon the tort but upon an action in unjust enrichment. In these final two instances, a reference merely to "waiver of tort" serves to prevent an understanding of whether the basis of the action is restitutionary damages for a tort or restitution for an unjust enrichment.

(ii) An action for restitutionary damages

In the leading case of *United Australia Ltd* v. *Barclays Bank Ltd*,[65] the House of Lords in discarding the fiction of implied contract recognised that an action for money had and received in *indebitatus assumpsit* could be based on the tort itself. A cheque, payable to United Australia, was fraudulently endorsed by the corrupt secretary of United Australia to a company, MFG, with which he was associated. MFG deposited the cheque into their account with Barclays Bank and it was credited by Barclays. United Australia initially sued MFG seeking repayment of the money as money had and received. After MFG went into liquidation, and before a trial against MFG, United Australia sued Barclays Bank for the *indebitatus assumpsit* count of money had and received and for compensatory damages for conversion and negligence. The trial judge and the Court of Appeal held that the action against Barclays Bank must fail. It was held that, having brought the first action against MFG for money had and received, United Australia had "waived the tort" and extinguished the wrong.

The House of Lords rejected these arguments in favour of the argument made by counsel for the appellants. The appellant's counsel, Denning KC, adopted remarks made extra-judicially by Lord Wright and argued that "[t]he *assumpsit* was a mere fiction, the substance of the claim being the wrong done".[66] The House of Lords agreed. Lord Atkin criticised the theory of implied contract as "fantastic resemblances of contracts"[67] and argued that "[w]hen the ghosts of

---

[64] *Bolton Partners* v. *Lambert* (1889) 41 Ch D 295; F Reynolds *Bowstead & Reynolds on Agency* (Sweet and Maxwell London 1996) 65.

[65] *United Australia* above note 61.

[66] *United Australia* above note 61, 5.

[67] *United Australia* above note 61, 29.

the past stand in the path of justice clanking their mediaeval chains the proper course for the judge is to pass through them undeterred".[68] He stated that the approach to be taken in that case was "a question of alternative remedies" for the one cause of action.[69] The claimant was free to seek money had and received for the tort as an alternative remedy to compensatory damages for the tort. The Lord Chancellor in *United Australia* took a similar approach:[70]

> "When the plaintiff "waived the tort" and brought assumpsit, he did not thereby elect to be treated from that time forward on the basis that no tort had been committed; indeed if it were to be understood that no tort had been committed, how could an action in assumpsit lie? It lies only because the acquisition of the defendant is wrongful and there is thus an obligation to make restitution . . . The election to bring an action for assumpsit . . . is the choice of one of two alternative remedies."

The effect of this approach was that the term "waiver of tort" was taken to mean that instead of bringing an action for compensatory damages for loss, the action was one for restitutionary damages based upon reversing the value transferred from the defendant's conversion of the claimant's cheque. Well before the *United Australia* case it was recognised that where the tort was relied upon the fiction really meant that the remedy the law is providing is for the tort itself.[71]

Very shortly after the decision, writing extra-judicially on the *United Australia* case, Lord Wright endorsed the analysis of the House of Lords as accepting that "in bringing an action for money had and received . . . [t]he cause of action was the wrong".[72] More recently, in delivering the advice of the Privy Council in *Tang Man Sit* v. *Capacious Investments Ltd*[73] and in the leading speech of the House of Lords in *Attorney General* v. *Blake*,[74] Lord Nicholls referred to the *United Australia* decision and stated that it meant that a "person whose goods were converted by another had a choice of two remedies against the wrongdoer" one based upon loss suffered, the other based upon gain made. In some cases the action for "money had and received" for a wrong is now referred to interchangeably with "restitutionary damages".[75]

(iii)   An action in unjust enrichment
The House of Lords in the *United Australia* case left open an alternative meaning for "waiver of tort". Instead of an election between remedies for a tort it

---

[68] *United Australia* above note 61, 29.

[69] *United Australia* above note 61, 30.

[70] *United Australia* above note 61, 18. See also 34 (Lord Romer) "What was waived by the judgment was not the tort but the right to recover [compensatory] damages for the tort."

[71] WA Keener "Waiver of Tort" (1892) 6 Harv L Rev 223, 223.

[72] Lord Wright "*United Australia Ltd* v. *Barclays Bank Ltd*" (1941) 57 LQR 184, 189. In *Commercial Bank of Sydney* v. *Mann* [1961] AC 1 (PC) 8 the Privy Council also stated that if the claim for conversion fails so too does the claim for money had and received.

[73] The claim for money had and received is "a waiver of the right to recover from MFG [compensatory] damages for the tort, not a waiver of the tort itself": *Tang Man Sit* v. *Capacious Investments Ltd* [1996] AC 514 (PC) 523.

[74] *Attorney General* v. *Blake* [2001] 1 AC 268 (HL) 280.

[75] *Daly* v. *Hubner* (High Court 9 July 2001) (Etherton J).

could mean an election between two causes of action. The tort could be waived by bringing an action in unjust enrichment instead of in tort. Lord Atkin left open this possibility[76] as did Lord Porter.[77] Lord Wright extra-judicially also acknowledged that there was another cause of action "variously named quasi contract, restitution, unjust enrichment" whose progress had been inhibited by "the fictitious *assumpsit* which tied it up with contract".[78]

In chapter three it was shown that an action for restitution for unjust enrichment might exist concurrently with an action for restitutionary damages for a tort. For example, a claimant who is defrauded of £100 might have concurrent claims in tort to reverse the transfer from the deceit and in unjust enrichment to reverse the transfer from the mistaken payment. Like restitutionary damages for wrongs, these actions for restitution in unjust enrichment were historically also hidden within the notion of "implied contract". In *Sinclair* v. *Brougham*[79] Lord Sumner's speech epitomised this fiction:

> "It was said that they paid their money under a mistake of fact, or for a consideration that has totally failed, or that it has been had and received by the society to their own use . . . All these causes of action are common species of the genus assumpsit. All now rest, and long have rested, upon a notional or imputed promise to repay."

The recognition of the category of unjust enrichment[80] therefore means that the phrase "waiver of tort" is ambivalent and liable to confuse. It might mean, as it did in the *United Australia* case, that the claimant has sought restitutionary damages instead of compensatory damages. In such a case the language should be rejected in favour simply of references to election between remedies. It might also mean that a claimant has alternative causes of action available to her. In this case references to "waiver of tort" should be eschewed in favour of the phrase "alternative analysis", coined by Professor Birks, to explain the possibility that an action might be brought in unjust enrichment as well as in tort.[81]

3) Explicit modern recognition in six cases

The modern recognition of restitutionary damages for torts began strongly with two judgments from Lord Denning (the successful counsel in the *United*

---

[76] He referred to "quasi-contract" on some occasions in contradistinction to tort: "having recovered in [quasi]contract it is plain that the plaintiff cannot go on to recover in tort": *United Australia* above note 61, 48. See also at 18 (Viscount Simon LC).

[77] *United Australia* above note 61, 50–51, 54. See also J Beatson "The Nature of Waiver of Tort" in J Beatson *The Use and Abuse* 206 who argues that *all* such awards are based in unjust enrichment and not tort.

[78] Lord Wright "*United Australia Ltd* v. *Barclays Bank Ltd*" (1941) 57 LQR 198–199. See also the speech of Lord Wright two years later in *Fibrosa Spolka Akcyjna* v. *Fairbairn Lawson Combe Barbour Ltd* [1943] AC 32 (HL).

[79] *Sinclair* v. *Brougham* [1914] AC 398 (HL) 452.

[80] Ch. 2 text accompanying note 52.

[81] P Birks *Introduction* 314–315. Cf P Jaffey *The Nature and Scope of Restitution* (Hart Publishing Oxford 2000) 371–373.

Australia case) in *Strand Electric and Engineering Co Ltd* v. *Brisford Entertainments Ltd*[82] and *Penarth Dock Engineering Co Ltd* v. *Pounds*.[83] The *United Australia* case had recognised that the gain-based *indebitatus assumpsit* count of money had and received was a remedy for a tort. In these cases Lord Denning recognised that damages in tort could be based upon the gain transferred to a defendant without referring to the counts of *indebitatus assumpsit*.

In *Strand Electric and Engineering Co Ltd* v. *Brisford Entertainments Ltd*[84] the defendant was negotiating the sale of a theatre. In order to make the theatre more marketable the defendant retained the claimant's switchboards. The claimant brought an action for the tort of detinue seeking the return of the switchboards (or their value) and payment of the full market hire rate for the period during which the switchboards were retained.

The trial judge, Pilcher J, assessed the damages on a compensatory basis and deducted an amount from the market hire rate to represent the possibility that the claimant would not have been able to hire the switchboards elsewhere. On appeal to the Court of Appeal the full market hire rate was awarded. Although the other judges appeared to adopt the fiction of viewing the award as one of compensatory damages, Denning LJ reasoned by analogy from the wayleave cases holding that if a gain-based award ("even though the owner has in fact suffered no loss")[85] is available for wrongful use of land, it should also be available in cases of wrongful use of goods. Denning LJ referred to the possibility of disgorgement damages[86] but held that the damages in this case were not to be measured by profit made but instead by restitutionary damages of "a hiring charge for the period of the detention".[87]

In *Penarth Dock Engineering Co Ltd* v. *Pounds*[88] the defendant stored his floating pontoon at the claimants' dock. The claimants were going to close the dock and they informed the defendant that the pontoon would have to be removed. By ignoring numerous requests to remove the pontoon the defendant committed the tort of trespass. Lord Denning MR, sitting at first instance, acknowledged that the claimants had not suffered any loss. They did not have to pay any extra rent for the dock, and were intending to shut it in any event. However he held that "the measure of damages is not what the plaintiffs have lost but what benefit the defendant obtained by having the use of the berth".[89] The "benefit the defendant obtained" was assessed at the value transferred; the market rate for the use of the claimants" dock (£32 5s) (which appears to have

---

[82] [1952] 2 QB 246.

[83] [1963] 1 Lloyds Rep 359.

[84] *Strand Electric* above note 82.

[85] *Strand Electric* above note 82, 254.

[86] "I can imagine cases where an owner might be entitled to the profits made by a wrongdoer by the use of a chattel": *Strand Electric* above note 82, 255.

[87] *Strand Electric* above note 82, 255 (Denning MR). See also at 252 (Somervell LJ) 256 (Romer LJ).

[88] *Penarth Dock* above note 83.

[89] *Penarth Dock* above note 83, 362. See also *Ministry of Defence* v. *Ashman* [1993] 2 EGLR 102 (CA) 104 (Kennedy LJ); *Swordheath Properties Ltd* v. *Tabet* [1979] 1 WLR 285 (CA) 288 (Megaw LJ).

been different from the particular sum that the defendant would have to pay elsewhere—£37 10s).

In *Ministry of Defence* v. *Ashman*,[90] Mr and Mrs Ashman had lived in a house leased at a substantial discount from the Ministry of Defence. The discount was due to Mr Ashman's position as a Flight Sergeant in the Royal Air Force. A condition of the lease was that if they separated and ceased to live together then the lease would be forfeit. The Ashmans separated and Mr Ashman left the accommodation. Mrs Ashman received notice to vacate the accommodation but she did not comply. The landlord (the Ministry of Defence) sought restitutionary damages (in the form of mesne profits) against Mrs Ashman for the period that she remained in the accommodation after the expiry of the lease.

The question was the appropriate rate at which the mesne profits should be calculated. The Ministry of Defence argued that it was the market price for the rental of the property. Mrs Ashman argued that the rate should be the lower discount accommodation rate which she would have paid if she were relocated elsewhere. The trial judge ordered that the rate was the market rate for that property. This objective measure reversing a transfer of value is consistent with the historic approach taken in such cases.

The Court of Appeal allowed the appeal and held that the discounted amount was appropriate. In the leading judgment, Hoffmann LJ acknowledged that "it has not been expressly stated that a claim for mesne profit for trespass can be a claim in restitution. Nowadays I do not see why we should not call a spade a spade".[91] However, Hoffmann LJ did not award the usual objective market value measure of the value transferred. He considered that the objective market value could be "subjectively devalued". As noted in chapter three, such subjective devaluation should be extremely rare in the law of wrongs although this type of reasoning might be more common in unjust enrichment. Lord Hoffmann stated:[92]

> "Such benefits may in special circumstances be subject to what Professor Birks, in his *Introduction to the Law of Restitution* has conveniently called *subjective devaluation*. This means that a benefit may not be worth as much to the particular defendant as to someone else. In particular, it may be worth less to a defendant who has not been free to reject it."

The particular factors allowing subjective devaluation were said all to be reasons why Mrs Ashman had no choice but to commit the wrong. They were that Mrs Ashman had no practical ability to leave the discounted accommodation and the fact that she had initially been occupying the premises with her husband at a rate discounted from the market.

---

[90] [1993] 2 EGLR 102 (CA).
[91] *Ministry of Defence* v. *Ashman* above note 90, 106.
[92] *Ministry of Defence* v. *Ashman* above note 90, 106.

With very similar facts, *Ministry of Defence* v. *Thompson*[93] was heard shortly afterwards by the Court of Appeal. Delivering the leading judgment, Hoffmann LJ again refused to award the market rental price and awarded the amount of the concessionary defence payments that Mrs Thompson had previously been making as evidence of the subjective value of the trespass to her. The lower concessionary rent was awarded because "[i]n the present case the only evidence before the judge was the former rent and the open market value".[94]

In *Gondal* v. *Dillon Newsagents Ltd*,[95] Mr Gondal operated a highly unsuccessful sub-post office service from a leased premises in a shopping complex. His service as a postmaster was terminated by the Post Office and he was replaced by Postal Management Services ("PMS") and their appointed postmaster, Mr Moore. However, the lessors of the complex where the sub-post office was situated allowed Mr Moore to operate in the premises without having validly terminated their lease with the Gondals. The Gondals sued the lessors and Mr Moore for trespass. In determining the damages which the Gondals should receive, the trial judge held that the amount for which the Gondals could have bargained and received from PMS for the assignment of the lease was £15,000. This figure represented the value PMS would have paid for the lease on foot (up to £10,000) as well as an amount for the assignment of the 15 year reversionary lease commencing in March 1993 (£5,000). This was therefore the "loss" which the Gondals had suffered and the amount of an award of compensatory damages which would have been available had it been sought. However, damages had not been sought on a compensatory basis and so this amount was not awarded. The Gondals had only sought damages on a restitutionary basis.[96] Judge Cooke held that restitutionary damages should be calculated by reference to what the trespasser had gained rather than what the claimant had lost. The trespassers had gained the ability to stay on in the premises without having to buy out the Gondals but they had never taken the benefit of the entry into the reversionary lease. As a result damages assessed on a restitutionary basis would only be £10,000.

Before the Court of Appeal liability was not contested. The issue was solely one of assessment of damages. The discussion of the Court of Appeal in relation to the appropriateness of the award of restitutionary damages was succinct. In the leading judgment, Simon Brown LJ (with whom Pill LJ and Sir John Vinelott agreed) upheld the award by Judge Cooke of £10,000 restitutionary damages. Simon Brown LJ quoted from *Ministry of Defence* v. *Ashman*[97] to the effect that this claim was mutually exclusive of a claim for compensatory damages and that the claimant must elect between the two measures which were both acknowledged remedies for trespass. He stated:[98]

[93] [1993] 2 EGLR 107 (CA).
[94] *Ministry of Defence* v. *Thompson* above note 93, 107.
[95] [2001] RLR 221.
[96] *Gondal* above note 95, 226.
[97] [1993] 2 EGLR 102, 105 (Hoffmann LJ).
[98] *Gondal* above note 95, 228.

"A restitutionary award, ie damages calculated according to the value of the benefit received by the occupier, is rightly decided not by reference to what subjectively the landlord would have otherwise done with his property, but rather by an objective determination of what the wrongful occupation was worth to the trespasser."

The *Gondal* case is also another example of the rejection of the lost opportunity to bargain fiction. The trial judge had found that if the parties had bargained the Gondals would have been able to extract £15,000. The Court of Appeal rejected this and held that £15,000 was not an available award of compensatory damages because "following [the Gondals'] huge initial outlay, they would never have agreed to accept remotely as little".[99] No compensatory damages were available for a lost opportunity to bargain that would never have been exercised.

Finally, in the leading speech in *Attorney General* v. *Blake*,[100] Lord Nicholls referred to many of the above cases of wayleaves, "user cases" and detention of goods and acknowledged that they are based upon the benefit obtained (transferred) by the wrongdoer. He stated that "these awards cannot be regarded as conforming to the strictly compensatory measure of damage for the injured person's loss unless loss is given a strained and artificial meaning".[101]

4) Obstacles

Three potential obstacles to restitutionary damages for torts must be considered. The first suggested obstacle is the existence of presumptions of loss such as the fiction of lost opportunity to bargain which was fortunately rejected in the *Gondal* case. These presumptions suggest that most cases of restitutionary damages can be explained as compensatory damages.[102] Although the lost opportunity to bargain fiction was rejected in chapter three, the fiction of creating a loss will be considered again below because a particular application of it persists strongly in the case of the tort of conversion. A second possible obstacle derives from the confused language of "waiver of tort" which, it was argued above, should be abandoned. It is sometimes said that some torts cannot be waived and this is used as a basis to restrict the availability of restitutionary damages. Finally, two cases are discussed which are often said to stand in the way of recognition of restitutionary damages. It is shown that the first, the litigation in *Phillips* v. *Homfray*, unequivocally *supports* restitutionary damages and the second, *Stoke on Trent City Council* v. *W & J Wass*[103] is wrong and has been effectively overruled.

---

[99] *Gondal* above note 95, 229.
[100] [2001] 1 AC 268 (HL).
[101] *Blake* above note 100, 279.
[102] See the rejection of this approach in ch. 3 text accompanying note 203–228.
[103] *Stoke-on-Trent City Council* v. *W & J Wass* [1988] 1 WLR 1406 (CA).

(a) *Confusion with compensatory damages*

In chapter three the difference between compensatory and restitutionary damages was explained. It was argued that the "fiction" of explaining restitutionary damages as compensatory by reference to a "lost opportunity to bargain" should be rejected. However, in relation to the tort of conversion there is one additional complication. In actions for conversion it is often an irrebuttable presumption that the loss suffered is at least the value of the property taken.[104] Professor Tettenborn has criticised this presumption as "arbitrary and unprincipled".[105] Such a measure of damages is often not compensatory for financial loss at all.

George Orwell once wrote of the thieving of coal by the unemployed from slag heaps discarded by the coal companies during the great depression. These companies suffered no financial loss; they had no need for the broken coal. But the companies were entitled to sue and sometimes did sue for the value of the coal (for the tort of conversion).[106] Although the award of the market value of the broken coal could be explained as an award of restitutionary damages, the irrebuttable presumption of loss in the tort of conversion would also value compensatory damages at the market price of the coal despite the fact that no real financial loss was suffered by the companies. Professor Tettenborn cites cases of this fictitious approach in conversion for which "there is little to be said".[107]

Nevertheless, because of this fiction in cases of conversion restitutionary damages will rarely be needed. Compensatory damages will often be at least the same amount. The two awards will only differ where restitutionary damages are given to reverse transfers of a "use" of the claimant's goods where market value remains unaffected. But, in any event, as the *United Australia* case illustrates, restitutionary damages (based on value transferred and not focussing upon the claimant's financial loss) are still an available alternative.

(b) *Torts that cannot be waived?*

In some cases in which a claim in *indebitatus assumpsit* was brought, and the reality of the claim was that it was based upon a tort, it was thought that it was too much of a fiction to suggest that the claimant had consented to the tortious act. Courts were not prepared to reason upon the basis of an implied contract. In the *United Australia* case for example, it was stated that "there are torts to which the process of waiver could not be applied; the tort of defamation, for example, or of assault, could not be dressed up into a claim in *assumpsit*".[108]

---

[104] The loss can be shown to be greater than the value of the goods if it is not too remote. For recent discussion of this see *Saleslease Ltd* v. *Davis* [2000] 1 All ER (Comm) 883 (CA).

[105] A Tettenborn "Damages in Conversion-The Exception or the Anomaly" [1993] CLJ 128, 145.

[106] G Orwell *The Road to Wigan Pier* (Penguin Harmondsworth 1937).

[107] A Tettenborn "Damages in Conversion—The Exception or the Anomaly" [1993] CLJ 128, 133. *Williams* v. *Archer* (1847) 5 CB 318; 136 ER 899; *BBMB* v. *Eda Holdings Ltd* [1990] 1 WLR 409 (PC). Cf *IBL Ltd* v. *Coussens* [1991] 2 All ER 133; *Brandeis Goldschmidt & Co Ltd* v. *Western Transport Ltd* [1981] QB 864 (CA).

[108] *United Australia Ltd* v. *Barclays Bank Ltd* [1941] AC 1 (HL) 13.

Lord Wright commented in his note on the *United Australia* case that he could not see how "this fiction could possibly be used in cases of money obtained by deceit or blackmail, or in cases other than the wrongful acquisition of the plaintiff's goods or property".[109] By 1952, Professor Winfield writing on the development of waiver of tort stated that, "the courts would not now be disposed to add to the list of torts which, it has been decided, can be waived".[110] Professor Birks has also tried to justify these apparent restrictions on the availability of restitutionary damages by arguing that some wrongs are "anti-harm" and others are "anti-enrichment". Wrongs such as assault, negligence and nuisance, which are anti-harm, should not permit restitutionary damages.[111] There are four reasons why such restrictions should be rejected.

(i) Rejection of implied contract

The limitations of "waiving the tort" arose from the tension inherent in the fiction of implying a contract where a wrong had been committed. It was seen above that recognising that the action lies for the tort itself and not for any implied contract should also entail rejection of the fiction that the tort is "waived". More importantly, it should entail rejection of any restrictions on recovery for the tort that sprang from that theory.

(ii) Historical inaccuracy

A second reason why "waiver of tort" should not be used is because references to some torts which could not be "waived" (in the sense of an action brought in *indebitatus assumpsit* for a gain-based remedy) are simply historically wrong. For example, Lord Wright referred to deceit as one of these torts. But deceit *was* a tort which courts had recognised could allow a claim in *indebitatus assumpsit*.[112]

(iii) Contrary to principle

Another reason why restitutionary damages should not be subject to any perceived historical limitations is that this would be entirely anomalous. As discussed in chapter three, if a transfer is deemed to be wrongful then *prima facie* the response should be that the law should permit it to be reversed. To do otherwise would be to legitimate the wrong. There is no reason in principle to treat one wrong differently from another.

(iv) Confusion

A final reason is simply the confusion that this view creates. It will be seen below that the Court of Appeal recently relied upon the inability to "waive the tort of deceit" as a reason to refuse recovery for *disgorgement* damages for deceit.[113]

---

[109] Lord Wright "*United Australia Ltd* v. *Barclays Bank Ltd*" (1941) 57 LQR 184, 195.

[110] P Winfield *The Law of Quasi-Contracts* (Sweet and Maxwell London 1952) 100.

[111] P Birks *Introduction* 328–332. Although, to the extent that Professor Birks was concerned with limits on *profit-stripping* as opposed to restitutionary damages, it is shown below that these awards of disgorgement damages should be available for nuisance, negligence and assault.

[112] *Russell* v. *Bell* (1842) 10 M & W 340, 352; 152 ER 500, 506; *Hill* v. *Perrott* (1810) 3 Taunt 274; 128 ER 109.

[113] *Halifax Building Society* v. *Thomas* [1996] Ch 217 (CA).

Yet disgorgement damages have long been available for the tort of deceit although the considerations in awarding them are different. The use of language of waiver of tort and the perceived limitations creates further confusion between restitutionary damages and disgorgement damages.

(c) Phillips *v.* Homfray

Much academic ink has been spilt over the litigation in *Phillips* v. *Homfray*.[114] The case is often considered an obstacle to the development of restitutionary damages. In *Ministry of Defence* v. *Ashman*[115] Lord Lloyd referred to *Phillips* v. *Homfray* and stated that "it is very doubtful, as the law now stands, whether the restitutionary remedy is available in the case of wrongful occupation of land." Commentators have described it as an "anti-restitution" case,[116] or an "obstacle"[117] to be "exorcised".[118] However, the case is no obstacle at all. Properly understood, it is an example of an *endorsement* of both restitutionary damages and disgorgement damages. This point has recently been powerfully made in an article by Mr Swadling, devoted exclusively to *Phillips* v. *Homfray*, to which reference will be made below.[119]

(i) The facts

Homfray, Fothergill and Forman ran a partnership, the Tredegar Iron Company, which in 1859 negotiated with Joseph and John Phillips (the claimants) for rights to mine the coal under their farm at 6s per ton. The negotiations failed but Tredegar Iron secretly began mining the coal under the claimants" land without their consent. After agreeing to sell the property to Tredegar Iron in 1863, the claimants became aware that Tredegar Iron had been extracting coal from under their land through the use of underground passages. The claimants refused to proceed with the sale. These facts gave rise to several pieces of litigation.

The first piece of litigation was a suit for specific performance of the contract of sale by Tredegar Iron and a cross-suit by the claimants for a declaration that the contract was binding and an injunction and associated orders. The matter came before the Vice Chancellor, Sir John Stuart, in 1871. The Vice-Chancellor declared that the contract for sale of the property was not binding and ordered it to be delivered up for cancellation. In relation to the injunction and associated orders the Vice-Chancellor granted the injunction[120] and directed that inquiries be taken as to:

---

[114] (1871) LR 6 Ch App 770; *Llanover* v. *Homfray* (1881) 19 Ch D 224, 228; *Phillips* v. *Homfray* (1883) 24 Ch D 439 (CA); *Phillips* v. *Homfray* (1890) 44 Ch D 694; *Phillips* v. *Homfray* [1892] 1 Ch 465.

[115] *Ashman* above note 97, 106.

[116] A Burrows *The Law of Restitution* 390; A Burrows "Contract, Tort and Restitution—A Satisfactory Division or Not" (1983) 99 LQR 217, 237–238.

[117] G Fridman *Restitution* (2nd edn. Carswell Ontario 1992) 362.

[118] *Goff and Jones* 778.

[119] W Swadling "The Myth of *Phillips* v. *Homfray*" in W Swadling and G Jones (eds) *The Search for Principle: Essays in Honour of Lord Goff of Chieveley* (OUP Oxford 1999) 277.

[120] *Phillips* v. *Homfray* (1871) LR 6 Ch App 770, 776.

1. The market value of the quantities of coal at the time of removal less an allowance for the defendants" carriage expenses (but not the expenses of removing the coal itself from the ground);
2. The quantities of coal transported through the passages under the Phillips" land;
3. The amount which should be paid for the use of the land for this transported coal; and
4. Whether the property of the Phillips' had suffered any, and if so how much, damage.

As Forman had died by the time of the action, the first inquiry was ordered against the estate of Forman as well as the other partners, Homfray and Fothergill. The second and third inquiries, directed at ascertaining the market value of the use of the land were directed at Homfray and Fothergill only. On appeal to the Lord Chancellor, the inquiries were upheld with a small variation (excluding from the inquiries the drainage and ventilation cost to Phillips' land.)[121]

(ii) The four inquiries

The first head of inquiry was directed towards ascertaining the market value of the coal taken. As Professor Birks and Mr Swadling have noted, this award was akin to an account of profits or disgorgement damages.[122] This is apparent from subsequent further litigation in the case. This litigation was 20 years later, and concerned whether interest could be recovered on the award given pursuant to the first inquiry.[123] Stirling J considered that interest could not be given upon the award which was one of money had and received.[124] The Court of Appeal agreed that interest could not be recovered after such a delay but each of the judgments emphasised that the inquiry was based on an *account* in equity not upon a count of money had and received.[125] The account in equity was an account of profits from the *non-monetary benefit* obtained. Lindley LJ stated that the award was "for the value of the coal raised—that is to say, the market price or value after making just allowances".[126] These disgorgement damages awards are considered below.[127]

[121] *Phillips* v. *Homfray* above note 120.
[122] P Birks "Restitution for Wrongs" in E Schrage (ed.) *Unjust Enrichment: The Comparative Legal History of the Law of Restitution* (2nd edn. Duncker & Humblot Berlin 1999) 171, 188; P Birks *Future* 64; W Swadling "The Myth of *Phillips* v. *Homfray*" in W Swadling and G Jones (eds) *The Search for Principle: Essays in Honour of Lord Goff of Chieveley* (OUP Oxford 1999) 277, 292.
[123] *Phillips* v. *Homfray* (1890) LR 44 Ch 694.
[124] *Phillips* v. *Homfray* above note 123, 700.
[125] *Phillips* v. *Homfray* [1892] 1 Ch 465 (CA) 470, 472, 473. See also W Gummow "Unjust Enrichment, Restitution and Proprietary Remedies" in P Finn *Essays on Restitution* (Law Book Co Sydney 1990) 60–67.
[126] *Phillips* v. *Homfray* [1892] 1 Ch 465 (CA) 470.
[127] The nature of these awards as disgorgement damages and not restitutionary damages is explained below, text accompanying notes 161–168.

The second and third "wayleave" inquiries were directed toward ascertaining the market value of the benefits transferred; the use of the claimant's land. These were awards of restitutionary damages. By allowing all inquiries to continue the Lord Chancellor affirmed the availability of both restitutionary damages for trespass (the second and third inquiries) and disgorgement damages for conversion (the first inquiry). The final inquiry was compensatory, being concerned with the *loss* to the claimant.

(iii) The stay of the last three inquiries

Matters became more complex when, following the ordering of the inquiries, Fothergill and Homfray died. The cross-suit was revived against Fothergill's executors but they brought proceedings for a stay of all the inquiries. Homfray's executors then followed this course. The basis for this new litigation was the rule *actio personalis moritur cum persona;* an action for a wrong does not survive the death of the wrongdoer. This rule was only applicable to torts[128] and no longer exists.[129]

Pearson J relied upon the *actio personalis* rule but held that only the fourth inquiry (compensatory damages for the damage to the land) should be stayed. A majority of the Court of Appeal after observing that "we have not now to consider the policy of the maxim . . . whatever its wisdom",[130] stayed all of the final three inquiries because, as a result of the maxim, there was no longer a surviving wrong for which restitutionary or compensatory damages could be given.

However, the first inquiry was not stayed. This is what led commentators to view *Phillips* v. *Homfray* as an anti-restitutionary "obstacle". Because disgorgement damages were allowed for the first inquiry (the value of the coal once it was removed) it was thought that *Phillips* v. *Homfray* meant that other gain-based awards for trespass (such as restitutionary damages) would not be available. However, nothing was ever said to cast any doubt on the earlier decision of Stuart V-C, which had been affirmed by the Lord Chancellor. That decision had *endorsed* the restitutionary damages award for the use of the land. This subsequent litigation was only concerned with the application of the *actio personalis* rule.

(iv) The first inquiry

Why was the first inquiry allowed to continue although the second, third and fourth inquiries were not? Mr Swadling has argued that "it was simply a tracing exercise designed to identify an asset belonging to the plaintiff still in the executor's hands".[131] As a result, a claim for disgorgement damages could be brought for that value against the executor as the executor continues to commit the wrong of conversion whilst he retains the claimant's property. As the action is

---

[128] *Sollars* v. *Lawrence* (1743) Willes 413, 421 (Willes CJ).

[129] This rule was abolished by the Law Reform (Miscellaneous Provisions) Act 1934.

[130] *Phillips* v. *Homfray* (1883) 24 Ch D 439 (CA) 456.

[131] W Swadling "The Myth of *Phillips* v. *Homfray*" in W Swadling and G Jones (eds) *The Search for Principle: Essays in Honour of Lord Goff of Chieveley* (OUP Oxford 1999) 277, 290.

brought against the executor and not the deceased, the *actio personalis* rule does not apply in these cases. Mr Swadling's explanation is also supported by a number of cases in which actions for detinue and trover were allowed against an executor that retained property of a claimant.[132]

Unfortunately this explanation cannot work for the first inquiry in *Phillips* v. *Homfray*. Allowing the first inquiry to remain must be regarded as an error for three reasons. First, there are explicit statements in later aspects of the *Phillips* v. *Homfray* litigation that the action was not one of conversion against the executor.[133] Secondly, even if it could be said that the coal (whilst in the ground) was a chattel (which it was not)[134] which had been converted in the "taking" by the deceased, the executor was only in the possession of the proceeds from the sale of that coal by the deceased. Lord Goff has stated that it is not possible to make someone a wrongdoer through the process of tracing.[135] Thirdly, the basis for the award of disgorgement damages is not present. The need for deterrence existed against the cynical tortfeasor, not against the innocent executor.

The dissenting reasoning of Baggallay LJ is the most unsound. Although Baggallay LJ endorsed the *actio personalis* maxim and thus struck out the fourth (compensatory) inquiry,[136] he allowed all the other inquiries as being cases of gain where "the wrongful act has resulted in a benefit capable of being measured pecuniarily".[137] But if the wrong has been extinguished why should restitutionary damages and disgorgement damages be allowed and not compensatory damages? They are both dependent upon the wrong. The weak answer ventured by Baggallay LJ was that the inquiries were sought in equity and the *actio personalis* maxim was not as harsh as at common law.[138]

(v) An unjust enrichment analysis
One other issue arises from the litigation. The question might be asked whether an alternative analysis in unjust enrichment might have been possible so that the second and third inquiries could have been continued. As noted, the *actio personalis* rule was only applicable to torts.[139] Could not an action for "ignorance" be brought in unjust enrichment? It appeared that this point was considered.

The majority in *Phillips* v. *Homfray (No 2)* posed the question "could the Plaintiffs have sued the deceased at law in any form of action in which 'not guilty' *would not* be the proper plea".[140] At the time the answer was "no". The answer given by the majority in *Phillips* v. *Homfray (No 2)* was due to historical reasons

---

[132] W Swadling "The Myth of *Phillips* v. *Homfray*" in W Swadling and G Jones (eds) *The Search for Principle: Essays in Honour of Lord Goff of Chieveley* (OUP Oxford 1999) 277, 289–290
[133] *Phillips* v. *Homfray* [1892] 1 Ch 465 (CA) 470 "if the action had been an action for trover or trespass . . . it could not have been continued against the executors" (Lindley LJ).
[134] *Jegon* v. *Vivian* (1871) LR 6 Ch App 742, 760.
[135] *Lipkin Gorman* v. *Karpnale Ltd* [1991] 2 AC 548 (HL) 573.
[136] *Phillips* v. *Homfray* (1883) 24 Ch D 439 (CA) 477.
[137] *Phillips* v. *Homfray* (1883) above note 136, 476.
[138] *Phillips* v. *Homfray* (1883) above note 136, 476.
[139] *Sollars* v. *Lawrence* above note 128, 421 (Willes CJ).
[140] *Phillips* v. *Homfray* (1883) above note 136, 463.

relating to the unavailability of *indebitatus assumpsit* in cases of trespass to land.[141] However, in cases not involving land, this action *was* available.[142] Thus, the majority refused to depart from statements of Lord Mansfield in *Hambly* v. *Trott*[143] that in such cases this (unjust enrichment) type of action would lie although an action in tort would have been extinguished by the *actio personalis* rule:

> "if a man take a horse from another, and bring him back again; an action for trespass would not lie against his executor, though it would against him; but an action for the use and hire of the horse would lie against the executor."

This action, best seen as 'ignorance' or 'lack of consent' in unjust enrichment,[144] was only unavailable in cases of trespass to land. It was in this context that the majority judgments referred to the fact that trespass to land was a tort which could not be waived.[145]

(d) Stoke on Trent City Council *v*. W & J Wass

The decision in *Stoke on Trent City Council* v. *W & J Wass*[146] must now be regarded as wrong. In that case the defendants wilfully committed the tort of nuisance by operating a market unlawfully in breach of the claimant's exclusive right to operate a market within a defined area. The trial judge, Peter Gibson J, held that no loss had resulted to the claimants' market but was prepared to award the sum of a reasonable licence fee (restitutionary damages). The Court of Appeal allowed the appeal holding that only nominal damages could be awarded as no financial loss had been suffered. Nourse LJ distinguished other restitutionary damages cases as either "in accordance with . . . a user principle [the use of the plaintiff's property]",[147] or as cases of financial loss.[148] Nicholls LJ took a similar approach, refusing to extend what he saw as anomalies.[149]

There is no anomaly at all once it is recognised that awards of restitutionary damages—which effect the reversal of a wrongful transfer—were not confined to property torts. Examples cited above include fraud and interference with

[141] JB Ames "Assumpsit for Use and Occupation" (1889) 2 Harv Law Rev 377, 380. See also A Corbin "Waiver of Tort and Suit in Assumpsit" (1910) 19 Yale LJ 221, 232. The limitation in cases of trespass to land was mostly related to the passing of Statute II Geo II c19 which extended some common law actions against trespassers to land. The effect of the interference of Parliament was that it displaced the development of the *indebitatus assumpsit* against trespassers at common law as it was thought that to further extend the remedies would usurp the role of Parliament. Cf WA Keener "Waiver of Tort" (1892) 6 Harv Law Rev 223, 239.

[142] See D Ibbetson *A Historical Introduction to the Law of Obligations* (OUP Oxford 1999) referring to cases which recognised that in other instances *indebitatus assumpsit* was available against an executor.

[143] (1776) 1 Cowp 371, 375; 98 ER 1136, 1138. Cf "this approach is not founded in principle": *Foster* v. *Stewart* (1814) 3 M & S 191, 196; 105 ER 582, 584.

[144] See ch. 2, text accompanying note 114–118.

[145] *Phillips* v. *Homfray* (1883) above note 136, 463.

[146] *Stoke-on-Trent City Council* v. *W & J Wass* [1988] 1 WLR 1406 (CA).

[147] *Stoke-on-Trent* above note 146, 1413.

[148] *Stoke-on-Trent* above note 146, 1414.

[149] *Stoke-on-Trent* above note 146, 1419.

contractual relations but most importantly, prior to the *Wass* case, restitutionary damages had been awarded for nuisance itself. In *Carr-Saunders* v. *Dick
McNeil Associates Ltd*,[150] restitutionary damages were awarded to reflect the
reasonable licence value transferred. Although Nourse LJ distinguished this as
a case where loss had been suffered, as discussed above, the award there is best
viewed as having been made independently of any loss which had been suffered.[151]

In the leading speech in the House of Lords in *Attorney General* v. *Blake*[152]
Lord Nicholls recanted from his judgment in the *Wass* case and recognised the
existence of gain-based restitutionary damages. Although the *Wass* case had
been followed in one Court of Appeal decision concerned with breach of contract[153] Lord Nicholls expressly disapproved of this later decision and held that
even for breach of contract a reasonable licence fee (restitutionary damages)
could be awarded where rights had been appropriated.[154]

B Disgorgement damages

A variety of different mechanisms have been, and continue to be, used by courts
to effect disgorgement damages for torts. Once all this different nomenclature is
viewed together it can be seen that disgorgement damages are widely available
to strip a defendant of profits cynically made. The mechanism and language
used by courts has been through awards of "money had and received", broad
references to "damages", awards of accounts of profits and awards deceptively
entitled "compound interest". In addition, the "blunt instrument" of exemplary
damages for cynical breach is sometimes used to effect the same deterrent purposes as disgorgement damages. Together these awards have effected disgorgement damages for cynical commission of torts as diverse as trespass, conversion,
libel, inducing breach of contract, intimidation, fraud and deceit.

1) Different labels

(a) "Compound interest"

As discussed in chapter three, considering the confusion in *Westdeutsche
Landesbank Girozentrale* v. *Islington LBC*,[155] the disgorgement measure of compound interest requires a defendant to disgorge profits wrongfully made.
Confusingly entitled equity's award of "compound interest" the award really
operates to strip profit (rather than award interest) and, like an account of profits,

---

[150] [1986] 1 WLR 922.
[151] See above text accompanying notes 29–34.
[152] *Attorney General* v. *Blake* [2001] 1 AC 268 (HL).
[153] *Surrey County Council* v. *Bredero Homes Ltd* [1993] 1 WLR 1361 (CA).
[154] *Blake* above note 152, 283.
[155] *Westdeutsche Landesbank Girozentrale* v. *Islington LBC* [1996] AC 669 (HL).

it is constantly stated that the award operates only to deter by stripping only the profits and that it does not operate further to punish.[156]

The only difference between this meaning of "compound interest" and an account of profits is that an award of "compound interest" will also be made where the defendant has used money obtained from a wrong in trade or commerce regardless of whether any profits are proved to have been made. Unless evidence to the contrary is shown, a court will *presume* that profits of compound interest have been earned because the use of money in trade or commerce will ordinarily attract compound interest.[157]

Fraud at common law is one of the wrongs for which this disgorging response of "compound interest" is available in equity to ensure that the deliberate wrongdoer cannot profit from his wrong.[158] In *Southern Cross Pty Ltd* v. *Ewing*,[159] a fraudster, M, who was a director of both companies C and D, misappropriated funds from company C and transferred them to company D. The Supreme Court of South Australia held that company C was not fixed with the fraud of M but that the recipient, company D, was sufficiently involved to be fixed with the fraud of M. Company D was required to account for the money and for "compound interest" of any profit obtained or presumed to have been obtained through the use of the money. White J considered that the principle of allowing compound interest for fraudulent misapplication of a company's property was akin to that of allowing an account of profits for a fraudulent misrepresentation. He referred to Lord Wright in *Spence* v. *Crawford*[160] (although Lord Wright was speaking in the context of rescission for fraudulent misrepresentation) who had stated that "in the case of fraud, the court will exercise its jurisdiction to the full in order, if possible, to prevent the defendant from enjoying the benefit of his fraud at the expense of an innocent plaintiff."

(b) *Broad awards of "damages"*

(i) Trespass

There were a large number of cases in the nineteenth century concerning the removal, in trespass, of coal under the land of the claimant.[161] The award of disgorgement damages (the value of the coal as a chattel in the defendant's hands) was often made in cases where coal had been removed in a wilful and

---

[156] See ch. 3 note 136.
[157] *Attorney General* v. *Alford* (1855) 4 De G M & G 843, 851–851;43 ER 737, 741; *Burdick* v. *Garrick* (1870) 5 LR Ch App 233, 241–242; *Equiticorp Industries Group* v. *The Crown* [1996] 3 NZLR 690 (HCNZ) 700–701; *General Communications Ltd* v. *Development Finance Corporation of New Zealand Ltd* [1990] 3 NZLR 406 (CANZ) 436; *National Bank of New Zealand Ltd* v. *Development Finance Corporation of New Zealand* [1990] 3 NZLR 257 (CANZ) 263.
[158] *President of India* v. *La Pintada Cia Navegacion SA* [1985] AC 104 (HL) 116; *Equiticorp Industries Group* v. *The Crown* [1996] 3 NZLR 690 (HCNZ) 700–701; *Southern Cross Pty Ltd* v. *Ewing* (1988) 91 FLR 271 (SCSA) 285 (White J), 307 (Von Doussa J).
[159] *Southern Cross Pty Ltd* above note 158, 285.
[160] *Spence* v. *Crawford* [1939] 3 All ER 271 (HL) 288.
[161] See text above accompanying notes 17–24.

cynical manner.[162] In *Powell* v. *Aiken*,[163] the Vice Chancellor, Sir Page Wood stated that this award effects "an account of profit realised . . . by the working of coal to give relief in respect of wrongs attended with profit to the wrong-doer." Similarly in *Jegon* v. *Vivian*[164] Lord Hatherley LC explained this award as based upon the fact that "this Court never allows a man to make a profit by a wrong."

In *Martin* v. *Porter*,[165] the defendant had wilfully removed coal from the claimant's land. The Court *en banc* approved of the order of Baron Parke that the claimant was entitled to both a wayleave for the use of the land (restitution-ary damages) and to the value of the coal once removed from the land. The award of the value of the coal when removed from the land was clearly not one of compensatory damages. Even the fiction, discussed in chapter three, of irre-buttably presuming the value of the goods converted to be a loss depended upon the value of the goods as they lay in the ground and not their value in the form of a chattel in the defendant's hands. Nor was the award one of restitutionary damages. The value of the coal, as removed from the land, was greater than a mere *right* to remove the coal. Alexander, counsel for the defendant, had argued that the award be reduced to the value of the coal in the ground or the value of a right to remove it. Alexander argued that "the expense . . . of working out so small a bed of coal. . . would have been double its saleable price" and that the value of the coal whilst in the land was "much below the sum paid into court".[166] But the court *en banc* refused to reduce the award to one which might have represented restitutionary damages (the market value of the right to mine the coal).

An argument was made in *Martin* v. *Porter*,[167] before the court *en banc*, that the award was excessive as it should include an allowance for the cost of remov-ing the coal. But the court refused this allowance. Baron Parke stated that "I am not sorry that this rule is adopted; as it will tend to prevent trespasses of this kind which are generally wilful". This refusal to give an allowance for the value of the work done adds to the disgorgement damages an additional element of punishment or exemplary damages.[168]

A United States example of a disgorgement damages award for trespass, dis-cussed in chapter two, is the decision of the Kentucky Court of Appeal in *Edwards* v. *Lee's Administrators*.[169] It will be recalled that Edwards had built a hotel on his land which attracted numerous tourists who came to visit a cave

---

[162] See the discussion above of *Phillips* v. *Homfray* (1871) LR 6 Ch App 770. Also *Morgan* v. *Powell* (1842) 3 QB 278; 114 ER 513; *Wild* v. *Holt* (1842) 9 M & W 672; 152 ER 284; *Bulli Coal Mining Co* v. *Osborne* [1899] AC 351 (HL).

[163] (1858) 4 K & J 343, 351; 70 ER 144, 147.

[164] (1871) LR 6 Ch App 742, 762.

[165] (1839) 5 M & W 351; 151 ER 149.

[166] *Martin* v. *Porter* above note 165, 353; 149.

[167] *Martin* v. *Porter* above note 165, 354; 150.

[168] *Jegon* v. *Vivian* (1871) LR 6 Ch App 742, 762 (Lord Hatherley LC).

[169] 96 SW 2d 1028 (1936 CA Ken).

that lay beneath his land. Edwards was aware that a third of the cave lay beneath Lee's land, but wilfully and cynically trespassed into this part of the cave.

Stites J, in the leading judgment was unable clearly to explain why the award that he preferred, a third of the net profits (disgorgement damages), should be accepted instead of a measure based on the rental value of the land (restitutionary damages). In chapter two it was explained that this was because he conflated the concepts of restitutionary damages and disgorgement damages and considered them both as part of an award based upon "unjust enrichment".[170] Although the error of this method was explained in chapter two, the profit-based result can still be justified. As an award of disgorgement damages it operated in the same manner as the coal cases; to strip a defendant of profits cynically made.

The *Edwards* case can be neatly contrasted to a recent United States case also concerning trespass. The contrasting decision is that of the 10th Circuit of the United States Court of Appeals in *Beck and Others* v. *Northern Natural Gas Company*.[171] "Northern" was a natural gas company which was commissioned by State and Federal Governments to store (by injection) natural gas in a sub-surface area known as the Viola formation. This storage was done by consent of the landowners. However, in trespass, a far greater amount was stored than agreed because of a "migration" of the gas to a lower formation for which permission to store had not been obtained. The Court of Appeals accepted the assessment of the trial judge that the fair market value of the storage was $2.3 million but that the profits generated as a result of the additional storage (through additional sales) was $12 million. However, for the innocent trespass, the court held that the "proper measure of damages was . . . fair rental value".[172]

This approach to trespass in the United States is identical to that in England. It is that disgorgement damages are awarded only where the wrong is committed cynically. In cases of conversion, US Courts take an identical approach.

(ii) Conversion
In *Olwell* v. *Nye & Nissen Co*[173] the appellant had purchased the respondents" egg-packing business. The respondents left an egg-washing machine on the premises which had been excluded from the sale of the business. The appellant cynically committed the tort of conversion by using the respondent's egg-washing machine (without the respondent's knowledge) to clean the eggs, a method far more effective than manually washing them. Although using the language of implied contract, the Supreme Court of Washington accepted that the profit must be disgorged.

The court referred to arguments of the appellant that an award of disgorgement damages would be excessive as "any damages awarded to the plaintiff

[170] Ch. 2, text accompanying note 88.
[171] *Beck and Others* v. *Northern Natural Gas Company* 170 F 3d 1018 (10th Cir 1999).
[172] *Beck* above note 171, 1024.
[173] 173 P 2d 652 (1946 SCW).

should be based on the use or rental value of the machine and should bear some reasonable relation to market value".[174] Mallery J, with whom the other Justices agreed, rejected these arguments and affirmed a comment from the *Restatement of Restitution:*[175]

> "the measure of restitution is determined with reference to the tortiousness of the defendant's conduct . . . If he was consciously tortious in acquiring the benefit, he is also deprived of any profit derived from his subsequent dealing with it."[176]

On the other hand, if the claimant is an innocent converter, the *Restatement* suggests that they cannot be recovered and only restitutionary damages are allowed.[177] In the result in the *Olwell* case it did not matter because the respondent had only sought the restitutionary damages award of the market rate of the use—$25 per month—so the award was limited to that amount.

(c) *Money had and received*

(i) Conversion

The disgorgement damages award for conversion in the United States described simply as "damages", might be achieved in English cases by the use of money had and received. In *Lightly* v. *Clouston*[178] Mansfield CJ acknowledged that:[179]

> "it has now been long settled, that in cases of sale, if the Plaintiff chooses to sue for the produce of that sale, he may do it: and the practice is beneficial to the defendant, because a jury may give in damages for the tort a much greater sum than the value of the goods."

This principle was constantly affirmed and money had and received became the method for disgorging the profits from the sale of converted goods.[180] However, as noted in chapter three, these are cases in which a disgorgement award of the profits from the sale might not be needed as the result could lead to the same award as one of restitutionary damages. Restitutionary damages can allow a claim to the profit through tracing into the higher value of the goods wrongfully sold as damages which are not too remote.[181] This award of restitutionary damages is allowed even in cases in which the conversion is innocent. Professor Burrows has noted that the award of restitutionary damages in such cases mirrors the same approach taken for restitution in unjust enrichment.[182]

---

[174] *Olwell* above note 173, 653.

[175] *Restatement of Restitution*, Introductory Note to Ch. 8, 595–596.

[176] *Olwell* above note 173, 654. There was a suggestion however that the profits in that case might be measured by expense saved, a concept which English law has not adopted (see ch. 3 text accompanying note 60–69).

[177] *Restatement of Restitution* §155, Illustration 2, 610–611.

[178] (1808) 1 Taunt 112; 127 ER 774; *Lamine* v. *Dorell* (1701) 2 Ld Ray 1216; 92 ER 303.

[179] *Lightly* v. *Clouston* above note 178; 775.

[180] *Lightly* v. *Clouston* above note 178; *Lamine* v. *Dorell* above note 178; *Oughton* v. *Seppings* (1830) 1 B and Ad 241; 109 ER 776; *King* v. *Leith* (1787) 2 TR 141, 145; 100 ER 78–79; *Parker* v. *Norton* (1796) 6 TR 695, 700; 101 ER 779–780; *Feltham* v. *Terry* (1772) Lofft 207, 208; 98 ER 613, 613.

[181] See ch. 3, text accompanying note 259.

[182] See A Burrows *The Law of Restitution* 384.

However, it should be noted that this award of traceable higher value in cases in which the wrong is not the cause of action have been argued to be an instance of restitution to vindicate a property right rather than to reverse an unjust enrichment.[183]

(ii) Deceit and fraud

Although it has been said that the "common law knows no generalised tort of fraud"[184] it is clear that fraud is actionable in some circumstances as a tort although there has been no representation. The deceit case of *Derry* v. *Peek*[185] introduced the requirement of a representation for the tort of deceit. However, common law fraud does not always require a representation. Thus, whilst there may be no *generalised* tort of fraud,[186] it is clear that, concurrently with the jurisdiction of equity, there is an extension of the tort of deceit in cases of bribery.[187] In these cases the tort consists of a wrong against the party whose relationship is abused by the bribed defendant (usually a principal or an employer) in order to receive the bribe.[188]

Reading v. *Attorney General*[189] is a classic illustration. In that case an army sergeant had sat on a lorry in uniform to allow lorries of alcohol to be smuggled through British check-points. He made over £20,000 in bribes. The profits from the bribery were sought by the Crown. At first instance Denning J held that the Crown were entitled to the profits either at common law or in equity.[190] Denning J did not specify the precise cause of action for which the profits were disgorged.

On appeal to the Court of Appeal, the court was unhappy with the common law analysis of Denning J and preferred to base their judgment on the finding of a breach of fiduciary duty in equity in "a very loose . . . sense".[191] In the House of Lords each of their Lordships endorsed the fiduciary analysis of the Court of Appeal. However Viscount Jowitt LC and Lord Porter accepted that the Crown were also entitled to recover the bribe from the sergeant at common law as money had and received.[192] Lord Oaksey also thought recovery was possible at common law although explaining it as based upon the now-rejected implied contract fiction. Like the decision of Denning J, there was no explanation in these speeches in the House of Lords of the basis on which the *common law* remedy of money had and received was made.

---

[183] See ch. 3 note 263.

[184] *Armitage* v. *Nurse* [1998] Ch 241 (CA) 250; *Walker* v. *Stones* [2001] 2 WLR 623 (CA) 656.

[185] *Derry* v. *Peek* (1889) 14 App Cas 337 (HL).

[186] The tort has close parallels to the Roman *actio doli* which was, however, a subsidiary action available for any fraud or deceit where no other action lay (B Nicholas *Introduction to Roman Law* (Clarendon Press Oxford 1962) 223).

[187] *Hovenden* v. *Millhoff* (1900) 83 LT 41 (CA); *Mahesan S/O Thambiah* v. *Malaysian Government Officers Co-Operative Housing Society* [1979] AC 374 (PC); *Petrotrade Inc* v. *Smith* [2000] 1 Lloyds Rep 486; *Fyffes Group Ltd* v. *Templeman* [2000] 2 Lloyds Rep 643.

[188] *Petrotrade* above note 187, 490; *Mahesan S/O Thambiah* above note 187, 383.

[189] [1951] AC 507 (HL).

[190] *Reading* v. *The King* [1948] 2 KB 268, 275 ("it is unnecessary to draw a distinction").

[191] *Reading* v. *The King* [1949] 2 KB 232 (CA) 236.

[192] *Reading* v. *Attorney General* (HL) above note 189, 513, 515–516.

One explanation of the decision came in *Mahesan S/O Thambiah* v. *Malaysian Government Officers Co-Operative Housing Society*.[193] In that case, an agent took a bribe to purchase land on behalf of his principal at an inflated price. The Privy Council held that the bribe exceeded the amount by which the price was inflated (the principal's loss). The principal sought recovery of the amount of the bribe as money had and received. Counsel for the principal relied upon the *Reading* case and argued that:[194]

> "When an agent has received the bribe his obligation is to hand it to the principal as money had and received and it is recoverable by the principal as such . . . By disgorging the bribe the agent loses nothing; the principal receives a windfall but there is nothing in that to preclude him from pursuing his remedy for fraud."

Delivering the advice of the Privy Council, Lord Diplock relied upon the reasoning in the *United Australia* case and accepted that the claimant could elect between compensatory damages for the tort of fraud or disgorgement damages in the form of money had and received.[195] Lord Diplock had difficulty with the notion that no loss might be suffered yet an award of profits might still be made for the tort of fraud. But he considered this meant that in cases where disgorgement damages are sought for bribery, loss was not really an element of this common law cause of action.[196] As Smith LJ had stated 76 years earlier, "when a purchaser finds out this state of things [the bribe] he may call upon his agent or the vendor to disgorge".[197]

The approach of Lord Diplock was followed at first instance by David Steel J in *Petrotrade Inc* v. *Smith*[198] where he held that the profit from a bribe should be disgorged. Unfortunately, David Steel J described the award simply as one for "money had and received" in "restitution" and did not explain that, like the compensatory damages award he recognised for the fraud, this was also an award arising from the tort at common law.[199]

The same should be true of the tort of deceit. Whilst the position in the United States is clear that a party that cynically makes profit from a fraudulent

---

[193] [1979] AC 374 (PC) 376. See also *Armagas Ltd* v. *Mundogas SA* [1986] AC 717 (CA) 742–743 (Robert Goff LJ); decision aff'd [1986] 1 AC 717 (HL).

[194] *Mahesan* above note 187, 376.

[195] Although at times Lord Diplock seemingly treated money had and received as independent of the law of tort, stating, for example, that "the same facts gave rise in law to two causes of action . . . for money had and received and the other for tort": *Mahesan* above note 187, 382.

[196] *Mahesan* above note 187, 380, 383. See *Fawcett* v. *Whitehouse* (1829) 1 Russ & M 132; 39 ER 51. Some common law authorities had relied upon the now-rejected concept of implied contract: *Boston Deep Sea Fishing and Ice Co* v. *Ansell* (1888) 39 Ch D 339 (CA) 367. Others did not: *Salford* v. *Lever* [1891] 1 QB 168 (CA); *Armagas Ltd* v. *Mundogas SA* [1986] AC 717 (CA) 742–743 (Robert Goff LJ); decision aff'd [1986] 1 AC 717 (HL).

[197] *Hovenden* v. *Millhoff* (1900) 83 LT 41 (CA) 42.

[198] *Petrotrade Inc* v. *Smith* [2000] 1 Lloyds Rep 486 490. This case is discussed in detail in ch. 6, text accompanying notes 51–53.

[199] Although he did appear to treat the award as arising because of the bribe and "the benefit which has accrued to the briber". *Petrotrade* above note 198, 490. See further J Edelman "Money Had and Received: Modern Pleading of an Old Count" [2000] RLR 547.

misrepresentation must disgorge that profit as "damages", there is little English authority on the point.[200] In *Kettlewell* v. *Refuge Assurance Company*[201] the claimant sued to recover life insurance premiums paid to a company as a result of fraudulent misrepresentations that if the premiums were paid for four years a policy would be given free thereafter. The claimant, Mrs Kettlewell, clearly obtained a benefit from the payment of the premiums as the insurance company would have been liable to pay out on the contract, despite the fraud if the life assured had died within the insurance period. However, Lord Alverstone CJ and Sir Gorell Barnes thought that all the premiums could be recovered as money had and received, to reverse the transaction, as they considered that the benefits conferred upon Mrs Kettlewell could be "ignored".

The approach of Buckley LJ did not take such a fictitious route. Buckley LJ acknowledged that benefits had been received by Mrs Kettlewell. As a result an award to reverse the transaction was not possible. Instead he stated that an award should focus upon the *profit* made by the defendant. He stated that "they, having by their agent's fraud got her money into their pocket, cannot be allowed to keep the *profit* as against her".[202]

(iii) Inducing breach of contract

In *Federal Sugar Refining Co* v. *US Sugar Equalization Board Inc*[203] the president of the defendant corporation induced a foreign buyer of sugar to break a contract with the claimant and buy from the defendant instead. This was done by wrongfully refusing the plaintiff an export licence to sell to the foreign buyer. The defendant sought to strike out the cause of action as the claimant had not pleaded that it was able to perform. Mayer DCJ rejected this on the basis that the claim was one for the profit the defendant made (as money had and received) and the inability of the claimant to perform was irrelevant. The Court also held that it did not matter that the claimant had suffered no loss.

Although disgorgement damages for the tort of inducing a breach of contract have not been accepted beyond the United States, the tort has been considered in Australia to give rise to the possibility of exemplary damages in cases of cynical breach.[204]

(d) *Exemplary damages compared*

In chapter one, the case of *Livingstone* v. *Rawyards Coal Company*[205] was considered. The respondent had innocently mined under the appellant's land. No

---

[200] The United States authority allows a claimant an election between profits made (disgorgement damages) or fair rental value of any property deceitfully obtained: *Lang* v. *Giraudo* 40 NE (2d) 707 (1942 SCM) 711. See also *Janigan* v. *Taylor* 344 F (2d) 781 (1965 CA 1st Cir) 786 and cases cited therein. For further discussion of the position in the United States see J Edelman "Unjust Enrichment, Restitution and Wrongs" [2001] Texas Law Rev 1869.

[201] [1908] 1 KB 545 (CA).

[202] *Kettlewell* v. *Refuge Assurance Company* [1908] 1 KB 545 (CA) 553.

[203] (1920) 268 F 575 (DCNY).

[204] *Whitfeld* v. *De Lauret & Co Ltd* (1920) 29 CLR 71 (HCA) 77.

[205] (1880) 5 App Cas 25 (HL).

damage was done to the appellant's land but the appellant had sought disgorgement of the profits made by the respondent from the mining. The House of Lords had held that the appellant was only entitled to nominal damages. However, the House of Lords indicated that if there had been evidence of "bad faith or sinister intention"[206] the appellant could have recovered the market value of the coal, in precisely the same manner as disgorgement damages were awarded in the trespass cases discussed above.

In *Broome* v. *Cassell & Co*,[207] Lord Diplock referred to the *Livingstone* case and acknowledged that the goals of this award of disgorgement damages were mirrored in the profit-stripping (second) limb of exemplary damages for cynical breach.[208] However, an award of exemplary damages sometimes goes further than disgorgement damages. Lord Diplock acknowledged in the *Broome* case that the additional refusal often to allow a deduction for the cost of working the coal was a purely punitive element[209] which might be given at common law[210] or in equity.[211] Lord Diplock saw this additional punishment as necessary for additional deterrence:[212]

> "to restrict the damages recoverable to the actual gain made by the defendant if it exceeded the loss caused to the plaintiff, would leave the defendant contemplating an unlawful act with the certainty that he had nothing to lose to balance against the chance that the plaintiff might never sue him or, if he did, might fail in the hazards of litigation."

Nevertheless, examples of where profit is stripped under the second limb of exemplary damages illustrate the fact, recognised by both Lord Nicholls and Lord Scott in the *Kuddus* case,[213] that the less objectionable disgorgement damages should also be available.[214]

(i)   Libel

In *Broome* v. *Cassell & Co*,[215] the claimant brought an action against the publishers of a book which had suggested that he was partly responsible for a naval disaster. The claimant and other high ranking naval officers had informed the publisher that the book was libellous but only minor modifications had been made prior to publication. The trial judge had directed the jury that they could award exemplary damages if satisfied that the action had been "calculated" by

---

[206] *Livingstone* above note 205, 31 (Earl Cairns LC), 34 (Lord Hatherley), 39 (Lord Blackburn).
[207] [1972] AC 1027 (HL) 1129.
[208] *Rookes* v. *Barnard* [1964] AC 1129 (HL).
[209] *Broome* above note 207, 1129.
[210] *Livingstone* above note 205.
[211] *Bulli Coal Mining Co* v. *Osborne* [1899] AC 351 (HL).
[212] *Broome* above note 207, 1130 (Lord Diplock).
[213] *Kuddus* v. *Chief Constable of Leicestershire Constabulary* [2001] 2 WLR 1789 (HL) 1807 (Lord Nicholls) 1819 (Lord Scott).
[214] Indeed, some cases on exemplary damages confine the award to the amount of the profits made as "a starting-point for assessing punitive damages": *Douglass* v. *Hustler Magazine Inc* 769 F 2d 1128 (1985 CA 7th Circuit) 1145.
[215] *Broome* above note 207, 1129.

the defendants to make a profit for themselves. In the House of Lords the award of exemplary damages was upheld and its goal, to strip these profits, was affirmed as valid.

(ii) Intimidation

The tort of intimidation involves a threat by A of an unlawful[216] act which intentionally induces B to act (or abstain from acting) in a way causing detriment to himself (two party intimidation in which B brings the action) or a third party C (three party intimidation in which C brings the action).[217] In *Rookes* v. *Barnard*[218] the claimant resigned his membership of a registered trade union. The union informed the employer corporation that if the claimant was not dismissed other employees would, in breach of contract, go on strike. Fearing the severe consequences of the threatened breach of contract, the corporation suspended the claimant from work and several weeks later dismissed him. The claimant commenced an action against a number of defendants, including several members of the union that had exerted the pressure on the corporation, for the tort of intimidation.

The House of Lords awarded a new trial on the issue of damages for the tort of intimidation in order to determine whether exemplary damages should be awarded. In doing so, the House of Lords implicitly approved the possibility of awarding exemplary damages if "in all the circumstances" the conduct fell within one of the limbs proposed by Lord Devlin, including the second limb—cynical breach.[219]

(iii) Other torts

Concurrently with the operation of common law disgorgement damages which operate to strip a defendant of profits from trespass, the second limb of exemplary damages has been used to strip profits made cynically in cases of trespass including unlawful eviction of tenants.[220] The second limb has been used for other torts including false imprisonment,[221] assault and battery,[222] malicious prosecution,[223] and misfeasance in public office[224] and, following the rejection of the cause of action test by the House of Lords in the *Kuddus* case, it is both generally available and regarded as a more extreme remedy than the less objectionable disgorgement damages.[225] Disgorgement damages should therefore also be available to strip profits and deter cynical and wilful wrongdoing for all these torts.

[216] *Allen* v. *Flood* [1898] AC 1 (HL).
[217] *Rookes* v. *Barnard* [1964] AC 1129 (HL).
[218] *Rookes* above note 217.
[219] *Rookes* above note 217, 1232.
[220] *Drane* v. *Evangelou* [1978] 1 WLR 455 (CA); *Law Commission 1997* 4.17. See also *Mehta* v. *Royal Bank of Scotland* [1999] 3 EGLR 153.
[221] *Huckle* v. *Money* (1763) 2 Wils KB 205; 95 ER 769.
[222] *Benson* v. *Frederick* (1766) 3 Burr 1845; 97 ER 1130.
[223] *Leith* v. *Pope* (1779) 2 Black W 1327; 96 ER 777.
[224] *Kuddus* v. *Chief Constable of Leicestershire Constabulary* [2001] 2 WLR 1789 (HL).
[225] *Kuddus* above note 224, 1807 (Lord Nicholls) 1819 (Lord Scott).

2) Obstacles

(a) Halifax *v.* Thomas

In *Halifax Building Society* v. *Thomas*[226] the appellant building society gave a mortgage to Thomas induced by fraudulent misrepresentations from him as to his identity and creditworthiness. After Thomas defaulted upon the mortgage the society discovered the fraud and commenced proceedings against him. The society obtained an order for possession of the mortgaged property. The property was sold for a high price leaving a surplus of more than £10,000. After the conviction of Thomas the Crown obtained a confiscation order for the value of the surplus.[227] The society argued that the surplus was its property and not the property of Thomas and that the confiscation order could not attach to it.

Before the Court of Appeal, the society argued, in two alternative submission, that it owned the surplus. The first relied upon a condition of the mortgage which provided that the mortgage was security for "all moneys which may be or become owing". It was argued that because of Thomas" fraud he was liable to account for any profits made and that this liability to account was money "owing" secured by the mortgage. As a result, the surplus from the sale[228] was also secured by the mortgage and belonged to the society. The second submission was that the society was entitled to a constructive trust over the profits of fraud in the same manner as such an award has been made for a breach of fiduciary duty. This argument related exclusively to proprietary relief and is considered in the concluding chapter in this book.

The Court of Appeal rejected the first argument for two reasons. First, because the provision in the mortgage did not cover liabilities other than debts to the society and so a liability to account did not entitle the society to displace the equity of redemption. Secondly, and strictly obiter dicta, because Thomas was, in any event, not liable to account to the Society for the profits made from his fraud. In the leading judgment, Peter Gibson LJ stated that:[229]

> "there is no decided authority that comes anywhere near to covering the present circumstances . . . on the facts of the present case, in my judgment, the fraud is not in itself a sufficient factor to allow the society to require Mr Thomas to account to it."

The obiter dicta assertion that there is no authority requiring disgorgement of profits of fraud is demonstrably wrong. The extended tort of deceit or fraud, in cases discussed above, clearly allowed disgorgement of profits. The same disgorgement exists in the jurisdiction to award "compound interest" for fraud in order "to disgorge a profit made . . . which should not have been made".[230]

---

[226] [1996] Ch 217 (CA).

[227] Section 79(3) of the Criminal Justice Act 1988.

[228] Pursuant to his equity of reversion under s. 105 of the Law of Property Act 1925.

[229] *Halifax Building Society* v. *Thomas* [1996] Ch 217 (CA) 227–228.

[230] *Westdeutsche Landesbank Girozentrale* v. *Islington LBC* [1996] AC 669 (HL) 723 (Lord Woolf).

Peter Gibson LJ made another incidental point. He considered that "there is an inconsistency between a person being [a contractual] creditor and yet claiming more than that to which he is contractually entitled".[231] However, there is no inconsistency once it is appreciated that the claim is based upon the tort and not a concurrently existing contract. The House of Lords have allowed disgorgement of profits for breach of fiduciary duty in circumstances in which a contract exists and a claim in tort should not be any different.[232]

(b) Re Simms

In *Re Simms*,[233] a builder had assigned his business and assets to a company in exchange for shares in the company. After the builder went bankrupt the trustee in bankruptcy succeeded in avoiding the transaction and sought the return of the chattels. This was not contested. In the meantime, the company had gone into receivership and the receiver had used those chattels to make significant profits from pre-existing contracts. The trustee sought an award representing the profits made as either "damages" (which the Court of Appeal treated as compensatory damages) or as money had and received. The Court of Appeal rejected this claim to the profits.

This case is not an obstacle to the award of disgorgement damages. The receiver had acted wrongfully, but not deliberately or cynically. Lawrence LJ stated that "it is not suggested that the receiver . . . acted otherwise than with the utmost good faith".[234] Further, the reasoning of the case relating to money had and received is infected with the rejected "implied contract" reasoning.[235] For instance, Lord Hanworth MR stated that "determining that the receiver was a trespasser . . . cut away the possibility of imputing the fiction of a promise to the receiver".[236]

(c) Hart *v*. Dutton

Hart v. *E P Dutton & Co Inc*[237] is another authority said to be an obstacle to recognition of disgorgement damages.[238] Merwin K Hart sued the publisher of a book, *Under Cover*, which held him out as a traitor during World War II. Hart sued for the profits the publisher had made through the sale of the book as money had and received. An action for libel was subject to a one year limitation period which had expired. Hart brought a claim for money had and received to strip the defendant of the profits, an action which he argued was based upon an implied contract and subject to the contract limitation period of 6 years.

[231] *Halifax Building Society* above note 229, 227.
[232] *Gluckstein* v. *Barnes* [1900] AC 240 (HL). See also C Mitchell "No Account of Profits for a Victim of Deceit" [1996] LMCLQ 314, 316.
[233] [1934] 1 Ch 1 (CA).
[234] *Re Simms* above note 233, 25.
[235] *Re Simms* above note 233, 20, 27, 32.
[236] *Re Simms* above note 233, 20.
[237] 93 NYS (2d) 871 (1949 DCNY); Affirmed *Hart* v. *E P Dutton & Co Inc* 98 NYS (2d) 773 (1950 SCNY).
[238] P Birks *Introduction* 328.

The claim to the profits was denied for two reasons. First, the limitation period could not be avoided as the claim for disgorgement damages, in the form of money had and received, was considered as effectively a claim to "damages" and therefore covered by the same limitation period as a claim for compensatory damages for torts. Secondly, the claim would have been rejected anyway because it was for the entirety of the publishers profits. Malpass J was uncomfortable making an award which involved an "inequitable" assertion of "a right to the fruits of the defendant's labour and investment even beyond that which may flow from the alleged libel".[239] These remarks should not be seen as suggesting that the award of disgorgement damages is not available to strip profits from a cynical libel. They should simply be seen as requiring that only *that part* of the profits resulting from the libel can be disgorged, not the profits from the entire book. An award operating to strip profits from *that* part of a book which is libellous is precisely what the award of exemplary damages did in the *Broome* case.[240] To the extent that the case suggests anything more than this, it has been criticised by Goff and Jones as "unpersuasive".[241]

CONCLUSION

This chapter has applied the theory, developed in the first three chapters of this book, to the branch of common law wrongs known as torts. It has been shown that in cases of torts the common law has used a number of different labels to reverse transfers and disgorge profits.

In the case of awards which seek to reverse transfers of value, once these differently labelled awards are examined together (under the label "restitutionary damages") it can be seen that the law has evidenced an intention to reverse all tortious transfers of value. In the case of those awards which seek to disgorge profits, again viewed as a single body, the label disgorgement damages can be applied to them and the common intention to strip profits from cynical tortfeasors (where compensatory damages are an inadequate remedy to deter wrongdoing) is immediately apparent.

---

[239] *Hart* v. *Dutton* above note 237, 877.
[240] *Broome* v. *Cassell & Co* [1972] AC 1027 (HL).
[241] *Goff and Jones* 782.

5

Breach of Contract

INTRODUCTION

THE DECISION OF the House of Lords in *Attorney General* v. *Blake*[1] marked a watershed not only for the award of gain-based remedies for breach of contract but, as has been seen in the earlier chapters of this book, for the more general discussion of gain-based damages for wrongs. Because of the importance of the decision (in which four Law Lords recognised the availability of disgorgement damages for breach of contract) this chapter will consider the awards of gain-based damages for breach of contract primarily in the context of the *Blake* case.

It will be demonstrated that the *Blake* case can be seen to have effected recognition of disgorgement damages on a principled basis, rationalising prior authority and making rules as to availability of disgorgement damages similar to other wrongs. However, as a result of the *Blake* case, there is one very significant difference between gain-based damages for a breach of contract and gain-based damages for other civil wrongs. The first two sections of this chapter examine the treatment of disgorgement damages and restitutionary damages respectively for breach of contract. It is shown that although there are powerful arguments for treating breach of contract in the same way as other civil wrongs, the House of Lords in the *Blake* case required an additional element before gain-based damages could be allowed.

In the leading speech in the *Blake* case, Lord Nicholls came close to recognising that breach of contract should be treated in the same way as other civil wrongs. He stated that "it is not easy to see why, as between parties to a contract, a violation of a party's contractual right should attract a lesser degree of remedy than a violation of his property rights".[2] Professor Friedmann has even argued that contractual rights *are* a form of property right.[3] However, even Professor Friedmann concedes that some cases, such as standard contracts of employment, involve contractual rights (of an employer to the labour of the employee) which are unlikely to be considered as property interests.[4] The additional limitation on gain-based damages for a breach of contract introduced by

---

[1] [2001] 1 AC 268 (HL).

[2] *Blake* above note 1, 283.

[3] D Friedmann "Restitution of Benefits Obtained Through the Appropriation of Property or the Commission of a Wrong" (1980) 80 Col Law Rev 504, 513. See also L Smith "Disgorgement of the Profits of Breach of Contract: Property, Contract and 'Efficient Breach' " (1995) 24 Can Bus LJ 121.

[4] D Friedmann "Restitution" above note 3, 520.

the House of Lords in the *Blake* case is a requirement that the claimant have a "legitimate interest" in the performance of the contract. This limitation upon gain-based damages, unique in cases of breach of contract, operates to deny the same protection to contractual interests which the law has traditionally afforded to other property rights, unless it is satisfied.

After the consideration of disgorgement damages and restitutionary damages in the first two sections, the final section of this chapter considers an action for breach of promise which is not in the traditional contractual form (either as a deed or supported by consideration). This action for breach of promise is hidden in the terminology of "estoppel" but should be treated in exactly the same manner as the law treats contracts supported by consideration or in the form of a deed.

Throughout this chapter it is assumed that a breach of contract is a wrong which consists of a breach of the promised duty to perform for which the remedy compensatory damages is possible. Arguments that breach of contract cannot be a wrong—because there is never a duty to perform—are rejected in the context of arguments which are raised against disgorgement damages.

A Disgorgement damages

1) *The* Blake *litigation*

(a) *History*

George Blake was a member of the British Secret Intelligence Service who, between 1951 and 1960, disclosed valuable and secret information to Russia. He was convicted in 1961 and sentenced to 42 years imprisonment in England. In 1966, after a dramatic escape from prison, he went to live in Moscow where he remains. In 1989 he entered into a contract with the publisher Jonathan Cape Ltd for the publication of a book of his memoirs entitled "No Other Choice". The publication of the book was in breach of the Official Secrets Act 1989[5] as well as an express prohibition in Blake's 1944 contract of employment against revealing any information (confidential or otherwise) obtained as an agent of the government. The book was published in 1990. Once the Crown was aware of the publication, it was too late to obtain an injunction to restrain publication as the book had been widely disseminated.[6]

In 1991 the Crown brought an action against George Blake and Jonathan Cape Ltd (as a third party) seeking remedies including disgorgement damages (as an account of profits) for breach of copyright and breach of fiduciary duty.[7]

---

[5] In fact, Blake's disclosure probably came before the Act came into force on 1 March 1990 so that the offence was properly covered by the Official Secrets Act 1911. This point was never taken during the litigation.

[6] *Attorney General* v. *Guardian Newspapers (No 2)* [1990] 1 AC 109 (HL).

[7] No claim was made for breach of confidence on the basis that although the information might have lost its confidentiality at the time of publication, George Blake was under a lifelong obligation

At first instance, Sir Richard Scott V-C held that the fiduciary duty owed by former members of the intelligence services did not extend to prohibit disclosure of information which was no longer confidential.[8] The Court of Appeal agreed with this finding. However, during the hearing before the Court of Appeal, the Court stated that it would like to hear argument on whether a public law claim could be made for an injunction to restrain the defendant from receiving any profits as a result of his crime.[9] The Court also asked the Crown if they wished to make an argument based upon whether the account of profits could be made on the basis of Blake's breach of contract rather than his breach of fiduciary duty. The Crown argued the public law issue but declined the opportunity to seek disgorgement damages (an account of profits) for Blake's breach of contract.[10]

In a joint judgment of the Court of Appeal, the Court stated that disgorgement damages (which they referred to as "restitutionary damages") would have been given if they had been sought. As George Blake had been unrepresented at first instance and before the Court of Appeal, and as the Court had allowed the Crown's public law claim for an injunction, the Court of Appeal also thought that there was "no possibility" of an appeal to the House of Lords.[11] The Court, therefore, considered it appropriate to examine the basis of such an award in detail. As the first explicit judicial discussion of disgorgement damages for a breach of contract, it prompted much academic discussion.[12]

Blake was contacted after the appeal and he gave instructions to apply for leave to appeal to the House of Lords. Leave was subsequently granted in relation to two issues.[13] The first was whether the Court of Appeal were right to extend the Attorney General's powers to obtain an injunction. The second was whether disgorgement damages could be awarded for a breach of contract.

For the first time in history, the House of Lords explicitly confronted the issue of disgorgement damages for a breach of contract.[14] There was an appeal and a cross-appeal. The appeal by Blake was against the award of an injunction and the cross appeal by the Crown, at the initiative of the Law Lords, sought disgorgement damages (an account of profits) for the breach of contract.

of confidence: *Attorney General* v. *Blake* [1998] Ch 439 (CA) 444; cf. *Attorney General* v. *Guardian Newspapers (No 2)* [1990] 1 AC 109 (HL). However, the Court of Appeal appeared to indicate that this concession was properly made: *Attorney General* v. *Blake* [1998] Ch 439 (CA) 454.

[8] *Attorney General* v. *Blake* (CA) above note 7.
[9] Extending *Gouriet* v. *Union of Post Office Workers* [1978] AC 435 (HL).
[10] *Attorney General* v. *Blake* (CA) above note 7, 456.
[11] *Attorney General* v. *Blake* (CA) above note 7, 456.
[12] G Virgo "Clarifying Restitution for Wrongs (Attorney General v Blake)" [1998] RLR 118, 125; C Mitchell "Remedial Inadequacy in Contract and the Role of Restitutionary Damages" (1999) 15(2) JCL 133; M Haliwell "Profits from Wrongdoing: Private and Public Law Perspectives" (1999) 62 MLR 271; M Chen-Wishart "Restitutionary Damages for Breach of Contract" (1998) 114 LQR 363.
[13] *Attorney General* v. *Blake* [1999] 1 WLR 1279 (Application for Leave).
[14] Their Lordships refused the Attorney-General leave to put the case on the alternative basis seeking "restitutionary damages for the criminal wrong". For such arguments see G Virgo *Restitution* 556.

Delivering the leading speech, Lord Nicholls (Lords Goff and Browne-Wilkinson agreeing, Lord Steyn delivering a concurring speech and Lord Hobhouse dissenting) held that disgorgement damages could be awarded against Blake to recover the profits from his breach of contract.[15] As a result, for the majority, the public law claim to an injunction did not arise. However, in the majority speeches Lords Nicholls and Steyn indicated that they would not have allowed that claim and Lord Hobhouse agreed on this point. Each speech indicated that the effect of such an injunction was confiscatory in nature and that there was no common law power to confiscate property.[16]

The focus of all the speeches was, therefore, on the award of disgorgement damages and when such an award is appropriate for a breach of contract. However, in the course of the leading speech, Lord Nicholls also considered gain-based awards for a breach of contract generally and, although not describing them as such, restitutionary damages.

(b) *The test proposed by the House of Lords*

In the leading speech Lord Nicholls considered that disgorgement damages could be awarded against Blake because the circumstances were exceptional. The circumstances of Blake's deliberate, criminal breaches of his contract combined with the fact that the undertaking was akin to a fiduciary obligation and the fact that the profits arose from his breaches of contract were together sufficient to allow an account to be taken of his profits. In discussing the other circumstances in which an account of profits would be available for a breach of contract, Lord Nicholls refused to prescribe any "fixed rules":[17]

> "The court will have regard to all the circumstances, including the subject matter of the contract, the purpose of the contractual provision which has been breached, the circumstances in which the breach occurred, the consequences of the breach and the circumstances in which relief is sought. A useful general guide, although not exhaustive, is whether the plaintiff had a legitimate interest in preventing the defendant's profit-making activity and, hence, in depriving him of his profit."

In his concurring speech, Lord Steyn also refused to lay down any firm rules, preferring that they be "hammered out on the anvil of concrete cases".[18]

Despite the apparent vagueness of this approach, throughout his speech Lord Nicholls did lay down a "general guide" for when disgorgement damages will be available for a breach of contract. A close analysis of his decision suggests that two requirements should be necessary to fulfil the "guidelines" required. The first requirement is one which is not necessary when gain-based disgorgement

---

[15] As discussed in ch. 3, Lord Nicholls described the award as an "account of profits" deliberately avoiding the Crown's preferred term, "restitutionary damages", and Lord Steyn described the award as disgorgement of profits: ch. 3 note 71, 81.

[16] *Attorney General* v. *De Keyser's Royal Hotel Ltd* [1920] AC 508 (HL); *Burmah Oil Co Ltd* v. *Lord Advocate* [1965] AC 75 (HL).

[17] *Blake* above note 1, 285.

[18] *Blake* above note 1, 291.

damages are sought for other civil wrongs. This is a requirement that the contractual provision breached must be one which courts are prepared to protect as a primary right. Lord Nicholls expressed this as a requirement that the defendant have a "legitimate interest in performance". Second, like other wrongs, it would seem that it is necessary that the breach be cynical so that compensatory damages would not be an adequate remedy. Each of these requirements is examined in detail below.

Lord Hobhouse dissented on the basis that if non-compensatory damages were to be introduced into the law of contract, "the consequences would be far reaching and disruptive" and he refused to "depart from principle".[19] However, he would have been prepared to award damages based upon a reasonable value of rights appropriated by Blake as compensation. As explained in chapter three, Lord Hobhouse, with respect, was incorrect to view cases awarding damages of a reasonable sum as "compensatory damages". The point will be reiterated below that these cases can only properly be seen as non-compensatory awards of restitutionary damages.

(i) A legitimate interest in performance

The first requirement for disgorgement damages in Lord Nicholls' speech was that the claimant has a legitimate interest in the performance of the contractual provision breached.[20] Lord Nicholls stated that this legitimate interest was required for the disgorgement damages remedy of an account of profits in the same way as a legitimate interest in performance was required for an order for specific performance or an injunction.[21] The difficult question is when a claimant has a legitimate interest in performance. The more stringent this test for "legitimate interest" the more exceptional disgorgement damages will be for a breach of contract.

The notion that, in some circumstances, a claimant might not have an "interest in performance" might derive support from Oliver Wendell Holmes, who thought that a claimant never had a legitimate interest in performance. Holmes considered that "the only universal consequence of a legally binding promise is that the law makes the promisor pay damages if the promised event does not come to pass".[22] He therefore considered that a promisee should be free to break his contract if he chooses.

It has been said that this is "a faulty analysis of legal obligations [because] . . . the promisee [always] has a legal right to the performance of the contract".[23]

---

[19] *Blake* above note 1, 298.
[20] *Blake* above note 1, 285.
[21] *Blake* above note 1, 285.
[22] OW Holmes *The Common Law* (Dover New York 1881) 301. See also OW Holmes "The Path of the Law" (1897) 10 Harv L Rev 457, 462; *Globe Refining Co* v. *London Western Oil Co* (1903) 190 US 540 (SCUS) 544 (Holmes J).
[23] *Coulls* v. *Bagot's Executor and Trustee Co Ltd* (1967) 119 CLR 460 (HCA) 504 (Windeyer J); *Beswick* v. *Beswick* [1968] AC 58 (HL) 91 (Lord Pearce); *Raymond* v. *Yarrington* 96 Tex 443, 451; 73 S W 800, 803 (1903 SC Tex).

However, the law has not always provided the promisee with remedies to protect adequately such a legal right to performance of the contract. Without adequate remedies to enforce or protect a right to performance, such a right sometimes appears empty or illegitimate.[24]

An example of inadequate protection being afforded to contractual rights, such that it might be said that there is no legitimate interest in performance, is when a claimant is not always entitled to insist upon performance following repudiation by the other party to a contract. In cases where the defendant has repudiated, it is said that the claimant must have a "legitimate interest in performance"[25] in order to be able to continue to perform and claim counter-performance, even if the counter-performance is only payment of the price.[26] The right only to compensation, and not to performance, is sometimes said to be one of the policies underlying the rejection of a general right to specific performance[27] and the refusal of exemplary damages for any breach of contract.[28] Unlike courts in Canada,[29] English courts refuse to award exemplary damages for a breach of contract even when, as the Ontario High Court have stated, the cynical breach of contract would allow the law "to say to the rich and powerful, 'do what you like, you will only have to make good the plaintiff's actual financial loss, which compared to your budget is negligible' ".[30] Another example is the fact that parties to a contract cannot insert provisions into the contract that operate to penalise and deter breach.[31] If the parties truly had a legitimate interest in performance then such penalty clauses would merely be a way of protecting that interest.

(ii) Compensation inadequate

Satisfaction of the first aspect of Lord Nicholls' test does not entitle a claimant to disgorgement damages. The second requirement is that the legitimate interest in contractual performance is insufficiently protected by compensatory damages. Lord Nicholls stated:[32]

---

[24] SM Waddams "Breach of Contract and the Concept of Wrongdoing" (2000) 12 SCLR (2d) 1.

[25] *White & Carter Councils* v. *McGregor* [1962] AC 413 (HL).

[26] *Clea Shipping Corporation* v. *Bulk Oil International Ltd ("The Alaskan Trader")* [1983] 2 Lloyds Rep 645.

[27] *Co-operative Insurance Society Ltd* v. *Argyll Stores (Holdings) Ltd* [1998] AC 1 (HL) 11 (Lord Hoffmann).

[28] *Thyssen Inc* v. *SS Fortune Star* 777 F 2d 57 (2nd Cir 1985) 63, approved in *Gray* v. *Motor Accident Commission* (1998) 196 CLR 1 (HCA). It has been noted that if it were to be properly recognised that a breach of contract is a breach of duty then exemplary damages *should* be available: N McBride "A Case for Awarding Punitive Damages in Response to Deliberate Breaches of Contract" [1995] Anglo-American LR 369, 390.

[29] *Royal Bank of Canada* v. *W Got* (2000) 178 DLR 385 (SCC). Cf *Gray* above note 28. This refusal to grant exemplary damages is criticised in J Edelman "Exemplary Damages for Breach of Contract" (2001) 117 LQR 539 where the Canadian position, which awards exemplary damages when all other remedies (including disgorgement damages) are inadequate, is advocated.

[30] *Natel* v. *Parisien* (1981) 18 CCLT 89 (HCO); See also *Brown* v. *Waterloo Regional Board of Commissioners of Police* (1982) 37 OR (2d) 277 (HCO) 292–293.

[31] *Dunlop Pneumatic Tyre Co Ltd* v. *New Garage & MotorCo Ltd* [1915] AC 79 (HL).

[32] *Blake* above note 1, 282, 285.

"It is equally well established that an award of [compensatory] damages, assessed by reference to financial loss, is not always 'adequate' as a remedy for breach of contract . . . Normally the remedies of damages, specific performance and injunction, coupled with the characterisation of some contractual obligations as fiduciary, will provide an adequate response to a breach of contract. It will only be in exceptional cases, where those remedies are inadequate, that any question of accounting for profits will arise."

The classic instance in which compensatory damages are inadequate as a remedy to protect rights is where the duties generated by those rights are cynically breached. Once the first part of Lord Nicholls' test is satisfied, it seems that breach of contract should be treated in the same manner as other wrongs and disgorgement damages should be available to deter cynical breaches of a defendant's legitimate right to performance. However, the only occasion in which Lord Nicholls referred to "cynical breach" he did note that by itself it was not sufficient for the disgorgement damages award of an account of profits.

(c) *Application of the test*

(i) A legitimate interest in performance

Lord Nicholls' speech refers to a number of cases and provides strong indicia of when each limb of his test will be satisfied. In relation to the first limb—the requirement of a legitimate right to performance—his speech highlights three examples.

Specific performance is the first example. Specific performance in English law is not a general remedy and is only available in limited circumstances. Where it is available it is explicit recognition of a right to performance and hence, a legitimate interest of the claimant in performance. Lord Nicholls referred to the case of *Lake* v. *Bayliss*[33] as endorsing an award of disgorgement damages in such circumstances.

In the *Lake* case the defendant had contracted to convey land to the claimant in exchange for the claimant withdrawing two claims against her. In breach of contract she sold the land to a third party. Her solicitor received the sale proceeds and an interpleader summons was brought to determine who was entitled to them. Although the claimant could have sued for the value of the proceeds as compensatory damages (assuming that they represented the value of the land), Walton J held that as the initial contract was specifically enforceable the defendant was a trustee of any proceeds received and must therefore account for them.[34] In approving this result, Lord Nicholls stated that it would not be necessary to characterise the defendant as holding the land on trust in order to disgorge the profits from the second sale. Relying on the breach of contract itself would be sufficient.[35]

Injunctions restraining breaches of negative contractual provisions also illustrate this right to performance. As Professor Burrows notes, an injunction

---

[33] [1974] 1 WLR 1073.
[34] *Lake* above note 33, 1076.
[35] *Blake* above note 1, 284.

"belongs on the reverse side of the coin from specific performance, which enforces a positive contractual promise".[36] This was the *Blake* case itself. Had the Crown discovered that the book was going to be published in time, an injunction would have been available. Such an injunction would amount to a requirement specifically to perform the covenant not to reveal information acquired during the course of employment in the Secret Services.

Lord Nicholls endorsed two other cases in this category. The first, *British Motor Trade Association* v. *Gilbert*,[37] concerned a defendant that had sought to sell his car in breach of a statutory scheme prohibiting second-hand sales of cars (without consent). An injunction had been obtained but the car was sold in breach of that injunction. Danckwerts J held that the scheme was not in restraint of trade as it was "in the interests of the general public and fair dealing".[38] Lord Nicholls endorsed the award in that case as an appropriate one to strip the defendant of profits made.[39]

The second case in this category endorsed by Lord Nicholls was *Reid-Newfoundland Co* v. *Anglo-American Telegraph Co Ltd*.[40] In that case a railway company had contracted with a telegraph company for the telegraph company to install a "special wire" for the railway company and their successors to use. The railway company promised not to use the wire to transmit any commercial messages except "for the benefit and account of the telegraph company".[41] Successors of the railway company, with notice of the covenant, later used the wire for their own business purposes. The Privy Council held that the successor company must account for the profits accruing from the use of the wire, comparing the liability to account for profits to that of a trustee in breach.[42] Although the successors to the railway company were not a party to the original contract, the Privy Council were not concerned with this distinction as the successors took the assignment of the railway company's rights with notice of the contractual restriction. Indeed, Lord Nicholls in the *Blake* case approved the account of profits in the *Reid* case as an award for a breach of contract, assuming the defendants to have been the original railway company.[43]

The difficulty with using the availability of an injunction to satisfy the "legitimate interest" requirement for disgorgement damages is that although injunctions to restrain breaches of negative contractual provisions are common the principles governing their availability are not certain. Lord Goodhart and Professor Jones have observed that "it is difficult to find any principle unifying

---

[36] A Burrows *Remedies* 403.
[37] [1951] 2 All ER 641.
[38] *British Motor Trade Association* v. *Gilbert* above note 37, 644.
[39] *Blake* above note 1, 284.
[40] [1912] AC 555 (PC).
[41] *Reid-Newfoundland Co* above note 40, 558.
[42] *Reid-Newfoundland Co* above note 40, 559 (Lord Robson). No precise evidence was given as to whether any actual profit had been made from the unauthorised use of the wire (as opposed to expense saved) but the matter was referred to a Registrar.
[43] *Blake* above note 1, 234.

the cases in which an English Court has restrained the breach of such commercial contracts".[44] With 150 years of judicial decisions on injunctions this question still remains much disputed.[45] Although in *Doherty* v. *Allman*[46] Lord Cairns LC described "the specific performance . . . of that negative right" as a "matter of right" this overstates the principle.[47] For instance, an injunction could be refused because of the claimant's own conduct,[48] where it would amount to indirect specific performance where specific performance is not available,[49] or where the breach is merely trivial.[50]

A third illustration of where the law recognises that a claimant has a right to performance is in cases of fiduciary relationships. Fiduciary relationships often arise in contractual situations. In such cases one contracting party is required to act exclusively in the interests of the other.[51] An injunction can be easily obtained to prevent a fiduciary acting contrary to the contract;[52] indeed it is said that an injunction can be obtained in these cases as of right.[53] In *CMS Dolphin Ltd* v. *Simonet*[54] Lawrence Collins J recently held that a director who diverted corporate opportunities to a new company, after having left the previous company, was liable to pay either compensation for the breach of fiduciary duty and breaches of his contract of employment or to account for profits from the breach of fiduciary duty. However, he noted that the profits could also have been stripped for the breach of an implied contractual term of fidelity because of this fiduciary context:

> "If there had been no effective remedy in relation to the allegations of breach of fiduciary duty, I would have held that the breach of the duty of fidelity . . . would have justified the remedy of an account of profits and not simply [compensatory] damages. In *Att. Gen.* v. *Blake* [2000] 3 W.L.R. 625, 639 (H.L.) Lord Nicholls said that one of the exceptional circumstances which would justify a restitutionary remedy for breach of contract was the characterisation of a contractual obligation as fiduciary and a finding that the claimant has a legitimate interest in preventing the profit-making activity of the defendant. This is such a case."

[44] G Jones, W Goodhart *Specific Performance* (2nd edn. Butterworths London 1996) 318.

[45] *Co-operative Insurance Society Ltd* above note 27, 14.

[46] (1878) 3 App Cas 719, 720.

[47] Meagher et al. *Equity* 568, 572.

[48] "He who comes to equity must come with clean hands": Cases cited in JM Paterson (ed.) *Kerr on Injunctions* (6th edn. Sweet and Maxwell London 1927) 413.

[49] Such as injunctions seeking to prevent the defendant working for anyone except the claimant: *Whitwood Chemical Co* v. *Hardman* [1891] 2 Ch 416; *Ehrman* v. *Bartholemew* [1898] 1 Ch 671. Although as Sir George Jessel MR noted, this area is beset by inconsistencies: *Fothergill* v. *Rowland* (1873) LR 17 Eq 132, 141; G Jones, W Goodhart *Specific Performance* (2nd edn. Butterworths London 1996) 318.

[50] *Harrison* v. *Good* (1871) LR 11 Eq 338, 352.

[51] It has been stated that the strict fiduciary *obligation* is ultimately an imposed and not an accepted one: P Finn "The Fiduciary Principle" in T Youdan (ed.) *Equity, Fiduciaries and Trusts* (Carswell Toronto 1989) 54.

[52] *Pacifica Shipping Co Ltd* v. *Andersen* [1986] 2 NZLR 328 (HCNZ).

[53] Meagher et al. *Equity* 532.

[54] (High Court 23 May 2001).

It is very unclear how far the law will recognise a legitimate interest in performance outside these three situations identified by Lord Nicholls. Even within the examples given by Lord Nicholls the law is not entirely clear. However, broad markers establish the nature of the "legitimate interest" in performance; there is no legitimate interest (which would allow disgorgement damages) where the contractual provision would not be protected by injunctions or specific performance. Common examples of this are contractual breaches which are trivial or in contracts for personal service where to enforce the contractual provision would unreasonably restrain the liberty of the defendant. The other usual requirement for specific performance, that "compensatory damages are inadequate" is duplicated in the second condition for disgorgement damages; the requirement of wilful or cynical breach.

(ii) Compensation inadequate

Even where there is a legitimate interest in performance, it is necessary, in the words of Lord Nicholls, that "normal remedies" will not "provide an adequate response to a breach of contract".[55] Normal remedies, such as compensatory damages, are inadequate when they are unable to protect the claimant's interest in having the contract performed.[56] As discussed in chapter one, the classic instance of this is where the contract is cynically breached. Where the defendant can wilfully breach a contract and make a gain which exceeds any loss to the claimant, compensatory damages will afford insufficient protection because, in the words of Lord Goff, they allow a defendant to "repudiate with impunity".[57]

In *Lumley* v. *Wagner*[58] Mr Lumley had secured an injunction to prevent his contracted singer, Ms Wagner, from singing for his rival Mr Gye during the period of her contract. There was a provision in her contract expressly forbidding her to sing for anyone else. Given that Mr Lumley had a legitimate interest in her performance (protected by the injunction), if Ms Wagner had sung for Mr Gye, could Mr Lumley have obtained disgorgement damages of the profit she made by doing so?

In the case of an innocent breach by Ms Wagner, which did not affect the contract with Mr Lumley, compensatory damages would suffice and no additional deterrence would be required. However, a cynical breach should entitle Mr Lumley to disgorgement damages. This is why Lord Nicholls observed that "something more" is required than "mere breach" of a negative obligation entitling the claimant to an injunction.[59] The "something more" was an inadequacy of compensatory damages which should be seen as the requirement of cynical breach.

---

[55] *Blake* above note 1, 285.

[56] S Worthington and R Goode "Commercial Law: Confining the Remedial Boundaries" in D Hayton (ed.) *Law's Future(s): British Legal Developments in the 21st Century* (Hart Publishing Oxford 2000) 293.

[57] *Alfred McAlpine Construction Ltd* v. *Panatown Ltd* [2001] 1 AC 518 (HL) 546.

[58] (1852) 1 De G M & G 604; 42 ER 687.

[59] *Blake* above note 1, 286.

(d) *The approaches of the House of Lords and the Court of Appeal compared*

The test of the Court of Appeal contrasts with the approach of the House of Lords because the Court of Appeal were prepared to recognise the availability of disgorgement damages in cases in which compensatory damages were inadequate. The Court of Appeal did not introduce a limitation of whether the claimant has a legitimate interest in performance. Implicit in the reasoning of the Court of Appeal was that there is always a legitimate interest in performance so that if compensatory damages were inadequate to remedy a breach of contract then profits would be stripped to protect that right.

The Court of Appeal considered that "compensatory damages are an inadequate remedy if regard is paid to the objects which the plaintiff sought to achieve" in two situations.[60] The first situation given was a case of "skimped performance" where the defendant saves expense (and often makes additional profit) by deliberately under-performing for the claimant, although the claimant might suffer no loss. The second was the *Blake* case itself where (endorsing a statement of Professor Birks) the Court of Appeal stated that "if you promise not to pursue a particular profit-making activity and you do pursue it, nothing is more apt than that you should make restitution of your profits".[61]

The instance of skimped performance is discussed in detail in relation to restitutionary damages below but the important point to note in comparing the approaches of the Court of Appeal and House of Lords is that in explaining why disgorgement damages should be available when compensatory damages are "inadequate", the Court of Appeal stated that "justice surely demands an award of substantial damages".[62] The "justice" is the necessity of adequately protecting contractual rights.

The House of Lords and the Court of Appeal therefore took similar approaches to disgorgement damages, in requiring an inadequacy of compensatory damages, although they differed in the additional "legitimate interest in performance" limitation imposed by the House of Lords. Although this limitation is criticised below as having no basis in rational principle, it might be said to be more consistent with the history of English contract law than an award of disgorgement damages unlimited by such a requirement. This consistency of the legitimate interest limitation is examined below in considering its legitimacy. However it should be noted that most other jurisdictions which have allowed disgorgement damages for a breach of contract have effectively imposed the same limitation. In the Unites States for instance, disgorgement damages have been awarded for breach of contractual provisions prohibiting competition with a former employer. In such cases, where an injunction is a common remedy to protect the legitimate right to performance of that negative covenant,

---

[60] *Attorney General* v. *Blake* [1998] Ch 439 (CA) 458.
[61] *Attorney General* v. *Blake* (CA) above note 60, 458; P Birks "Restitutionary Damages for Breach of Contract: *Snepp* and the fusion of law and equity" [1987] LMCLQ 421, 434.
[62] *Attorney General* v. *Blake* (CA) above note 60, 457.

courts have held that "the defendant cannot sustain any gain by such wilful mis-conduct on his part".[63] Even in Civilian jurisdictions such as Germany, where a prima facie or general right to specific performance is recognised, a claim to profits from breach of contract is only available when specific performance would have been possible.[64]

(e) *Remoteness of damages*

In chapter three it was explained that recognition of disgorgement damages will require the development of rules of remoteness of damages for those damages awards. It was argued that a sure path forward would be to mirror those rules of remoteness developed in relation to compensatory damages. In cases in which compensatory damages are sought for a breach of contract, the usual rules of remoteness are less clear than when compensatory damages are sought for torts.[65] In tort cases, where a wrong was committed deliberately (such as the wrong of deceit) it was observed that the remoteness rule is not the usual "reasonable fore-seeability" test but one of "directness of consequences".[66] In a case of a deliberate cynical breach of contract this "direct consequences" test could also be applied.

This seems to be the effect of examples and remarks in the Court of Appeal and House of Lords in the *Blake* case. The Court of Appeal, referring to the case of *Teacher* v. *Calder*,[67] emphasised that a test based upon cynical breach was necessary but not sufficient. It was also necessary that "the profits in question are occasioned directly by the breach".[68]

In *Teacher* v. *Calder*[69] the appellant had advanced £15,000 to the respondent for the use in the respondent's timber business. The appellant was to receive interest and a share of the profits from the business. In breach of contract the respondent used the money in a distillery venture instead of his timber business

---

[63] *YJD Restaurant Supply Company* v. *Dib* 413 NYS (2d) 835 (SCNY 1979) 837; *Oscar Barnett Foundry Co* v. *Crowe* 86 A (2d) 915 (1910); EA Farnsworth "Your Loss or My Gain? The Dilemma of the Disgorgement Principle in Breach of Contract" (1985) 94 Yale LJ 1339, 1367. See also the application of the same approach in these cases in the High Court of Ireland and by Deane J in dissent in the High Court of Australia: ; *Hickey* v. *Roche Stores (Dublin) Ltd (No 1)* (1976) [1993] RLR 196 (HCI); *Hospital Products Ltd* v. *US Surgical Corporation* (1984) 156 CLR 41 (HCA) (Deane J dissenting).

[64] Section 281BGB "Delivery of a substitute in case of impossibility". This section should be read with s. 275 which limits the reach of impossibility to cases where the impossibility of performance is due to the defendant's fault; *Oberlandesgericht* (OLG—Court of Appeal) Celle NJW (1954) 679; K Rusch "Restitutionary Damages for Breach of Contract—A Comparative Analysis of English and German Law" (2001) 118 Sth African L J 59, 71; J Kondgen "Immaterialschadenseratz, Gewinnabschöpfung oder Privatstrafen als Sanktionen für Vertragsbruch? Eine rechtsvergleichend-ökonomische Analyse" [1992] RabelsZ 696.

[65] Different tests have been proposed as to whether the reasonable contemplation is of an event which is "not unlikely": *Koufos* v. *C Czarnikow Ltd* [1969] 1 AC 350 (HL) 399, 410–411, 417; H Beale (Gen ed.) *Chitty on Contracts* (1999 Sweet and Maxwell London) 1291 or whether it is a "serious possibility or real danger": *Koufos* v. *C Czarnikow Ltd* [1969] 1 AC 350 (HL) 414–415, 425.

[66] *Doyle* v. *Olby (Ironmongers) Ltd* [1969] 2 QB 158 (CA); *Smith New Court* v. *Scrimgeour Vickers (Asset Management) Ltd* [1997] AC 254 (HL).

[67] [1899] AC 451 (HL).

[68] *Attorney General* v. *Blake* (CA) above note 60, 458.

[69] *Teacher* above note 67.

and made significant profits. The appellant argued that the respondent was liable to disgorge the profits made in the distillery business that could be traced from the money provided for the timber business. In the only speech which addressed the issue, Lord Davey stated that the "money withdrawn was not [the appellant's] in any sense, and he had no interest in it except to have it employed in the respondent's timber business".[70]

In the *Blake* case the Court of Appeal, on a point with which Lord Nicholls agreed in the House of Lords,[71] affirmed the correctness of this result on the basis that the breach of contract in the *Teacher* case merely provided the defendant with an opportunity for profit and did not put it out of his power to perform his contractual obligations.[72] Indeed Lord Davey in the *Teacher* case had observed that the money withdrawn was to some extent replaced by money borrowed from the bank.[73] The profits did not arise sufficiently "directly" from the breach of contract.

The same point was made by Lord Denning, at first instance, in *Reading* v. *The King*.[74] This case was discussed in chapters three and four. It will be recalled that Reading, an army sergeant, had sat in a lorry in his army uniform to allow alcohol to be smuggled through British checkpoints. The speeches in the House of Lords relied upon money had and received at common law as one basis for stripping the profits made from bribes received by Reading. One explanation of the basis of this award of money had and received is that it was an award of disgorgement damages for Reading's breach of contract. Denning J, at first instance, (and Lord Porter in the House of Lords)[75] possibly had this in mind when he stated that the claim of the Crown "rests on the fact that it is the employer . . . and on that account says that it is entitled to the money".[76] Denning J referred to the concerns of remoteness and posed a similar "directness of consequences" test:

"if a servant, in violation of his duty of honesty and good faith, takes advantage of his service to make a profit for himself, in this sense, that the assets of which he has control, or the facilities which he enjoys, or the position which he occupies, are the real cause for his obtaining the money, as distinct from being the mere opportunity for getting it, that is to say, if they play the predominant part in his obtaining the money, then he is accountable for it to the master. It matters not that the master has not lost any profit nor suffered any damage."

Other examples can be given. In one case, counsel for the applicant, Robert Goff QC (who later sat as a Lord in the *Blake* case) argued that the owners of a ship that repudiated a time charter-party to re-hire the ship on a rising market

---

[70] *Teacher* above note 67, 468.
[71] *Blake* above note 1, 285.
[72] *Attorney General* v. *Blake* (CA) above note 60, 458.
[73] *Teacher* above note 67, 468.
[74] [1948] 2 KB 268, 275.
[75] *Reading* above note 74, 516.
[76] *Reading* above note 74, 275.

should be liable for the disgorgement damages remedy of an account of profits. Kerr J rightly refused to make this award. The profit was not directly occasioned by the breach. The breach was in withdrawing the ship, not in subsequently rehiring it.[77]

This discussion illustrates the reason why disgorgement damages should be refused in cases of breach of contract which merely create an opportunity for profit rather than the profit itself. The remoteness limitation. The profits do not derive directly from the wrong where, in the words of Lord Denning, they do not "play a predominant part" in the making of the profit.

2) Objections

There are four arguments that are specifically raised against allowing disgorgement damages for a breach of contract. The first argument takes several forms. Each form of this argument seeks to reject disgorgement damages on the basis that there is no right to performance of a contract; the only right is said to be to compensatory damages if performance is not rendered. Lord Nicholls' legitimate performance interest limitation upon disgorgement damages seems to concede partly to this view; the suggestion that a claimant does not always have a legitimate interest supposes instances in which the claimant has no right to performance.

The other three arguments against disgorgement damages for a breach of contract are more easily dismissed. The second argument is one of "floodgates". The argument is that if disgorgement damages are allowed commercial uncertainty will result and that this is unacceptable in the very commercial area of contract law.[78] The third and fourth arguments are that these awards might allow a claimant to escape her duty to mitigate and that they might allow a claimant the benefit of the skill and initiative of the defendant, of which the defendant should not be deprived save in exceptional circumstances.

(a) There is never a "legitimate interest" in performance

(i) Efficient breach
Suppose X has entered into a contract with Y for the sale of 100 widgets, which only X can supply. Y offers to pay £100 for the widgets and will suffer £10 loss without them. Subsequently Z offers X £200 for the widgets. The doctrine of efficient breach suggests that it is socially desirable for X to break his contract with Y for the supply of the widgets and supply them instead to Z. The doctrine suggests that the best position for society would be reached by a rule that required X only to compensate Y for the £10 loss if X sells the widgets to Z. This

[77] See also *Occidental Worldwide Investment Corp* v. *Skibs A/S* ("*The Siboen and the Sibotre*") [1976] 1 Lloyds Rep 293. See also *University of Nottingham* v. *Fishel* [2001] RPC 367 discussed below text accompanying note 93.
[78] *Surrey County Council* v. *Bredero Homes Ltd* [1993] 1 WLR 1361 (CA) 1370 (Steyn LJ); G Treitel *The Law of Contract* (10th edn. Sweet and Maxwell London 1999) 868.

rule would leave X with an additional £90 profit from the sale to Z. The reason why efficient breach suggests this is the most desirable social result is because this approach is said to allow resources to find their best (or most efficient) use without making anyone worse off.[79] Z, who is prepared to pay more for the widgets, is considered a more efficient place for the widgets to be than with Y who is no worse off, as any losses from the lack of widgets will be compensated.

The doctrine of efficient breach therefore seeks to justify the idea that a party has the right to break a contract and choose to pay compensatory damages instead of rendering performance. If the argument were to be accepted disgorgement damages, rooted in notions of deterring breaches of contractual performance rights, would never be appropriate. Compensatory damages should always suffice.

The theory of efficient breach has come under attack in recent times. There are several reasons why it should be rejected. First, its economic basis is very questionable. Secondly, it is anomalous in its perceived application only to a breach of contract. Thirdly, as an absolute proposition it has never been accepted by the common law.

To begin with, the theory itself is very questionable. Ronald Coase made this point 40 years ago. Coase argued that in the absence of transaction costs, society would have equal benefit from a contract regardless of where entitlements fall.[80] He suggested that where resources would be more efficiently employed elsewhere, parties to a contract will compromise for release. Thus, efficient breach is not needed to preserve efficiency. The promisee will release the promisor for a share of the gain without the need for a doctrine of efficient breach.

One of the strongest proponents of efficient breach has now changed his mind. Initially arguing extra-judicially that any gain-based award is inefficient,[81] RA Posner now argues:[82]

"The promisor broke his promise in order to make money . . . we can deter this kind of behaviour by making it worthless to the promisor, which we can do by making him hand over all his profits from the breach to the promisee; no lighter sanction will deter."

However, despite this concession, RA Posner still suggests that disgorgement damages should not be available where the third party truly needs the resources. This is the case where A breaks his contract with B to supply B with 1,000 widgets for £10 each because C, whose factory will close without the widgets, offers A £20 per widget.[83]

---

[79] This situation is known in economic literature as "pareto optimality" : G Calabresi and A Melamed *Property Rules, Liability Rules and Inalienability: One View of the Cathedral* (1972) 85 Harv L Rev 1089, 1094.

[80] R Coase "The Problem of Social Cost" (1960) 3 Journ Law and Econs 1.

[81] RA Posner *Economic Analysis of Law* (1st edn. Aspen New York 1977) 95–96.

[82] RA Posner *Economic Analysis of Law* (5th edn. Aspen New York 1998) 130–131.

[83] This is a simplified version of Posner's example: RA Posner *Economic Analysis of Law* above note 82, 133.

RA Posner acknowledges that a Coasian situation could have resulted in the same outcome without permitting or encouraging such a breach; C could have bargained with B for the widgets. But he argues that this would introduce additional transaction costs, a factor that was excluded in the Coase theorem. The argument is that transaction costs in such a "bi-lateral monopoly" are prohibitive; efficient breach is seen as a way of avoiding those extreme transaction costs.[84] But efficient breach, although reducing transaction costs, increases litigation costs. These costs arise from the difficulty in coming to agreement upon the compensation the disappointed promisee will receive after the promisor breaches the contract. Indeed litigation has been said to be the ultimate bilateral monopoly.[85]

The second aspect of efficient breach that can be criticised is its anomalous application by its proponents only to contract law. The comparison with other wrongs is striking. No one has ever made an argument for a doctrine of "efficient conversion" or "efficient theft", although the economic justification for these notions would be just the same.[86]

Finally, it is clear that, as an *absolute* proposition, a right to breach a contract and instead pay compensatory damages has never been accepted in contract law. The right to specific performance is the antithesis of a right to breach for it recognises that a person cannot simply pay compensation upon breach but must actually perform the primary duty. Oliver Wendell Holmes had argued that specific performance was not given until the promise had been broken and therefore it was not truly performance of the primary obligation at all as the promise could not be performed in the manner promised.[87] On this point Holmes has been shown to be wrong. Courts can decree specific performance as soon as a party threatens to refuse to perform.[88]

(ii) Preserving individual liberty

A second possible justification for a right to choose to breach a contract and pay compensatory damages is that this preserves individual liberty and autonomy. Dr Worthington and Professor Sir Roy Goode argue that "the common law tradition. . . reflects a conviction that individual liberty reigns supreme".[89] They argue that specific performance has been strongly restricted for this reason.[90] Sir Guenter Treitel, writing after the decision of the Court of Appeal in the *Blake*

[84] R O'Dair "Restitutionary Damages for Breach of Contract and the Theory of Efficient Breach: Some Reflections" (1993) 46 CLP 113, 131.

[85] L Smith "Disgorgement of the Profits of Breach of Contract: Property, Contract and 'Efficient Breach' " (1995) 24 Can Bus LJ 121,134; IR MacNeil "Efficient Breach of Contract: Circles in the Sky" (1982) 68 Vir L Rev 947, 968.

[86] D Friedmann "The Efficient Breach Fallacy" (1989) 18 JLS 1, 4–6.

[87] OW Holmes *The Common Law* (Dover New York 1881) 236.

[88] W Gummow *Change and Continuity: Statute Equity and Federalism* (OUP Oxford 1999) 49; *Turner* v. *Bladin* (1951) 82 CLR 463 (HCA); *Hasham* v. *Zenab* [1960] AC 316 (PC) 329–330.

[89] S Worthington and R Goode "Commercial Law: Confining the Remedial Boundaries" in D Hayton (ed.) *Law's Future(s): British Legal Developments in the 21st Century* (Hart Publishing Oregon 2000) 289.

[90] S Worthington and R Goode "Commercial Law" above note 89, 290.

case, argued against disgorgement damages for the same reason. He cited as an example the imposition upon individual liberty of an award of disgorgement damages against an employee who breaks a contract to go and work for a higher salary for another employer.[91]

The example given by Sir Guenter is an extreme one. Consider a fixed term employment contract that provides that the employee shall work for the employer for three years at a salary of £50,000 per year. After the first year the employee leaves and goes to work for a competitor at double the salary. Should the employee be liable to disgorge the additional £100,000? The unreasonableness of such an award, which operates to deter breach, is that it would create an impediment to social mobility and infringe individual liberty.

In some circumstances the decision of the House of Lords in the *Blake* case might lead to this result which disturbs Professors Goode and Treitel and Dr Worthington. But in the usual instance of breach of contract the profits made will probably be too remote from the breach. As explained above, in considering the remoteness rules for disgorgement damages for breach of contract,[92] if the employee in Sir Guenter's example leaves the service of the employer, any additional salary is unlikely to be a direct consequence of the breach but better seen as an independent consequence of the new employment. This was precisely the approach taken in a case decided between the decisions of the Court of Appeal and House of Lords in the *Blake* case. In *University of Nottingham* v. *Fishel*,[93] Dr Fishel had breached his employment contract by performing external consultancy work without the consent of his employer. However, the contract had not expressly provided that Dr Fishel was not to perform any external work and the profits were therefore not directly occasioned from his breach. For Elias J, this was the crucial reason why the obiter dicta of the Court of Appeal in the *Blake* case did not apply.[94]

A second reason why disgorgement damages will be exceptional in cases of breach of employment contracts is that on the test of the House of Lords, disgorgement damages will only be possible where there is a legitimate interest in performance. Injunctions and specific performance (two of the indicia of a legitimate interest in performance suggested in the *Blake* case) are commonly refused to prevent breach of standard employment contracts where enforcement would be too great an infringement of personal liberty.[95]

However, there will be instances in which an employee *can* be stripped of profits made. The *Blake* case is itself a classic illustration. Blake's profits were made directly as a result of a breach of a contractual prohibition and were not too remote. He was forbidden to reveal secrets and his profits were made as a

---

[91] G Treitel *The Law of Contract* (10th edn. Sweet and Maxwell London 1999) 868.
[92] Text accompanying notes 65–77 above.
[93] [2001] RPC 367.
[94] *University of Nottingham* above note 93, 393–394.
[95] *Whitwood Chemical Co* v. *Hardman* [1891] 2 Ch 416; *Ehrman* v. *Bartholemew* [1898] 1 Ch 671; *Mortimer* v. *Beckett* [1920] 1 Ch 571; *Page One Records Ltd* v. *Britton* [1968] 1 WLR 157.

result of doing just that. The Crown also had a legitimate interest in the extra-ordinary service provided by Blake and, had they sought it in time, there is no question they could have obtained an injunction.[96] More generally, consider the opera singer Ms Wagner who wanted to breach her (short term) contract with Mr Lumley, which expressly forbade her singing for anyone else, by singing for Mr Gye at a rival opera house. If Mr Gye offered Ms Wagner a greater sum of money (which could also cover compensatory damages for any losses Mr Lumley would suffer) then this is a classic case in which compensatory dam-ages would be inadequate to deter Ms Wagner's breach. In cases where there is a legitimate interest in enforcing such an exclusivity clause then disgorgement damages *should* be allowed. Mr Lumley did have a legitimate interest in the per-formance of Ms Wagner which was demonstrated in the fact that Mr Lumley obtained an injunction preventing her from singing for Mr Gye.[97] Why is the infringement of liberty in the granting of the injunction any less than the infringement of liberty in stripping profits made by Ms Wagner if in fact she had gone and sung for Mr Gye? It must surely be greater in that it prevents social mobility rather than merely providing a financial deterrent to it.[98]

This conclusion is also supported by older cases where disgorgement dam-ages were awarded against an apprentice who breached the very personal con-tracts of employment with a master. In one such case, an apprentice left the employment of his master and made profits working on a ship at sea. The court held that the profits must be disgorged although the judgment held that the master had property in the profits, not merely a personal action for them.[99]

(iii) The legitimacy of the legitimate interest limitation

A related, but less extreme, version of the above two arguments against dis-gorgement damages is that they are a form of "monetarised specific perform-ance" but that not all contracts are specifically enforceable.[100] Hence, it is argued, disgorgement damages should only be available in cases in which the law recognises this interest in performance. The limitation of a legitimate inter-est in performance might initially be seen as a concession to this argument.

The analogy is imperfect. Disgorgement damages go further than specific performance in some cases by allowing a claimant to recover more than per-formance itself could have generated (as, for example, in the *Blake* case itself). The comparison has also been criticised on the basis that bars to specific performance

---

[96] See JT Brennan "Injunction Against Professional Athletes Breaching their Contracts" (1967) 34 Brooklyn L Rev 61; EA Farnsworth "Your Loss or My Gain? The Dilemma of the Disgorgement Principle in Breach of Contract" (1985) 94 Yale LJ 1339, 1371 analysing a case which stripped a hair-dresser "of exceptional talent" of profits from a higher salary as disgorgement damages (see *Roth* v. *Speck* 126 A 2d 153 (DC 1956)).

[97] *Lumley* v. *Wagner* (1852) 1 De G & M 604; 42 ER 687.

[98] D Friedmann "Restitution of Benefits Obtained Through the Appropriation of Property to the Commission of a Wrong" (1980) 80 Col LR 504, 521 fn 87.

[99] *Barbar* v. *Dennis* (1795) 1 Salk 68; 91 ER 63. See also *Hill* v. *Allen* (1747) 1 Ves Sen 82; 27 ER 906.

[100] *Law Commission* 1997 3.46; J Beatson *Use and Abuse* 16–17.

should not apply to *monetary*, non-specific remedies.[101] For instance, bars such as hardship and uncertainty or the fact that a court cannot supervise specific ongoing orders do not make sense when applied to monetary remedies.[102]

The comparison is only meaningful in that disgorgement damages and specific performance both require rejection of the notion that a claimant has a choice between breaching the contract and paying compensatory damages. The question for specific performance is how far a right of performance should be specifically protected and the question in awarding disgorgement damages is how far a right to performance should be protected by deterring its breach where compensatory damages cannot.

In introducing the notion of a legitimate interest in performance above, several examples where courts seem to recognise that a claimant has no legitimate interest in performance were given. These examples were that a claimant is not entitled to insist upon performance following repudiation of the other party of a contract unless the claimant has a "legitimate interest" in performance;[103] the refusal of English law to allow agreed "penalty clauses" or exemplary damages[104] to deter breach of contract;[105] and the fact that one of the policies underlying the rejection of a general right to specific performance is said to be a right only to compensatory damages.[106]

On the other hand, sometimes the law appears to recognise that there is a general right to performance of a contract. In *Cooper v. Jarman*,[107] Jarman had entered into a contract with a builder for the construction of a house. The house had only been partly completed when Jarman died. After Jarman's death, the builders completed the work and were paid by the administrator of Jarman's estate. Although the report is unclear on the point, it appears that the contract price of completing performance was less than the compensatory damages the builders could have recovered if the administrator had repudiated the contract. The question was whether the estate should bear the full cost of performing the contract or whether it should only bear the cost of any compensatory damages claim brought as that was the expense they could have chosen if the contract had been repudiated. The issue was therefore whether the administrator had a duty

---

[101] R Nolan "Remedies for Breach of Contract: Specific Performance and Restitution" in F Rose (ed.) *Failure of contracts: Contractual, Restitutionary and Proprietary consequences* (Hart Publishing Oxford 1997) 41–42; D Friedmann "Restitution of Benefits Obtained Through the Appropriation of Property to the Commission of a Wrong" (1980) 80 Col LR 504, 514; LD Smith "Disgorgement of the Profits of Breach of Contract: Property, Contract and 'Efficient Breach' " (1995) 24 Can Bus LJ 121, 137.

[102] *Surrey County Council v. Bredero Homes Ltd* [1993] 1 WLR 1361 (CA) 1370 (Steyn LJ).

[103] *White & Carter Councils v. McGregor* [1962] AC 413 (HL).

[104] *Thyssen Inc v. SS Fortune Star* 777 F 2d 57 (2nd Cir 1985) 63, approved in *Gray v. Motor Accident Commission* (1998) 196 CLR 1 (HCA).

[105] *Dunlop Pneumatic Tyre Co Ltd v. New Garage & MotorCo Ltd* [1915] AC 79 (HL).

[106] *Co-operative Insurance Society Ltd v. Argyll Stores (Holdings) Ltd* [1998] AC 1 (HL) 11 (Lord Hoffmann).

[107] (1866) LR 3 Eq 98.

to perform (and complete) a contract, even where it was one for personal services which would not be specifically enforceable.

Lord Romilly MR held that all the costs paid out for the completion of the building were properly expenses of the estate. He stated that the administrator has "a clear duty to perform".[108] In a case with very similar facts, the Privy Council approved this result and Lord Romer stated that "the breaking of an enforceable contract is an unlawful act . . . it can never be the duty of an executor or an administrator to commit such an act".[109] If there were no legitimate interest in performance, especially of contracts in these cases where specific performance is not possible, then an executor should be able to breach such contracts.

Another example where the law appears to recognise an unlimited right to contractual performance is the tort of inducing a breach of contract. This tort is committed where a defendant acts in a manner that induces a contracting party to commit a breach of contract. If a breach of contract were ever to be legitimate, then the law could never condemn third parties for inducing such a breach.[110] The same is true of the tort of intimidation, which, like the tort of inducing breach of contract, also supports the view that breach of contract is a wrongful act. The tort of intimidation requires a threat by a defendant to do something unlawful, (usually to a third party) and includes a threat to break a contract with the claimant or a third party. If breaking a contract were ever lawful tort law would not prohibit this conduct.[111]

A third example is that in some cases substantial damages are now recognised as available where although no financial loss is suffered by the claimant, the damages are measured by the value of cure, to remedy the lost *performance*.[112] Ironically, at the same time as implicitly acknowledging a limited legitimate interest in performance in the context of disgorgement damages, Lord Nicholls recognised this measure of damages for a breach of contract based upon the value of performance lost rather than financial loss.[113]

In other areas, the courts are equivocal. It might be thought that an example of the refusal by courts properly to protect a right to performance is in cases where a promisor returns to the promisee to ask for payment of a higher price in exchange for rendering the promised performance. Such a variation of the contract is void for want of consideration. This might be thought to reject the legitimate interest concept because if there were cases in which the promisee had

---

[108] *Cooper* v. *Jarman* above note 107, 102.

[109] *Angullia (Ahmed) bin Hadjee Mohamed Salleh Angullia* v. *Estate and Trust Agencies (1927) Ltd* [1938] AC 624 (PC) 635.

[110] T Weir *Economic Torts* (Clarendon Press Oxford 1997) 4–5. "A violation of a legal right committed knowingly is a cause of action . . . it is a violation of a legal right to interfere with contractual relations recognised by law": *Quinn* v. *Leatham* [1901] AC 495 (HL) 510.

[111] *Allen* v. *Flood* [1898] AC 1 (HL).

[112] *Alfred McAlpine Construction Ltd* v. *Panatown Ltd* [2001] 1 AC 518 (HL); *Ruxley Electronics and Construction Ltd* v. *Forsyth* [1996] AC 344 (HL) although the contrary result was reached in the *Ruxley* case because the performance measure was said to be "unreasonable".

[113] *Attorney General* v. *Blake* [2001] 1 AC 268 (HL) 285.

no legitimate interest in performance, then the promise of actual performance should constitute valuable consideration in these cases. However, this principle is becoming more relaxed in modern times by allowing variations where the consideration received by the promisee is a "practical benefit".[114] The notion of a "practical benefit" being conferred by a promise, in exchange for performance of a pre-existing contractual duty, might implicitly endorse a right to breach by suggesting that there was no duty to complete in the first place.[115]

The application of the doctrine of economic duress is also equivocal. Although the doctrine of economic duress protects a claimant against threats by a defendant to withhold performance if further payment or benefit is not rendered (which argument suggests a rejection of efficient breach), the cause of action for economic duress is only satisfied if the court considers that it was "not legitimate" for a promisee to ignore the threat and seek compensatory damages.[116] If the promisee always had a right to performance then these threats could never be legitimate.

The result of all this discussion is that although there is no policy justification for the legitimate interest limitation, and it is inconsistent with approaches to breach of contract in other areas, the law has simply not taken a consistent stance toward protecting a claimant's apparent right to performance of contractual obligations in the way other rights are protected (for instance by tortious duties).

The approach of the House of Lords in the *Blake* case might therefore be seen as a cautious yet consistent extension of the law. Contractual rights could, in the future, be properly protected by construing the legitimate interest limitation narrowly and treating most contracts as giving rise to legitimate rights in performance. If this approach is taken, an account of profits should usually be available as a remedy to deter breach whenever compensatory damages are inadequate (limited by remoteness requirements). Indeed, the Lando Commission on European Contract Law[117] has recommended recognition of a general *prima facie* right to specific performance,[118] similar to that recognised in Civilian jurisdictions.[119] And in Civilian jurisdictions such as Germany, where specific performance is a prima facie right, disgorgement damages are liberally available.

---

[114] *Williams* v. *Roffey Bros & Nicholls (Contractors) Ltd* [1991] 1 QB 1 (CA); *Musumeci* v. *Winadell Pty Ltd* (1994) 34 NSWLR 723 (SCNSW). Cf *Re Selectmove Ltd* [1995] 1 WLR 474 (CA).

[115] E McKendrick *Contract Law* (Macmillan London 2000) 93–94.

[116] *Pao On* v. *Lau Yiu Long* [1980] AC 614 (PC); *Dimskal Shipping Co SA* v. *International Transport Workers' Federation (The Evia Luck)* [1992] 2 AC 152 (HL).

[117] O Lando and H Beale (eds) *Principles of European Contract Law* (Kluwer Law International The Hague 1999).

[118] O Lando and H Beale (eds) *Principles of European Contract Law* above note 117, 391, 394.

[119] In German and French law it is said to be axiomatic that where performance can be compelled an order for such performance can generally be obtained (including where the obligation is *vertrebar* or capable of substitute performance): §887 Code of Civil Procedure (Germany), Article 1184 par 2 Code Civil (France); §888 Code of Civil Procedure and Article 1142 of the Code Civil (exceptions). See also K Zweigert and H Kotz *Introduction to Comparative Law* (OUP Oxford 1998) 472. Lord Hoffmann has observed that the differences might not be that great: *Co-operative Insurance Society Ltd* above note 106.

(b) *Commercial uncertainty and the private nature of contract*

Dr Worthington and Professor Goode also seek to justify a refusal of disgorgement damages by arguing that commercial uncertainty and loss of autonomy will deter parties from entering into contracts.[120] Similarly Sir Guenter Treitel[121] and Steyn LJ[122] have argued against disgorgement damages because of the unsettling effect they might have on commercial law. Lord Nicholls also regarded this as a powerful objection and a reason why the remedy of disgorgement damages should be more limited and "exceptional".[123]

Three responses can be made to this view. First, it is difficult to see why people should be able to be deprived of valuable contractual rights in the interests of commercial certainty; this argument is certainly never made against tortious duties. The difference in approach is sometimes justified on the basis that tortious duties are owed to the public generally but that breach of contract is not aimed at "the public generally"[124] (as it is a "private wrong").[125] The need for commercial certainty in such a private relationship is said to be more important than in cases of tortious wrongdoing. But tortious duties may be owed to individual persons. For example a tortious duty not to trespass onto land is owed only to the person in possession.[126] In addition the facts establishing a breach of contract may also establish a tort.[127]

Secondly, it is difficult to see why commercial uncertainty will necessarily result. If the fear is that the institution of contracting will be inhibited by deterring cynical breaches the answer must surely be to question why the honest person would be deterred from entering into a contract?[128] Nor is the award arbitrary or any more uncertain than compensatory damages. A prospective defendant will know precisely what the award will be; the amount of profits made as a result of the breach. In *Snepp* v. *United States*[129] the Supreme Court stated that the award of disgorgement damages:[130]

> "deals fairly with both parties by conforming relief to the dimensions of the wrong. . . the remedy is sure and swift . . . and since the remedy reaches only funds attributable to the breach, it cannot saddle the [contract breaker] with exemplary damages out of all proportion to his gain."

---

[120] S Worthington, R Goode "Commercial Law: Confining the Remedial Boundaries" in D Hayton (ed.) *Law's Future(s): British Legal Developments in the 21st Century* (Hart Publishing Oxford 2000) 309.
[121] G Treitel *The Law of Contract* (10th edn. Sweet and Maxwell London 1999) 868.
[122] *Surrey County Council* v. *Bredero Homes Ltd* [1993] 1 WLR 1361 (CA) 1370.
[123] *Blake* above note 113, 285.
[124] *Stack Electric Inc* v. *DiNardi Construction Corporation* 555 NYS 2d 346 (1991 SCNY).
[125] *Fisher* v. *Yaakov* 575 NYS 2d 310 (1991 SCNY).
[126] J Swanton "The Convergence of Tort and Contact" (1989) 12 Syd LR 40, 41.
[127] *Jaggard* v. *Sawyer* [1995] 1 WLR 269 (CA).
[128] DW Carroll "Four Games and the Expectancy Theory" (1981) 54 S Cal L Rev 503, 516; Mason and Carter *Restitution* 694.
[129] *Snepp* v. *United States* 100 SC 763 (1980 SCUS) 768.
[130] *Snepp* above note 129, 768.

It is true that some uncertainty might result from the fact that it might not always be possible to predict precisely when the breach *causes* the profit, but this is no more uncertain than causation and remoteness tests for compensatory damages.

(c) *Discouraging mitigation of loss*

A further argument against disgorgement damages is that they operate to discourage mitigation of loss.[131] That is, the law will effectively hedge such a claimant from risk so a claimant will rarely seek to mitigate. If disgorgement damages are available, it is argued, a claimant will be discouraged from entering the market to purchase the bargained-for item unless the price falls.

This argument is misconceived. Suppose A contracts to purchase 10 barrels of oil from B at £10 a barrel and B repudiates the contract (for which A terminates) by selling the oil to C at £15, a price £5 above the market price of £10. Assuming disgorgement damages to be available, the only possible disgorgement damages award against B is £5 profit for each barrel as this is the only profit that B has made. This remains the case even if the market price later rises to £30. A's failure to mitigate is borne by A alone.

It might be argued that A could take advantage of a rise in the market if B made a profit on a rising market. Thus, if following the repudiation B had not sold the oil to C but held the oil and later took advantage of the market rise to £30, it might be that A could claim this profit as disgorgement damages. Assuming that the later profit can be stripped and that it is not too remote, in failing to mitigate A will still be subjecting himself to the risks and uncertainty of the subsequent conduct of B.

(d) *Defendant's skill and effort*

This policy concern of stripping a defendant of the value of skill and effort is, at first glance, a most powerful argument against awarding disgorgement damages (where there is a right to performance) limited only by a requirement of "cynical" breach. Professor Beatson considers this one reason for making disgorgement damages "exceptional".[132] The Law Commission also cited this argument,[133] and one of the Commissioners once argued that in cases of breach of contract disgorgement damages should only be allowed for "expense saved" but not for profit made[134] because "making profit in excess of what the plaintiff would have made requires skill and initiative which arguably deserves reward".[135]

---

[131] *Law Commission 1997* 3.46.

[132] J Beatson *Use and Abuse* 16.

[133] *Law Commission 1997* 3.46.

[134] A Burrows *Remedies for Torts and Breach of Contract* (1st edn. Butterworths London 1987) 273.

[135] However, Professor Burrows abandoned this view on the basis that it is difficult to distinguish between cases of expense saved and profit made and that the tort cases do not make such a distinction: A Burrows *Remedies* 310.

The simple answer to this objection, discussed in chapter three, is that disgorgement damages should always operate to ensure a liberal allowance for skill and effort by the defendant so that only the profits flowing from the wrong are disgorged.[136] In the cases where the allowance is denied, the denial of the allowance was explained as a punitive or exemplary damages award. In fact, it has been observed that the *Blake* case itself probably carried this punitive aspect in its denial of an allowance to George Blake for his skill and effort in writing his book.[137] However, this point was not argued on appeal and the reality of the case was that the Crown was concerned to recover the profits which were *owed* to George Blake; he still retained considerably large sums which had already been paid to him.

B Restitutionary Damages

1) *The meaning of restitutionary damages*

(a) *Wrongful transfer of contractual rights*

Like disgorgement damages for breach of contract, courts might have taken the position that restitutionary damages for breach of contract should operate in the same way as for torts although the value wrongfully transferred is contractual *rights*. The operation of restitutionary damages could have been recognised simply by treating contractual rights transferred in the same way as other rights such as property rights. If this were accepted, the expropriation of a claimant's right to contractual performance should entitle restitutionary damages in precisely the same way as torts involving expropriation of the claimant's property.

There are strong arguments that this is the approach the law should take. Lord Nicholls stated in the *Blake* case that "it is not easy to see why, as between parties to a contract, a violation of a party's contractual rights should attract a lesser degree of remedy than a violation of his property rights".[138] Professor Friedmann also has made this point in posing, and answering in the affirmative, the question:[139] "when performance is promised under a contract, is the promisee 'entitled' to it in such a way that if this performance is withheld, appropriated, or otherwise 'taken', the promisee can be regarded as having been deprived of an interest that 'belonged' to him?".

However, in the *Blake* case, Lord Nicholls did not need to consider whether the award of restitutionary damages (which, as the market value of the right to

---

[136] "It would be inequitable . . . to take the profit without paying for the skill and labour which has produced it": *Phipps* v. *Boardman* [1964] 1 WLR 993, 1018 (Wilberforce J).

[137] D Friedmann "Restitution for Wrongs: The Measure of Recovery" [2001] Tex L Rev 1879, 1900.

[138] *Attorney General* v. *Blake* [2001] 1 AC 268 (HL) 283 citing an article arguing for broad recognition of *disgorgement* damages for a breach of contract on this basis: L Smith "Disgorgement of the Profits of Breach of Contract: Property, Contract and 'Efficient Breach' " (1995) 24 Can Busi L J 121.

[139] D Friedmann "Restitution of Benefits Obtained Through the Appropriation of Property or the Commission of a Wrong" (1980) 80 Col LR 504, 515.

relax the secrecy provision, would have been less than that of disgorgement damages) should be made. As he acknowledged, "the Crown seeks to go further" and claim disgorgement damages (an account of profits)—the entirety of the profits made.[140] The imposition by the House of Lords in the *Blake* case, of a "legitimate interest" limitation on disgorgement damages for a breach of contract should probably be taken as doing the same for restitutionary damages. Just as it was considered that disgorgement damages can only be justified in deterring breach of contractual rights where those rights are "legitimate", so too restitutionary damages can only be justified in reversing the transfer of valuable contractual rights where those rights are "legitimate".

The presence of a legitimate interest limitation explains why no substantial remedy was, or could be, given in a case such as *Tito* v. *Waddell*.[141] In that case, British Phosphate Commissioners, in breach of contract, had failed to make good an obligation to replant mined land on Ocean Island in the Pacific (known to its inhabitants as Banaba). The Banaban plaintiffs at the time of litigation had relocated to another larger island unaffected by the mining. Damages were sought in that case on the basis of either (1) the cost to replant, or (in a submission added on the 96th day of the hearing) (2) a reasonable sum which the Commissioners could have paid to be released from their obligation to replant (i.e. the value of the rights transferred).

In relation to the first damages claim, Megarry V-C held that the appropriate measure of compensatory damages for the failure to replant was not the cost that the British Phosphate Commissioners had saved from not replanting but the diminution of the value of the land resulting from that failure.[142] This was because the Banabans had not replanted nor had they shown any intention to replant the land. It will be seen below that this first measure sought was not in fact a compensatory measure but a measure valued on the basis of the cost of performance. Megarry V-C confused the two measures in treating the performance damages claim as one for compensatory damages.

The second damages claim was the restitutionary damages measure. Counsel cited the case of *Wrotham Park Estate Co Ltd* v. *Parkside Homes Ltd*[143] which was approved by Lord Nicholls in the *Blake* case as a restitutionary damages case.[144] Megarry V-C rejected the claim because "not unless the British Phosphate Commissioners would be liable to replant would there be any liability from which the British Phosphate Commissioners would seek release."[145] In other words, without a "legitimate interest" in performance the Banaban claimants could not seek restitutionary damages based on the value of contractual rights subtracted from them.

---

[140] *Blake* above note 138, 284.
[141] [1977] 1 Ch 106.
[142] *Tito* above note 141, 333–334.
[143] *Tito* above note 141, 335. *Wrotham Park Estate Co Ltd* v. *Parkside Homes Ltd* [1974] 1 WLR 798.
[144] Below text accompanying notes 175–186.
[145] *Tito* above note 141, 336.

In the United States, where the principle of restitutionary damages for a breach of contract is well established, a limitation exists which is much alike the legitimate interest limitation. The United States *Restatement (Second) of Contracts*[146] requires a "total breach" or "repudiation", before an injured party is entitled to "restitution of any benefit that he has conferred on the other party by way of part performance or reliance". "Total breach" is defined as a breach of contract that "so substantially impairs the value of the contract to the injured party that it is just in the circumstances to allow him to recover damages based on [the value of the appropriated] . . . remaining rights to performance".[147] The circumstances in which it is "unjust" to allow the injured party to recover therefore are similar to the requirement of "legitimate interest". Just as trivial breaches of contract or breaches of standard personal service contracts are cases in which the injured party has no legitimate interest in performance,[148] so too would the breach in these cases be held not to "substantially impair" the value of the contract. In the words of Stevens J in the United States Supreme Court:[149]

> "Restitution is an available remedy only when the breach is of vital importance. . . . In the case of a breach by non-performance, . . . [t]he injured party, however, can not maintain an action for restitution of what he has given the defendant unless the defendant's non-performance is so material that it is held to go to the 'essence' [of the contract]."

(b) *Examples of restitutionary damages*

One example of restitutionary damages, *British Motor Trade Association* v. *Gilbert*,[150] was mentioned above as it was cited as a disgorgement damages case by Lord Nicholls. But the case was really treated in the judgment of the trial judge as one of restitutionary damages (although a disgorgement damages remedy would have reached the same result). A covenant prohibited purchasers of new cars from the claimant from selling those cars within two years without the claimant's consent. Consent would only be given if the car were first offered for resale (at the original list price and tax less depreciation) to the claimant. The defendant bought a Jaguar for £1,263 and, in breach of contract, sold it for a considerable profit less than a month later to a third party without offering it to the claimant.

The trial judge, Danckwerts J, upheld the validity of the scheme and ordered the payment of the difference between the price paid for the car and the open market value, estimated at £2,100. The reason why the award is better seen as restitutionary damages and not disgorgement damages is because Danckwerts J

---

[146] American Law Institute *Restatement (Second) of Contracts* (American Law Institute Minnesota 1981) §373.

[147] *Restatement* above note 146, §236, §243.

[148] See text to note 91–99 above.

[149] *Mobil Oil Exploration & Producing SouthEast Inc* v. *United States* 120 S Ct 2423 (2000 SCUS) 2440, stating that damages are the usual remedy for breach.

[150] [1951] 2 All ER 641.

regarded the evidence of the price at which the defendant had sold the car as only relating to evidence of the open market value and the actual profit of the defendant was not a concern:[151]

> "one way and another, therefore, it seems that, if I am to take the value in the open market, whether I treat it as what can be obtained surreptitiously at the present time, or a legitimate purchase price in 1953 discounted, I would come to the conclusion that the market value would be £2,100."

Danckwerts J awarded restitutionary damages despite observing that it was "anomalous to apply the open market value in all cases without regard to the special circumstances of the plaintiff".[152] In other words, the circumstances of the claimant were not applied as the claimant had suffered no financial loss from the sale. But the defendant had appropriated or transferred the claimant's contractual right to buy back the car. The market valued that right at £836, the excess of the market price over the price paid.

To pretend that the damages in *British Motor Trade Association* v. *Gilbert* were compensatory for the appropriation of the exclusive right to re-purchase the car is fictitious.[153] The claimants had no intention of purchasing a like car on the open market. Indeed the very reason for the contractual restriction was to *prevent* such a market arising. To the *claimant* the loss was negligible; it was the policy behind it that was important. But the value that was transferred was £836.

A second example of restitutionary damages for breach of contract was considered in chapter three: *Moses* v. *Macferlan*.[154] It will be recalled that Macferlan, ignoring a promise not to sue Moses if Moses indorsed several notes, did sue Moses and recovered the money indorsed in a Court of Conscience. Moses paid and then sued Macferlan to recover the money paid as a result of the judgment, and recovered in an action for money had and received which reversed the value of the payment.

In chapter three it was explained that the only basis upon which this award of the money transferred was made was the breach of contract.[155] Lord Mansfield emphasised this when he considered the objection that the cause of action was trying to avoid the doctrine of *res judicata* by seeking the return of a payment made by compulsion of due process of law. He stated that the answer to this objection was that "unquestionably an action might be brought on the agreement".[156]

---

[151] *British Motor Trade Association* above note 150, 644.
[152] *British Motor Trade Association* above note 150, 645.
[153] Cf. *Mouat* v. *Betts Motors Ltd* [1959] AC 71 (PC) 82.
[154] *Moses* v. *Macferlan* (1760) 2 Burr 1005; 97 ER 676.
[155] P Birks "Restitutionary Damages for Breach of Contract: *Snepp* and the fusion of law and equity" [1987] LMCLQ 421, 429–430. See also Anon "*Moses* v. *Macferlan*—Is it Sound Law" (1915) 24 Yale LJ 246, 249–250 and JP Dawson *Unjust Enrichment* (Little Brown & Co Boston 1951) 11. See ch. three, text accompanying notes 176–180.
[156] *Moses* v. *Macferlan* (1760) 2 Burr 1005, 1010; 97 ER 676, 679.

(c) *Cases of "expense saved"*

A consequence of this analysis is that some cases of "skimped performance" might be analysed as cases of restitutionary damages. An example of a skimped performance case is the famous case of *City of New Orleans* v. *Firemen's Charitable Association.*[157] The claimant discovered after the contract had concluded that the defendant had not provided the full firefighting service; the number of firemen and hoses and the length of hosepipe fell short of the amount required by the contract. Although the court ruled that no more than nominal damages were required as the plaintiff could point to no loss which had been suffered,[158] the Court of Appeal in the *Blake* case considered the result unjust. The Court of Appeal thought that this was the sort of case in which disgorgement damages (which they described as "restitutionary damages") could disgorge the extra profit made.[159]

As noted in chapter three, the stripping of profits has never operated by measuring profit as "saved expense". Lord Nicholls in the House of Lords observed that such profit-stripping "does not fall within the scope of an account of profits as ordinarily understood" and thought that a remedy should instead be recognised which is based on "performance" lost.[160] However, an award of *restitutionary* damages might sometimes be available in these cases. The City of New Orleans was entitled to valuable contractual rights. The Fireman's Charitable Association deprived them of those rights and the value transferred, was the market value of those rights.

A number of cases in England,[161] Canada[162] and the United States[163] have allowed recovery of the value of skimped performance and might be explained in this manner. A difference between the award of the full amount of "skimped performance" and the award of restitutionary damages might, however, sometimes exist. The expense saved by the Firemen's Charitable Association might have been hundreds of thousands of dollars but the enhanced market value of the additional performance which was skimped might have been far less. These cases of "skimped performance", as Lord Nicholls suggests, are probably best seen as a remedy based upon "perfection" or "performance" damages rather than restitutionary damages.

---

[157] 9 So 486 (1891 SC Lou).

[158] A claim for failure of consideration also failed because the claimants were seeking restitution of the entire price paid despite the fact that the services had been provided.

[159] *Attorney General* v. *Blake* [1998] Ch 439 (CA) 458.

[160] *Blake* above note 138, 286. See the above discussion of performance damages in text accompanying notes 201–216.

[161] *Radford* v. *De Froberville* [1977] 1 WLR 1262; *Dean* v. *Ainley* [1987] 3 All ER 748; *Joyner* v. *Weeks* [1891] 2 QB 31 (CA).

[162] *Arbutus Park Estates* v. *Fuller* (1976) 74 DLR (3d) 257 (SCBC).

[163] *Groves* v. *John Wunder Co* 286 NW 235 (1939 SC Minn); *Coca-Cola Bottling Co of Elizabethtown* v. *Coca-Cola Co* 988 F 2d 386 (3rd Cir CA 1993). Cf *Peevyhouse* v. *Garland Coal Mining Co* 382 P 2d 109 (SC Okla 1963) although the minority in that case noted that without a substantial award the defendant "would be taking from the plaintiff the benefits of the contract and

(d) *Measuring the contractual value transferred*

Because restitutionary damages, in the sense of wrongful transfers of contractual rights, have rarely been explicitly considered in English law there has been little discussion about valuation difficulties which arise in assessing the value of contractual rights transferred. The only law to guide the situation is the detailed consideration given to this topic in the United States *Restatement (Second) of Contracts*.[164]

(i) Contractual rights to non-monetary benefits

The usual operation of restitutionary damages in cases where non-monetary benefits are wrongfully transferred to a defendant reverses that transfer by allowing the claimant the market value of those wrongfully transferred benefits. This award represents their objective value.[165] However, where restitutionary damages are sought for breach of contract, the substance of the wrongful transfer from the claimant is *contractual rights* to non-monetary benefits (as a result of a defendant's refusal to perform) and the valuation of such rights is more difficult. The objective value of those rights to the defendant could be made at their market value or at contract prices. The position taken in the United States appears to be the most principled approach. Where the contract has assigned a clear value to those rights then that should be taken as the objective value of the contractual rights to the defendant. That is the value that the defendant, in the marketplace, placed on those rights. But where the contract does not assign a precise value to the contractual rights appropriated by the defendant then a market valuation should be used.

The first question then is how valuation of *non-monetary* benefits should be made. The *Restatement (Second) of Contracts* usually assesses the value of the rights to the non-monetary benefit to be received at the contract price.[166] In one case A paid $5,000 to B in advance for 2,000 barrels of flour at a contract price of $7 per barrel. The market price fell to $5.50 and A claimed restitutionary damages of $5,000 when B failed to deliver the flour. B argued that the value of the rights appropriated should be assessed at the lower market rates. The court held that the entire $5,000 must be returned to A.[167] Under the contract B had rights to $14,000 and A had rights to 2,000 barrels. A had received none of the

---

placing those benefits in [the hands of the] defendant which has failed to perform its obligations" 382 P 2d 109, 116 (SC Okla 1963).

[164] *Restatement (Second) of Contracts* above note 146.

[165] It has been seen that in extraordinary circumstances that objective value transferred might be *subjectively* devalued.

[166] *Mobil Oil* above note 149, 2430; *Restatement (Second) of Contracts* above note 146, §373, Comment a, Illustration 1.

[167] *Bush* v. *Canfield* (1818) 2 Conn 485 (SCConn). Note that Hosmer J dissented on the basis that such an award of damages was not concerned with compensation for loss. Hosmer J (at 491) stated that "the verdict of the jury, in opposition to the contract of the parties, reverses their condition. It rescues the plaintiff's from their loss, and deprives the defendant of his gain." This is precisely the role of restitutionary damages.

rights which corresponded to his $5,000 payment, rights appropriated by B's breach of contract; A was therefore entitled to the return of the $5,000.[168]

On the other hand, where there is no contractual assessment of the value of the corresponding contractual right for the non-monetary benefit conferred (perhaps because the corresponding benefit had been partly conferred and the contract price cannot be apportioned) then market price would be appropriate. This is illustrated in relation to valuation of contractual rights to monetary benefits.

(ii) Contractual rights to monetary benefits
Suppose that the claimant performs work as a consultant for the defendant after which the defendant repudiates the contract and refuses to pay. The rule is that where the claimant has completely conferred a non-monetary benefit on the defendant and the defendant refuses payment, the claimant's right to payment is limited to its contractually assessed value. Even if the market value of the benefit conferred upon the defendant is far greater than the contract price, the claimant is limited to the agreed contract price.[169] This corresponds perfectly with the same example in the case of contractual rights to non-monetary benefits. In both cases the contract has given a financial assessment of the contractual rights appropriated and that is the assessment of the value transferred.

However, where the claimant has not completed the work before the repudiation (such as the refusal to pay) by the defendant, the contract will rarely provide for the value of the corresponding right to monetary payment which the defendant has denied the claimant. For instance, where A is dismissed at the end of 11 months of a 12 month fixed-term contract, assessment is at market value and the terms of the contract are only indicators of the market value.[170]

2) Restitutionary damages in the Blake case

There is a second aspect to the *Blake* case that will have great impact on the landscape of remedies for breach of contract. This is the discussion of awards of restitutionary damages. In his speech, Lord Nicholls avoided the term restitutionary damages and at times elided restitutionary damages and disgorgement damages.[171] For instance, in considering property torts, Lord Nicholls stated that an account of profits was equity's measure of gain-based award whereas the common law always awarded market value. Lord Nicholls thought this was simply an "accident of history".[172] The falsity of this statement has already been shown in this book. It was shown in chapter four, in relation to torts, that the common law makes "damages" awards to strip profits as well as damages awards of reasonable market value. Chapter six will show that both awards have also been made in equity.

[168] The criticism that this result allows a claimant to escape from a bad bargain is considered below.
[169] *Restatement (Second) of Contracts* above note 146, §373, Comment b, Illustration 5.
[170] *Restatement (Second) of Contracts* above note 146, §373, Comment d, Illustration 12.
[171] P Jaffey "Disgorgement for Breach of Contract" [2000] RLR 578, 583–585.
[172] *Blake* above note 138, 280.

However, Lord Nicholls did confront restitutionary damages directly by considering the conflicting decisions of *Wrotham Park Estate Co Ltd* v. *Parkside Homes Ltd*[173] and *Surrey County Council* v. *Bredero Homes Ltd*.[174] In *Wrotham Park Estate Co* v. *Parkside Homes*,[175] a parcel of land had been sold subject to a restrictive covenant prohibiting development. Parkside Homes had purchased the land from the initial purchaser with notice of the restrictive covenant. It was accepted by the parties that the restrictive covenant bound Parkside Homes. It was also accepted that although the Wrotham Park Estate Company was only the successor to the initial vendor, the benefit of the restrictive covenant had passed to the Wrotham Park Estate Company. Parkside Homes developed the land and sold homes on it making profits of £50,000.

Brightman J awarded damages of £2,500 in lieu of an injunction under the equivalent of Lord Cairns' Act.[176] The Wrotham Park Estate Company were deprived of a valuable right (to restrict development). The value of that right, transferred to the defendant, was assessed at £2,500. As Brightman J stated it was a "sum of money as might reasonably have been demanded by the plaintiffs from [the defendant] as a quid pro quo for releasing the covenant".[177]

Although there was strictly no contract between the parties in the *Wrotham Park* case (and hence the cause of action cannot truly be seen as one for breach of contract) their rights arose from the original contract and the result should have been exactly the same if the litigation had been between the parties to the initial contract.[178] The best analysis of the decision is that the market value of the right to relax the restrictive covenant, £2,500 was wrongfully transferred to the defendant. Restitutionary damages reversed that wrongful transfer. Indeed, Brightman J reached this result by analogising from tort cases which had awarded wayleaves and other awards of the market value of the use of property where no loss was suffered.[179]

In *Surrey County Council* v. *Bredero Homes Ltd*[180] a developer developed land in breach of a restrictive covenant requiring any development to conform to existing planning permission. The permission provided that only 72 houses were to be built on the land but 77 had been built. The council suffered no loss from the additional houses which were built and the Court of Appeal awarded only nominal damages.

Each of the judgments in the Court of Appeal distinguished the *Wrotham Park* case. Dillon LJ distinguished the *Wrotham Park* case on the basis that it

---

[173] [1974] 1 WLR 798.
[174] [1993] 1 WLR 1361 (CA).
[175] *Wrotham Park* above note 173.
[176] Chancery Amendment Act 1858, now s. 50 Supreme Court Act 1981.
[177] *Wrotham Park Estate Co* above note 173, 815.
[178] "The measure of damages cannot depend on whether the proceedings are between the original parties to the contract or their successors in title" *Attorney General* v. *Blake* [1998] Ch 439 (CA), 457.
[179] *Wrotham Park Estate Co* above note 173, 813.
[180] *Surrey County Council* above note 174.

180 Breach of Contract

was concerned with damages under Lord Cairns' Act.[181] No mention was made of the fact that Lord Wilberforce had observed in the House of Lords in *Johnson* v. *Agnew*[182] that damages under Lord Cairns' Act are awarded on the same basis as damages at common law. Rose LJ similarly viewed the failure to seek an injunction as preventing a substantial claim to damages. Steyn LJ distinguished the *Wrotham Park* case as a case concerning property rights, although he accepted that it was correctly decided and that it would be a fiction to explain it on the basis of a loss of bargaining opportunity.[183]

Faced with these two conflicting authorities, and a mixed reception to the *Surrey* case,[184] Lord Nicholls did not seek to draw artificial distinctions between the cases and he expressly preferred the *Wrotham Park* analysis. He stated that "in a suitable case damages for breach of contract may be measured by the benefit gained by the wrongdoer from the breach. The defendant must make a reasonable payment in respect of the benefit he has gained".[185] He noted that there was a tendency to label these awards as "restitution" and accepted that they "cannot be regarded as conforming to the strictly compensatory measure of damages unless loss is given a strained and artificial meaning".[186]

Lord Hobhouse in the *Blake* case, although dissenting on the availability of disgorgement damages, would have been prepared to award damages against Blake of the objective value of relaxing the contractual secrecy provision. However, in doing so he confused various different remedies for breach of contract. First, he referred to the profit-stripping disgorgement damages award of an account of profits as an example of restitutionary damages.[187] This is to confuse restitutionary damages and disgorgement damages, an error described in detail in chapter three. Because of this conflation Lord Hobhouse thought it necessary to explain the objective value to relax the contractual provision in terms other than restitutionary damages. Lord Hobhouse explained the award as one of compensatory damages.

In explaining awards of value transferred as compensatory, Lord Hobhouse therefore viewed the award in the *Wrotham Park* case as one of compensatory damages for loss. He argued that "what the plaintiff has lost is the sum which he could have extracted from the defendant".[188] But Brightman J in the *Wrotham Park* case had held that the claimants would never have consented to relaxation of the covenant.[189] As discussed in chapter three, attempts to justify the award in the *Wrotham Park* case as compensatory damages (for a "lost

---

[181] *Surrey* above note 174, 1367.
[182] [1980] AC 367 (HL) 400.
[183] *Surrey* above note 174, 1369–1370.
[184] Compare R O'Dair "Remedies for Breach of Contract: A Wrong Turn" [1993] RLR 31 and A Burrows "No Restitutionary Damages for Breach of Contract" [1993] LMCLQ 453.
[185] *Attorney General* v. *Blake* [2001] 1 AC 268 (HL) 283–284.
[186] *Blake* above note 185, 279.
[187] *Blake* above note 185, 297.
[188] *Blake* above note 185, 298.
[189] *Wrotham Park Estate Co* above note 173, 815.

opportunity to bargain")[190] proceed by a fiction which suggests that the claimant "lost" the market value of an opportunity to bargain that it would never have exercised, an analysis which was rejected by the Court of Appeal in *Gondal* v. *Dillon Newsagents Ltd*.[191] The same fiction is the only way in which the award of restitutionary damages, favoured by Lord Hobhouse in the *Blake* case, could be justified. Just as the claimants would never have consented to a relaxation of the covenant in the *Wrotham Park* case, neither would the Crown have been prepared to relax the secrecy provisions in the *Blake* case.[192] Indeed Lord Hobhouse compounded this confusion by referring to awards concerned with "perfection" and "performance" and stating that they were cases of compensatory damages as well.[193] Those "performance" damages awards are discussed below.

3) Restitutionary damages in the United States

The same award of restitutionary damages for a breach of contract has a long pedigree in the United States and, as noted above, is entrenched in the *Restatement (Second) on Contract*.[194]

In a similar case to the *Blake* case in the United States, an award of restitutionary damages was given. In *Structural Dynamics Research Corp* v. *Engineering Mechanics Research Corp*[195] the defendants were former employees of an engineering research company and left the company taking with them valuable trade secrets which, in breach of contractual promises to their former employer, they used themselves in their new employment. The Michigan District Court held that they, and their new employer who had induced their breach of contract, had not made a profit from the breach of contract but had objectively gained from the use of the secrets and that they were liable for the reasonable value (described as a reasonable royalty) of the rights transferred. This was assessed at 15 per cent of the gross sales of the new employer. The Court stated that "the reasonable royalty measure of damages . . . very simply means the actual value of what has been appropriated".[196]

A more difficult example is *Mobil Oil Exploration & Producing SouthEast Inc* v. *United States*.[197] In that case oil companies had paid $158 million to the United States government in exchange for a right to explore for and develop oil

---

[190] RJ Sharpe and SM Waddams "Damages for lost opportunity to bargain" (1982) 2 OJLS 290. See *Tito* v. *Waddell (No 2)* [1977] Ch 106, 335; *Jaggard* v. *Sawyer* [1995] 1 WLR 269 (CA); *Gafford* v. *Graham* (1998) 76 P & CR 18.

[191] [2001] RLR 221. See ch. 4 text accompanying notes 95–99.

[192] *Blake* above note 185, 287.

[193] *Blake* above note 185, 298.

[194] *Restatement (Second) of Contracts* above note 146. See *Bush* v. *Canfield* (1818) 2 Conn 485 (SCConn).

[195] 401 F Supp 1102 (ED Mich 1975).

[196] *Structural Dynamics* above note 195, 1119. See also *University Computing Co* v. *Lykes-Youngstown Corp* 504 F (2d) 518 (5th Cir 1974).

[197] 120 S Ct 2423 (2000 SCUS).

on the coast of North Carolina. However, before all the preliminary steps and approvals were taken as required under the contract, the United States government passed legislation which had the effect of imposing substantial additional requirements before any exploration could be undertaken. The United States argued that the oil companies would never have met the contractual requirements in order to explore for the oil and hence that they suffered no loss. A majority of the Supreme Court held that the actions of the United States government amounted to a repudiatory breach that was so substantial as to entitle the remedy of "restitution" of the $158 million. The Supreme Court held that the fact that no loss might have been suffered was irrelevant as the remedy sought was not damages for loss, but for "restitution".[198] The United States government had, by their repudiation, deprived the oil companies of valuable rights. The government's repudiation effectively transferred those rights back to itself. The award of restitutionary damages reversed that transfer by awarding the oil companies the value of those rights, $158 million:[199]

> "the oil companies gave the United States $158 million in return for a contractual promise to follow the terms of pre-existing statutes and regulations. The new statute prevented the Government from keeping that promise. The breach 'substantially impaired the value of the contracts' . . . And therefore the Government must give the companies their money back."

4) Restitutionary damages distinguished from other remedies

(a) Restitutionary damages and "performance" damages

Although the opportunity existed for Lord Nicholls to have analysed the "skimped performance" cases in terms of restitutionary damages, his Lordship did not need to do so. Lord Nicholls referred to the *City of New Orleans* case and explained that recovery in that case of the value of the skimped performance was possible by extending recognition of the well understood principle that if a shopkeeper provides defective goods the claimant is entitled to claim the difference in value between the performance promised and the performance received. Lord Nicholls noted that the same principle should apply to services.[200] This is a measure of damages which operates as a monetary measure of *performance*. The Supreme Court of Canada has referred to this type of award as a monetary measure of specific performance which is a "substitute for an order of specific performance".[201]

The performance damages award has this in common with restitutionary damages: it does not focus upon compensating for financial loss. It focuses upon

---

[198] *Mobil Oil* above note 197, 2430, 2437.
[199] *Mobil Oil* above note 197, 2437–2438.
[200] *Blake* above note 185, 286. The same approach was taken by Lord Millett in *Alfred McAlpine Construction Ltd* v. *Panatown Ltd* [2001] 1 AC 518 (HL) 586.
[201] *Semelhago* v. *Paramadevan* [1996] 2 SCR 415 (SCC).

the cost of completing the promised performance.[202] Lords Goff and Millett have noted that it has support from a large number of commentators[203] and, before 1996, a number of authorities had made this award although most did so by contorting findings of financial loss to reach a performance loss award.[204] Two significant House of Lords authorities have now recognised this award and acknowledged that it is not based in notions of financial loss. The first of such cases is *Ruxley Electronics and Construction Ltd* v. *Forsyth*.[205] In that case the claimants had contracted to build a swimming pool with a depth at one end of 7 foot 6 inches. The pool was only built to the depth of 6 feet. The defendant refused to pay the outstanding contract price and counterclaimed for the cost of rebuilding the pool although there was no adverse effect on the value of the property from the lesser depth. The House of Lords treated the question as an overall one of reasonableness. Intention to rebuild was only one aspect of this award so that performance damages might be available even where no financial loss had been suffered because there was no intention to complete the performance.[206]

Although "performance damages" were recognised, they were refused in the *Ruxley* case as "unreasonable". A majority of the House of Lords again recognised the existence of these damages in *Alfred McAlpine Construction Ltd* v. *Panatown Ltd*.[207] In that case two Law Lords (Lords Goff and Millett) accepted,[208] and one (Lord Browne-Wilkinson) was prepared to assume[209] the validity of, performance damages. The proposition which these three |Lords accepted was that a promisee could recover damages for the cost of correcting defective performance rendered under a contract to perform work on the

---

[202] In this sense it might even be artificial to describe it as "damages". As a monetary substitute for specific performance the remedy seems to be a primary rather than a secondary right and might align more naturally as a primary "perfection" response in the same way as specific performance or the common account against a trustee. Nevertheless the term "damages" is used because it is said to be triggered by the wrong of breach of contract. See also S Elliott "Compensation Claims Against Trustees" (D.Phil Thesis University of Oxford 2001); Mason and Carter *Restitution* 714–715.

[203] *Alfred McAlpine Construction Ltd* v. *Panatown Ltd* [2001] 1 AC 518 (HL) 548 (Lord Goff) 587 (Lord Millett). See B Coote "*Dunlop* v. *Lambert*: The Search for a Rationale" (1998) 13 JCL 91; IN Duncan Wallace "Third Party Damage: No Legal Black Hole?" (1999) 115 LQR 394 and "Defects and Third Parties: No Peace for the Wicked" (1999) 15 Const LJ 245; G McMeel "Complex Entitlements: The *Albazero* Principle and Restitution" [1999] RLR 20. See also B Coote "The Performance Interest, Panatown and the Problem of Loss" (2001) 117 LQR 81.

[204] *Radford* v. *De Froberville* [1977] 1 WLR 1262 (cost of building a wall which was not built but would have added no value to the land); *Dean* v. *Ainley* [1987] 3 All ER 748 (cost of properly waterproofing patio awarded although it would only nominally enhance the value of the house); *Joyner* v. *Weeks* [1891] 2 QB 31 (CA) (Cost to perform repairs awarded although apartment was to be demolished). Cf *Conquest* v. *Ebbetts* [1896] AC 490 (HL) holding that the "rival" measures of compensatory damages or damages to effect a cost of cure could, in fact, both be legitimate measures.

[205] [1996] AC 344 (HL).

[206] *Ruxley* above note 205, 354, 355, 365–372. See especially B Coote "Contract Damages, *Ruxley*, and the Performance Interest" [1997] CLJ 537.

[207] [2001] 1 AC 518 (HL)

[208] *McAlpine* above note 207, 548 (Lord Goff), 587 (Lord Millett).

[209] *McAlpine* above note 207, 577.

property of another.[210] Lords Clyde and Jauncey dissented from this view, and Professor Burrows has strongly criticised it,[211] on the basis that no financial loss was suffered. But each of their Lordships were fully aware of this and conceived of themselves as awarding damages not based on financial loss but upon loss of performance.[212] In the *Blake* case, Lord Hobhouse also referred to the *Ruxley* case and although explaining it as a case of "compensation", explained that it is not "compensatory" in the sense of "relating to a loss as if there has to be some identified physical or monetary loss to a plaintiff" he considered that compensation in this sense means "a substitute for performance".[213] It is far better in such cases to eschew the use of the words "compensation" or "loss" altogether and acknowledge that the remedy is concerned with correcting performance and not with compensation, a concept traditionally associated with financial loss.

It might be noted that the recognition of performance damages, acknowledging and valuing a right to performance, might seem inconsistent with the "legitimate interest" limitation upon restitutionary damages and disgorgement damages which conceded that there are some interests in contractual performance that should not be protected. However, the corresponding limitation in the case of performance damages is the "reasonableness" requirement. Indeed, in the *Panatown* case, Lord Millett acknowledged that a key aspect of the test of reasonableness is a requirement that the claimant have a "legitimate interest" in performance.[214]

The performance damages remedy recognised in the *Ruxley* and *McAlpine* cases is different from restitutionary damages. Had the performance damages remedy been given in each of those cases it would have been a different measure from any possible restitutionary damages award. In both cases the work had been done defectively but the contractual value transferred, in terms of gain by the defendant from the defective work, was minimal. For instance, the market value of the contractual right to the deeper pool in the *Ruxley* case was negligible. It would not have affected the overall contract price.

Although damages awards in the skimped performance cases can also be analysed as instances of "performance damages", this does not mean that there

---

[210] Although Lord Browne-Wilkinson held that recovery was not possible in the case itself because the existence of a duty of care deed between the defendant and the third party owner of the land meant that there was no damage to the performance interest of the claimant: *McAlpine* above note 207, 577–578

[211] A Burrows "No Damages for a Third Party's Loss" [2001] 1 OUCLJ 107.

[212] *McAlpine* above note 207 "A, although not himself suffering the physical or pecuniary damage . . . has suffered his own damage being the loss of his performance interest" (Lord Browne-Wilkinson) 577; "damages may be measured by the cost of obtaining alternative performance" (Lord Millett) 587.

[213] *Blake* above note 185, 298.

[214] *McAlpine* above note 207, 592. The same criticism as might be levelled at the "legitimate interest" limitation on restitutionary damages (that it fails to recognise that there is always an interest in performance) has been levelled at this limitation on "performance" damages cases: G Jones "The Recovery of Benefits Gained from a Breach of Contract" [1983] 99 LQR 443.

is no additional role for restitutionary damages.[215] Cases such as the *Wrotham Park* case and the *British Motor Trade Association* case illustrate that there is still a need for restitutionary damages outside the sphere of the skimped performance cases. As Lord Millett observed in the *McAlpine* case,[216] there is room for both restitutionary damages and performance damages: "in some cases one approach may be more appropriate, in others the other. They will often produce the same measure of damages though they will not always do so."

(b) *Restitutionary damages and restitution for failure of consideration*

Much discussion in chapter two focused upon the alternative analysis between restitutionary damages for wrongs and restitution for unjust enrichment. Throughout this book it has been seen that where the cause of action is not clearly specified an award of restitution can often be analysed as an award of restitutionary damages for a wrong or restitution for an unjust enrichment.

The same is true in cases of breach of contract. In many of these cases the same restitutionary result can be reached with an analysis based upon the unjust factor of failure of consideration in unjust enrichment. However there are distinct differences between the two causes of action. The cause of action for failure of consideration, in a contractual context, allows the recovery of benefits conferred when the contractual consideration fails. "Consideration" in these cases bears a different meaning from its contractual meaning, "it is, generally speaking, not the promise which is referred to as the consideration, but the performance of the promise".[217] The basic operation of the unjust factor of failure of consideration in a contractual context allows the reversal of enrichments transferred where the promised contractual performance, which is usually the basis of the agreement, has not been rendered. However there are key limitations upon failure of consideration actions which mean that its operation might not be co-extensive with an action for restitutionary damages for breach of contract.

The first limitation is a close parallel to the requirement of "legitimate interest" where restitutionary damages are sought for a breach of contract. This is the requirement that the contract must be discharged.[218] This requirement has been explained on the basis that, until the contract is discharged, the defendant might still be ready, willing and able to perform so that there has been no enrichment.[219] It has also been explained as preventing the subversion of contractual bargains while the contract remains on foot.[220] Whatever the reason, it provides a neat parallel with the restitutionary damages requirement that there must be

---

[215] Cf. A Kull "Disgorgement for Breach, the 'Restitution Interest' and the Restatement of Contracts" [2001] 79 Tex Law Rev 2021, 2035.

[216] *McAlpine* above note 185, 588.

[217] *Fibrosa Spolka Akcjna* v. *Fairbairn Lawson Combe Barbour Ltd* [1943] AC 32 (HL) 48 (Viscount Simon LC); A Burrows *The Law of Restitution* 251.

[218] *Thomas* v. *Brown* (1876) 1 QBD 714.

[219] *Goff and Jones* 503; A Burrows *The Law of Restitution* 257; G Virgo *Restitution* 331.

[220] P Birks *Introduction* 47.

a legitimate interest in performance. The parallel arises on facts where a claimant might be entitled to a remedy of either restitutionary damages for breach of contract or restitution for failure of consideration. In such a case, the condition for the latter—that the claimant terminate the contract—requires the defendant's breach to be particularly serious; a requirement which will often correlate to a legitimate interest in the defendant's performance (the condition for the former).[221]

Another limitation on failure of consideration actions is the requirement that the failure of consideration be total. This requirement, although subject to significant exceptions (such as when the consideration can be apportioned or when "counter-restitution is simple")[222] the scope of which have yet to be worked out,[223] operates to limit claims for failure of consideration perhaps beyond those of restitutionary damages for breach of contract.

A final difference, and one which might mean that many cases of restitutionary damages for breach of contract cannot be alternatively analysed as instances of restitution for failure of consideration in unjust enrichment, arises in circumstances in which the contract is discharged not by breach but by performance. In these cases, the most common example being those of skimped performance, the conventional analysis suggests that the contract must govern the rights of the parties; it is only in cases where the contract is discharged by breach that failure of consideration can operate.[224] Although this limitation has been criticised,[225] Professor McKendrick has noted that it is independent of a claim for restitutionary damages for breach of contract where such a limitation does not exist, and should not be imposed, when those damages are sought simply because the final measure might be the same.[226]

An argument has been made that many of the awards considered above should not be seen as restitutionary damages for a breach of contract but as restitution for failure of consideration. Professor Burrows, for instance, referring to a case where the claimant contracts to buy a car paying money in

---

[221] G Treitel *The Law of Contract* (10th edn. Sweet & Maxwell London 1999) 713 referring to the requirement as one of "substantial failure" which provides a perfect parallel for the same requirement for restitutionary damages in the United States. Other commentators adopt more common terminology and divide breaches which allow termination into cases of breaches of conditions and serious breaches of intermediate terms: E McKendrick *Contract Law* (4th edn. MacMillan London 2000) 207.

[222] *David Securities Pty Ltd v. Commonwealth Bank of Australia* (1992) 175 CLR 353 (HCA) 383; *Goss v. Chilcott* [1996] AC 788 (PC) 798.

[223] See K Barker "Restitution of Passenger Fare: The Mikhail Lermontov" (1993) LMCLQ 291; P Birks "Failure of Consideration" in F Rose (ed.) *Consensus Ad Idem: Essays in the Law of Contract in Honour of Guenter Treitel* (Sweet & Maxwell London 1996) 195; E McKendrick "Total Failure of Consideration and Counter-Restitution: Two Issues or One?" in P Birks (ed.) *Laundering and Tracing* (Clarendon Press Oxford 1995) 217; J Edelman "The New Doctrine of Partial Failure of Consideration" (1997) 15 Aust Bar Rev 229.

[224] E McKendrick "Breach of Contract and the Meaning of Loss" (1999) 52 CLP 37, 70.

[225] S Smith "Concurrent Liability in Contract and Unjust Enrichment: The Fundamental Breach Requirement" (1999) 115 LQR 245; G Mead "Restitution within Contract?" (1991) 11 Legal Studies 172.

[226] E McKendrick "Breach of Contract and the Meaning of Loss" above note 224, 71.

advance, recites facts akin to the *Mobil Oil* case and argues that the cause of action could only be a failure of consideration. When the defendant fails to deliver, Professor Burrows argues that the money can only be recovered in an action for failure of consideration because "the breach cannot be regarded as the cause of the defendant's gain, since if there had been no breach, the defendant would still have made that gain from the contract."[227] But this misconceives the gain made by the defendant. The gain is not the initial payment received but the valuable right to performance which the defendant has taken from the claimant. The defendant receives restitution of the payment made for that right because that is the (contractually determined) value subtracted from the defendant's rights.

Further, it is apparent from all the United States cases considered as restitutionary damages that they are being considered as "an alternative remedy for breach of contract"[228] and not as a remedy for failure of consideration in unjust enrichment. As noted in chapters two and three, despite the similarities and often concurrent availability of the awards of restitutionary damages for a wrong (here breach of contract) and restitution for unjust enrichment (here failure of consideration) it is vital to keep these causes of action and remedies distinct.

5) Objections to restitutionary damages

Whilst restitutionary damages and disgorgement damages are conflated by commentators and the courts it is difficult to isolate any additional objections which have been made to restitutionary damages independently of disgorgement damages for breach of contract. However, two objections to restitutionary damages for breach of contract which operate differently from the case of disgorgement damages are that restitutionary damages encourage a failure to mitigate any loss suffered and that they allow escape from a bad bargain.

The same example given for disgorgement damages can illustrate this objection. Person A contracts to purchase 10 barrels of oil from person B at £10 a barrel paying in advance. B repudiates by selling the oil to C at a price of £15 being £5 above the market value. Even ignoring the legitimate interest limitation, do restitutionary damages encourage A not to purchase the oil from an alternative source but to wait in case the price falls? The answer must be "no". If the United States rule is followed the value of the contractual right taken from A will be assessed at contractual prices. If A waits to see if the price falls instead of mitigating, he does so at his own risk. Restitutionary damages will remain at £10 a

---

[227] A Burrows *Remedies* 308. Elsewhere, Professor Burrows argues that the "giving back" of contractual rights in the context of rescission is not restitutionary: A Burrows *The Law of Restitution* 32–33. Cf. P Birks *Introduction* 163: "the power to revoke rights conceded under the vitiated contract is itself a restitutionary right".

[228] J Dawson "Restitution or Damages" (1959) 20 Ohio St Law Journ 175, 189; *Restatement (Second) of Contracts* above note 146, §373, Comment a.

barrel. Even if the United States rule is not followed and restitutionary damages are assessed at market value, the market value will be that at the time of breach. If A fails to mitigate and the price rises, A will bear that additional cost.

The second objection is that restitutionary damages allow the claimant to escape from a bad bargain. This was noted above in explaining the effect of valuing the contractual rights transferred at contract prices. But this objection is not fatal. Exactly the same "evasion of a bad bargain" occurs where the award of restitution is given for failure of consideration in unjust enrichment, often on exactly the same facts. This has been justified on the basis that "there is no need for the law of restitution [unjust enrichment] to bow to contract".[229] It could also be said that there is no need for restitutionary damages to bow to compensatory damages for a breach of contract.

C Other breaches of promise

There is another cause of action which has not been discussed in this chapter but which closely resembles a contract. This is the action for breach of a promise which is referred to as promissory "estoppel". In England, it is usually (although anomalously) said that estoppel can only be used as a cause of action in instances of "proprietary estoppel"; where the promise made concerns land.[230]

Much confusion surrounds the remedy that is given for an action for breach of promise in these circumstances. Where an unambiguous promise is made which the promisor intends the promisee to rely upon, and the promisee does so rely to his detriment, then it is now recognised that the money award made is to satisfy the expectations of the promisee.[231] Such an award is compensatory damages as calculated for a breach of contract. There is no reason why the breach of the estoppel-promise should be treated differently from a breach of a contractual promise supported by consideration or a breach of a promise made in a deed. In Australia, where the action to enforce the estoppel-promise is not confined to promises involving land, the two actions have indeed been treated in the same manner.[232] Restitutionary damages and disgorgement damages should be available for all these different forms of breach of promise.

---

[229] A Burrows *The Law of Restitution* 266.

[230] *Gillett* v. *Holt* [2001] Ch 210 (CA); *Central London Property Trust* v. *Hightrees House Ltd* [1947] KB 130 (CA); *Crabb* v. *Arun District Council* (1976) Ch 179 (CA).

[231] *Gillett* v. *Holt* above note 230, rejecting *Taylor* v. *Dickens* [1998] 1 FLR 806; *Re Basham decd* [1986] 1 WLR 1498; *Giumelli* v. *Giumelli* (1999) 196 CLR 101 (HCA) 111.

[232] J Edelman "Remedial Certainty or Remedial Discretion in Estoppel after Giumelli" (1999) 15 JCL 179; *Giumelli* v. *Giumelli* (1999) 161 ALR 473 (HCA).

CONCLUSION

Attorney General v. *Blake* is a bold decision, which, in allowing disgorgement damages for a breach of contract, marks a consistent and cautious change to the landscape of contractual remedies. The precise effect of the decision and cases in which disgorgement damages will be allowed in the future will have to be worked out in future cases. However, Lord Nicholls has left powerful guidelines for the nature of a test which can now develop. The guiding criteria suggest the same requirements for disgorgement damages (that compensatory damages are inadequate to deter a failure to perform which, this book has argued, exists in cases of cynical breach) and restitutionary damages (available generally to reverse wrongful transfers of value) as other wrongs. But there is one major difference.

The difference lies in another limitation imposed by the *Blake* case upon disgorgement damages and, by implication, also upon restitutionary damages for breach of contract. This additional limitation sets breach of contract apart from other civil wrongs. In order for the same approaches to apply as for other civil wrongs the claimant must first have a legitimate interest in performance of the contractual obligation which is breached. In some instances this interest in performance is clear (for instance, where a claimant is entitled to specific performance or an injunction to restrain a breach of that contractual provision or under fiduciary duties). But beyond these recognised cases it is very difficult to tell when the law will consider that a claimant has a legitimate interest in performance.

6

Equitable Wrongs

INTRODUCTION

IT WAS SHOWN in chapter two that the category of "wrongs" should not be limited to common law wrongs but should also include conduct treated as wrongful in equity. The Law Commission, in recommending that gain-based damages be available for equitable wrongs, listed the causes of action in equity that it considered equitable wrongs. These causes of action were breach of fiduciary duty (which includes breach of trust), breach of confidence and knowing assistance in a breach of fiduciary duty.[1] These equitable wrongs are all considered in this chapter with two modifications. First, it will be argued that the wrong of "knowing assistance in a breach of fiduciary duty" should be recognised as a broader wrong of "knowing participation in a breach of fiduciary duty". Secondly, one additional wrong, the wrong of actual fraud (encompassing both deceit and bribery) which exists concurrently at common law and in equity, will also be considered.

Because equitable wrongs, unlike torts, are often not recognised as part of a law of wrongs, section A of this chapter considers the nature of these wrongs. Sections B and C follow the same format as the other chapters and show that, as in the case of common law wrongs, restitutionary damages are generally available for equitable wrongs (in section B) and disgorgement damages are available where compensatory damages are inadequate sufficiently to deter (section C).

A The equitable wrongs

1) Breach of trust and fiduciary duty

In a certain type of relationship, characterised by the presence of a large degree of trust and confidence, equity recognises strict duties, the breach of which is wrongful. These relationships are described as "fiduciary". The classic instance of a fiduciary relationship is the trustee/beneficiary relationship where a trustee is entrusted with the legal ownership of property to which a beneficiary is entitled in equity.[2] However, the word "trust" is sometimes used in a very loose

---

[1] *Law Commission 1997* Appendix A, Draft Bill.

[2] *Hardoon v. Belilios* [1901] AC 118 (PC) 123 (Lindley LJ): "All that is necessary to establish the relation of trustee and cestui que trust is to prove that the legal title was in the plaintiff and the equitable title in the defendant."

sense encompassing all fiduciary relations. It is this broad sense in which directors are sometimes referred to as "trustees"[3] and said to be "trustees of company property".[4] In the same way the term "constructive trustee" has also been (mis)used to describe fiduciary relations not characterised by a separation of legal and equitable ownership.[5]

The degree of trust and confidence inherent in the fiduciary relationship is reflected in the particular vulnerability of the fiduciary to the principal. In the words of Professor Finn (as his Honour then was), a fiduciary relationship exists because the "circumstances . . . are such that one party is entitled to expect that the other will act in his interest in and for the purposes of the relationship".[6]

It is well established that a breach of fiduciary duty can arise although the fiduciary might have acted with the very best of intentions. It does not matter that the fiduciary has conducted himself honestly[7] or that the claimant might not have been able to make the profit himself.[8] The fiduciary is held to a "level higher than that trodden by the crowd"[9] in order "to preclude the fiduciary from being swayed by considerations of personal interest and from accordingly misusing the fiduciary position for personal advantage".[10] The institution of trust and confidence is regarded as such an important one that the rule is strict to prevent the possibility of departure from it.

The fiduciary comes under particular duties of which one distinguishing obligation is the obligation of loyalty. A fiduciary's obligation of loyalty has several facets. A fiduciary must act in good faith; he must not make a profit out of his trust; he must not place himself in a position where his duty and his interest may conflict; he may not act for his own benefit or the benefit of a third person without the informed consent of his principal.[11]

It was once thought that liability for breach of fiduciary duty was based in notions of property. However, any doubts were resolved in *Attorney General*

---

[3] L Sealy "The Director as Trustee" [1967] CLJ 83.

[4] *Agip (Africa) Ltd* v. *Jackson* [1990] Ch 265, 290.

[5] See, for instance *Chan* v. *Zacharia* (1983) 53 ALR 417 (HCA) 433 (Deane J); *Regal (Hastings) Ltd* v. *Gulliver* [1967] 2 AC 134 (HL); *Boardman* v. *Phipps* [1967] 2 AC 46 (HL) . This "type of constructive trust is merely the creation by the court . . . to meet the wrongdoing alleged: there is no real trust and usually no chance of a proprietary remedy": *Coulthard* v. *Disco Mix Club Ltd* [2000] 1 WLR 707, 731. See also *Selangor United Rubber Estates Ltd* v. *Cradock (No 3)* [1968] 1 WLR 1555, 1582. The criticism of the lax use of this term has also been made by commentators on a number of occasions: see P Millett "Restitution and Constructive Trusts" in W Cornish et al *Restitution* 200 and also the discussion and authorities in L Smith "Constructive Trusts and Constructive Trustees" [1999] CLJ 294.

[6] P Finn "The Fiduciary Principle" in TG Youdan (ed.) *Equity, Fiduciaries and Trusts* (Carswell Toronto 1989) 1, 47.

[7] *Regal (Hastings) Ltd* v. *Gulliver* [1967] 2 AC 134 (HL); *Boardman* v. *Phipps* [1967] 2 AC 46 (HL).

[8] *Keech* v. *Sandford* (1726) Sel Cas T King 61; 25 ER 223; *Boardman* v. *Phipps* above note 7.

[9] *Meinhard* v. *Salmon* (1928) 164 NE 545 (SCUS) 546 (Cardozo CJ).

[10] *Warman International Ltd* v. *Dwyer* (1995) 182 CLR 544 (HCA) 557–558; *Chan* v. *Zacharia* (1984) 154 CLR 178 (HCA) 198–199

[11] *Bristol and West Building Society* v. *Mothew* [1998] Ch 1 (CA) 18; *Arklow Investments* v. *Maclean* [2000] 1 WLR 594 (PC) 599.

for Hong Kong v. *Reid*,[12] where the Privy Council made it clear that the fiduciary liability was independent of any question of interference with property held by the fiduciary.[13] That case was discussed in detail in chapter three. It will be recalled that the breach of fiduciary duty in that case was that the defendant, a public prosecutor, took bribes to obstruct prosecutions in breach of his fiduciary duty to the Crown, his employer. The Privy Council held that the bribes had to be disgorged but as the defendant had purchased land with the bribes a proprietary remedy was given over the land. The breach of fiduciary duty in that case—receiving bribes—clearly did not involve property of the claimant (principal).

2) Dishonest participation in a breach of fiduciary duty

The equitable wrong characterised here as "dishonest participation in a breach of fiduciary duty" has previously been treated as three different equitable wrongs. Most courts and commentators refer to two wrongs of "knowing receipt of property in breach of trust" and "knowing assistance in a breach of trust" and occasionally a wrong of "knowing participation in a breach of fiduciary duty". It is argued below that the latter is a wrong which subsumes the former two and the test for "knowledge" should be a unitary test of dishonesty.

The argument that the law should recognise a unitary wrong of dishonest participation in breach of fiduciary duty is made in four steps. First, it is shown that the best, and prevailing, view should be that the test for knowledge in cases of knowing receipt of proceeds in breach of trust and knowing assistance in a breach of trust should be a requirement of dishonesty. Secondly, it is shown that there is no reason to confine knowing receipt and knowing assistance to cases of breaches of trust and that courts and commentators have now accepted that these wrongs extend to breaches of fiduciary duty generally. Thirdly, there is no need to differentiate between dishonest receipt of property in breach of fiduciary duty and dishonest assistance in a breach of fiduciary duty. These two aspects of the equitable wrong should be, and are being, combined into a single equitable wrong of dishonest participation in a breach of fiduciary duty. Finally, it is shown that this approach does not affect any possible *alternative analysis* in unjust enrichment based upon a defendant's receipt of a claimant's equitable property.

---

[12] [1994] 1 AC 324 (PC). See also *Keech* v. *Sandford* above note 8, where the trustee was not only compelled to hold the lease on trust for the infant but also all profits made despite the fact that the infant's request for renewal of the trust was refused.

[13] A narrow majority of the House of Lords in *Boardman* v. *Phipps* had earlier held that it was not necessary for a breach of fiduciary duty that there be an interference with the property of the fiduciary: *Boardman* v. *Phipps* above note 7, 102 (Lord Cohen), 127 (Lord Upjohn) cf at 107 (Lord Hodson), 115 (Lord Guest).

(a) *Dishonest receipt and dishonest assistance in a breach of trust*

In *Barnes* v. *Addy*[14] two solicitors had assisted in preparing a transfer of trust property on the appointment of a new trustee. The new trustee had misapplied the trust money and had then gone bankrupt. The question before the Court of Chancery was whether the solicitors were liable.

Lord Selborne LC held that they were not. In a very famous obiter dictum he formulated the principle that liability only arises if "those agents receive and become chargeable with some part of the trust property, or . . . they assist with knowledge in a dishonest and fraudulent design on the part of the trustees.[15] This traditional formulation was subsequently taken to establish two "limbs" or wrongs of knowing receipt and knowing assistance.

(i) Knowing assistance

The wrong of knowing assistance was considered in detail by the Privy Council in 1995. In *Royal Brunei Airlines* v. *Tan*[16] the defendant was the managing director of a company which had misapplied trust money by paying it into the company's current account instead of a trust account. The company became insolvent and the defendant was sued for having knowingly allowed the money to be paid into the wrong account. In delivering the advice of the Privy Council, Lord Nicholls stated that the difference between the two "limbs" of *Barnes* v. *Addy* is that the first contemplates liability based upon receipt of trust property whilst, in the second, "liability as an accessory is not dependent upon receipt of trust property".[17]

The question as to what constituted sufficient "knowledge" for "knowing assistance" had been a vexed question before the *Tan* case. The competing views usually referred to the degrees of knowledge listed by Peter Gibson J in *Baden, Delvaux and Lecuit* v. *Société Général pour Favoriser le Développement du Commerce et de l'Industrie en France SA*:[18]

> "(i) actual knowledge; (ii) wilfully shutting one's eyes to the obvious; (iii) wilfully and recklessly failing to make such inquiries as an honest and reasonable man would make; (iv) knowledge of the circumstances which would indicate the facts to an honest and reasonable man; (v) knowledge of the circumstances which would put an honest and reasonable man on inquiry."

One view was that only "dishonesty" (usually the first three degrees of knowledge) would suffice for liability. The other view was that negligence (usually all five degrees) was sufficient. In the *Tan* case, the Privy Council affirmed that the criterion was one of dishonesty[19] and that the reference to a "dishonest and

---

[14] (1874) 9 LR Ch App 244.
[15] *Barnes* v. *Addy* above note 14, 252.
[16] [1995] 2 AC 378 (PC).
[17] *Royal Brunei Airlines* v. *Tan* above note 16, 382.
[18] [1983] BCLC 325, 427.
[19] *Selangor United Rubber Estates Ltd* v. *Cradock (No 3)* [1968] 1 WLR 1555, 1591 (Ungoed Thomas J). See also *Gold* v. *Rosenberg* (1997) 152 DLR (4th) 385 (SCC) 394.

fraudulent design" did not encompass conduct which was "not innocent . . . but still short of dishonesty".[20] Lord Nicholls preferred that references not be made to the degrees of "knowledge"[21] and that in a commercial setting dishonesty will depend upon what is "commercially unacceptable conduct".[22] Knowingly allowing the money to be paid into the wrong account was sufficient to amount to "dishonesty" although mere carelessness would not have been.[23] This test, from Lord Nicholls' advice, requiring "dishonesty" in cases of knowing assistance, has now been accepted as authoritative in England.[24]

(ii) Knowing receipt
The difficulty that remains is that the test for the level of knowledge in knowing receipt cases is still unsettled. Every authority on the cause of action of "knowing receipt" has held that there is a requirement of knowledge,[25] but unlike knowing assistance cases since the *Tan* case, the extent of this required knowledge is unclear. The cases range from recognising a requirement of dishonesty through mere carelessness even to the possibility of strict liability. It will be seen below that much of this difficulty arises because two different causes of action are being conflated. In chapter two it was explained that dishonest receipt of property in breach of fiduciary duty should be a *wrong* (assimilated with that of "knowing assistance" in a breach of fiduciary duty) into a unitary wrong of "knowing participation" and the possibility of a separate strict liability action in unjust enrichment should be recognised.[26] This unjust enrichment action is explained further below.

Although Lord Nicholls separated the two limbs of *Barnes* v. *Addy* in the *Tan* case more recent authorities have favoured treating a wrong of knowing receipt in the same way as knowing assistance and hence applying the same dishonesty test to both. In *Dubai Aluminium Co Ltd* v. *Salaam*,[27] claims were brought against a number of parties in respect of a sham services transaction designed to transfer money from the Dubai Aluminium Company to companies controlled by the defendants Mr Salaam and Mr Amhurst. The claims included claims against Mr Salaam and Mr Amhurst for both knowing assistance and knowing receipt. The trial judge, Rix J, accepted that the level of knowledge required for

---

[20] *Belmont Finance Corporation Ltd* v. *Williams Furniture Ltd* [1979] Ch 250 (CA) 274 (Goff LJ).
[21] *Royal Brunei Airlines* v. *Tan* above note 16, 392.
[22] *Cowan de Groot Properties Ltd* v. *Eagle Trust Plc* [1992] 4 All ER 700, 761 (Knox J).
[23] *Royal Brunei Airlines* v. *Tan* above note 16, 389.
[24] *Dubai Aluminium Co Ltd* v. *Salaam* [2001] QB 113 (CA); *Houghton* v. *Fayers* [2000] Lloyds Rep Bank 145 (CA); *Twinsectra Ltd* v. *Yardley* [1999] Lloyds Rep Bank 438 (CA).
[25] See the survey of the conflicting degrees of knowledge in *Goff and Jones* 743–744. In addition to those cases cited see *Citadel General Assurance Co* v. *Lloyds Bank Canada* [1997] 3 SCR 805 (SCC); *Gold* v. *Rosenberg* above note 19; *Dubai Aluminium Co Ltd* v. *Salaam* [1999] 1 Lloyds Rep 415; *Twinsectra Ltd* v. *Yardley* above note 24; *Houghton* v. *Fayers* above note 24, 148; *Bank of America* v. *Arnell* [1999] Lloyd's Rep Bank 399; *Bankgesellschaft Berlin AG* v. *Makris* (High Court 22 Jan 1999) (Creswell J); *Bank of Credit and Commerce International (Overseas) Ltd* v. *Akindele* [2001] Ch 437 (CA).
[26] See further ch. 2 text accompanying note 115.
[27] *Dubai* v. *Salaam* above note 25.

knowing assistance was "dishonesty" as advised by the Privy Council in the *Tan* case. However, he also held that the test for the level of knowledge in a case of knowing receipt was the same.[28] An appeal to the Court of Appeal did not consider this point.[29]

Twinsectra Ltd v. *Yardley*[30] is another recent example. In that case Mr Sims, a solicitor, gave a personal undertaking in order that Twinsectra Ltd would make a loan to Yardley. Sims was closely associated with Yardley but gave the undertaking after Yardley's own solicitor, Mr Leach, had refused to give it. The undertaking included a promise that Sims would retain the loan monies until they were required by Yardley for the acquisition of a property and that they would only be used for such an acquisition. Yardley subsequently received another loan on better terms and allowed Sims to take over the Twinsectra loan and repayment of it. In breach of the undertaking the loan monies provided by Twinsectra were then transferred to Mr Leach's client account and paid from there to other sources including companies controlled by Yardley.

In the Court of Appeal, claims of knowing receipt were made against Mr Yardley, the companies he controlled (which had received money from the loan) and Mr Leach.[31] Claims of knowing assistance were also made against Mr Leach for allowing the funds to be distributed through his client account. The Court of Appeal held that the Twinsectra loan monies were held by Mr Sims on trust to be used for the purpose provided in the undertaking. The Court treated the liability of Mr Leach for knowing receipt and knowing assistance interchangeably, considering both claims as depending upon whether Mr Leach had acted dishonestly, and accepting that he had, held that this satisfied the requirements of knowing receipt and knowing assistance.[32] Likewise, the Court of Appeal held that the companies, controlled by Mr Yardley, were "by reason of Mr Yardley's state of mind . . . dishonest recipients of the monies paid over to Mr Leach by Mr Sims in breach of his fiduciary obligations".[33]

In *Bank of America* v. *Arnell*[34] a counterfeit cheque, in favour of a company, (Bluepark International Ltd) controlled by Mr Arnell, had been presented to the claimant bank, Bank of America. The cheque was honoured by the Bank of America and subsequently much of the money from Bluepark's account was transferred from the company's account to Mr Arnell's personal account at Lloyds Bank. One manner in which the money was transferred was through an acquaintance of Mr Arnell's, Miss Hadden. Miss Hadden knew nothing about the transaction, only that she was paid £750 in order to allow Mr Arnell to deposit £25,750 in her account and immediately withdraw £25,000. A number

---

[28] *Dubai* v. *Salaam* above note 25, 453.
[29] *Dubai* v. *Salaam* (CA) above note 24.
[30] *Twinsectra Ltd* v. *Yardley* above note 24.
[31] Sims was bankrupt and no claim was made against him.
[32] *Twinsectra Ltd* v. *Yardley* above note 24, 465.
[33] *Twinsectra Ltd* v. *Yardley* above note 24, 466.
[34] *Bank of America* v. *Arnell* above note 25.

of claims were brought against Mr Arnell but of concern here is the claim brought against Miss Hadden for knowing receipt.

The difficulty faced by the Bank of America was in establishing that the money paid into Miss Hadden's account from Bluepark was actually the same money as had been paid by Bank of America to Bluepark. Instead, the Bank of America relied upon the fact that Mr Arnell owed a fiduciary duty as the beneficial owner of Bluepark. The Bank of America sought to make Miss Hadden liable for the £25,750 as a knowing recipient of funds which had been paid in breach of this fiduciary duty. Aikens J however held that this claim failed. Referring to the *Twinsectra* case he stated that:[35]

> "The fundamental question that the court has to ask now is: was the recipient acting *honestly* when she received the funds? . . . In my judgment she was not acting dishonestly. She was naïve and was duped, but she was innocent."

On the other hand, other authorities have followed an earlier Court of Appeal case, *Belmont Finance Corp* v. *Williams Furniture Ltd (No 2)*,[36] and held that dishonesty is not required; carelessness will suffice.[37] This approach was taken by the Court of Appeal in obiter dicta in one knowing receipt case even after the *Tan* case had resolved that dishonesty was the standard for knowing assistance. In *Houghton* v. *Fayers*[38] this finding was made by the Court of Appeal in an application for summary judgment.

In *Houghton* v. *Fayers*,[39] Mr Fayers had set up a company, Fayers Legal Services Ltd ("FLS"), ostensibly for the purpose of funding third party litigation for a share in any damages. A large number of people invested in the company but never recovered any of their investment. One transaction involved a gross over-payment for services rendered, many of which were for Mr Fayers personally and not for the benefit of FLS. Part of the payment (£75,075) was made to Mr Day and the trial judge, Collins J, had held that Mr Day was liable for having dishonestly received the money which was paid in breach of fiduciary duty. Delivering the leading judgment of the Court of Appeal, Nourse LJ affirmed this finding (to the extent of the £75,075 received) but held that:[40]

> "it was unnecessary for a finding of dishonesty to be made against Mr Day. It was enough for FLS to establish that he knew or ought to have known that the money had been paid to him in breach of Mr Fayers' fiduciary duty to FLS. That point was made very clearly by Buckley LJ in *Belmont Finance Corp* v. *Williams Furniture Ltd*."

---

[35] *Bank of America* v. *Arnell* above note 25, 406.
[36] *Belmont Finance Corp* above note 20, 405.
[37] *Rolled Steel Products (Holdings) Ltd* v. *British Steel Corporation* [1986] 1 Ch 246 (CA) 307–307; *Karak Rubber Co Ltd* v. *Burden (No 2)* [1972] 1 WLR 602, 632; *Agip (Africa) Ltd* v. *Jackson* [1990] Ch 265, 291; *Gold* v. *Rosenberg* above note 19, 798.
[38] *Houghton* v. *Fayers* above note 24.
[39] *Houghton* v. *Fayers* above note 24.
[40] *Houghton* v. *Fayers* above note 24, 148.

Most recently in *Bank of Credit and Commerce International (Overseas) Ltd*
v. *Akindele*[41] the Court of Appeal recognised the conflict between the two
approaches. The defendant, Chief Akindele, agreed to provide $US 10 million to
one of the claimant companies, BCCI Holdings, through another of the
claimant companies, ICIC Overseas. The loan was structured as a purchase of
shares which, after a period of at least two years, ICIC Overseas would sell at a
price which would give Chief Akindele a 15 per cent compounded return. The
claimants were the liquidators of the two companies which alleged that the
transaction was in breach of fiduciary duties owed to the companies. The breach
lay in arranging a loan transaction to appear on the balance sheet to be a purchase of equity. The claims brought included claims for knowing receipt and
knowing assistance in breach of fiduciary duty.

Delivering the judgment of the Court of Appeal, Nourse LJ recognised the conflict in the cases, although unfortunately the only English case after the *Tan* case
to which he referred was his own decision in *Houghton* v. *Fayers*.[42] Nourse LJ
suggested a resolution in a single test for the state of mind of the defendant which
was that "the recipient's state of knowledge must be such as to make it unconscionable for him to retain the benefit of the receipt".[43] In the result, it did not
matter in the *Akindele* case, as the Court of Appeal held that there was no evidence which could have led Chief Akindele to have questioned the propriety of the
transaction.[44]

"Unconscionability" is unmanageable without the express insertion of a
standard. It is impossible to tell what the term actually means. Indeed, Lord
Nicholls had discussed unconscionability in the *Tan* case and concluded that
"unconscionable" simply means dishonest and if it does mean something different "it is not clear what that something different is".[45] If a unitary test based
upon "unconscionability" is to have any meaning it must collapse into a test
based upon dishonesty bringing knowing receipt in line with knowing assistance.

(b) *Dishonest receipt and dishonest assistance in a breach of
fiduciary duty*

(i) Dishonest assistance in a breach of fiduciary duty
An expansion has occurred in the case of knowing assistance in a breach of trust
to encompass cases of knowing assistance in a breach of fiduciary duty generally. In extra-judicial speeches, Lord Hoffmann, Lord Nicholls, and a number
of other judges and commentators, have noted that "knowing participation" is
the "equitable counterpart of the common law tort of interfering with contractual relations".[46] The analogy with interfering with the plaintiff's contractual

[41] *Akindele* above note 25.
[42] *Houghton* v. *Fayers* above note 24. See also *Akindele* above note 25, 451–452.
[43] *Bank of Credit and Commerce International (Overseas) Ltd* v. *Akindele* above note 25, 455.
[44] *Bank of Credit and Commerce International (Overseas) Ltd* v. *Akindele* above note 25, 458.
[45] *Royal Brunei Airlines* v. *Tan* [1995] 2 AC 378 (PC) 392.
[46] Lord Hoffmann "The Redundancy of Knowing Assistance" in P Birks (ed.) *The Frontiers of Liability* (Vol 1 OUP Oxford 1994) 27, 29; Lord Nicholls "Knowing Receipt: The Need for a New

rights in equity should not be limited to interfering with the plaintiff's *trust* rights but should extend to the plaintiff's rights owed to him by a defendant fiduciary generally.[47] The law having already reached the conclusion that fiduciaries generally, like trustees, are both to be held to the highest standards, interference or assistance in a breach of a fiduciary duty between, for example, an agent and a principal should be treated no more lightly than a trustee and a beneficiary.

This approach of viewing knowing assistance claims as related to breaches of fiduciary duty and not merely breaches of trust can be seen in several recent cases.[48] In one of these, *Satnam Ltd* v. *Dunlop Heywood Ltd*,[49] the claimant property development company, Satnam Investments ("Satnam") had an option to purchase a site with development potential. When Satnam went into liquidation, the site's owners exercised their contractual right to cancel the option. A surveying company which had been acting for Satnam then informed a rival development company, Morbaine Ltd of the development potential of the site. Morbaine purchased the site. After the discharge of its receivers Satnam brought actions against its surveyors and Morbaine for breach of fiduciary duty and participation in a breach of fiduciary duty respectively.

The trial judge held that both the surveyors and Morbaine were liable although there was no finding made that Morbaine had been aware of the breach of fiduciary duty or had been dishonest. Morbaine appealed to the Court of Appeal. The Court of Appeal accepted that liability could be imposed for knowing assistance in a breach of fiduciary duty, but allowed the appeal because no finding of dishonesty had been made against Morbaine. Relying upon the *Tan* case, Nourse LJ in the leading judgment stated that "mere knowledge that [an] opportunity has been afforded in breach of someone else's fiduciary duty is not enough"; dishonesty is required.[50]

Unfortunately, in *Petrotrade Inc* v. *Smith*[51] a significant limitation was suggested upon dishonest assistance in a breach of fiduciary duty. In that case, Mr Smith, the operations manager of an oil-trading company, Petrotrade, accepted a bribe from a company, Alpina, in order to appoint that company as Petrotrade's port agent to handle the arrival of its chartered vessels at Antwerp. David Steel J held Mr Smith liable both for the loss suffered by Petrotrade at common law for "fraud" or a broader version of the tort of deceit not requiring

Landmark" in W Cornish et al *Restitution* 231, 244; C Harpum "Accessory Liability for Procuring or Assisting a Breach of Trust" (1995) 111 LQR 545, 546; *Fyffes Group Ltd* v. *Templeman* [2000] 2 Lloyds Rep 643.

[47] *El Ajou* v. *Dollar Land Holdings plc* [1994] 2 All ER 685 (CA).
[48] See also *Logicrose Ltd* v. *Southend United Football Club Ltd* [1988] 1 WLR 1256, 1261 (Millett J); G Jones "Bribes and Bribers" [1989] CLJ 22; *Satnam Ltd* v. *Dunlop Heywood Ltd* [1999] 3 All ER 652; *Grupo Torras SA* v. *Al-Sabah (No 5)* [2001] Lloyd's Rep. Bank. 36 (CA) describing knowing assistance as " a fault-based liability as an accessory to a breach of fiduciary duty."
[49] [1999] 3 All ER 652.
[50] *Satnam Ltd* v. *Dunlop Heywood Ltd* above note 48, 671.
[51] [2000] 1 Lloyds Rep 486.

a representation[52] or for disgorgement of the profits made.[53] A claim for disgorgement of the profits had also been sought for the equitable wrong of knowing assistance in a breach of fiduciary duty. David Steel J refused this claim
because the profits were not the property (or traceable property) of Petrotrade.
The bribes had been paid by Alpina. This view confines cases of dishonest assistance to instances where the assistance is in the misapplication of property.

This approach has been strongly criticised by Dr Mitchell and said to possibly
derive from a misunderstanding of the formula that dishonest assistants are liable
to account as constructive trustees; a formula which is used in these cases simply
to mean a liability to account in the manner of a trustee.[54] It is akin to the now-
rejected view that a breach of fiduciary duty must involve a misapplication of
property of the fiduciary.[55] This limitation also has little support in other authorities. In *Satnam Ltd* v. *Dunlop Heywood Ltd*,[56] Nourse LJ did refer to the two
limbs from the *Barnes* v. *Addy* case as both requiring a misappropriation of "trust
property or traceable proceeds of trust property".[57] However, as noted above,
when discussing liability for dishonest assistance in the breach of fiduciary duty
in that case, although no property had been acquired (all that was acquired was
information), Nourse LJ stated that "we would not have wanted to shut out the
possibility of such a claim's being successful".[58] Later cases have referred to this
statement as a reason to doubt the existence of such a limitation,[59] or, as will be
seen below, in recognising the existence of a broad wrong of dishonest participation in a breach of fiduciary duty, implicitly rejected such a limitation.[60]

(ii) Dishonest receipt in breach of fiduciary duty
The trend toward expanding dishonest receipt from instances of breach of trust
to all instances of breach of fiduciary duty has also been evident in England for
some time. The acceptance that the wrong extends to cases of breaches of fiduciary duties generally can be seen in two of the knowing receipt cases discussed
above, *Houghton* v. *Fayers*[61] and *Bank of Credit and Commerce International
(Overseas) Ltd* v. *Akindele*.[62] Neither of these cases involved breaches of trust by

---

[52] *Petrotrade Inc* v. *Smith* [2000] 1 Lloyds Rep 486 490. See ch. 4, text accompanying note 184.

[53] Although it was not explicitly recognised that the action was one for disgorgement damages
for the fraud and David Steel J simply referred to it as an action for "money had and received for the
bribe": *Petrotrade* above note 52, 490. See further, J Edelman "Money Had and Received: Modern
Pleading of an Old Count" [2000] RLR 547.

[54] C Mitchell "Civil Liability for Bribery" (2001) 117 LQR 207, 210. See above text accompanying note 5.

[55] See above text accompanying note 12.

[56] [1999] 3 All ER 652.

[57] *Satnam* above note 48, 671.

[58] *Satnam* above note 48.

[59] *Gencor ACP Ltd* v. *Dalby* [2000] 2 BCLC 734, 757; *Brown* v. *Bennett* [1999] 1 BCLC 649 (CA)
657–659; See also *Goose* v. *Wilson Sandford & Co (No 2)* [2001] Lloyd's Rep P N 189 (CA) 210: "the
formulation of the principle by Lord Nicholls of Birkenhead does not embrace such a requirement."

[60] *Fyffes Group Ltd* v. *Templeman* [2000] 2 Lloyds Rep 643;

[61] *Houghton* v. *Fayers* above note 24.

[62] [2000] 3 WLR 1423 (CA) .

a trustee; both were concerned with knowing receipt of proceeds from breaches of a director's fiduciary duty to his company.[63] Cases of dishonest receipt of property, like those of dishonest assistance, should not be confined to receipt of trust property or assistance in a breach of trust but should encompass fiduciary duties generally. The final step to a complete understanding of this wrong is to appreciate that both these aspects of liability can be merged into a wrong of "dishonest participation in a breach of fiduciary duty".

(c) *Dishonest participation in a breach of fiduciary duty*

The suggestion of assimilating the two limbs of *Barnes* v. *Addy* into a single wrong was first put forward extra-judicially by Lord Nicholls:[64] "receipt of property is incidental, in the sense that it is merely the form which the dishonest participation takes".[65] There is much to commend this view. One significant advantage is that it is otherwise difficult to draw the line between cases of receipt of property and cases of assistance in transfer of property. It is a very difficult question whether and when knowing receipt amounting to concealment of property falls within dishonest assistance.[66]

A unitary equitable wrong of dishonest participation should apply not only to cases of breach of trust but also to cases of breach of fiduciary duty. In Australia courts refer to this equitable wrong as "knowing participation in a breach of fiduciary duty".[67] The same issue arises of the required degree of knowledge, as is encountered in cases of knowing receipt and knowing assistance. But, like the two limbs of the *Barnes* v. *Addy* case, it is becoming clear that this broader wrong, which subsumes knowing receipt and knowing assistance, requires a level of knowledge amounting to dishonesty.

Recognition of this broader wrong occurred recently in England in *Fyffes Group Ltd* v. *Templeman*.[68] Mr Templeman was the marine operations manager for Fyffes Group Ltd ("Fyffes"). He negotiated a contract with Seatrade for weekly shipments of Fyffes' bananas from South America and the Caribbean to the United Kingdom and Europe. Unknown to Fyffes, Mr Templeman received secret commissions from 1992 to 1996 which amounted to $1.4 million, paid to a company he controlled in Cyprus. Fyffes sought to recover the amount of the secret commissions from Seatrade as money had and received, damages for the tort of fraud, and equitable compensation and an account of profits for Seatrade's dishonest assistance in Mr Templeman's breaches of fiduciary duty.

---

[63] See also *Gencor ACP Ltd* v. *Dalby* [2000] 2 BCLC 734; *Brown* v. *Bennett* [1999] 1 BCLC 649 (CA).

[64] Lord Nicholls "Knowing Receipt: The Need for a New Landmark" in W Cornish et al. *Restitution* 231.

[65] Lord Nicholls "Knowing Receipt: The Need for a New Landmark" above note 64, 244.

[66] *Agip (Africa) Ltd* v. *Jackson* [1990] Ch 265, 293; *Heinl* v. *Jyske Bank(Gibraltar) Ltd* [1999] Lloyds Rep Bank 511 (CA) 523.

[67] *Consul Development Pty Ltd* v. *DPC Estates Pty Ltd* (1975) 132 CLR 373 (HCA) 397; *Warman International Ltd* v. *Dwyer* (1995) 182 CLR 544 (HCA).

[68] *Fyffes Group Ltd* above note 60.

Toulson J held that Fyffes were entitled to compensatory damages for any loss suffered as a result of any more favourable terms granted due to the bribes, for the common law wrong of the tort of fraud and the equitable wrong of dishonest participation in a breach of fiduciary duty. However, disgorgement damages were not awarded as Toulson J held that any additional profit made as a result of more favourable terms due to the wrong committed was already awarded as compensatory damages for the equivalent loss suffered by Fyffes. However, in the course of argument about these disgorgement damages, Seatrade had sought to distinguish knowing receipt from knowing assistance and argued that disgorgement damages should only be available for the former. Toulson J quoted from the Australian authorities which accept a broad wrong of knowing participation in a breach of fiduciary duty (for which disgorgement damages are available) and rejected the proposed distinction.

(d)   *A different action in unjust enrichment*

There is a view that a cause of action based upon receipt of property belonging to another in equity should be recognised as a strict liability cause of action in unjust enrichment (subject to the defence of change of position).[69] This view has many academic supporters.[70] It is suggested that these cases, like those of "ignorance"[71] at common law, are unjust enrichment claims to the value of equitable property transferred without the claimant's knowledge. Like the unjust enrichment claim for "ignorance", there is no requirement of any degree of knowledge on the part of the defendant recipient. Liability is strict subject to defences, including change of position.

The case which lends the most support to this approach is *Ministry of Health* v. *Simpson*.[72] In that case a provision in the will of the deceased, Mr Diplock, directed his executors to distribute the residue of his estate according to their choice of charitable or benevolent objects. Pursuant to this provision gifts were made to a range of charities. It was held that the disposition was void because it permitted gifts to non-charitable objects (by allowing distribution of the residue to objects which were benevolent but not charitable).[73] As a result the residue

---

[69] The extent to which there is a requirement of an assertion of ownership, such that the liability is not truly strict is not examined here either: See *Agip (Africa) Ltd* v. *Jackson* above note 66, 291–293.

[70] P Birks "Accessory Liability" [1996] LMCLQ 1,2; Lord Nicholls "Knowing Receipt: The Need for a New Landmark" in WR Cornish et al *Restitution* 231; P Birks "Property and Unjust Enrichment" [1997] NZLR 623, 651–653; P McGrath "Knowing Receipt and Dishonest Assistance: A Wrong Turn" [1999] LMCLQ 343; C Harpum "The Basis of Equitable Liability" in P Birks (ed.) *The Frontiers of Liability* (Vol 1 OUP Oxford 1994) 9; Lord Hoffmann "The Redundancy of Knowing Assistance" in P Birks (ed.) *The Frontiers of Liability* (Vol 1 OUP Oxford 1994) 27, 29. Cf. L Smith "W(h)ither Knowing Receipt" (1998) 114 LQR 394; L Smith "Unjust Enrichment, Property, and the Structure of Trusts" (2000) 116 LQR 412. Others are more ambivalent: S Gardner "Knowing Assistance and Knowing Receipt: Taking Stock" (1996) 112 LQR 56.

[71] See ch. 2, text accompanying notes 114–118.

[72] [1951] AC 251 (HL) affirming *Re Diplock* [1948] Ch 465 (CA).

[73] *Chichester Diocesan Fund and Board of Finance Inc* v. *Simpson* [1944] AC 341 (HL).

was the subject of an intestacy. Instead of distributing the residue to the charities the executors should have distributed them to Mr Diplock's next of kin.
Although the executors could not recover the payments from the charities as
they were made under a mistake of law, the Court of Appeal and House of Lords
held that that the next of kin could recover from the charities. The charities were
personally and strictly liable to repay everything they had received.

Professor Smith has recently mounted a powerful argument against the use of
this case[74] to support a strict liability claim for receipt of property in breach
of trust.[75] However, it is unnecessary to examine this debate, and the existence
of a strict liability claim in unjust enrichment, which has been recently doubted
by the Court of Appeal.[76] The reason for this is that unless one is to argue that
all of the existing authorities on knowing receipt are wrong to require fault (or
knowledge), it is clear that independent of the existence of a strict liability unjust
enrichment claim, there must be an equitable wrong based upon the receipt[77]
which does not arise until the necessary element of knowledge is satisfied.[78]
Indeed, this dual analysis has been conceded by three of the proponents of a
strict liability unjust enrichment claim including Lord Nicholls.[79]

Much of the difficulty in this area arises from the fact that these two different
causes of action are being conflated and a dual analysis is not recognised. The
view that knowing assistance and knowing receipt should always be considered
as different causes of action is a manifestation of this view. It can be seen in
numerous statements which assume that knowing receipt is a cause of action in
unjust enrichment and state that it is an action only for restitution.[80] All this
confusion can be avoided by recognising that two different actions exist or, at
least, that an action based upon the dishonest receipt of equitable property is
part of the broader equitable wrong of dishonest participation in a breach of
fiduciary duty. In 1918 this point was made in *John* v. *Dodwell and Co Ltd*.[81]

---

[74] See also *G L Baker Ltd* v. *Medway Building and Supplies Ltd* [1958] 1 WLR 1216. Reversed on appeal in relation to a pleading point [1958] 1 WLR 1216 (CA) 1231, 1239. Dicta in support can also be seen in *Koorootang* v. *ANZ Banking Group* [1998] 3 VR 16 (SCV) 105 (Hansen J).

[75] L Smith "Unjust Enrichment, Property, and the Structure of Trusts" (2000) 116 LQR 412.

[76] *Bank of Credit and Commerce International (Overseas) Ltd* v. *Akindele* [2000] 3 WLR 1423 (CA).

[77] L Smith "Unjust Enrichment, Property, and the Structure of Trusts" (2000) 116 LQR 412, 428–434.

[78] *Agip (Africa) Ltd* v. *Jackson* [1990] Ch 265, 291.

[79] Lord Nicholls "Knowing Receipt: The Need for a New Landmark" in WR Cornish et al. *Restitution* 231; P Birks "The Role of Fault in the Law of Unjust Enrichment" in W Swadling and G Jones (eds) *The Search for Principle—Essays in Honour of Lord Goff of Chieveley* (OUP Oxford 1999) 235, 269; *Goff and Jones* 745–746. Cf P Birks "Property and Unjust Enrichment" [1997] NZLR 623, 651–653.

[80] *Royal Brunei Airlines* v. *Tan* [1995] 2 AC 378 (PC) 386; *Citadel* v. *Lloyds Bank* above note 25, 836–837; S Gardner "Knowing Assistance and Knowing Receipt: Taking Stock" (1996) 112 LQR 56, 85. See also *Grupo Torras SA* v. *Al-Sabah* [2001] Lloyd's Rep. Bank 36 (CA) describing knowing receipt as a receipt-based liability which may, on examination, prove to be either a vindication of per-sistent property rights or a personal restitutionary claim based on unjust enrichment by subtraction.

[81] [1918] AC 563 (PC).

In *John* v. *Dodwell and Co Ltd*[82] the manager of Dodwell and Co had bought shares for himself but had paid with cheques drawn against Dodwell's account. The appellant sharebrokers, partners in E John and Co, received the cheques and paid them onto the sellers of the shares. They were not fraudulent in receiving the amount of the cheques but they did have knowledge that the manager was drawing on Dodwell's account without apparent authority. However, when Dodwell brought their action they were met with the defence under a Ceylonese Ordinance that limited claims "for any loss, injury or damage" to 10 years. The Privy Council held that this limitation period applied to an action to recover the proceeds of the cheque for conversion but an action to recover the money based upon knowing receipt of property which the manager held on trust for Dodwell was not an action "for any loss, injury or damage".[83] However, Viscount Haldane LC acknowledged that a different cause of action did exist which *was* based upon loss. Such a cause of action was based upon dishonest or fraudulent assistance or receipt in breach of fiduciary duty for which dishonest participants or recipients might be held liable. Viscount Haldane LC stated that "mere notice of want of title is not enough, unless there is such notice of actual fraud as extends to the defendant a fiduciary obligation to disclose what it becomes fraudulent on his part to conceal".[84] Viscount Haldane LC explained that such a cause of action is quite independent and separate from one that is merely seeking restitution of trust property independently of any wrongdoing.[85]

3) Breach of confidence

The wrong of breach of confidence requires that "he who has received information in confidence shall not take unfair advantage of it".[86] The basis of the equitable wrong of breach of confidence has been much debated. In 1851, in *Morison* v. *Moat*,[87] Turner V-C stated of the basis of the wrong that "in some cases it has been referred to as property, in others as contract, and in others again . . . as founded upon trust or confidence."

---

[82] *John* v. *Dodwell* above note 81.
[83] *John* v. *Dodwell* above note 81, 569–570. See also *British American Elevator Co* v. *Bank of British North America* [1919] AC 658 (PC).
[84] *John* v. *Dodwell* above note 81, 574.
[85] *John* v. *Dodwell* above note 81, 576.
[86] *Seager* v. *Copydex (No 1)* [1967] 1 WLR 923 (CA) 931 (Lord Denning MR). In fact the doctrine might go further than this and extend to someone who has, without authorisation, *taken* information which is confidential: Compare *Franklin* v. *Giddins* [1978] Qd R 72 (SCQ) and *obiter dicta* in *Lord Ashburton* v. *Pape* [1913] 2 Ch 469 (CA) 475 with *Malone* v. *Metropolitan Police Commissioner* [1979] Ch 344 and the Law Commission which described the use of breach of confidence in these cases as "very doubtful": Law Commission *Breach of Confidence* (1981 Law Comm No 110) 24.
[87] (1851) 20 LJ Ch 513, 522.

Although it is sometimes difficult to distinguish the obligation of confidence from a property right,[88] the doctrine is not solely based in concepts of property.[89] This is the reason why this doctrine is not considered in chapter seven, "Intellectual Property Wrongs", although many books often consider it as part of this area.[90]

In *Prince Albert* v. *Strange*,[91] one of the earliest cases on breach of confidence, the defendant had come into the possession of copies and impressions of etchings made by the claimant for the claimant's private use. The Lord Chancellor, Lord Cottenham, held that it was not necessary for the plaintiff to establish a property right in the copies made in order to receive an injunction, the order operating "to prevent what this Court considers and treats as a wrong".[92] Lord Cottenham LC stated that the wrong "by no means depends solely upon the question of property, for a breach of trust, confidence, or contract, would of itself" be sufficient.[93] It has therefore been invoked in cases where marital secrets are revealed[94] or government secrets leaked.[95]

It is also clear that the basis of the equitable wrong of breach of confidence is not contract. It is well established that there can be a breach of an obligation of confidence where there is no contract between the parties.[96] Nor is the wrong rooted in a relationship of trust and confidence. Although the Court of Appeal (followed by at least one commentator) has suggested that the duty to respect confidence is a fiduciary duty[97] this approach should be rejected. The duty of confidence exists independently of any continuing relationship between the parties, or even any relationship at all between them. A complete stranger that comes into possession of clearly confidential information is still subject to the duty to respect it. For this reason the Privy Council obiter dicta recently cast doubt on this suggestion of the Court of Appeal.[98]

Although the precise basis of the doctrine of breach of confidence is not resolved, several points are now clear. First, the information (in the form in

[88] P Birks *Introduction* 343; ES Weinrib "Information and Property" (1988) 38 UTLJ 117. In *Attorney General* v. *Guardian Newspapers (No 2)* [1990] 1 AC 149 (HL) 281 Lord Goff preferred to leave this question open.
[89] "Its rational basis does not lie in proprietary right" but in "an obligation of conscience arising from the circumstances in or through which the information was communicated or obtained": *Moorgate Tobacco Co* v. *Phillip Morris Ltd* (1984) 156 CLR 414 (HCA) 438; *Cadbury Schweppes Inc* v. *FBI Foods Ltd* [1999] SCR 142 (SCC) 169; *E I Du Pont de Nemours Powder Co* v. *Masland* 244 US 100 (1917) (SCUS) 102.
[90] W Cornish *Intellectual Property*.
[91] (1849) 1 Mac & G 25; 41 ER 1171.
[92] *Prince Albert* v. *Strange* above note 91, 46; 1179.
[93] *Prince Albert* v. *Strange* above note 91, 44; 1178.
[94] *Duchess of Argyll* v. *Duke of Argyll* [1967] Ch 302.
[95] *Attorney General* v. *Jonathan Cape Ltd* [1976] QB 752.
[96] *Saltman Engineering Co Ltd* v. *Campbell Engineering Co Ltd* (1948) [1963] 3 All ER 413 (CA); *Attorney General* v. *Guardian Newspapers (No 2)* above note 88.
[97] *Attorney General* v. *Blake* [1998] Ch 439 (CA) 454; G Virgo *Restitution* 530–531.
[98] *Arklow Investments* v. *Maclean* [2000] 1 WLR 594 (PC) 600. See also *LAC Minerals Ltd* v. *International Corona Resources Ltd* (1989) (1989) 61 DLR (4th) 14 (SCC).

which it is used) must be confidential, and not freely available.[99] Secondly, compensatory damages (as equitable compensation) are available for breach of confidence.[100] Finally, provided the defendant received the information in circumstances in which he had knowledge that it was confidential, it does not matter if the subsequent use of the information is inadvertent.[101]

4) Fraud

Like the tort of fraud at common law, the equitable wrong of "fraud" is difficult to define. The equitable wrong clearly overlaps with the common law torts of deceit and fraud and hence includes cases of fraudulent misrepresentation[102] and cases of bribery.[103] A complication of terminology in relation to this equitable wrong is that equity sometimes uses the term "fraud" in other instances even in which the claimant has not acted improperly. For instance, unjust enrichments such as undue influence or unconscionable bargains are sometimes referred to as instances of "equitable fraud". Justices Meagher, Gummow and Lehane state that in equity the use of the word "fraud was "infinite" in the sense that it was discerned in quite disparate circumstances so as to make the concept appear amphibolous".[104] The equitable wrong of fraud is considered here only in the narrow sense of its concurrent operation with the common law tort of fraud. So the unjust factor of induced mistake by innocent misrepresentation, sometimes referred to as "equitable fraud" or "moral fraud",[105] does not fall within the concept of fraud in equity as considered in this chapter. Chapter two explained in detail why the cause of action for innocent misrepresentation is not a wrong but is an unjust enrichment. It suffices to note here that innocent misrepresentation is not part of the wrong of fraud considered in this chapter because "a case of innocent misrepresentation may be regarded rather as one of misfortune than as one of moral obliquity. There is no deceit or intention to defraud".[106]

---

[99] *James v. James* (1872) 41 LJ Ch 353; *Reuters Telegram Co v. Byron* (1874) 43 LJ Ch 661; *Saltman Engineering Co Ltd v. Campbell Engineering Co Ltd* [1963] 3 All ER 413 (CA) 415 (Lord Greene MR); *Seager v. Copydex (No 1)* [1967] 1 WLR 923 (CA) 932; *Coco v. A N Clark (Engineers) Ltd* [1969] RPC 41, 49; *Woodward v. Hutchins* [1977] 1 WLR 760; *O Mustad & Son v. Dosen (Note)* [1964] 1 WLR 109.

[100] *Aquaculture Corporation v. NZ Green Mussel Co* [1990] 3 NZLR 299 (NZCA); *Cadbury Schweppes Inc v. FBI Foods Ltd* above note 89, 179.

[101] *Attorney General v. Guardian Newspapers (No 2)* above note 88, 268.

[102] See ch. 2 text accompanying note 18; *Peek v. Gurney* (1873) LR 6 HL 377 (HL) 390, 393; *Ramshire v. Bolton* (1869) 8 LR Eq 294; *Slim v. Croucher* (1860) 1 De G F & J 518, 524; 45 ER 462, 465 (Lord Campbell LC).

[103] *Fawcett v. Whitehouse* (1829) 1 Russ & M 132; 39 ER 51; *Mahesan S/O Thambiah v. Malaysian Government Officers Co-Operative Housing Society* [1979] AC 374 (PC) 376.

[104] Meagher, Gummow and Lehane *Equity* 336. The Oxford English Dictionary (2nd edn. Clarendon Press Oxford 1989) defines "amphibolous" as "ambiguous; of double or doubtful character".

[105] *Redgrave v. Hurd* (1881) 20 Ch D 1 (CA) 12–13.

[106] *Spence v. Crawford* [1939] 3 All ER 271 (HL) 288. See ch. two, text accompanying notes 173–177.

B Restitutionary damages

1) Breach of fiduciary duty

The award of restitutionary damages has effectively been made for breach of fiduciary duty in some circumstances in which rescission is sought. The primary method used to reverse fraudulent transactions in equity is rescission. Rescission itself cannot be fitted into any understanding of "damages". This is because rescission is a proprietary remedy which is devisable,[107] assignable[108] and has been said to allow priority in insolvency and bankruptcy[109] although this latter point is now in doubt.[110] However, there have been suggestions that, as a proprietary remedy, rescission should be more limited and more recognition should be given to a monetary award in lieu of proprietary rescission. This monetary award, in cases of wrongs, is restitutionary damages. The proprietary award is not a money "damages" award for a wrong but a property response for the wrong. This property response is examined and explained in chapter eight.

It was noted in chapter three that this money remedy has also been referred to as "pecuniary rescission",[111] "the monetary equivalent of a rescissionary remedy",[112] "rescissory damages"[113] or "damages in lieu of rescission".[114] In each case the remedy operates to reverse a wrongful transaction as restitutionary damages. Indeed the restitutionary damages award can also accompany a proprietary award of rescission. In *Alati* v. *Kruger*[115] for example the High Court of Australia ordered rescission of a transaction, involving a sale of a fruit business, which was induced by a fraudulent misrepresentation. Although the lease of the fruit business was restored to the fraudulent seller the buyer had had the *use* of the business. The proprietary reversal of the transaction did not take into account the reversal of the *use* of the business. Even though the business ran at a loss, the High Court of Australia ordered that, in default of agreement between the parties, an inquiry be directed as to the (objective) amount which "ought to be allowed in favour of the said defendant" for the claimant's use of the property.[116] This money award is restitutionary damages.

---

[107] *Stump* v. *Gaby* (1852) 2 De GM & G 623; 42 ER 1015; *Gresley* v. *Mousley* (1859) 4 De G & J 78; 45 ER 31. As is the interest of the other party to the return of the counter-performance: *Re Sherman Deceased* [1954] 1 Ch D 653.

[108] *Dickinson* v. *Burrell* (1866) LR 1 Eq 337; *Melbourne Banking Corp* v. *Brougham* (1882) 7 App Cas 307.

[109] *Re Eastgate* [1905] 1 KB 465; *Tilley* v. *Bowman Ltd* [1910] 1 KB 745. See R Goode *Principles of Corporate Insolvency Law* (2nd edn. Sweet and Maxwell London 1997).

[110] *Re Goldcorp Exchange Ltd* [1995] 1 AC 74 (PC).

[111] P Birks "Unjust Factors and Wrongs" [1997] RLR 76.

[112] *Hodgkinson* v. *Simms* [1994] 3 SCR 377 (SCC) 384.

[113] *Randall* v. *Loftsgaarden* 478 US 647 (1986) 657 (SCUS).

[114] Misrepresentation Act 1967, s 2(2).

[115] (1955) 94 CLR 216 (HCA) 229.

[116] *Alati* v. *Kruger* above note 115.

McKenzie v. *McDonald*[117] involved a transaction exchanging a farm for a shop. The claimant, Mrs McKenzie, was a widow who had asked a land and property salesman, Mr McDonald, to sell her farm and advised him of the price she required. After confirming that the farm was worth that price, Mr McDonald wrote to Mrs McKenzie unduly depreciating the farm. Later he proposed an exchange of the farm for his shop (which he significantly overvalued) plus an amount of cash. After the exchange Mr McDonald sold the farm at its true (enhanced) price. Mrs McKenzie brought an action seeking rescission of the exchange.

Dixon AJ held that as the farm had been sold to a bona-fide purchaser rescission was impossible. However the same effect could be given in money terms by awarding to Mrs McKenzie the amount by which the shop was overvalued as well as the amount by which the land was undervalued.[118] This was effectively an award of restitutionary damages, operating to reverse the transaction rather than compensate for any loss, although the term "equitable compensation" was used.[119]

In *Tang Man Sit* v. *Capacious Investments Ltd*[120] Mr Tang committed a breach of trust by secretly letting 16 houses which were to be assigned to Capacious Investments. When the time came for execution of the assignment the homes were therefore incumbered with the leases. One of the remedies to which the Privy Council allowed Capacious to elect, was "damages" (two different heads of damages were allowed) for "the wrongful use and occupation" of the land by Mr Tang.[121] These damages for the wrongful use and occupation, are best seen as restitutionary damages. On the evidence had Mr Tang not secretly let out the houses, Capacious Investments would not have done so and thus suffered no financial loss from the use and occupation.[122] The market rate of the use and occupation awarded has been explained throughout this book as restitutionary damages whether for the tort of trespass[123] or, as here, for a breach of trust.

---

[117] [1927] VLR 134 (SCV).

[118] In fact part of the award provided that rescission (in its proprietary sense) could be effected if the defendant wished to retake possession of the shop he was entitled to do so by paying the proper value (less the amount which was paid as part of the award): *McKenzie* v. *McDonald* above note 117, 148.

[119] *McKenzie* v. *McDonald* above note 117, 147. See also *Hill* v. *Rose* [1990] VR 129 (SCV); *Coleman* v. *Myers* [1977] 2 NZLR 225 (HCNZ).

[120] [1996] AC 514 (PC).

[121] *Tang Man Cit* above note 120, 519.

[122] It was noted that before Mr Tang's breach of trust, "the houses stood empty. There were complications over Mr Kung's [the owner of Capacious Investments Ltd] estate": *Tang Man Cit* above note 120, 518.

[123] Ch. 3 text accompanying note 19.

2) Dishonest participation in breach of fiduciary duty

In many cases of dishonest participation in breach of fiduciary duty, a remedy of restitutionary damages will not be needed. The participant might not have *received* anything from the claimant. In many other circumstances compensatory damages will suffice as the claimant's loss and defendant's gain will often coincide. Nevertheless, an example of an award of restitutionary damages for dishonest participation in a breach of fiduciary duty is *Twinsectra Ltd* v. *Yardley*,[124] It will be recalled that Mr Leach and associated companies had knowingly (and dishonestly) received the proceeds of a loan in breach of the terms of the trust upon which it was held. The Court of Appeal held that Mr Leach and the associated companies that dishonestly received the proceeds of the loan were liable to refund the amount of the loan proceeds. The form of the order simply stated that Mr Leach and the Companies were liable "personally to account" for the proceeds, but the Court of Appeal acknowledged that that "formula for equitable relief" was a liability to account for the property which *they* held (rather than any loss which might have been suffered) "as though [they were] a trustee".[125]

3) Breach of confidence

In *Cadbury Schweppes Inc* v. *FBI Foods Ltd*[126] the question of assessment of damages for breach of confidence arose before the Supreme Court of Canada. Caesar Canning had been licensed by Duffy-Mott to manufacture a drink called "Clamato" containing clams and tomatoes. The actual manufacture was done by FBI Foods under a sub-agreement with Caesar-Canning. Cadbury Schweppes subsequently acquired the shares in Duffy-Mott and gave 12 months notice of termination of the licence agreement. Following the end of the licence both Caesar Canning and FBI Foods were to be left free to compete with Cadbury Schweppes but were contractually prohibited from manufacturing a drink containing clams or with a title containing "-mato".

In the 12 months following the termination of the agreement, Caesar Canning used its confidential knowledge of the recipe for Clamato to develop a similar drink (although omitting clams) called Caesar Cocktail. Caesar Cocktail was co-packaged by FBI Foods[127] and an action was brought by Cadbury Schweppes against FBI Foods for breach of confidence.

The trial judge found that the respondents had not suffered financial loss as the period of one year, between notice of termination of the licence and actual termination, would have been sufficient time to develop the drink. However she

---

[124] [1999] Lloyds Rep Bank 438 (CA).
[125] *Twinsectra Ltd* v. *Yardley* above note 24, 467.
[126] [1999] 1 SCR 142 (SCC).
[127] In fact FBI Foods later purchased the assets of Caesar Canning.

awarded as damages "in the interest of fairness" the cost of a consultant to develop the drink over that year period.[128] This award could only be restitutionary damages. It was the market value of the information acquired. Disgorgement damages were not awarded as the plaintiffs had "waived any claim to disgorgement (or an accounting) or profits".[129]

In making the award effecting restitutionary damages, the trial judge followed the approach of Lord Denning MR in *Seager* v. *Copydex (No 2)*[130] where his Lordship recognised that a measure of damages for breach of confidence could be made according to the benefit or "springboard" transferred to the defendant. Lord Denning argued that in case of information which was "nothing very special", the value of the information was to be obtained by reference to the cost of a competent consultant for the period it would have taken to obtain the information.[131] If the information was "something special" its value would be the price a willing buyer would pay in the market and if it were "something very special" its value would be based upon the capitalised value of a royalty.[132]

The Supreme Court, on appeal in the *FBI Foods* case, accepted that in the case of information which was "not very special", such as the Clamato recipe, "the 'consulting fee' approach . . . is a proxy for the market value of the confidential information".[133] However, in the Supreme Court a greater award based on compensatory damages was made, and the trial judge's finding that no loss was suffered was overruled. The restitutionary damages award was therefore ignored.[134]

It has been recognised in England that the approach suggested by the trial judge in the *FBI Foods* case and by Lord Denning in the *Seager* case is *not* compensatory. In *Universal Thermosensors Ltd* v. *Hibben*[135] the then Vice-Chancellor, Sir Donald Nicholls, referred to the damages which Lord Denning MR granted on the basis of the "springboard" doctrine:[136]

> "an award of damages in such circumstances would not be a novelty. There are several fields where the courts have awarded damages to a plaintiff whose property is wrongfully used by another even though the plaintiff has not suffered any pecuniary loss by such user. The cases concerning this principle [are] sometimes called the 'user principle'."

In the Supreme Court of Canada, La Forest J, in a previous breach of confidence case, had recognised that, "in contrast to an account of profits" (which is not measured by the value transferred from the defendant) this type of "measure

---

[128] *Cadbury Schweppes Inc* v. *FBI Foods Ltd* above note 126, 176.
[129] *Cadbury Schweppes Inc* v. *FBI Foods Ltd* above note 126, 155.
[130] [1969] 1 WLR 809 (CA).
[131] *Seager* v. *Copydex (No 2)* above note 130, 813.
[132] *Seager* v. *Copydex (No 2)* above note 130, 813.
[133] *Cadbury Schweppes Inc* v. *FBI Foods Ltd* above note 126, 182.
[134] *Cadbury Schweppes Inc* v. *FBI Foods Ltd* above note 126, 176.
[135] [1992] 3 All ER 257 (CA).
[136] *Universal Thermosensors Ltd* v. *Hibben* above note 135, 271–272 (footnote omitted).

of restitutionary recovery is the gain the [defendant] made at the plaintiff's expense".[137] He had contrasted this restitutionary recovery with disgorgement damages (as an account of profits) and with recovery of a compensatory remedy which "has recently been introduced into the law of confidential relationships".[138]

4) Fraud

It was seen in chapter four that restitutionary damages awards have been given for fraud as awards of money had and received in lieu of rescission at common law.[139] For instance, in chapter four the case of *Kettlewell* v. *Refuge Assurance Company*[140] was considered. The claimant sued to recover life insurance premiums paid to a company. The payments were made as a result of fraudulent misrepresentations made by their agent that if the premiums were paid for four years a policy would be given free. The majority of the Court of Appeal, Lord Alverstone CJ and Sir Gorell Barnes, thought that the award of money had and received followed from a rescission of the transaction. They awarded the full value of the premiums as the intangible benefits conferred upon Mrs Kettlewell (the fact that the policy would have been paid if the insured had died within the period) were considered to be of no real value.

Whether the award of restitutionary damages is for the tort of fraud at common law or for fraud in equity (including bribery and fraudulent misrepresentations) should make no difference. In *Kupchak* v. *Dayson Holdings*,[141] the Kupchaks had been induced by fraudulent misrepresentations by Dayson Holdings as to a motel's revenues to exchange properties and a mortgage for shares in the motel owned by Dayson Holdings Ltd. By the time the case came to court the proprietary remedy of rescission was impossible as a half interest in one property had been conveyed by Dayson and apartments on it had been torn down. The Court of Appeal of British Columbia awarded a money remedy instead for what they referred to as the wrong of fraud (which involves a fraudulent misrepresentation) in equity. Although the monetary award made was referred to as "compensation" it was acknowledged, in the words of Davey JA (with whom Norris JA agreed), that the award was "an incident . . . of rescission".[142] In other words, its purpose was not truly to compensate the Kupchaks for any loss that they had suffered but it was to reverse the transaction in money terms.

---

[137] *LAC Minerals Ltd* v. *International Corona Resources Ltd* above note 98, 45.
[138] *LAC Minerals Ltd* v. *International Corona Resources Ltd* above note 98, 46.
[139] *Clarke* v. *Dickson* (1858) El Bl & El 148; 120 ER 463; *Kettlewell* v. *Refuge Assurance Company* [1908] 1 KB 545 (CA).
[140] [1908] 1 KB 545 (CA).
[141] (1965) 53 WWR 65 (CABC).
[142] *Kupchak* above note 141, 70.

C Disgorgement damages

1) Breach of fiduciary duty

As discussed in chapter three, disgorgement damages are available for a breach of fiduciary duty even in circumstances of innocence. The institution of trust and confidence requires such a degree of protection as to warrant strict liability for breach of fiduciary duty including strict liability for disgorgement damages; compensation alone is insufficient.

In *Boardman* v. *Phipps*[143] the appellants were the solicitor to a trust and a beneficiary under that trust. The trust owned shares in a company. In the course of representing the interests of the trust, information was acquired which allowed the appellants to obtain a large number of shares (amounting to a controlling interest) in the company for themselves. Although there was no possibility that the trust would have acquired further shares,[144] and although the trust *benefited* from the increase in value of the shares from the appellants' acquisition, the House of Lords held that the appellants' acquisition amounted to a breach of fiduciary duty. The breach of fiduciary duty consisted of making an unauthorised profit with information obtained in a fiduciary capacity. Informed consent of the beneficiaries had not been properly obtained. The appellants were held liable to disgorge the profits representing the higher value of the shares as well as the more remote (but still reasonably foreseeable) profits made from capital distributions from the shares.

It was irrelevant that it was never "suggested that the appellants acted in any other than an open and honourable manner".[145] The reasons for the rule were stressed by Lord Hodson , quoting from Lord Herschell in *Bray* v. *Ford*:[146]

> "It does not appear to me that this rule is, as has been said, founded upon principles of morality. I regard it rather as based on the consideration that human nature being what it is, there is danger, in such circumstances, of the person holding a fiduciary position being swayed by interest rather than duty, and thus prejudicing those whom he was bound to protect."

It was made clear in *Regal (Hastings) Ltd* v. *Gulliver*[147] that this strong deterrent principle, which allows disgorgement damages beyond circumstances of cynical breach, is not confined to trustees and applies equally to all fiduciaries.[148]

---

[143] [1967] 2 AC 46 (HL).

[144] *Boardman* v. *Phipps* above note 143, 119 (Lord Upjohn).

[145] *Boardman* v. *Phipps* above note 143, 105 (Lord Hodson) "they acted with complete honesty throughout": at 104 (Lord Cohen).

[146] [1896] AC 44 (HL) 51–52; See *Boardman* v. *Phipps* above note 143, 111. See also *Costa Rica Railway Co Ltd* v. *Forwood* [1901] 1 Ch 746 (CA) 761; *Guinness plc* v. *Saunders* [1990] 1 All ER 652 (HL) 660 (Lord Templeman); *Regal (Hastings) Ltd* v. *Gulliver* [1967] 2 AC 134 (HL) 155 (Lord Wright).

[147] *Regal (Hastings) Ltd* v. *Gulliver* above note 146.

[148] Although the action failed against one director, Gulliver, who made no profit and the solicitor, Garton, who had procured full knowledge and consent of the company.

2) *Dishonest participation in a breach of fiduciary duty*

In *Warman International Ltd* v. *Dwyer*[149] a claim was made for disgorgement damages of profits made by parties which had dishonestly participated in a breach of fiduciary duty. Dwyer had been the manager of the claimant company, Warman International Ltd, whose business included an agency agreement with an Italian manufacturer for the distribution of gearboxes. In breach of fiduciary duty Dwyer negotiated with the manufacturer to enter a joint venture for both assembly and distribution of the gearboxes. Dwyer then resigned from Warman and the Italian manufacturer terminated the agency agreement with Warman. The manufacturer then entered into the joint venture agreement with Dwyer through a company, BTA, which was established for this purpose. A number of Warman employees left Warman to work for BTA. A second company, ETA, was formed by Dwyer to distribute a range of other products in conjunction with the joint venture. The High Court of Australia held that Dwyer had breached his fiduciary duty to Warman. It also held that ETA and BTA had "knowingly profited from Dwyer's breach of fiduciary duty".[150] The profit from that wrong was assessed to be the profits from the first two years of the companies' operation and disgorgement damages of that amount were awarded.

In *Cook* v. *Deeks*[151] the directors of the Toronto Construction Company had the opportunity to obtain a railway construction contract for that company, in which the claimant was a shareholder. They diverted the opportunity to the Dominion Construction Company, in which they were shareholders but the claimant had no interest. The Privy Council held that the directors acted in breach of their fiduciary duty to the Toronto Construction Company and must account to it for their profits from the transaction. The Privy Council also held that the Dominion Construction Company should account to the Toronto Construction Company for its profits and disgorgement damages were awarded against the Dominion Construction Company as a dishonest participant in a breach of fiduciary duty. Lord Buckmaster LC stated that[152] "the Dominion Construction Company acquired the rights of . . . the directors with full knowledge of all the facts, and the account must be directed."

3) *Breach of confidence*

It is clear that disgorgement damages are available where a defendant breaches a duty of confidence by deliberately exploiting confidential information with a view to profit. In *Attorney General* v. *Guardian Newspapers (No 2) ("Spycatcher")*[153]

---

[149] (1995) 182 CLR 544 (HCA).
[150] *Warman International Ltd* v. *Dwyer* above note 149, 562.
[151] [1916] AC 554 (PC).
[152] *Cook* v. *Deeks* above note 151, 565.
[153] [1990] 1 AC 149 (HL).

the Attorney-General sought disgorgement damages (an account of profits)[154] from the newspaper *Sunday Times* which serialised substantial parts of Peter Wright's book *Spycatcher*. The *Sunday Times* published it as a serial despite knowing that an injunction was in force to prevent the book from being published in England. Disgorgement damages were awarded against the newspaper.

Lord Keith acknowledged the deterrent basis for the award as preventing cynical breach, stating that "its availability may also, in general, serve a useful purpose in lessening the temptation for recipients of confidential information *to misuse it for financial gain*".[155] The other Lords agreed that there should be disgorgement damages and Lord Brightman added that there should possibly still be "an allowance for those copies of the paper which omitted the offending instalment" even though that omission was "part of a deceit to hoodwink the government".[156]

In *Peter Pan Manufacturing Corporation* v. *Corsets Silhouette Ltd*[157] disgorgement damages were awarded where two styles of brassiere were manufactured based upon patterns and information provided in confidence during a licence. Although Pennycuick J stated that an account of profits for a breach of confidential information follows "as a matter of right"[158] this comment should be viewed in the context that the information had been consciously used and the brassieres could not have been manufactured without the conscious breach. Strict liability for disgorgement damages could only be justified if the courts regarded the institution of confidences as akin to that of the fiduciary relationship of trust and confidence. However, no relationship need exist between the parties in cases of breach of confidence. The party about whom the information is known might even be oblivious to the fact of the defendant's possession of the information. It is difficult to see how this equitable wrong is an institution in need of a greater degree of protection than, for example, the tort of deceit. In *Cadbury Schweppes Inc* v. *FBI Foods Ltd*[159] the Supreme Court of Canada made this observation:[160]

> "The overriding deterrence objective applicable to situations of particular vulnerability . . . does not operate here. If different policy objectives apply, one would not expect the remedy necessarily to be the same."

In *Seager* v. *Copydex Ltd (No 1)*[161] disgorgement damages (an account of profits) were also claimed but Lord Denning MR refused to make the award

---

[154] Injunctions were also sought against any further publication by *The Guardian, The Observer* and *The Sunday Times* but these were refused.

[155] *Attorney General* v. *Guardian Newspapers (No 2)* above note 153, 262.

[156] *Attorney General* v. *Guardian Newspapers (No 2)* above note 153, 266. Lord Keith (262) and Lord Jauncey (293–294) refused to allow a separate claim to the money paid to Peter Wright to secure the right to publish the extracts. But as the money had been paid it should surely be taken into account in assessing the profit: *Goff and Jones* 36.

[157] [1964] 1 WLR 96.

[158] *Peter Pan Manufacturing Corporation* v. *Corsets Silhouette Ltd* above note 157, 106.

[159] [1999] SCR 142 (SCC).

[160] *Cadbury Schweppes Inc* v. *FBI Foods Ltd* above note 159, 164.

[161] [1967] 1 WLR 923 (CA).

where the information, although knowingly received by the defendant in confidence, had been used inadvertently. Lord Denning MR stated that "it may not be a case for injunction or even for an account".[162]

4) Fraud

In *Paragon Finance* v. *D B Thackerar & Co*[163] the defendant firm of solicitors had acted for both the claimant mortgage lenders and the borrowers who were purchasers of a block of flats. However, the solicitors were aware that the borrowers were in fact only sub-purchasers who were purchasing the flats at a highly inflated price from the true purchaser. After the collapse of the property market and significant losses, the claimants commenced actions against the defendant solicitors alleging negligence, breach of contract and breach of fiduciary duty. They later sought to add a number of other claims, including fraud. The relevant Supreme Court Rule[164] provided that leave to amend would only be given if the new cause of action arose out of the same facts, or substantially the same facts as a cause of action already pleaded. The Court of Appeal were therefore required to consider whether a claim for liability to account as a constructive trustee for equitable fraud was a wholly different cause of action from negligence, breach of contract or breach of fiduciary duty.

The Court of Appeal refused leave to amend. In relation to the fraud claim the court considered that it did not involve substantially the same facts as the other claims because it involved an allegation of intentional wrongdoing. Merely because it was framed in artificial language of "constructive trusteeship" did not change the nature of the action for fraud in equity. In delivering the judgment of the Court of Appeal with which the other Lord Justices agreed, Millett LJ explained that "there is no logical basis for distinguishing between an action for [compensatory] damages for fraud at common law and the corresponding claim in equity . . . founded on the same fraud".[165] However, in obiter dicta Lord Millett discussed the availability of disgorgement damages for fraud in equity and stated that the reference to a constructive trust arising from fraud in equity was misleading:[166]

> "Equity has always given relief against fraud by making any person sufficiently implicated in the fraud accountable in equity. In such a case he is traditionally though I think unfortunately described as a constructive trustee and said to be 'liable to account as constructive trustee'. Such a person is not in fact a trustee at all, even though he may be liable to account as if he were."

---

[162] *Seager* v. *Copydex (No 1)* above note 161, 932.
[163] [1999] 1 All ER 400 (CA).
[164] RSC Ord 20 r5(2)(5).
[165] *Paragon Finance* v. *D B Thackerar & Co* above note 163, 413.
[166] *Paragon Finance* v. *D B Thackerar & Co* above note 163, 409. See also footnote 5 and accompanying text above.

Like common law fraud, instances of bribery and secret commissions entitled a claimant to disgorgement damages in equity against the bribee.[167] Indeed, in *Reading* v. *Attorney General*,[168] considered in chapter four in the context of the so-called tort of fraud, Lord Denning expressly stated that it did not matter whether the profits were sought at common law or in equity.

Finally, in *Fawcett* v. *Whitehouse*,[169] a partner had received a secret commission in the process of negotiating a lease for the partnership. The Lord Chancellor held that it must be given up, stating that "this is what must be called in a Court of Equity a fraud on the part of the Defendant".[170] Although the award was a proprietary declaration of trust, the rationale for the award was the same as that for disgorgement damages; in the words of the Lord Chancellor, "to prevent a private advantage".[171]

CONCLUSION

This chapter has shown that gain-based awards for conduct regarded as wrongful in equity correspond precisely (although not always in name) to those gain-based awards for common law torts. It has been shown that there is an acceptance that transfers which are regarded as wrongful should be reversed. Although in equity such transfers are sometimes reversed by proprietary awards, a matter discusssed further in chapter eight, a money award (of restitutionary damages) is also available.

In relation to disgorgement damages it has been shown that, again like torts, they are available in order to effect deterrence which cannot be effected by compensatory damages (commonly referred to in equity as "equitable compensation"). Like torts, this need for deterrence arises in circumstances of cynical and wilful wrongdoing. However, there is one additional circumstance in the field of equitable wrongs where this additional need for deterrence arises. This is in cases where one person has reposed a high degree of trust and confidence in another such that the other is expected to act only in that person's interest. In these cases, the need to deter is so great that this fiduciary institution requires that profits be stripped even from innocent, non-cynical, wrongdoers who breach fiduciary duties.

---

[167] See the discussion of Lord Diplock in *Mahesan S/O Thambiah* v. *Malaysian Government Officers Co-Operative Housing Society* [1979] AC 374 (PC) 376.

[168] [1951] AC 507 (HL). Chapter 4, text accompanying note 190.

[169] (1829) 1 Russ & M 132; 39 ER 51.

[170] *Fawcett* v. *Whitehouse* above note 169, 149; 39 ER 51, 58.

[171] *Fawcett* v. *Whitehouse* above note 169, 147; 39 ER 51, 57.

7

Intellectual Property Wrongs

INTRODUCTION

INTELLECTUAL PROPERTY WRONGS are treated in this book as a separate chapter because they are a distinct body of wrongs deriving from a number of sources. Some originate in equity, some at common law, some from both sources. Many are now governed (at least partly) by statute. Intellectual property wrongs are different from property torts considered in chapter four because the property in question is intangible.[1] Although this distinction should not result in intellectual property wrongs being treated any differently from other wrongs, their particular history has meant that some differences have arisen historically. Although there is recognition of both restitutionary and disgorgement damages for these wrongs, the principles governing these two remedies for intellectual property wrongs are not as consistent as they are for common law torts and equitable wrongs. This necessitates their treatment as a separate chapter.

Section A of this chapter briefly examines the history and nature of each intellectual property wrong to be considered before the awards of restitutionary damages and disgorgement damages for these wrongs are discussed. It is only the history of the intellectual property wrongs at common law and in equity that is considered, rather than the considerable influences of international treaties and European law.[2] This is because the history of the origins of these wrongs in relation to gain-based damages relates to the remedies that common law and equity have traditionally provided. These remedies are commonly preserved in the various legislation.

The remainder of the chapter assesses the availability of restitutionary damages and disgorgement damages for intellectual property wrongs. Section B considers restitutionary damages and explains that the statutory provisions are usually consistent and conform to the model advocated in this book: they should always be available consequent upon a wrong. Because of recent statutory additions, section C considers the limitations that have been imposed upon restitutionary damages in some cases of innocent infringements. The effect of

---

[1] It has, however been argued that such intangible rights are "just the same as houses and other estates": RR Bowker *Copyright: Its History and Its Law* (Houghton Mifflin Boston 1912) 23. Cf. "[the courts] have not in British jurisdictions thrown the protection of an injunction around all the intangible elements of value . . . the exclusive right to invention, trade marks, designs, trade names and reputation are dealt with in English law as special heads of protected interests and not under a wide generalisation": *Victoria Park Racing* v. *Taylor* (1937) 58 CLR 479 (HCA) 509.

[2] W Cornish *Intellectual Property* 18–31.

218   *Intellectual Property Rights*

these provisions is that although restitutionary damages are available for all breaches of trade marks and passing off, it is likely that the innocence of the infringement is a defence to restitutionary damages for copyright, design and patent infringements.

Section D examines awards of disgorgement damages for these intellectual property wrongs. It will be recalled from chapter four that, like other wrongs, in cases of wrongs amounting to infringements of non-intellectual proprietary rights, disgorgement damages are not available unless the breach of duty is cynical. It is clear that disgorgement damages are allowed for cynical infringements of all intellectual property rights. There is one exception. This is the case of copyright infringement where disgorgement damages are allowed for *any* infringement. Despite the fact that older copyright legislation provided that remedies for copyright infringement should be the same as for other property infringements, actions for breach of copyright have allowed disgorgement damages even in cases of innocent copyright infringement. However, the copyright legislation has been amended and the position could now be different limiting deterrent measures to cases in which they are needed.

A History of the different intellectual property wrongs

In this section the different intellectual property wrongs are discussed. In each case (except passing off which is left to the general law) they are now governed by a similar regime; a statute provides for a broad range of remedies, and states that the remedial regime for the intellectual property wrong in question is to operate in the same manner as infringements of other property rights. This suggests that awards of restitutionary damages and disgorgement damages should correspond precisely to the availability of those awards for torts such as trespass, conversion or interference with property. However, it will be seen in section B, C and D, further statutory provisions have complicated this issue.

1) Copyright and design infringement

The wrongs of copyright infringement and design infringement consist of the copying, issuing of copies or adapting a claimant's original work.[3] Copyright infringement is a cause of action granted pursuant to a statutory right (since 1709[4]) protecting literary works.

The modern Copyright Patents and Design Act 1988 (the "1988 Act") has its origins in the Copyright Act 1911 (the "1911 Act") which was repealed and re-enacted in the Copyright Act 1956 (the "1956 Act"). For an infringement of copyright the 1911 Act simply provided that the copyright owner "shall be entitled to

---

[3] Copyright Patents and Design Act 1988, s.16–18, 21.
[4] Statute of Anne, 8 Anne c19.

all such remedies by way of injunction or interdict, damages, accounts, and otherwise, as are or may be conferred by law for the infringement of a property right." The 1956 Act re-enacted most of the 1911 Act and again provided for the same broad range of remedies specifying that they are available as they would be in "corresponding proceedings in respect of infringements of other proprietary rights".[5]

The 1988 Act maintained this broad range of remedies.[6] It also introduced provisions as to design infringement, which are similar to those for copyright infringement. Like the provisions relating to infringement of copyright, the starting point in the legislation is that an infringement of a design right allows all relief as is available in respect of any other property right.[7]

2) Passing off and trade mark infringement

Because of their close link, these two intellectual property wrongs of passing off and trade mark infringement are considered together in this chapter. The cases have rarely distinguished between them although they are slightly different. In the case of passing off, the law protects the property in the goodwill in the product or business to which the name, mark, process and method of manufacture all contribute.[8] In the case of a registered trade mark, the law protects the property in the mark itself. In many cases there will be little difference[9] as the mark will often also involve the name, and passing off the product or business will usually involve passing off the mark.[10] Indeed, section 2(2) of the Trade Marks Act 1994 expressly preserves the law of passing off.

The Trade Marks Act 1994 has its origins in the Trade Marks Registration Act 1875. The Trade Marks Registration Act 1875 did not change any of the developed law in relation to remedies for infringement of trade marks. It simply provided for a system of registration of trade marks. Likewise, the Trade Marks Act 1994 does not affect the developed law on remedies for infringement. As with instances of copyright and design infringement, the 1994 Act provides that remedies for trade mark infringement are available in the same manner as infringement of other proprietary rights.

Although these two intellectual property wrongs are treated together, it is essential to contrast the different attitudes that have historically been taken to these wrongs at common law with the attitudes taken to them in equity. Although the common law and equity now take the same approach to passing

---

[5] Copyright Act 1956, s. 17(1).

[6] Copyright Patents and Design Act 1988 s. 96(2).

[7] Copyright Patents and Design Act 1988 s. 229(2).

[8] "The power to attract and retain customers": P Cane *Tort Law and Economic Interests* (2nd edn. Clarendon Press Oxford 1991) 61.

[9] For instance *J Bollinger* v. *Costa Brava Wine Company* [1960] Ch 262.

[10] "Both trade marks and trade names are in a certain sense property, and the right to use them passes with the goodwill of the business": *Singer Manufacturing Company* v. *Loog* (1882) 8 App Cas 15 (HL) 33 (Lord Blackburn).

off and trade mark infringement, many earlier cases were influenced by the different conceptions of the two court systems to these wrongs.

(a) *Treatment at common law and in equity*

The position at common law and in equity traditionally varied. Common law treated trade mark infringement and passing off as actions based in the tort of deceit and evidence of fraudulent intent was required. Courts of equity regarded the wrongs as based in property and they were treated as wrongs of strict liability. Following the introduction of a statutory register in 1875 the common law courts began to treat the wrongs in the same way as their equitable counterparts and recognise passing off and trade mark infringements as wrongs of strict liability like other intellectual property wrongs.

(i) The traditional view

The common law wrong of interference with a trade mark originated in the tort of deceit.[11] As a part of the tort of deceit, liability rested upon proof of a "purpose to deceive" and knowledge by the defendant of the existence of the claimant's trade mark was essential to the action.[12] Courts of equity also regarded it as wrongful to interfere with a trade mark but did not require proof of deceit. Equity courts "would enjoin even a defendant who had adopted the mark or name in all innocence: the goodwill at risk was easily characterised as property".[13]

In *Bourne* v. *Swan & Edgar Ltd*[14] the claimant was a vendor of ladies' corsets and baby linen. The claimant's registered trade mark was a swan with two cygnets on a background of bulrushes with the word "Swanbill". The defendants carried on a similar business and habitually used the figure of a swan including in production of a corset called "Swan Corset". The claimant brought an action for trade mark infringement and the defendant cross-claimed for rectification of the register arguing that the association of corsets with swans was not sufficiently distinctive to register as a trade mark. Corsets and swans had been used as symbols on many corsets for years and were understood by the public to represent corsets generally.

Farwell J was not persuaded that the defendants' use of the swan infringed the claimant's trade mark in equity. The claimant never used a swan without the word "Swanbill" underneath it and the claimant had not established "title to the figure of a swan of every sort and description in every capacity".[15] Nevertheless, Farwell J considered the position at common law and in equity in detail.

---

[11] *Southern* v. *How* (1618) Pop 143; 79 ER 1243, Doderidge J remarked that of a case where "a clothier . . . had gained great reputation for his making of his cloth . . . used to set his mark to his cloth, whereby it should be known to be his cloth: and another clothier perceiving it, used the same mark to his ill-made cloth on purpose to deceive him, and it was resolved that the action did well lie".

[12] *Derry* v. *Peek* (1889) 14 App Cas 337 (HL).

[13] W Cornish *Intellectual Property* 599.

[14] [1903] 1 Ch 211.

[15] *Bourne* v. *Swan & Edgar Ltd* above note 14, 228.

Farwell J stated that the action at common law had to be distinguished from a suit in equity. He considered that "at law the proper remedy is by an action on the case for deceit: and proof of fraud on the part of the defendant is of the essence of the action: but this Court [of equity] will act on the principle of protecting property alone".[16] He emphasised that "it certainly is not now, and since Lord Cottenham's decision in *Millington* v. *Fox* never was in the old Court of Chancery or in the Chancery Division, necessary to prove fraud".[17] He acknowledged that it is not even necessary, in equity, to prove that anyone has been deceived. The action in equity simply requires that it is likely that someone will be deceived.[18]

Farwell J was however confronted by several decisions which seemed to suggest that fraud was required for any action for passing off or trade mark infringement, even in equity. One of these decisions was that of the House of Lords in *Payton & Co Ltd* v. *Snelling, Lampard & Co Ltd.*[19] In that case the appellants had sold coffee in canisters with particular labels and colours and the words "Royal Coffee". The respondents, also coffee wholesalers, began to package their coffee also in canisters bearing similar colours and the words "Flag Coffee". The House of Lords refused an injunction on the basis that there was no evidence of fraud, nor evidence that anyone was deceived.[20]

In another decision of the House of Lords, *Singer Manufacturing Company* v. *Loog*,[21] an action was brought against the respondent for an injunction and damages. The respondent was an agent which had sold sewing machines with the name "Singer" on them and used the word "Singer" in connection with their business, a name which the appellant had long used on its sewing machines. The appellant obtained an injunction to prevent the label "Singer" being applied to the sewing machines but the case proceeded to the House of Lords on the question of whether the respondent was entitled to use the word in connection with the respondent's business and advertising. The courts below had accepted evidence that no wholesaler would have been deceived by this labelling in business and advertising and that it was unlikely that the use of the word "Singer" in these contexts would be seen by any retailer. The House of Lords affirmed this finding and statements were made that no "actionable wrong" is committed where a trade mark is used innocently[22] or when there is "no evidence of fraudulent purpose or intent".[23]

---

[16] *Bourne* v. *Swan & Edgar Ltd* above note 14, 227; *Edelsten* v. *Edelsten* (1863) 1 De G J & S 185, 199; 46 ER 72, 78 (Lord Westbury LC).

[17] *Bourne* v. *Swan & Edgar Ltd* [1903] 1 Ch 211, 223. See also *Edelsten* v. *Edelsten* (1863) 1 De G J & S 185, 199; 46 ER 72, 78 (Lord Westbury LC) -the only requirement for the suit in equity is that "the Court be satisfied that the resemblance is such as would be likely to cause one mark to be mistaken for the other".

[18] *Bourne* v. *Swan & Edgar Ltd* above note 17, 227.

[19] [1901] AC 308 (HL).

[20] This being a matter for the judge's assessment not a matter to be adduced by leading evidence: *Payton & Co Ltd* above note 19, 311.

[21] (1882) 8 App Cas 15 (HL).

[22] *Singer Manufacturing Company* above note 21, 31 (Lord Blackburn).

[23] *Singer Manufacturing Company* above note 21, 26 (Lord Selborne LC)

Farwell J explained these cases as common law cases. He referred to passages in Lord Blackburn's speech in *Singer Manufacturing Company* v. *Loog*[24] which recognised a difference between protection afforded to trade marks at common law and in equity. Lord Blackburn also referred to a case of trade mark infringement in equity in which an injunction was granted although "there was no evidence to show that the defendants were even aware of the existence of the plaintiffs".[25] He considered this an example of where there "may be a difference between law and equity".[26]

(ii) Strict liability

In 1875 a registry was established for trade marks and the wrong became a statutory wrong.[27] Remedies for trade mark infringement were not provided in the statutes establishing the registry. The registration of a trade mark was "deemed to be equivalent to public use of the trade mark"[28] and "prima facie evidence of exclusive use".[29] The basis of the new statutory wrong was recognised as the protection of property and not deceit. This recognition of this basis soon spread to passing off cases.[30]

The Trade Marks Registration Act 1875 did not immediately result in change. In some cases courts of common law still refused compensatory damages for trade mark infringement because of absence of fault.[31] Likewise there was considerable confusion in cases of passing off. In *Draper* v. *Trist*,[32] Draper had acquired from Trist the goodwill in a business named "Hubert H P Trist" involving sales of brake linings. Trist subsequently began trading as "H H P Trist" and "Tristbestos & Co". Draper obtained judgment against Trist by consent and an inquiry as to damages was ordered. The only question was whether it was competent for the Court of Appeal to infer substantial loss from the passing off. The Court of Appeal held that it was. However, in the course of the judgments there was considerable discussion as to the nature of the action for passing off.

The Court of Appeal was divided as to whether passing off was a wrong of strict liability. Goddard LJ stated that he had "considerable doubt" as to whether "it is the law that damages can be claimed for an innocent passing off".[33] However, Clauson LJ was unprepared to answer the question "in general terms",[34] and Sir Wilfred Greene MR stated that "both in claiming damages and

---

[24] *Singer Manufacturing Company* above note 21, 29.

[25] *Millington* v. *Fox* (1838) 3 My & Cr 338; 40 ER 956.

[26] *Singer Manufacturing Company* above note 21, 30.

[27] Trade Marks Registration Act 1875 incorporated into the Patents, Designs and Trade Marks Act 1883. See now Trade Marks Act 1994.

[28] Patents, Designs and Trade Marks Act 1883, s. 75.

[29] Trade Marks Registration Act 1875 s. 3; Patents, Designs and Trade Marks Act 1883, s. 76.

[30] *A G Spalding & Bros* v. *A W Gamage Ltd* (1915) 32 RPC 273 (HL) 283 (Lord Parker); *Draper* v. *Trist* (1939) 56 RPC 429 (CA) 442 (Goddard LJ).

[31] *Slazenger & Sons* v. *Spalding & Bros* [1910] 1 Ch 257.

[32] *Draper* v. *Trist* above note 30, 442.

[33] *Draper* v. *Trist* above note 30, 443.

[34] *Draper* v. *Trist* above note 30, 441.

in claiming purely equitable relief, whether by way of injunction or by way of account of profits, or both, fraud is not a necessary element in the transaction".[35]

Contrary to the view of Goddard LJ, a consensus notion of trade mark infringement and passing off as wrongs of strict liability slowly emerged. After a series of cases,[36] including obiter dicta in the House of Lords,[37] it became accepted that knowledge or fraud was not an element of liability for compensatory damages for passing off or trade mark infringement at common law and in equity alike. In *Gillette* v. *Edenwest*,[38] this point was finally laid to rest. The defendant had purchased and re-supplied a consignment of counterfeit razor blades which imitated the well-known Gillette brand. Gillette sought compensatory damages for passing off and trade mark infringement. In an application for summary judgment one basis upon which the defendant sought to defend the claim for compensatory damages was that it was unaware that the razor blades infringed the Gillette mark.

Blackburne J considered authorities both prior and subsequent to the Trade Marks Registration Act 1875 concerning the requirement of knowledge in an action seeking compensatory damages for passing off or trade mark infringement. Blackburne J held that "as regards infringement of a registered trade mark. . .it is well settled law, and has been for very many years, that innocence on the part of the infringer is no defence to an action for damages".[39] Blackburne J also stated that the wrongs of passing off and trade mark infringement should be treated in the same way: "both wrongs are very closely related and both may, as in the instant case, spring out of the same act. Indeed it is not obvious to me in the instant case whether there would be any difference between the damages recoverable".[40]

3) Patent infringement

The award of patents conferring a trading monopoly has ancient roots with precedents as early as the time of Elizabeth I.[41] The infringement of such a statutory patent was regarded as wrongful by courts of both Common Law and Chancery. The common law courts considered the wrong as a tort although the right arose from statute.[42]

It was not until the Patent Law Amendment Act 1852 that provision was made in statute for remedies for infringement of patents. That Act was the origin of the modern Patents Act 1977 and was based upon a Report of a Select

[35] *Draper* v. *Trist* above note 30, 434.
[36] *Heath* v. *Gorringe* (1924) 41 RPC 457; *Fialho* v. *S D Simond & Co Ltd* (1937) 54 RPC 193; *Sony Corporation* v. *Anand* [1982] FSR 200.
[37] *A G Spalding & Bros* v. *A W Gamage Ltd* (1915) 32 RPC 273, 283.
[38] [1994] RPC 279.
[39] *Gillette* above note 38, 290.
[40] *Gillette* above note 38, 291. See also *Sony Corporation* v. *Anand* [1982] FSR 200, 206.
[41] WR Cornish *Intellectual Property* 111; *Statute of Monopolies* 1624.
[42] *Watson* v. *Holliday* (1882) 20 Ch D 780, 784 (Kay J).

Committee.[43] In the Patent Law Amendment Act 1852 the approach was simply to make the remedies which had been available in equity for patent infringement available in courts of common law. Section 42 provided that it shall be lawful "to make such Order for an injunction, inspection or accoun . . . as such Court or Judge may see fit." No mention was made of compensatory damages. The Patents Act 1907 later expanded these provisions as to remedies and provided that a patentee was entitled to an injunction, inspection or an account of profits upon any terms that the court shall see fit.[44] It also introduced a provision allowing "damages" for infringement of patents.[45]

The introduction of the claim for damages followed statutory recognition in the United States[46] that limiting a claimant to recovery of the defendant's profits only could work injustice, particularly where large losses have been suffered and only small profits made.[47] The current provision lists all the possible claims leaving the circumstances of their availability to be determined by the common law; "damages", an account of profits, injunctions, declarations and orders for delivery up and destruction.[48]

B Restitutionary damages

In this section, the award of restitutionary damages focuses to a great extent upon the award of reasonable licence fees or reasonable royalties as a measure of damages for the infringements. In chapter three, it was explained that such awards are best seen as restitutionary damages (reversing the objective value transferred) because the awards could only be made to fit a compensatory mould by the use of the fiction of a lost opportunity to bargain.[49] The fiction is evident where the bargain between the particular parties would have been struck at a rate higher than the market (because of the claimant's powerful bargaining position), at a rate lower than the market, or would never have been struck at all. In each case the court ignores the true loss of opportunity and awards the market value of rights transferred. In the cases of intellectual property infringements discussed below, examples are again given of recognition by courts of this true restitutionary basis of the damages award.

---

[43] *Report of the Select Committee on Patents* (British Parliamentary Press London 1851).
[44] Patents Act 1907 s. 34. This replaced s. 30 of the Patents, Designs and Trade Marks Act 1883 which had followed the Patent Law Amendment Act 1952.
[45] Patents Act 1907 s. 33.
[46] Act of July 8, 1870, c30 s. 55, 16 Stat 198, 206.
[47] *Birdsall* v. *Coolidge* 93 US 64 (1876 SCUS) 69.
[48] Patents Act 1977 s. 61(1).
[49] Ch. 3 text accompanying notes 203–228.

1) Infringement of copyright and design rights

As mentioned above, the Copyrights, Designs and Patents Act 1988 (the "1988 Act") provided no specific remedies for copyright or design infringement but in both cases simply provided that the same remedies should be available as for infringement of any other property right.[50] Restitutionary damages are available for all property torts as explained in chapter four (trespass, conversion or wrongful interference with goods under the *Torts (Interference with Goods) Act 1977*[51]) so this provision should be interpreted to mean that restitutionary damages are available for design infringement or copyright infringement. Although no case on the 1988 Act has awarded restitutionary damages, such damages have effectively been awarded under similar provisions of a related statute.

In *Rickless* v. *United Artists*[52] the claimants were the representatives of a deceased actor, Peter Sellers, who had appeared in four well known films, known as "the Pink Panther" films, produced by the defendants. After the death of Mr Sellers, the defendants decided to make a fifth film using unexhibited clips from the previous four movies. The claimants brought actions against the defendants including an action under section 2 of the Dramatic and Musical Performers Protection Act 1958. Section 2 is a parallel measure to s182 of the 1988 Act and it states that it is an offence to make "a cinematograph film directly or indirectly from or by means of the performance of a dramatic or musical work without the consent in writing of the performers." However, no civil remedy is provided.

Hobhouse J, whose judgment was approved by the Court of Appeal, held that alternative remedies of a reasonable royalty and an account of profits were available. However Hobhouse J was of the view that the reasonable royalty was a compensatory damages award. It was for this reason that Hobhouse J explained the measure as the amount the "parties would have agreed, if they had been forced to bargain".[53]

As noted in chapter three, this fictitious view that a reasonable royalty is a measure of compensatory damages was again maintained by Lord Hobhouse in the House of Lords in *Attorney General* v. *Blake*[54] in considering cases which had awarded restitutionary damages for a breach of contract. This fiction has now been rejected including in the leading speech of Lord Nicholls who considered and affirmed the existence of restitutionary damages including in reference to a case of patent infringement.[55]

---

[50] Copyrights, Designs and Patents Act 1988 s. 96(2) (copyright infringement), s. 229(2) (design infringement).
[51] Torts (Interference with Goods) Act 1977 s. 3(2)(c).
[52] [1988] QB 40 (CA), affirming Hobhouse J [1986] FSR 502.
[53] *Rickless* v. *United Artists* [1986] FSR 502, 524.
[54] [2001] 1 AC 268 (HL).
[55] *Blake* above note 55, 279.

In the United States there is also authority rejecting the fictitious "compensatory" justification of reasonable royalty awards. In *Vermont Microsystems Inc* v. *Autodesk Inc*[56] this issue arose in the context of a claim for misappropriation of trade secrets. Autodesk produced highly sophisticated computer software to be used by engineers and architects. Its premier software product, a program entitled AutoCAD, had nearly 80% of the market. Vermont Microsystems ("VMI") initially produced only hardware accessories but in 1989 decided to concentrate on software accessories that could be used with the AutoCAD program.

In 1991 one of VMI's former employees, Mr Berkes who had worked on these accessories, joined Autodesk. Although Mr Berkes initially was assigned to projects which bore no relation to VMI's areas of operation, by 1992 VMI learned that his assignments had changed and that his new work implicated VMI trade secrets involving AutoCAD accessories. VMI sued Autodesk and Mr Berkes alleging copyright infringement and misappropriation of trade secrets. Although VMI abandoned its copyright infringement claim, it was successful in its claim for trade secret misappropriation and the measure of damages would have been the same for the copyright infringement.

The District Court had held that the measure of damages was to be based on the rate which the claimant would have charged for a royalty for the AutoCAD accessories secrets. The Court of Appeals insisted that this measure of damages for such an infringement be ascertained objectively and stated that a claimant's possibly extortionate demands would not be considered: [57]

> "Apparently, the district court equated 'the amount VMI would have charged' with 'reasonable royalty', a common form of award in trade secret cases. *See Taco Cabana Int'l Inc* v. *Two Pesos Inc*, 932 F.2d 1113, 1128 (5th Cir. 1991), *aff'd*, 505 U.S. 763 (1992). This was an error. A reasonable royalty award attempts to measure a hypothetically agreed value of what the defendant wrongfully obtained from the plaintiff . . . the court calculates . . . a fair licensing price at the time that the misappropriation occurred."

2) *Passing off and trade mark infringement*

No legislation governs the law relating to passing off and the remedies for infringement of a trade mark are left to the common law by section 14 of the Trade Marks Act 1994. Section 14 simply provides that for trade mark infringement "all such relief by way of damages, injunctions, accounts or otherwise is available to the plaintiff as is available in respect of infringement of any other property right."

In *Dormeuil Freres SA* v. *Feraglow Ltd*[58] an action was brought for an infringement of the claimant's trade mark and passing off in relation to cloth manufactured by the defendant under the claimant's "Dormeuil" label. The

---

[56] 88 F 3d 142 (1996 2nd Cir CA).
[57] 88 F 3d 142 (1996 2nd Cir CA). See also *Georgia-Pacific Corp* v. *US Plywood-Champion Papers Inc*, 446 F.2d 295 (1970 2nd Cir CA) 296–297, *cert denied*, 404 U.S. 870 (1971 SCUS).
[58] [1990] RPC 449.

defendants conceded that an infringement had occurred and consented to an inquiry as to the damages. An appeal was brought to Knox J from an interim payment order by a Master. The claimants had sought compensatory damages based upon lost profits from lost sales as a result of the infringements and, in the alternative, damages measured by a reasonable royalty.

Knox J considered whether a "reasonable royalty" method of assessment of damages could be applied to a trade mark infringement and passing off case. However, the question did not have to be conclusively decided. The application was simply an appeal from an order for an interim payment.[59] However Knox J refused to acknowledge the possibility of restitutionary damages measured by a reasonable royalty for three reasons.[60]

First, that there was no reported authority granting such a measure in a case of trade mark or passing off cases. Secondly, Knox J was concerned that all the defendants' sales might not have been made by the claimants (so the reasonable royalty award might even exceed the claimants' loss of profits). Thirdly, the royalty measure would not be appropriate if the claimant's loss of sales (compensation measure) were *greater* and therefore the claimant had elected to seek compensatory damages.

The first two of Knox J's objections to restitutionary damages are all that stand in the way of their recognition of trade mark infringement and passing off. The third is a different question of election between remedies, which is explained in the concluding chapter in this book. In relation to the second objection this "difficulty" merely stems from the fact that Knox J was viewing the award of a reasonable royalty as compensatory. As a compensatory award it would indeed be anomalous if the measure of damages exceeded the loss suffered by a claimant, especially in the circumstances of the claimant which would not have exercised any opportunity to bargain for a royalty. But once viewed as restitutionary damages there is no anomaly at all. The damages are based on the defendant's (transferred) gain.

In relation to the first objection, Knox J himself acknowledged that although this measure of damages had not actually been awarded before, this was not fatal. Indeed, he acknowledged that the award had been made in cases of *patent* infringement (see below).[61] In fact, obiter dicta support exists for damages of a reasonable royalty in a case where an interlocutory injunction was sought for passing off[62] and in the United States this award of a reasonable royalty is a common award for trade mark infringement.

In the United States, in *Sands, Taylor & Wood* v. *Quaker Oats Co*[63] the District Court for Illinois had found that the Quaker Oats Company had

---

[59] RSC Order 29, Rules 9,10, 11.

[60] *Dormeuil Freres SA* v. *Feraglow Ltd* above note 58, 464.

[61] *Dormeuil Freres SA* v. *Feraglow Ltd* above note 58, 464.

[62] *IPC Magazines* v. *Black & White Music Corporation* [1983] FSR 348, 354 (although the reasonable royalty was referred to as a compensatory award).

[63] 34 F 3d 1340 (7th Cir, 1994).

infringed the appellants trade mark, "Thirst-Aid" by making references in advertisements to "Thirst-Aid" while promoting their competing product "Gatorade". The District Court had determined that 10 per cent of Quaker's profits were due to the references to "Thirst-Aid" and that disgorgement damages of 10 per cent should be paid. A submission seeking a reasonable royalty was rejected because, the District Court held, this would involve speculation on what the parties would have hypothetically agreed when the parties had never considered the point. On appeal to the 7th Circuit Court of Appeals, the Court of Appeal allowed the appeal holding that the starting point should be a reasonable royalty and an award of disgorgement of profits could be considered only if any additional need for deterrence were required.[64]

After remand to the District Court to determine the reasonable royalty the case was again appealed on the manner of calculating the reasonable royalty. The District Court had held that the reasonable royalty measure should be calculated on the basis of a need to deter wrongdoing. The 7th Circuit Court of Appeals emphasised that this was not the basis for such restitutionary damages. The Court of Appeals suggested that the basis for the restitutionary damages was compensation, but it was acknowledged that this was a legal fiction:[65]

"Determination of a 'reasonable royalty' after infringement, like many devices in the law, rests upon a legal fiction. Created in an effort to 'compensate' when [lost] profits are not proveable, the 'reasonable royalty' device conjures a 'willing' licensor and licensee, who like Ghosts of Christmas Past, are dimly seen as 'negotiating' a 'license'. There is, of course, no actual willingness on either side, and no license to do anything, the infringer being normally enjoined . . . from further manufacture, use, or sale of the patented product."

3) Patent infringement

Section 61(1) of the Patents Act 1977 provides that

". . . civil proceedings may be brought in the court by the proprietor of a patent in respect of any act alleged to infringe the patent and. . . in those proceedings a claim may be made-

(a) for an injunction restraining the defendant. . .from any apprehended act of infringement . . .;

(b) for an order for him to deliver up or destroy any patented produce . . .;

(c) for damages in respect of the infringement;

(d) for an account of profits derived by him from the infringement;

(e) for a declaration . . . that the patent is valid and has been infringed by him."

In *General Tire Co v. Firestone Tyre Co Ltd*[66] General Tire had invented a process for making tyre tread and patented it in the United Kingdom. Firestone infringed the patent and the only question that reached the House of Lords was

---

[64] *Sands, Taylor & Wood* above note 63, 1343.
[65] *Sands, Taylor & Wood* above note 63, 1350.
[66] [1975] 1 WLR 819 (HL).

the method of assessment of damages. Counsel for the appellant, who included Dr McGregor QC,[67] only sought compensatory damages under section 61. As a result, although a reasonable royalty was awarded to General Tire, it was considered as a compensatory award and the House of Lords attempted to ascertain the bargain that would have been struck between General Tire and Firestone so as to fit the award within the compensatory pleadings.[68]

Nevertheless, it is clear that the reference to "damages" in the legislation includes the earlier cases of restitutionary damages. *Watson Laidlaw & Co Ltd* v. *Pott Cassells & Williamson*[69] involved the infringement of a patent by sale of approximately 130 machines in Java, for use in the process of manufacturing sugar, which were closely based on the respondent's patent. At first instance, the Lord Ordinary gave an award of substantial damages but did not support it on any particular basis. In the leading speech in the House of Lords, Lord Shaw was prepared to assume in that case that the Respondents would not have "done the Java trade in the 130 machines sold in that island by the infringers . . . [so] the Respondents have lost no trade which they could have obtained".[70] The question was whether a substantial damages award made by the Lord Ordinary could be supported. However, in his opinion, the award could be supported as restitutionary damages:[71]

> "It is not exactly the principle of restoration, either directly or expressed through compensation, but is the principle underlying price or hire. It plainly extends—and I am inclined to think—not infrequently extends—to Patent cases. But, indeed, it is not confined to them. For whenever an abstraction or invasion of property has occurred, then, unless such abstraction or invasion were to be sanctioned by the law, the law ought to yield a recompense under the category or principle, as I say, of price or hire. If A, being a liveryman, keeps his horse standing idly in the stable, and B, against his wish or without his knowledge, rides or drives it out, it is no answer to A for B to say: 'Against what loss do you want to be restored? I restore the horse. There is no loss. The horse is none the worse; it is better for the exercise.' "

The other Lords took a different approach. Lords Kinnear and Atkinson considered the case as one based upon assessment of loss and the Earl of Halsbury dissented on the basis that there was no evidence to support any damages award given in the decision of the Lord Ordinary.

The approach of Lord Shaw echoed precisely obiter dicta comments of Fletcher Moulton LJ in the Court of Appeal in *Meters Ltd* v. *Metropolitan Gas Meters Ltd.*[72] The defendant, who sold gas meters, had sold an advanced gas meter very similar in design to the claimant's "Simplex" meter and which

---

[67] See ch. 1 for a criticism of the views of Dr McGregor in H McGregor (ed.) *McGregor on Damages* (16th edn. Sweet & Maxwell London 1997).
[68] *General Tire Co* above note 66, 824–825, 833.
[69] (1914) 31 RPC 104 (HL) 119.
[70] *Watson Laidlaw & Co Ltd* above note 69, 119.
[71] *Watson Laidlaw & Co Ltd* above note 69.
[72] (1911) 28 RPC 157.

infringed the claimant's patent. The Court of Appeal had to consider an appeal from an award by a Master, which had been upheld by Eve J, allowing the claimant a proportion of the profits made on every infringing article. The defendant argued that the claimant had not shown that any loss had been suffered and, in any event, some of the sales by the defendant would not have been made by the claimant such as those made to regular customers of the defendant. Each of the judges in the Court of Appeal rejected this argument on the basis that the method employed was a legitimate method of assessing loss. Moulton LJ justified the award by referring to the basis of restitutionary damages.

Moulton LJ recognised that the damages might have been sought not on the basis of the actual loss of the claimant but "by the sum which would have had to have been paid in order to make the manufacture of that article lawful" and continued:[73]

> "Persons may deliberately combine to manufacture surreptitiously and to sell to other persons, the whole object being not to go to the plaintiff, because the very object of the wrongful acts was to avoid that. Not one of those manufactured articles would have been purchased from, or manufactured by, the plaintiff. Could it be suggested that this might be done with impunity?"

Where the claimant was in the habit of licensing the use of the patented item Moulton LJ thought it clear that the court can also award damages measured by that licence fee. But even when the claimant did not licence the item Moulton LJ stated that it was probably a "rule of law" that damages could be assessed at a reasonable rate to be paid in order to licence the use of those items.[74]

In *Catnic Components Ltd* v. *Hill & Smith Ltd*[75] this approach was applied. The defendants had infringed the claimant's patent on cavity wall lintels. An infringement had been found and the matter came before Falconer J simply as an assessment of damages. The claimants sought damages measured in a number of ways including significant loss of profits from the defendant's sales and a royalty assessed at 20 per cent of the sale price which they would have charged to licence use by a competitor. The defendants claimed that the damages should be nominal as they alleged that the claimant had not lost any sales from their infringing conduct. However, the defendants conceded that they were liable to pay a reasonable royalty on all the infringing items of two per cent of gross sales or three per cent of net sales.

Falconer J held that the claimants were entitled to compensatory damages for loss of manufacturing profits for those infringing sales which would have been sales made by the claimants. However, in relation to those infringing sales which would *not* have been sales of the claimants (and hence did not reflect any loss suffered by the claimants) a reasonable royalty was awarded.[76] Falconer J

---

[73] *Meters Ltd* v. *Metropolitan Gas Meters Ltd* above note 72,164.
[74] *Meters Ltd* v. *Metropolitan Gas Meters Ltd* above note 72, 165.
[75] [1983] FSR 512.
[76] *Catnic Components* above note 75, 521–522.

held that the reasonable royalty should be assessed at the rate which was "fair and reasonable" and he awarded it at 10 per cent of gross sales value.[77]

Like the United States, where the position has been long settled,[78] English recognition of restitutionary damages for patent infringement is now assured following subsequent acceptance of the approach of Falconer J,[79] and explicit endorsement of the comments of Lord Shaw in *Attorney General* v. *Blake*[80] as an acceptable measure of gain-based damages for a patent infringement.

C Restitutionary damages for innocent infringement

1) Copyright and design right infringements

An interesting situation exists in relation to restitutionary damages for intellectual property infringements that does not exist for any other wrong. In relation to copyright, design and patent infringement, a new defence has been introduced of "innocent infringement" that will probably apply to restitutionary damages.

The Copyright Act 1956 first introduced a restriction on "damages" for copyright or design infringement where the defendant did not know and had no reason to believe that copyright subsisted in the work infringed.[81] The Copyright Act 1988 maintained this position:

> "Section 97(1) Where in an action for infringement of copyright it is shown that at the time of the infringement the defendant did not know, and had no reason to believe, that copyright subsisted in the work to which the action relates, the plaintiff is not entitled to damages against him, but without prejudice to any other remedy."

The same provision was made in relation to infringement of design rights.[82]

Whether these provisions will apply to prevent an action for restitutionary damages depends upon the construction of the word "damages". One construction might be to view the word "damages" narrowly, encompassing only compensatory damages and not including restitutionary damages. Another would be to view the definition of "damages" as not coterminous with compensation and simply as a money award for a wrong.

An argument in favour of reading the provision down derives from the general remedial provisions for breach of copyright which provide that the same

---

[77] *Catnic Components* above note 75, 533.

[78] The Patents Act 1922 (US) was the statutory entrenchment of the common law position that the award of a reasonable royalty was the *minimum* award of damages which should be made even if the claimant suffers no loss of profits: *Tegers* v. *Tegers Inc* 458 F 2d 726 (1972 7th Cir CA); *Foster* v. *American Machine & Foundry Co* 492 F 2d 1317 (1974 2nd Cir CA).

[79] *Gerber Garment Technology Inc* v. *Lectra Systems Ltd* [1995] RPC 383, 412–413; *Allen & Hanburys Ltd's (Salbutamol) Patent* [1987] RPC 327 (CA).

[80] [2001] 1 AC 268 (HL) 279.

[81] Copyright Act 1956 s. 17(2).

[82] Copyright Patents and Design Act 1988 s. 233(1).

remedies should be available as in the case of infringement of any other property right. If the reference to "damages" is viewed as simply meaning "compensatory damages" then restitutionary damages could be allowed in cases of innocent infringement of copyright or design rights as they are in cases of infringement of other property rights such as torts of trespass, conversion or interference with goods.[83]

On the other hand, the intention behind the provision seems to have been to create a defence to the strict liability for intellectual property infringements. Such a defence does not exist to a liability for compensatory damages for trespass, conversion or statutory liability for interference with goods. It would seem that it was intended that such a defence apply to restitutionary damages awards as well. This is because in other areas restitutionary damages have been specifically preserved for innocent breaches. In relation to *secondary* design infringements (such as importation or secondary sale of infringing items), the Copyright Act 1988 provides that "the only remedy available against him in respect of the infringement is damages not exceeding a reasonable royalty in respect of the act complained of".[84] The logic behind allowing innocence as a defence to restitutionary damages in some instances but not in others is difficult to see.

2) *Patent infringement*

Exactly the same situation arises in instances of patent infringement. In the Patents Act 1907, which was the first statutory reference to damages for patent infringement, a restriction on damages was provided in the case of an innocent infringement. This was a defence to "an action for damages but not to an injunction".[85] This defence was expanded[86] upon in the Patents Act 1977 in section 62(1):

> "In proceedings for an infringement of a patent damages shall not be awarded, and no order shall be made for an account of profits, against a defendant . . . who proves that at the date of the infringement he was not aware, and had no reasonable grounds for supposing, that the patent existed."

This raises the same question as was encountered in relation to copyright infringement. Should the reference to "damages" be constrained and read down so that innocence is not a defence to restitutionary damages? Again, it would seem to do too much violence to the statutory intent to take this approach.

3) *Passing off and trade mark infringement*

The intellectual property wrongs of passing off and trade mark infringement are, however, different. No statutory provision is made in relation to any defences.

---

[83] See ch. 4.
[84] Copyright Patents and Design Act 1988 s. 233(2)
[85] Patents Act 1907 s. 33.
[86] The modern provision reintroduces this restriction on "damages" awards not initially present in the Patent Law Amendment Act 1852 (see s. 42), introduced in the Patents Act 1907 but which was omitted again in the Patents Act 1949.

As was seen, the only provision at all is in the Trade Marks Act 1994[87] which, in the same manner as copyright and patent legislation, provides that "all such relief by way of damages, injunctions, accounts or otherwise is available to the plaintiff as is available in respect of infringement of any other property right."

In addition to the availability of restitutionary damages for innocent breaches of other property rights, the fact that courts have finally concluded (in considering liability for compensatory damages) that both passing off and trade mark infringement are wrongs of strict liability would suggest that restitutionary damages are available in cases of innocent breach.

D Disgorgement damages

1) Generally

In cases of infringement of intellectual property generally, equity traditionally allowed disgorgement damages in the form of accounts of profits whenever an injunction to prevent further infringement was available.[88] Professor Cornish refers to the account of profits in these cases as "a corollary of the injunction".[89]

Various reasons were traditionally advanced to justify this approach. The usual rationale advanced was that disgorgement damages (as an account of profits) were awarded because of the difficulty of calculating compensatory damages. The questions are often "of great nicety and difficulty" and it was thought that the account of profits was an easy way to compensate, and the difficulties of determining when it should be available avoided by its award simply whenever an injunction was granted. As an injunction was available in circumstances of innocent infringement an account of profits should also be allowed in those circumstances as a means of compensation.

In a passing off case Lord Eldon stated that a "Court of Equity . . . is not content with an action for damages; for it is nearly impossible to know the extent of the damage . . . the remedy [is] by an injunction and account".[90] In *Colburn v. Simms*[91] Sir James Wigram V-C stated as follows:

---

[87] Trade Marks Act 1994 s. 14.

[88] "The right to an account of profits is incident to the right to an injunction in copy and patent right cases": *Stevens* v. *Gladding* 58 US 447, 455 (1854 SCUS); *Lever* v. *Goodwin* (1887) 36 Ch D 1, 7 (Cotton LJ); *Callaghan* v. *Myers* 128 US 617 (1888 SCUS). *Smith* v. *London and South Western Railway Co* (1854) Kay 408; 69 ER 173; *Prices' Patent Candle Co* v. *Bauwen's Patent Candle Co* (1854) 4 K & J 727; 70 ER 302.

[89] WR Cornish *Intellectual Property* 76.

[90] *Hogg* v. *Kirby* (1803) 8 Ves Jun 215, 223; 32 ER 336, 339. The fictitious reasoning by which Lord Eldon LC reached this conclusion—an account of profits being the means by which equity "compensates"—is criticised in ch. three text accompanying notes 100–109.

[91] (1843) 2 Hare 543, 560; 67 ER 224, 231.

"The Court, by the account, as the nearest approximation which it can make to just-ice, takes from the wrongdoer all the profits he has made by his piracy, and gives them to the party that has been wronged. In doing that the Court may often give the inno-cent party more, in fact, than he is entitled to, for *non constat* that a single additional copy of the more expensive book would have been sold if the injury by the same of the cheaper book had not been committed."

This compensatory fiction was considered in chapter three and rejected.[92] The two reasons for its rejection were the fact that the account of profits remains available even where it can be shown that no loss had been suffered by the claimant at all and the fact that equity now *can* award compensatory damages.

In addition, chapter three also considered the circumstances in which dis-gorgement damages should apply. It was shown that there is no justification for institutional protection, comparable to the instance of fiduciary relations, which could justify a disgorgement damages award for innocent infringements of property rights (where an injunction might be appropriate).

A more sophisticated rationale for allowing an account of profits in cases of innocent infringement was advanced in a trade mark case by Sir John Romilly MR. The explanation was that disgorgement damages could be allowed for an "innocent" trade mark infringement by a *presumption* of conscious wrong-doing. He stated that "if it be found that there has been a colourable imitation of a trade mark, it follows that the person making it intended to imitate the genuine trade mark".[93] This fiction of fraud was created because Sir John was concerned that without strict liability to account "a man by carefully abstaining from inquiring whose trade mark he was imitating, and by refusing to hear any-thing about it, might escape from all liability".[94] However, as was seen in chap-ter three, a reckless disregard for property rights of others with a view to gain would still justify disgorgement damages based upon cynical breach. Nor could Sir John's fiction explain why the presumption could not be rebutted by the defendant showing that he was truly innocent.

The problem is that the failure to reject these fictions meant that disgorge-ment damages were accepted as available for innocent infringement of intellec-tual property wrongs. They remained available even once it was recognised that compensatory damages could be awarded. And although, as will be seen below, Lord Westbury LC constrained the availability of disgorgement damages in passing off cases to instances of intentional wrongdoing this was not applied consistently across the body of intellectual property wrongs and the inconsist-ency was entrenched into the statutes.

---

[92] Ch. 3, text accompanying notes 203–228.
[93] *Cartier* v. *Carlisle* (1862) 31 Beav 292, 298; 54 ER 1151, 1153.
[94] *Cartier* v. *Carlisle* above note 93.

2) *Copyright and design infringement*

(a) *The Copyright Act 1956*

As discussed above, the Copyright Act 1956 was the precursor to the modern Copyrights, Designs and Patents Act 1988. The Copyright Act 1956 provided that all relief was available as in the case of "infringements of other proprietary rights".[95] There was a restriction on the award of (compensatory) damages where the defendant did not know and had no reason to believe that copyright subsisted in the work infringed. However this restriction specifically excluded an account of profits. It provided that in cases of innocence[96]

> "The plaintiff shall not be entitled under this section to any damages against the defendant in respect of the infringement, but shall be entitled to an account of profits in respect of the infringement whether any other relief is granted under this section or not."

This provision probably represented the view that an account of profits should be available whenever an injunction is awarded. As will be seen below, although the traditional view that an account of profits was available as a corollary to an injunction (which was available to restrain even innocent infringement) was rejected by the middle of the 19th century, almost 100 years later the Copyright Act 1956 overlooked these developments and was drafted according to the traditional view.

Cases on the Copyright Act 1956 allowed an account of profits for innocent copyright infringement as the Act required. In *Potton Ltd* v. *Yorkclose Ltd*,[97] for example, Millett J also held that an account of profits could be awarded against an innocent copyright infringer under the Act. There, the defendants infringed the claimant's copyright in designs for construction of houses. The defendants admitted the infringements although denying that they were knowingly committed. However an account was ordered irrespective of this denial.

(b) *The Copyrights, Designs and Patents Act 1988*

Although the modern Copyrights, Designs and Patents Act 1988 (the "1988 Act") only exempted compensatory damages in cases of innocence, an account of profits was not expressly preserved. Although the Copyright Act 1956 had specifically exempted an account of profits from this innocence exception there was no mention of such an exemption in the 1988 Act. Section 97(1) simply provided that no liability for "damages" would be incurred in cases of innocence but "without prejudice to any other remedy".

It might therefore be thought that section 97(1) should now allow only an injunction in cases of innocent breach and that disgorgement damages would

---

[95] Copyright Act 1956 s. 17(1).
[96] Copyright Act 1956 s. 17(2).
[97] [1990] FSR 11, 15 discussed in ch. three, text accompanying notes 50–51. See also *Redwood Music* v. *Chappell & Co Ltd* [1982] RPC 109, 132 (Goff J).

require evidence of cynical breach.[98] Unfortunately the only case which has considered this issue held that the 1988 Act did not effect any change.

In *Wienerworld Ltd* v. *Vision Video Ltd*[99] the claimants alleged that they were the owners of copyright and/or exclusive licensees of film copyrights which they alleged had been infringed by the defendant. The claimants sought summary judgment for an account of profits and compensatory damages (at their election). The point in issue was whether the defendant was entitled to discovery of the claimant's documents in order to decide whether to oppose this right of election. The defendant argued that discovery should be allowed because the claimant should not be entitled to an account of profits for an innocent infringement. However, as no defence of innocence was raised this argument was rejected. Yet, in obiter dicta Judge Burton QC considered that no change had been effected to the Copyright Act 1956 by the 1988 Act. Judge Burton QC held that it made no difference that the defence of innocence in the 1988 Act did not specifically exempt an account of profits (as it did in the Copyright Act 1956). Therefore he considered that the defence of innocence still applied.

In relation to design rights, the argument for requiring evidence of cynical breach for disgorgement damages is more difficult. A primary design infringement[100] is made subject to the defence of innocence expressly only in cases of "damages".[101]

Contrary to the views of Judge Burton QC, in cases of copyright infringement liability for disgorgement damages should arise in the same manner as for infringements of other property rights (as the section provides). Without express provision allowing an account of profits in cases of innocent infringement, cynical breach should be required as it is for infringement of other property rights. The same argument can be made in relation to design rights; the defence of innocence is only required in cases of liability for compensatory damages because proof of wilful or cynical breach is an *element* of the proof required for disgorgement damages.

3) Passing off and trade mark infringement

(a) Before 1875

Like the other intellectual property wrongs, influenced by the fictional justifications for the account of profits, disgorgement damages for passing off or trade mark infringement in equity could traditionally be awarded in the absence of

---

[98] Disgorgement damages also being unavailable for secondary infringements where knowledge is an element of the offence: "Possessing or dealing with an infringing copy": s. 23 or "Providing means for making infringing copies": s. 24.

[99] [1998] FSR 832.

[100] In relation to a secondary design infringement s. 233(2) excludes disgorgement damages altogether.

[101] The limiting provision applies by s. 229(4) which makes s. 229 subject to s. 233.

fault. In *Cartier* v. *Carlisle*[102] an injunction and account were ordered to prevent the defendant selling cotton with labels similar to those of the claimant. The defendants swore an affidavit that they had no knowledge of the claimant's labels and should therefore escape liability. Sir John Romilly MR stated that the account must be awarded even in cases of innocent infringement, as it is always available as incidental to an injunction. He awarded an account of all the profit attributable to the use of the mark during the entire six year period of the infringement as "the fact of the Defendant not knowing to whom the trade mark he copies belongs does not, in the slightest degree, affect the right of the owner to an injunction and to an account of the profits".[103]

As discussed above, Sir John Romilly MR reached this conclusion by the fiction that "if it be found that there has been a colourable imitation of a trade mark, it follows that the person making it intended to imitate the genuine trade mark".[104] Although the common law required proof of fraud or deceit Sir John considered the effect of this fiction to effect the rule "at law and equity to be the same".[105]

Edelsten v. *Edelsten*,[106] decided only a year later, reached a different conclusion without reference to the *Cartier* case. The *Edelsten* case concerned a defendant that manufactured inferior wire and identified its product by attaching an anchor to the "tally" on the wire. The use of the anchor was an infringement of the claimant's famous anchor and crown trade mark that was always attached to the claimant's wire of the finest quality. The claimant sought orders including an injunction to prevent the attachment of the anchor and an account of profits. Lord Westbury LC granted the injunction and account of profits due to the wilful infringement of the trade mark but stated, obiter dicta, that where a claimant, A, who[107]

> "has acquired property in a trade mark, which is afterwards adopted and used by B in ignorance of A's right, A is entitled to an injunction; yet he is not entitled to an account of profits or compensation, except in respect of any user by B after he became aware of prior ownership."

Lord Westbury did acknowledge that although *at law* the origins of the wrong were in the action on the case for deceit (so that proof of fraud was the essence of the action) equity "will act on the principle of protecting property alone, and it is not necessary for the injunction to prove fraud in the defendant".[108] All that was necessary in equity was that the public be likely to mistake the claimant's product for the defendant's.

---

[102] (1862) 31 Beav 292, 298; 54 ER 1151, 1153 (Romilly MR). Cited with approval in *Potton Ltd* v. *Yorkclose Ltd* [1990] FSR 11, 15 (Millett J).

[103] *Cartier* v. *Carlisle* above note 102, 298; 1153.

[104] *Cartier* v. *Carlisle* above note 102.

[105] *Cartier* v. *Carlisle* above note 102, 297; 1153.

[106] (1863) 1 De G J & S 185; 46 ER 72.

[107] *Edelsten* v. *Edelsten* above note 106, 199; 78.

[108] *Edelsten* v. *Edelsten* above note 106. Lord Westbury reiterated this point less than 12 months later in *Hall* v. *Barrows* (1863) 4 De G J & S 150; 46 ER 873.

The only case that Lord Westbury referred to during argument was *Millington* v. *Fox*.[109] However, that case did not decide the point either way. In that case the claimants sought an injunction and an account of profits for trade mark infringement. The claimant was a steel manufacturer and the defendant had begun marking its rival steel with the claimant's mark: "Crowley" steel and "Crowley Millington" steel. The defendant was not aware that the claimant's mark designated a particular brand but thought it was just a common method of identifying a type of steel.

Lord Cottenham LC held that although no fraud was present the claimants would have been entitled to an injunction.[110] However, the defendants had sent a letter stating that they had now ceased to use the marks and would not do so in future. This had the effect that it was not proper to apply for the injunction and the only purpose of the suit that the Lord Chancellor could see was to obtain an account of profits. However, the account of profits was withdrawn before the trial because it would only have been very small and, without referring to whether it would have been awarded if it had been significant, the Lord Chancellor referred to this withdrawal as "very proper".[111]

Two apparently contradictory lines of authority therefore existed after *Edelsten*. Certainly the stronger view was that an account of profits, like an injunction, was generally available for innocent infringements. In the year following *Edelsten*, claimants again appeared before Sir John Romilly MR seeking an account of profits in a case of innocent trade mark infringement.

In *Moet* v. *Couston*[112] the defendants were wine merchants and had innocently purchased and sold in England a consignment of champagne labelled as "Moet's Champagne". Moet, the claimant, brought an action against the defendants for an injunction and an account of profits for the infringement of the "Moet" trade mark. Both his decision in *Cartier* and the decision of the Lord Chancellor in *Edelsten* were cited to the Master of the Rolls. In a very short judgment, Sir John followed the Lord Chancellor's decision in the *Edelsten* case and refused the account because the defendants had no knowledge that the champagne was not truly Moet's. No mention was made by Sir John of his own previous decision in the *Cartier* case.

The position before 1875 had therefore developed that disgorgement damages were only available for cynical infringement of trade marks infringement and cynical passing off.

(b) *After 1875*

As discussed above, after the establishment of the registry in 1875 for trade marks, it eventually became recognised that the basis of the new statutory

---

[109] (1838) 3 My & Cr 338; 40 ER 956.
[110] *Millington* v. *Fox* above note 109, 352; 962.
[111] *Millington* v. *Fox* above note 109, 355; 963.
[112] (1864) 33 Beav 578; 55 ER 493.

wrong, like that of passing off, was the protection of property and not the common law basis originating in the tort of deceit.[113] Passing off and trade mark infringement were, alike at common law and in equity, wrongs of strict liability. The question was whether the traditional approach denying disgorgement damages unless the infringement was cynical would still be maintained.

In *Gillette UK Ltd* v. *Edenwest Ltd*[114] as discussed above, in an action for compensatory damages Blackburne J comprehensively examined all the authorities and concluded that passing off and trade mark infringements were wrongs of strict liability. However Blackburne J expressly avoided the question of whether disgorgement damages could be awarded in circumstances of innocence stating that "different issues arise".[115] However he acknowledged that there are cases in which an account of profits had been refused because the breach was innocent[116] (in line with Lord Westbury's initial suggestions).

In *A G Spalding & Bros* v. *A W Gamage Ltd*[117] the issue was again raised in obiter dicta. The claimants, Spalding, manufactured footballs and sued the defendants who had passed off certain of their old footballs as Spalding balls. The defendants had purchased a number of Spalding's discarded "Orb" balls and had advertised and sold them as Spaldings "Improved Orb" balls. The defendants then withdrew the balls and the advertisement but continued to sell the balls as "Orb" balls. The House of Lords accepted that an injunction against the sale of the balls as "Orb" balls should be granted and that an inquiry into compensatory damages should proceed. Although the only issue was one of compensatory damages, Lord Parker, (with whom Lords Atkinson and Sumner agreed) after stating that passing off was a wrong of strict liability, commented that "the complete innocence of the party . . . may be a reason for limiting the account of profits to the period subsequent to the date at which he became aware of the true facts".[118]

This approach was again taken in *Colbeam Palmer Ltd* v. *Stock Affiliates Pty Ltd*[119] by Windeyer J, sitting as a single judge in the High Court of Australia. In that case, the claimant produced painting sets under the name "Craft Master". The defendant also sold painting sets which bore that mark unaware of the claimant's presence. The reason for the identical name arose out of an agreement whereby the two companies would both sell the product as "Craft Master" but would not compete in a number of specified countries. Australia was one of the few countries not mentioned and each company was initially unaware when the other began selling in Australia. Although the defendant became aware and notified the claimant of the issue it was not for another four years before the

---

[113] *A G Spalding & Bros* v. *A W Gamage Ltd* (1915) 32 RPC 273 (HL) 283 (Lord Parker); *Draper* v. *Trist* (1939) 56 RPC 429 (CA) 442 (Goddard LJ).
[114] [1994] RPC 279.
[115] *Gillette UK Ltd* v. *Edenwest Ltd* above note 114, 290.
[116] *Ellen* v. *Slack* (1880) 24 Sol Jo 290.
[117] (1915) 32 RPC 273 (HL) 283.
[118] *A G Spalding & Bros* above note 117, 283.
[119] (1968) 122 CLR 25 (HCA).

claimant notified the defendant that the sales were infringing its trade mark and the defendant discovered that its sales infringed the claimant's trade mark. However, by the time the action was brought for infringement of trade mark, the trade mark had expired. The claimants sought an injunction and account of profits.

Windeyer J held that as the trade mark had expired an injunction could not be awarded. However, based on the fact that the trade mark was previously valid he was prepared to award an account of profits. This award was limited to the period from which the defendant knew of the claimant's rights. Windeyer J approved of the *Edelsten* and *Moet* cases and suggested that nothing had changed by the introduction of the register. He stated that:[120]

> "The account of profits retains its characteristics of its origin in the Court of Chancery. By it a defendant is made to account for, and is then stripped of, profits which he has made which it would be unconscionable that he retain. These are profits made by him dishonestly, that is by his knowingly infringing the rights of the proprietor of the trade mark . . . The account is limited to the profits made by the defendant during the period when he knew of the plaintiff's rights. So it was in respect of common law trade marks. So it still is in respect of registered trade marks: *Edelsten* v. *Edelsten* (1863) 1 De G J & S 185 (46 ER 72) ; *Slazenger & Sons* v. *Spalding & Bros* (1910) 1 Ch 257; *Moet* v. *Couston* (1964) 33 Beav 578 (55 ER 493). I think that it follows that it lies upon a plaintiff who seeks an account of profits to establish that profits were made by the defendant knowing that he was transgressing the plaintiff's rights."

If accepted, this approach would treat passing off and trade mark infringement in the same way as all other strict liability property infringements. Compensatory damages would be available for infringement of the property right but disgorgement damages would require evidence of cynical breach. It would also be consistent with the position prior to the Trade Marks Registration Act 1875, after the implicit concession by Sir John Romilly.

This approach was also bolstered in 1994 in the new Trade Marks Act 1994 which provided in section 14(2):

> "In an action for infringement all such relief by way of damages, injunctions, accounts or otherwise is available to [the plaintiff] as is available in respect of the infringement of any other property right"

Like the property rights considered in chapter four, this provision suggests that disgorgement damages should only be available in cases of cynical breach.

Unfortunately, in the latest case on this Act, *Microsoft Corp* v. *Plato Technology Ltd*,[121] Judge Steinfeld QC held that either damages *or* an account of profits were to be calculated in the same fashion following an innocent passing off and trade mark infringement of several counterfeit Windows 95 Microsoft software programs. However, the innocence point was not contested

---

[120] *Colbeam Palmer Ltd* above note 119, 34–35.
[121] [1999] FSR 834. .

and on appeal to the Court of Appeal (in relation to the nature of the injunction awarded) the Court simply referred to this finding of Judge Steinfeld QC without argument.[122]

It would seem that the best approach for a court to take would be to follow the balance of historical authority, and the position in relation to other property wrongs, such as trespass, conversion and interference with goods, as mandated by the Trade Marks Act 1994. This would have the effect of limiting the availability of disgorgement damages only to cases of cynical breach.

4) Infringement of patent

As was seen above, the Patents Act 1977 introduced a defence of innocence to a case of breach of patent and applied it to an account of profits. This provision should be wholly unnecessary. Like the balance of authority for copyright and design infringement, passing off and trade mark infringement, disgorgement damages should not be awarded for the infringement of a patent unless the infringement is shown to be wilful or cynical.

However, although there are a number of cases where disgorgement damages (an account of profits) are awarded for an infringement of a patent[123] no case has considered this issue in the context of a claim by a defendant that the infringement was innocent. Indeed, in *Dart* v. *Décor Corp*[124] it was assumed that an account of profits was prima facie allowed whether or not the infringement was wilful. Thus, the introduction of the defence of innocence in the Patents Act 1977 will operate to ensure that disgorgement damages are only available in cases of cynical breach (although the burden of proof is reversed).

CONCLUSION

This chapter has not sought exhaustively to examine every single statutory, common law or equitable wrong that might involve an infringement of a defendant's intellectual property rights. The focus has been upon the main intellectual property rights. It has been argued that the principles in each case should be consistent and, as most of the legislation provides, should correspond with the principles concerning infringements of property rights generally. However, in the three categories examined there is some inconsistency.

In relation to disgorgement damages the authority is mixed. The best view seems to be that disgorgement damages are available only for cynical breaches

---

[122] *Microsoft Corp* v. *Plato Technology Ltd* (1999) 22 IPD 22108.

[123] Several of these were discussed in ch. three in the context of assessment of disgorgement damages: *Celanese International Corp'n* v. *BP Chemicals Ltd* [1999] RPC 203; *Siddell* v. *Vickers* (1892) 9 RPC 152, 163; *Dart* v. *Décor Corp* (1993) 116 ALR 385 (HCA).

[124] (1993) 116 ALR 385 (HCA). The relevant Australian provisions were to the same effect as the Patents Act 1977: Patents Act 1990 (Cth) ss. 122, 123 and Patents Act 1952 (Cth) ss. 118, 124.

of copyright, design rights, trade marks and in cases of passing off. The issue has not arisen in the context of infringement of patent rights but provision of an innocence defence to an account of profits for breach of patent should militate against any award of disgorgement damages for non-cynical breach of patent.

In relation to restitutionary damages, even with their obiter dicta acceptance in the leading House of Lords speech by Lord Nicholls, in the context of patent infringement, there remains the anomaly that, unless a strained interpretation is placed on the word "damages" in the relevant statutes, it is a defence to restitutionary damages that the breach of copyright, design right or patent was innocent. On the other hand, trade mark infringement and passing off cases are left to be treated in the same way as other property rights which, as chapter four has shown, suggests that restitutionary damages should be available regardless of the character of the breach. This inconsistency invites a comparison with German law, which allows a claim for restitutionary damages (a fair licence fee) for infringement of *any* intellectual property right, treating such rights as akin to other property rights.[125]

Despite these inconsistencies, what emerges is a pattern of liability which instantiates the model advocated in this book. Except for the defence of innocence in cases of copyright, design right and patent infringement, restitutionary damages, with their compelling rationale of reversing wrongful transfers, are always available to reverse any wrongful transfer of intellectual property rights. Disgorgement damages exist to strip a defendant of profits made cynically and therefore to deter wrongdoing committed with a view to profit. The trend of authority for intellectual property wrongs generally supports this as it suggests that an account of profits (the usual form of disgorgement damages in this area) will only be available for a cynical and wilful infringement of intellectual property rights.

---

[125] §812 BGB. K Zweigert & H Kötz *Introduction to Comparative Law* (3rd edn. Clarendon Press Oxford 1998) 545.

8

Conclusions

THIS BOOK HAS explored the nature and legitimacy of gain-based damages and this final chapter explains the conclusions and their implications. The conclusions are fourfold. First, the common view that "damages" are only awarded to compensate for loss is a fallacy. Damages serve other purposes. Exemplary damages primarily operate to punish and deter. Nominal damages operate to affirm the infraction of a legal right. Both of these measures of damages, especially exemplary damages which were examined in chapter one, are legitimate. Because of the different purposes of damages awards, it was argued in chapter one that the word "damages" should be taken to mean nothing more than a monetary award which is given for a wrong.

Secondly, it is possible, desirable and sometimes essential to appreciate that the law recognises a classification of "wrongs". Wrongs are causes of action that have this in common: remedies are given for them because they are characterised as breaches of duty. Although it is sometimes extremely difficult to identify whether a particular cause of action is a wrong, it is at least clear that this category is broader than the common law category "tort" and includes breaches of contract and breaches of equitable and statutory duties. The category of "wrongs" is not closed. New wrongs might be developed or causes of action such as those currently thought to be causes of action in unjust enrichment might be alternatively analysed as new wrongs.

The third conclusion reached is that an examination of the remedies given throughout the law of wrongs reveals that the law commonly recognises two different gain-based awards. These two awards were entitled "restitutionary damages" and "disgorgement damages". Although compensatory damages are the usual form of relief for wrongdoing, restitutionary damages and disgorgement damages are alternative measures which a claimant might seek. Restitutionary damages reverse a wrongful transfer of value and are the corresponding remedy in the law of wrongs to restitution in the law of unjust enrichment. They subtract from a defendant any (usually objective) benefit transferred from a claimant. They differ from compensatory damages in that the claimant need not have suffered any financial loss—the only requirement is that some objective benefit has been wrongfully obtained by the defendant through the claimant's assets or rights or their use. Disgorgement damages, on the other hand, are not concerned with whether there has been any transfer of value or not. They operate, independently of any transfer, to strip a defendant of any profit made.

The final conclusion in this book is that these two forms of gain-based damages are explained by different policies and thus arise in different circumstances. Restitutionary damages, concerned with reversing wrongful transfers of value, should always be available where a wrongful transfer has occurred. Once a transfer of value is deemed wrongful, the response of the law should always be to reverse that transfer. Disgorgement damages, focusing only upon stripping gain from a defendant, are best explained as concerned with deterrence of wrongdoing. Such deterrence, by stripping profits from a wrongdoer, is justified in two circumstances where the law considers compensatory damages to be inappropriate to deter. First, when a wrong is committed with a view to gain, deterrence of other like wrongdoing is achieved by stripping all gain made from that wrongdoer. Secondly, in the case of fiduciary relations, the importance of ensuring that the fiduciary is constantly vigilant and cannot be swayed by self-interest, requires a higher standard of deterrence so that even profits made innocently, but wrongfully, will be stripped.

In examining the existence and legitimacy of gain-based damages at common law this involved consideration of torts in chapter four (although passing off was considered separately with infringements of intellectual property) and breaches of contract in chapter five. Equitable wrongs of breach of fiduciary duty, breach of confidence, knowing participation in a breach of fiduciary duty (a wrong which *includes* "knowing assistance" and "knowing receipt of property" in breach of trust or fiduciary duty) and actual fraud were all considered in chapter six. Finally, intellectual property wrongs (most of which are now regulated, at least in part, by statute) were considered in chapter seven. In all of these diverse areas of the law of wrongs the availability of restitutionary damages and disgorgement damages was shown to conform to the theoretical rationales of reversing transfers and deterring wrongdoing.

One significant exception to the broad theory enunciated in chapter three was the wrong of breach of contract. In this case, it was seen that both restitutionary damages and disgorgement damages were limited by an additional requirement that the defendant have a "legitimate interest" in performance. Although this requirement was criticised, it is consistent with the approach historically taken to breaches of contract where, in some circumstances, contractual rights have not been afforded the same extent of protection as other rights such as those protected in the law of torts.

Neither of the labels "restitutionary damages" or "disgorgement damages" have achieved general recognition by courts although both have been used judicially. But the exact nomenclature is not important. What is important is that it is recognised that two different forms of damages exist, both of which are based upon gain to a defendant but motivated by different policies. The importance of giving each of these two forms of damages *some* label or description arises because historically numerous different names have been given to awards for wrongs which have a common restitutionary purpose (reversing transfers) or a common disgorgement purpose (stripping profits). By recognising that two different forms of gain-based damages exist, each based upon different policies, these many different gain-based awards for wrongs can then be recognised as sharing either of these two purposes—and labelled either restitutionary damages or disgorgement damages—so that like responses can be treated alike.

This final chapter explores two significant consequences of these conclusions. One consequence of the failure to differentiate between restitutionary damages and disgorgement damages is that there has been very little attention paid to questions of election or proprietary consequences in the context of distinguishing between these different measures. The first part of this section considers issues of election arising in the context of gain-based damages and suggests a principled solution. The second part explains how an appreciation of the two forms of gain-based damages illustrates that there are two corresponding forms of proprietary remedy. However the basis upon which proprietary remedies should be made available *in addition to* personal remedies is an extremely difficult question. The cases are not consistent and various different solutions have been proposed.

A Election

1) The governing principle

There are numerous issues of election which this short conclusion does not consider. The consideration below merely raises the questions of election that will need to be considered in light of the recognition of two forms of gain-based damages. The primary issue raised (and considered below) is the question of election between different remedies for a wrong once two forms of gain-based remedies are recognised. Incidental issues which can only benefit from this analysis, but which are not considered, are the manner by which election is required[1] or rules of election between remedies for different *causes of action* such as actions in unjust enrichment.[2] The primary question that is raised by the recognition of two forms of gain-based damages is the extent to which election is necessary between restitutionary damages, disgorgement damages, compensatory damages and exemplary damages.

In principle the answer is not difficult. Each of compensatory damages, restitutionary damages, disgorgement damages and exemplary damages serve central

---

[1] A process governed by principles which, as Lord Nicholls has acknowledged is "no more than practical applications of a general and overriding principle . . . namely that proceedings should be conducted in a manner which strikes a fair and reasonable balance between the interests of the parties".*Tang Man Sit* v. *Capacious Investments Ltd* [1996] AC 514 (PC) 522.

[2] Although the analysis below should inform this question. For instance, there is a very powerful argument that rules governing election between restitution for unjust enrichment and concurrent remedies for wrongs should mirror the rules governing restitutionary damages and other remedies for wrongs considered below. See also J Stevens "Election between Alternative Remedies" [1996] RLR 117; A Burrows "Solving the Problem of Concurrent Liability" [1995] CLP 103.

purposes. Compensatory damages are primarily concerned to compensate a defendant for financial loss suffered. Restitutionary damages are primarily concerned to reverse wrongful transfers of value received by a defendant. Disgorgement damages are primarily concerned to strip profits and deter wrongdoing. Exemplary damages are concerned to punish and to deter. At a more theoretical level, the first three measures of damages can all be explained as concerned with corrective justice[3] although exemplary damages cannot.[4] Each remedy also *incidentally* performs the functions of the other remedies. To the extent that all damages remedies involve a subtraction from the wealth of the defendant, they are all punitive and all operate to deter. Indeed, the very factor determining the availability of disgorgement damages, as explained in chapter three, is that compensatory damages are inadequate *fully to deter* wrongdoing in some cases.[5] The highest in quantum of all of these remedies operates to serve the purposes of the others, except where exemplary damages require a measure of *additional* punishment. The only situations in which an election should *not* be required, and the remedies should be cumulative, is where they focus upon different wrongful acts.

2) Disgorgement damages and restitutionary damages

In *Tang Man Sit* v. *Capacious Investments Ltd*[6] Mr Tang committed a breach of trust by secretly letting, as homes for the elderly, 16 houses which were to be assigned to Capacious Investments. When the time came for execution of the assignment the homes were therefore incumbered with the leases. The Court of Appeal of Hong Kong made a declaration that the claimant, Capacious Investments, was the equitable owner of the properties and this was not challenged. The difficulty arose in the money remedies sought by the claimant.

The claimant sought an account of the profits (disgorgement damages) secretly made from the rental of the properties and "damages" arising from the secret use and letting of the 16 houses. The "damages" sought were broken into two heads. Head A was damages for "the wrongful use and occupation" and head B was damages for the financial loss from the decreased value of the property because it was incumbered with leases.[7] The value of the damages under head A was almost $8 million and under head B was $11 million. It appeared that the profits received were several million less than the $8 million market rate sought under head A. Leaving aside the issue of when the claimant was required to elect,[8] the Privy

---

[3] E Weinrib *The Idea of Private Law* (Harvard Univ Press Mass 1995) 135.

[4] E Weinrib "Restitutionary Damages as Corrective Justice" (2000) 1 Theoretical Inquiries in Law 1, 11; L Smith "Restitution: The Heart of Corrective Justice" (2001) 79 Texas Law Rev 2115.

[5] See ch. 3, text accompanying notes 113–126.

[6] *Tang Man Cit* above note 1.

[7] *Tang Man Cit* above note 1, 519.

[8] Overruling the Hong Kong Court of Appeal on this point the Privy Council advised that the claimant was only required to elect when "the judge is asked to make orders against the defendant": *Tang Man Cit* above note 1, 521. See also *Warman International Ltd* v. *Dwyer* (1995) 182 CLR 544 (HCA) 570.

Council advised that the claimant was entitled to elect between an account of profits and (both head A and head B) "damages" but could not have both as they were inconsistent remedies.[9]

Head A of the "damages", damages for the wrongful use and occupation, are best seen as restitutionary damages. On the evidence, had Mr Tang not secretly let out the houses, Capacious Investments would not have done so and thus suffered no financial loss from the use and occupation.[10] The market rate of the use and occupation award has been explained throughout this book as restitutionary damages. The difficulty is in understanding why an award of an account of profits (disgorgement damages) was inconsistent with both awards of damages (restitutionary damages (head A) and compensatory damages (head B)) but, within the "damages" award, the (head A) restitutionary damages was not "inconsistent" with the (head B) compensatory damages.[11] This is another case where the solution to this question is only possible by separating out the different claims and using the different nomenclature of restitutionary damages, disgorgement damages and compensatory damages.[12]

The claim for disgorgement damages and the claim for restitutionary damages under head A were both concerned with the wrongful use and occupation of the land. The restitutionary damages award, being greater than the disgorgement damages award, *incidentally* performed the function of the disgorgement damages award and ensured that any profits made from the use and occupation of the land were disgorged. But the loss caused by the incumbering of the land related to a different matter. The wrong of use and occupation of the land can be seen as a separate breach of trust to the incumbering of the properties, the latter of which continued even after Mr Tang was no longer using the land. This is why the compensatory damages (head B) and the restitutionary damages (head A) were not "inconsistent".

In the same fashion, where the claims to disgorgement damages and the claim to restitutionary damages focus upon *different* wrongful acts then no election between them will be required. In *Ex Parte James*[13] for instance, Lord Eldon held that land had been acquired by a solicitor (from a bankrupt's estate) in breach of fiduciary duty. The solicitor let out the land for a period and then occupied it for a further period. Lord Eldon awarded restitutionary damages of an occupation rent from the time he took possession as well as disgorgement damages (an account of rents and profits) from the time previous to that when he leased out the property.

---

[9] *Tang Man Cit* above note 1, 525.
[10] It was noted that before Mr Tang's breach of trust, "the houses stood empty. There were complications over Mr Kung's [the owner of Capacious Investments Ltd] estate": *Tang Man Cit* above note 1, 518.
[11] *Tang Man Cit* above note 1, 526.
[12] See ch. 3, text accompanying note 132.
[13] *Ex Parte James* (1803) 8 Ves 337, 351; 32 ER 385, 390.

3) Disgorgement damages and compensatory damages

In the Court of Appeal for Hong Kong in the *Tang Man Cit* case, it was held that the disgorgement damages were only inconsistent with head A (restitutionary damages) and not the independent wrong which caused the head B loss.[14] The requirement of election between disgorgement damages and compensatory damages only exists where they are concerned with the same act.[15] In these cases an election is always required.

Warman International Ltd v. *Dwyer*,[16] discussed in chapter six,[17] is a good example of this requirement. In that case the High Court of Australia held the claimant must elect between an account of profits made by the defendants and compensation for their loss. The wrongful act which generated the profits was the participation in the breach of fiduciary duty by a former agent in setting up an independent company and terminating the agency arrangement. This was the same as the act which created the losses.

The higher of the two awards would concurrently *effect* both purposes of disgorging profits and compensating for loss even if the *purpose* of the award was only the former (disgorgement damages) or the latter (compensatory damages).[18] It is therefore orthodox, and entirely principled, that when both compensatory damages and disgorgement damages are sought for the same wrongful act the claimant must elect between them. This applies whether the disgorgement damages are described as an account of profits[19] or where the same profit-stripping function is performed at common law and referred to as "damages" or "money had and received".[20]

---

[14] *Tang Man Cit* above note 1, 519–520.

[15] In *Smith* v. *Thompson* [1895] 1 Ch 71, a trustee had taken a bribe and (subsequently) negligently and wrongfully invested the trust property. He was held liable to account for (disgorge) the bribe as well as to compensate the beneficiaries for loss from the investment, the two being treated as separate acts by Kekewich J.

[16] (1995) 182 CLR 544 (HCA).

[17] Ch. 6, text accompanying note 149.

[18] It has been argued that there is no inconsistency between compensatory damages and disgorgement damages because one is concerned with loss and the other with gain. But the inconsistency arises from the fact that the higher of the two awards *in its effect* fulfils the purpose of the other award. Cf A Tettenborn "Bribery, Corruption and Restitution—The Strange case of Mr Mahesan" (1979) 95 LQR 68, 74–75; P Birks "Inconsistency between Compensation and Restitution" (1996) 112 LQR 375. See also *Law Commission* 1997 48–49.

[19] *Redrow Homes Ltd* v. *Betts Brothers Plc* [1999] 1 AC 197 (HL) 209; *Colbeam Palmer Ltd* v. *Stock Affiliates Pty Ltd* (1968) 122 CLR 25 (HCA) 32; *Neilson* v. *Betts* (1871) LR 5 HL 1 (HL); *De Vitre* v. *Betts* (1873) LR 6 HL 319 (HL) *Warman International Ltd* v. *Dwyer* (1995) 182 CLR 544 (HCA) 570. See also s. 61(2) Patents Act 1977.

[20] *Mahesan S/O Thambiah* v. *Malaysian Government Officers Co-Operative Housing Society* [1979] AC 374 (PC); *Petrotrade Inc* v. *Smith* [2000] 1 Lloyds Rep 486.

4) *Restitutionary damages and compensatory damages*

As noted, in the *Tang Man Cit* case, no election between restitutionary damages and compensatory damages was required because the wrong for which the restitutionary damages were sought (the breach of trust in the use and occupation of the land) was functionally a separate act to the incumbering of the properties; the latter of which continued even after Mr Tang was no longer using the land. It will be recalled from chapter four that in *Whitwham* v. *Westminster Brymbo Coal and Coke Co*,[21] the defendant had caused damage to the claimant's land by dumping waste upon it from the defendant's colliery. The Court of Appeal held that the claimant was entitled to compensation for the damage caused to the land as well as an *additional* wayleave award or restitutionary damages for the "value transferred"; the market value of the *use* of the land. Again, the causing of damage to the land was an independent claim from the claim relating to the *use* of the land.

On the other hand, if the two remedies are sought for the same wrongful act then the claimant must elect for the higher. Thus, if the claimant in the *Whitwham* case had also sought compensatory damages for the loss of the ability to let the land (for example under a pre-existing contract) this award would have been inconsistent with the restitutionary damages. Numerous cases have affirmed that an election between compensatory damages and restitutionary damages is required in such circumstances.[22] In *Dormeuil Freres SA* v. *Feraglow Ltd*[23] Knox J stated that "if the loss of sales basis were the higher result the royalty basis [restitutionary damages] would not be the subject of any inquiry. The two are necessarily mutually exclusive. There could not be any question of the plaintiff recovering both."

The same approach applies in cases where restitutionary damages are sought for wrongful use of goods. It is only where the remedies are concerned with different wrongful acts that they will both be allowed. Damages (either compensatory or restitutionary) for the *use* of land are different from damages for injury, or loss of, the land itself. Likewise with goods. In *Strand Electric and Engineering Co Ltd* v. *Brisford Entertainments Ltd*,[24] Denning LJ allowed a claim for restitutionary damages for the wrongful use of goods. However, Denning LJ noted that "if the goods are retained by the wrongdoer up till judgment, the hiring charge runs up to that time, and *in addition the owner will get the return of the goods or their value at the time of judgment*".[25] Again, in *Lacon*

---

[21] [1896] 2 Ch 538 (CA).
[22] *Ministry of Defence* v. *Ashman* [1993] 2 EGLR 102 (CA) 105; *Gondal* v. *Dillon Newsagents Ltd* [2001] RLR 221.
[23] [1990] RPC 449, 464.
[24] [1952] 2 QB 246, 255.
[25] Italics added. See also *Rosenthal* v. *Alderton & Sons Ltd* [1946] KB 374.

v. *Barnard*[26] the claimant recovered restitutionary damages in trespass for the "taking and driving" of the defendant's sheep and this was held by the court not to be a bar to a separate claim for compensatory damages in conversion for the selling of the sheep. In each case therefore it is simply a question of identifying whether the remedy relates to the same act. If it does then the claimant should be required to elect for the money remedy of the highest quantum. That remedy will incidentally serve the function of the others.

5) *Exemplary damages*

The one exception to this operation of election principles is exemplary damages. The primary concerns of exemplary damages, as discussed throughout chapter one, are punishment and deterrence where the less extreme remedies such as compensatory damages, restitutionary damages or disgorgement damages do not operate sufficiently to punish and deter.[27] There never seems to have been a requirement in English law that a claimant elect for exemplary damages. They have always been seen as an *additional* remedy.

However, it was shown in chapter one that one category of exemplary damages parallels the availability of disgorgement damages. The second limb of exemplary damages is available where the defendant cynically makes a profit by wrongdoing. The recognition and availability of disgorgement damages should mean that this profit-stripping deterrent function of exemplary damages should indeed be subject to election in the same manner as disgorgement damages. Indeed where exemplary damages and disgorgement damages are both sought in these circumstances they are both fulfilling the same purposes *directly* and not merely incidentally. In cases where disgorgement damages operate to strip profits, exemplary damages should only be awarded if there is a further or additional need to punish. Lord Scott, in *Kuddus* v. *Chief Constable of Leicestershire Constabulary*,[28] relied on this reasoning in attempting to show that exemplary damages were an anomaly. Lord Nicholls in the *Kuddus* case also stated that the availability of disgorgement damages should now mean that exemplary damages in this category are largely unnecessary.[29]

---

[26] (1676) Cro Car 35; 79 ER 635. The same result can be seen in the United States where a constructive trust was declared over tortiously acquired property and a reasonable rental for the period was also allowed to reflect the rights transferred over that time to market hops; hop growers had established a market for these rights: *Scymanski* v. *Dufault* 491 P 2d 1050 (1972 SCW).

[27] *Kuddus* v. *Chief Constable of Leicestershire Constabulary* [2001] 2 WLR 1789 (HL) 1811 (Lord Hutton).

[28] "Lord Devlin's second category, cases in which the defendant's wrongful conduct has made a profit for himself which exceeds the compensation payable to the victim of the conduct, has been largely overtaken by developments in the common law. Restitutionary damages [Disgorgement damages] are available now in many tort actions as well as those for breach of contract. The profit made by a wrongdoer can be extracted from him without the need to rely upon the anomaly of exemplary damages": *Kuddus* above note 27, 1819.

[29] *Kuddus* above note 27, 1807.

The circumstances in which exemplary damages should still be available *in addition* to an award of disgorgement damages is where there is an additional need to punish. Lord Diplock also referred to this possible need for an additional punitive sum in *Broome* v. *Cassell & Co*:[30]

> "To restrict the damages recoverable to the actual gain made by a defendant, if it exceeded the loss to the plaintiff, would leave a defendant contemplating an unlawful act with the certainty that he had nothing to lose to balance against the chance that the plaintiff might never sue him or, if he did, might fail in the hazards of litigation."

It is for the same reason that it was seen, in chapter four, that the law sometimes denies an allowance in many of the older cases involving a cynical removal of coal from the defendant's property. This denial of an allowance effects a punitive award beyond the actual profits made by the defendant.[31]

The effect of this is that exemplary damages are not an exception to this analysis at all but simply a case where the other remedies cannot incidentally operate to sufficiently punish and deter. Recently, the Supreme Court of Canada allowed exemplary damages for a breach of contract because deterrence could not "be achieved through the award of compensatory damages".[32] In that case no profit had been made by a wilful breach of contract when the defendant bank obtained a court order for a receiver against a debtor without notifying the debtor. But the conduct was "a serious affront to the administration of justice"[33] The only cases which could possibly be seen as exceptions, and perhaps wrongly decided, are instances where compensatory damages have been awarded *in addition* to exemplary damages where the exemplary damages were simply operating to strip profits made from the same wrong and not to effect any further punishment or deterrence.[34]

B Proprietary claims

1) The problem

A second area of the law in which the thesis and conclusions in this book will have considerable impact is in the highly contentious area of "proprietary restitutionary awards" for wrongs. Like gain-based damages awards, gain-based proprietary awards for wrongs have generally been treated alike and labelled "restitutionary proprietary awards".[35] However, proprietary awards for

---

[30] [1972] AC 1027 (HL) 1130.

[31] See ch. 4, text accompanying note 168.

[32] *Royal Bank of Canada* v. *W Got & Associates Electric Ltd* (2000) 178 DLR 385 (SCC) 394–395. See J Edelman "Exemplary Damages for Breach of Contract" (2001) 117 LQR 19.

[33] *Got* above note 32, 394–395.

[34] The classic instance of such a case is *Rookes* v. *Barnard* [1964] AC 1129 (HL).

[35] *Goff and Jones* 81–93; P Birks *Introduction* 53; A Burrows *The Law of Restitution* 40–45; G Virgo *Restitution* 592.

wrongs mirror the personal gain-based damages. The proprietary awards might be disgorgement proprietary awards (corresponding to disgorgement damages) or restitutionary proprietary awards (corresponding to restitutionary damages). In the law of unjust enrichment, there are also restitutionary proprietary awards which parallel the personal award of restitution.

The effect of recognition of a proprietary award has many consequences additional to the recognition of personal damages awards. A proprietary award confers priority in insolvency, it has implications in private international law, for limitation periods, in the criminal law[36] and for land registration.[37] For these reasons, in many cases courts have been reluctant to give proprietary awards. The issue of the availability of gain-based proprietary awards is far from clear. Some authors argue that for personal awards of restitution a corresponding gain-based proprietary award should be generally available.[38] At the other extreme are arguments that gain-based proprietary awards, primarily because they confer priority in insolvency, cannot be justified.[39] The issue is currently a matter of intense debate and has received much attention particularly in the judicial and extra-judicial work of Lord Millett.[40]

This concluding section cannot resolve this extremely difficult debate to which entire monographs have been devoted.[41] Instead, this section seeks to show that any analysis of proprietary awards in the law of wrongs must differentiate between restitutionary proprietary awards and disgorging proprietary awards. It also notes that the trend in English law, powerfully driven by Lord Millett, mirrored in developments in the Supreme Court of Canada, is moving toward a principled model of recognition of these gain-based proprietary awards. The model suggests that gain-based proprietary awards should be available where the corresponding personal award (restitution in the case of unjust enrichment and restitutionary damages or disgorgement damages in the law of wrongs) is inadequate.

---

[36] *Moynes* v. *Cooper* [1956] 1 QB 439; *Ilich* v. *R* (1987) 162 CLR 110 (HCA). See G Williams "Mistake in the Law of Theft" (1977) CLJ 62; G Williams "Theft, Consent and Illegality" [1977] Crim LR 127; D Fox "The Transfer of Legal Title to Money" [1996] RLR 60.

[37] *Collings* v. *Lee* [2001] 2 All ER 332 (CA); *Attorney General for Hong Kong* v. *Reid* [1994] 1 AC 324 (PC).

[38] In the context of claims in unjust enrichment: R Chambers *Resulting Trusts*; P Birks *Introduction* 54–64; D Paciocco "The Remedial Constructive Trust: A Principled Basis for Priority over Creditors" (1989) 68 Can Bar Rev 315. Cf *Westdeutsche Landesbank Girozentrale* v. *Islington LBC* [1996] AC 669 (HL).

[39] W Swadling "Property and Unjust Enrichment" in JW Harris (ed.), *Property Problems: From Genes to Pension Funds* (Kluwer Law International London 1997) 130.

[40] In addition to the cases and articles cited below see the discussion of the resulting trust in P Millett "Tracing the Proceeds of Fraud" (1991) 107 LQR 71; 76, 80; P Millett "Equity—The Road Ahead" (1995) TLI 35.

[41] R Chambers *Resulting Trusts*.

2) *Two types of gain-based proprietary awards*

(a) *Proprietary restitutionary awards*

(i) Rescission

A wrongful transfer in the law of wrongs is reversed (whatever the nomenclature used) by an award of restitutionary damages. However, reversal can also be effected by a proprietary award of rescission. Although the mechanics of effecting rescission at common law and rescission in equity have traditionally differed[42] there is no doubt that rescission of a transaction could operate to revest property rights in the party from whom they had been transferred either due to a wrongful transfer or due to an illegitimate transfer in the law of unjust enrichment.[43]

In *Hunter BNZ Finance Ltd* v. *CG Maloney Pty Ltd*,[44] the plaintiff was defrauded into paying a cheque to a rogue who deposited the cheque in his account at Westpac Bank. The claimant was held to have rescinded the wrongful and fraudulent transfer (the giving of the cheque) and Westpac Bank were liable for conversion of this cheque. The New South Wales Court of Appeal held that the proceeds of the cheque held in the fraudster's account at Westpac were the property of the claimant consequent upon the rescission.[45]

Rescission and the revesting of property in the *Hunter* case was effected by the commencement of the legal proceedings.[46] However, at common law it might also be effected by retaking possession. In *Re Eastgate*[47] the vendor sold furniture and other goods to a rogue who bought without intending to pay. The retaking of possession of the goods by the vendor was held to be valid and an effective rescission.[48] In the same way, a defrauded purchaser is entitled to rescind and revest property in goods by an act sufficient to communicate rescission. In *Street* v.

---

[42] Primarily rescission at common law was a self-help remedy requiring an affirmative act of rescission and in equity a declaration was required by the court that the transaction is rescinded. See the detailed discussion of these differences in *Alati* v. *Kruger* (1955) 94 CLR 216 (HCA) 223–224.

[43] *Load* v. *Green* (1846) 15 M&W 216, 221; 153 ER 828, 830; *Clough* v. *London and North Western Railway Co* [1871] LR 7 Ex 26, 32; *Car and Universal Finance Co Ltd* v. *Caldwell* [1965] 1 QB 525; *Hunter BNZ Finance Ltd* v. *CG Maloney Pty Ltd* [1988] 18 NSWLR 420 (NSWCA) 432–433. The principle has also been affirmed in cases where a third party gains a paramount interest in the property before rescission, so preventing title revesting; see for example *White* v. *Garden* (1851) 10 CB 919; 138 ER 364; *Stevenson* v. *Newnham* (1853) 13 CB 285; 138 ER 1208; *Kingsford* v. *Merry* (1856) 11 Ex 577; 156 ER 960 reversed on other grounds (1856) 1 H&N 503; 156 ER 1299 and subsequently aff'd *Pease* v. *Gloahec* [1866] LR 1 HL 219 (PC) 230; *Truman (Limited)* v. *Attenborough* [1910] 26 TLR 601; *Whitehorn Bros* v. *Davison* [1911] 1 KB 463 (CA).

[44] *Hunter* above note 43.

[45] *Hunter* above note 43, 433–434, 437.

[46] *Clough* v. *London and North Western Railway Co* [1871] LR 7 Ex 26.

[47] [1905] 1 KB 465.

[48] See also *Moyce* v. *Newington* [1878] 4 QBD 32, 35. Counsel for both parties in *Car and Universal Finance Co Ltd* v. *Caldwell* [1965] 1 QB 525 (CA) accepted that rescission could be effected by retaking possession of goods, though Davies LJ noted (at 558) that apart from *Re Eastgate* no very clear authority had been cited for this conclusion.

Blay,[49] Lord Tenterden CJ stated that fraud entitled a purchaser "by his own act alone" to terminate the contract, revest title and recover the price.

Like common law, equity can also revest property rights in order to reverse a wrongful transaction. In *Alati* v. *Kruger*[50] the purchaser of a fruit shop business claimed to be entitled to rescind the contract in equity due to fraudulent misrepresentations made by the vendor. The lease was re-assigned to the vendor and property and chattels returned. Although the purchaser had possession and use of the premises for some time this was not a bar to rescission because a money allowance of restitutionary damages for the reasonable value of the use could be made as well as the proprietary award.[51]

In equity this proprietary restitutionary reversal (whether given to reverse a wrongful transfer or a transfer pursuant to unjust enrichment) has been described in various terms. It has been described as "equitable title",[52] a "constructive trust"[53] and as a "resulting trust".[54] Whichever of these labels is chosen, it should not distract from the fact that the same proprietary award can be used to effect the reversal of a transaction at common law.

(ii) Proprietary awards without rescission

There is another way in which wrongful transactions can be reversed with a proprietary award. In some cases equity recognises not merely a right to rescind but a full proprietary ownership right in the claimant *from the moment of the transfer*. Lord Millett has described these cases as subject to two requirements. First there must be no intention to make the transfer on the part of the claimant. Secondly, the wrong must be a breach of trust or fiduciary duty.[55] These requirements are discussed further below but a recent case serves to illustrate.

In *Collings* v. *Lee*,[56] L was the agent for the sale of a property and, as such, owed fiduciary duties to the vendor including duties to transfer the property to a purchaser. In breach of that duty, L created a fictitious purchaser and transferred the property to himself registering himself as proprietor. Despite L's fraud he became the legal owner by the act of registration.[57] L then gave a mortgage over the land to the defendant building society. The defrauded claimant contested the validity of the mortgage. The legislation provided that the register could be rectified by a claimant with an overriding equitable interest, so the

---

[49] (1831) 2 B&Ad 456; 109 ER 1212. See also *Murray* v. *Mann* (1848) 2 Ex 538; 154 ER 605; *Grimoldby* v. *Wells* [1875] LR 10 CP 391.

[50] *Alati* above note 42.

[51] *Alati* above note 42, 224. See also *El Ajou* v. *Dollar Land Holdings plc* [1993] 3 All ER 717.

[52] *Alati* v. *Kruger* (1955) 94 CLR 216 (HCA) 224.

[53] *Daly* v. *Sydney Stock Exchange* (1985) 160 CLR 371 (HCA) 390; *Greater Pacific Investments Pty Ltd (in liq)* v. *Australian National Industries Ltd* (1996) 39 NSWLR 143 (NSWCA) 152–153; *Lonrho plc* v. *Fayed (No 2)* [1992] 1 WLR 1, 11–12.

[54] *El Ajou* v. *Dollar Land Holdings plc* [1993] 3 All ER 717, 734; *Twinsectra* v. *Yardley* [1999] Lloyds LR Banking 438 (CA) 462.

[55] P Millett "Restitution and Constructive Trusts" in W Cornish *Restitution* 217.

[56] [2001] 2 All ER 332 (CA)

[57] Land Registration Act 1925 s. 5.

question became whether the claimant had an equitable proprietary interest in the land.

The Court of Appeal held that neither the transfer nor the registration divested the claimant of her equitable interest. L held the property on trust. The Court of Appeal distinguished cases of rescission in which consent had been given but that consent was impaired from cases where no consent was given at all. In the former cases the transaction had to be avoided, in the latter the equitable ownership arises to reverse the transaction from the time of the transfer.[58] However a strong argument could be made that the claimant in *Collings* did consent to the transfer, her consent was merely defective as she thought she was transferring to a bona fide third party.[59]

The cause of action to which the Court of Appeal referred was the wrong of breach of fiduciary duty.[60] Like many wrongs the case could be alternatively analysed as one in unjust enrichment. But, whether the wrong or the unjust enrichment is the cause of action, the difficulty with the analysis in *Collings* is that it seems to be a case of *impaired* consent (akin to the cases of rescission) rather than *absence* of consent. An action in unjust enrichment would have been on the ground of "mistake" rather than total "ignorance". The action that the Court of Appeal relied upon, in the law of wrongs, was the breach of fiduciary duty but that breach procured a transaction with impaired consent and not a complete absence of consent. L consented to a transfer of the property, it was simply that the transfer was thought to be made to a genuine purchaser (who did not exist) rather than the fraudster defendant.[61]

(iii) When is the transfer reversed?

It is clear from the above that in cases where there is *no* intention to pass property the reversal of the transfer arises from the time of the transferred possession of the property. The Court of Appeal in *Collings v. Lee* were explicit about this. Delivering the advice of the Privy Council in *Air Jamaica Ltd v. Charlton*,[62] Lord Millett, described the interest in cases of no consent as equitable ownership under a resulting trust:

> "like a constructive trust, a resulting trust arises by operation of law, though unlike a constructive trust it gives effect to intention. But it arises whether or not the transferor intended to retain a beneficial interest—he almost always does not—since it responds to the absence of any intention on his part to pass a beneficial interest to the recipient. It may arise even where the transferor positively wished to part with the beneficial interest. The cases of *voidable* transfer of property are more difficult."

---

[58] *Collings* above note 37, 337.

[59] W Swadling "What's in a Name" (2002) 65 MLR (forthcoming).

[60] *Collings* above note 37, 337.

[61] An analogy might, however, be stretched with cases in which property is said not to pass because of a fundamental mistake which is sometimes referred to as "without" consent. Professor Treitel, drawing from Lord Atkin, refers to these as mistakes *nullifying consent* and mistakes *negativing* consent: See G Treitel *The Law of Contract* (10th edn. Sweet & Maxwell London 1999) 232; *Bell v. Lever Bros Ltd* [1932] AC 161 (HL) 217.

[62] [1999] 1 WLR 1399 (PC) 1412.

In relation to transfers made with only *vitiated* or impaired consent, Dr Chambers has argued, with much support from the older cases,[63] that a right to rescind in equity confers immediate equitable ownership in the property upon the occurrence of the voidable transaction.[64] Certainly the right to rescind does bear similar characteristics to equitable ownership. It is devisable,[65] assignable[66] and has been said to allow priority in insolvency and bankruptcy[67] although this latter point is now open to doubt.[68] Dr Chambers also powerfully argues that in many of the cases of vitiated (but not absent) consent in the law of unjust enrichment, equitable ownership vests at the time of the vitiation of consent. In the most famous of these cases, *Chase Manhattan N.A v. Israel-British Bank (London) Ltd*,[69] Golding J thought that even a case of mistake with vitiated consent was enough for an immediate ownership right.[70] However Lord Browne-Wilkinson in the *Westdeutsche* case considered that such a mistake could not be sufficient.[71]

In *Phillips v. Phillips*,[72] Lord Westbury LC implicitly rejected the view of Lord St Leonards LC in *Stump v. Gaby*[73] stating that the right to rescind is "an equity as distinguished from an equitable estate"[74] and hence susceptible to a defence of bona fide purchase of a *later* equitable estate. The term "mere equity" or "equity" has also been preferred to distinguish this right.[75] In recent times the Court of Appeal, particularly in judgments of Lord Millett, have affirmed this view[76] and it has been stated in the House of Lords that a defrauded vendor of

---

[63] *Stump v. Gaby* (1852) 2 De GM & G 623;42 ER 1015; *Gresley v. Mousley* (1859) 4 De G & J 78; 45 ER 31; *Dickinson v. Burrell* (1866) LR 1 Eq 337; *Melbourne Banking Corp v. Brougham* (1882) 7 App Cas 307; *Gross v. Lewis Hillman Ltd* [1970] Ch 445.

[64] R Chambers *Resulting Trusts* 116–142.

[65] *Stump v. Gaby* above note 63; *Gresley v. Mousley* above note 63. As is the interest of the other party to the return of the counter-performance: *Re Sherman Deceased* [1954] 1 Ch D 653.

[66] *Dickinson v. Burrell* (1866) LR 1 Eq 337; *Melbourne Banking Corp v. Brougham* (1882) 7 App Cas 307.

[67] *Re Eastgate* [1905] 1 KB 465; *Tilley v. Bowman Ltd* [1910] 1 KB 745; R Goode *Principles of Corporate Insolvency Law* (2nd edn. Sweet and Maxwell, London 1997).

[68] See below text accompanying note 82.

[69] [1981] 1 Ch 105.

[70] In fact Goulding J considered this not as a case of a restitutionary proprietary right but as one of a persistent proprietary right which simply had not been transferred ([1981] 1 Ch 105, 119, 120). But it could only have been the mistake that *generated* the equitable proprietary right. Lord Browne-Wilkinson made this criticism in *Westdeutsche Landesbank Girozentrale v. Islington LBC* [1996] AC 669 (HL) 714.

[71] *Westdeutsche Landesbank Girozentrale v. Islington LBC* [1996] AC 669 (HL) 715. Although Lord Browne-Wilkinson suggested that *retention* of the money after learning of the mistake might be sufficient.

[72] *Phillips v. Phillips* (1861) 4 De 6 F&J 208; 45 ER, 1164.

[73] *Stump* above note 65.

[74] *Phillips* above note 72, 218; 1167.

[75] *Cave v. Cave* (1880) 15 Ch D 639, 649; *Bainbrigge v. Browne* (1881) 18 Ch D 188, 197; *Cloutte v. Storey* [1910] 1 Ch D 18, 24; *National Provincial Bank v. Ainsworth* [1965] AC 1175 (HL) 1254; *Latec Finance v. Hotel Terrigal Pty Ltd (in liq)* (1965) 113 CLR 265 (HCA) 281, 277–278, 291, cf 282, 284.

[76] *Lonrho plc v. Fayed (No 2)* [1992] 1 WLR 1; *El Ajou v. Dollar Land Holdings plc* [1993] 3 All ER 717, 735; *Bristol and West Building Society v. Mothew* [1998] Ch 1(CA) 22–23; *Twinsectra v. Yardley* [1999] Lloyds LR Banking 438 (CA); *Collings v. Lee* above note 37, 337.

goods "retains no proprietary interest in the chattel" which presumably means that the right to rescind does not confer an immediate right of ownership either at common law or in equity.[77] Nevertheless, as noted above, the right of rescission does confer such ownership, and effect the reversal of the transaction, once *exercised*. Thus, as Brennan J stated in *Daly v. Sydney Stock Exchange Ltd*:[78]

> "The vendor cannot insist in an *equitable interest* in the property if he does not choose to enforce his *equity* to avoid the sale. If a decree setting aside the conveyance is made, the plaintiff's equitable title is treated 'as having been, from the first, a trustee for the grantor, who, therefore has an equitable estate not a mere right of suit'."

There is therefore a fiction that once a transaction is rescinded, and the transfer reversed, the property subject to that transaction will be treated *as if* it had always belonged to the claimant. This fiction has substantial consequences. One effect of the fiction is that it is said to allow a tracing claim into the traceable substitute of the money or property.[79] That *other* money or other property will also be treated as if it were always the property of the claimant. The use of the fiction is also the only way to explain why a right of rescission can be exercised against a liquidator to allow priority over unsecured creditors in insolvency.[80] In *Re Eastgate*,[81] Bigham J stated that "the trustee acquired the interest of the bankrupt in the property subject to the rights of third parties. One of those rights in this case was the right of the vendors of goods to disaffirm the contract and to retake possession of the goods." The return of the property is presumably not a prohibited preference as it is treated as always having belonged to the claimant once the right to rescind is exercised. But even with the use of this fiction it is difficult to see how, at the moment of rescission the conversion of the equity to rescind into equitable ownership is not a preference.

However, both aspects of this fiction have now been seriously questioned by the Privy Council; the use of the fiction to date the proprietary interest from the time of the transfer of property and the use of the fiction to justify the effect of the rescission as conferring a proprietary interest in insolvency and bankruptcy.[82] Further, the fiction has been rejected in the context of holding that the defendant should not be treated as being under the same "fiduciary duties" as a true trustee who holds the property of another in equity[83] and in holding that a

---

[77] *Barclays Bank* v. *Boulter* [1999] 1 WLR 1919 (HL) 1925 (Lord Hoffmann). Although Professor Birks has referred to this as "highly contentious" and "not necessary for the decision": P Birks "At the Expense of the Claimant: Direct and Indirect Enrichment in English Law" (2000) Oxford U Comparative L Forum 1 at ouclf.iuscomp.org, text after note 70.

[78] (1985) 160 CLR 371 (HCA) 387–390. See also *Greater Pacific Investments Pty Ltd (in liq)* v. *Australian National Industries Ltd* (1996) 39 NSWLR 143 (NSWCA) 152–153.

[79] *El Ajou* v. *Dollar Land Holdings plc* [1993] 3 All ER 717, 734; *Daly* v. *Sydney Stock Exchange* (1985) 160 CLR 371 (HCA) 390; *Twinsectra* v. *Yardley* [1999] Lloyds LR Banking 438 (CA) 462.

[80] *Re Eastgate* [1905] 1 KB 465; *Tilley* v. *Bowman Ltd* [1910] 1 KB 745. See R Goode *Principles of Corporate Insolvency Law* (2nd edn. Sweet and Maxwell, London 1997).

[81] *Re Eastgate* above note 80, 470; *Tilley* v. *Bowman Ltd* above note 80.

[82] *Re Goldcorp* [1995] 1 AC 74 (PC).

[83] *Bristol and West Building Society* v. *Mothew* [1998] Ch 1 (CA) 23.

defendant is not liable for conversion prior to a claimant's election to rescind.[84] It seems that as this fiction is slowly being abolished the courts are moving toward complete recognition that a revested right of ownership, reversing a wrongful transaction in the law of wrongs (or illegitimate transaction in the law of unjust enrichment), can arise in a claimant upon rescission. However, that right only arises from the date of the rescission and not the date of the wrongful (or, in the law of unjust enrichment, illegitimate) transfer of property.

(b) *Proprietary disgorgement awards*

The term "constructive trust" is often also used to describe a proprietary claim which operates to disgorge a profit wrongfully made. It is the corresponding proprietary award to the personal award of disgorgement damages. But it is not always clear whether it means a constructive trust as a proprietary response or a personal response of *liability to account in the manner of a constructive trustee*[85] although in some cases it is apparent that it is being used in a proprietary sense.[86] The personal response is disgorgement damages; the proprietary response is a disgorging proprietary award.

Attorney General v. *Reid*[87] is a good example. It will be recalled from chapter three that a corrupt prosecutor had received bribes to obstruct prosecutions and invested some of those bribes in properties in New Zealand which appreciated in value. The Crown sought a *proprietary* right in the properties so that a caveat could be lodged on the basis of the breach of fiduciary duty by its employee, Reid. Lord Templeman, delivering the advice of the Privy Council, upheld the caveat and allowed the proprietary disgorging award to strip the fiduciary of "any surplus in excess of the initial amount of the bribe because he is not allowed by any means to make a profit out of a breach of duty".[88]

A difficulty with the reasoning in the *Reid* case is that if it were the case that a disgorgement proprietary award could be given to effect deterrence, then proprietary disgorgement awards should be available where needed to deter other wrongs. Proprietary disgorgement should be available to deter torts committed cynically and wilfully just as it is available to deter breaches of fiduciary duty.

---

[84] *Lipkin Gorman* v. *Karpnale plc* [1991] 2 AC 548 (HL) 573 (Lord Goff); *Bristol and West Building Society* v. *Mothew* [1998] Ch 1 (CA) 23 (Millett LJ); *Trustee of the Property of Jones* v. *Jones* [1997] Ch 159 (CA). See also L Smith *Tracing* 197.

[85] See, for instance *Chan* v. *Zacharia* (1983) 53 ALR 417 (HCA) 433 (Deane J); *Regal (Hastings) Ltd* v. *Gulliver* [1967] 2 AC 134 (HL); *Boardman* v. *Phipps* [1967] 2 AC 46 (HL). This "type of constructive trust is merely the creation by the court . . . to meet the wrongdoing alleged: there is no real trust and usually no chance of a proprietary remedy": *Coulthard* v. *Disco Mix Club Ltd* [2000] 1 WLR 707, 731. See also *Selangor United Rubber Estates Ltd* v. *Cradock* [1968] 1 WLR 1555, 1582. The criticism of the lax use of this term has been made on a number of occasions- see the authorities cited in L Smith "Constructive Trusts and Constructive Trustees" [1999] CLJ 294.

[86] *Keith Henry & Co Pty Ltd* v. *Stuart Walker & Co Pty Ltd* (1958) 100 CLR 342 (HCA) 350; *Featherstonhaugh* v. *Fenwick* (1810) 17 Ves Jr 298; 34 ER 115; *Clegg* v. *Edmondson* (1857) 8 De GM & G 787, 807; 44 ER 593, 601.

[87] [1994] 1 AC 324 (PC).

[88] *Reid* above note 87, 331

The proprietary award in both cases is operating to serve the same deterrent purpose. But, in the absence of a breach of fiduciary duty, courts have refused to impose a proprietary disgorgement remedy.

In *Re Polly Peck International plc (In Administration) (No 5); Marangos Hotel Co Ltd* v. *Stone*,[89] the respondents had committed the tort of trespass by illegally expropriating the appellants' hotels, apartments and other property. The appellants sought the disgorgement of the profits made by this expropriation. However, as the defendants were insolvent, the claim was never put as a personal claim to the profits. A constructive trust (a disgorgement proprietary remedy) was sought in order to gain priority over the other creditors in the insolvency. The appellants conceded that there was no "pre-existing equitable interest" but sought a proprietary remedy based upon "ex post facto imposition by the court, in its discretion, of a remedial constructive trust".[90] The Court of Appeal rejected this argument on the basis that it would interfere with the statutory insolvency scheme under the Insolvency Act 1986. As Nourse LJ stated "[y]ou cannot grant a proprietary right to A, who has not had one beforehand, without taking some proprietary right away from B".[91]

The *Polly Peck (No 5)* case was technically only concerned with a discretionary proprietary remedy which arose *only at the time of insolvency* and not at the time of the trespass. However, the Court of Appeal has also refused to extend the "institutional" proprietary remedy, which does arise at the time of the wrong, beyond cases of breach of fiduciary duty. This occurred in *Halifax Building Society* v. *Thomas*.[92] That case was discussed in chapter four and criticised for the failure to recognise that the personal remedy of disgorgement damages is available in cases of deliberate cynical torts. However, in an independent submission the appellant had also sought a proprietary disgorgement remedy.

It will be recalled that the appellant was a Building Society that had made a mortgage to Thomas as a result of fraudulent misrepresentations made by Thomas as to his identity and creditworthiness. After Thomas defaulted upon the mortgage the Society had obtained an order for possession of the mortgaged property which was sold for a surplus in excess of £10,000. After the conviction of Thomas a confiscation order was made in favour of the Crown Prosecution Service for the value of the surplus.[93] The Society argued that the surplus was its property and thus that the confiscation order did not attach. One submission (which did not rely upon any disgorgement damages remedy) was that the society, as a victim of fraud, was entitled to a constructive trust over the profits of the fraud in the same manner as a constructive trust was awarded over the profits of a breach of fiduciary duty in *Attorney General for Hong Kong* v. *Reid*.[94]

---

[89] [1998] 3 All ER 812.
[90] *Polly Peck* above note 89, 825 (Mummery LJ).
[91] *Polly Peck* above note 89, 832.
[92] [1996] Ch 217 (CA).
[93] Section 79(3) of the Criminal Justice Act 1988.
[94] *Reid* above note 87.

The Court of Appeal rejected this argument. Peter Gibson LJ noted the criticism of the proprietary award in the *Reid* case. However, he was content to state that in the instant case "there was no fiduciary relationship . . . [the relationship was] merely that of debtor and secured creditor".[95] He supported this reasoning by the fact that Parliament had already acted in a way to "prevent a fraudster benefiting from his wrong" by enacting the Criminal Justice Act 1988 and courts should not indulge in "parallel creativity".[96] Interestingly, Peter Gibson LJ did acknowledge the existence and possibility of a restitutionary proprietary claim based upon *value transferred*. He stated that if the mortgage had been *avoided*, the flat (and its sale proceeds) might have become the property of the Society, as the traceable product of its own property. However, avoidance had not been sought.[97]

Another example of the refusal of a proprietary disgorgement award is in cases of breach of contract. In the *Blake* case, the House of Lords awarded the disgorgement damages award of an account of profits for the breach of contract. However, Lord Nicholls went out of his way to note that this did remedy did not confer any proprietary entitlement upon the Crown to Blake's profits.[98]

Aside from breach of fiduciary duty then, there are only isolated other instances in which a proprietary disgorging award extends to other wrongs for which disgorgement damages are available. In *Potton Ltd* v. *Yorkclose Ltd*[99] for instance, Millett J held that an account of profits could be awarded for the infringement of a claimant's copyright. Millett J also stated that "profits made thereby belong in equity to the plaintiffs".[100]

3) *A principle governing the award of both gain-based proprietary awards?*

The position to which English law (particularly in the judgments, speeches and extra-judicial writings of Lord Millett) appears to be moving is to a principle that a gain-based proprietary remedy will be available only where a personal (gain-based damages) remedy is not adequate. This position is not explored or criticised in detail in this concluding chapter (although it is noted that it is a

---

[95] *Halifax* above note 92, 229.

[96] *Chief Constable of Leicestershire* v. M [1989] 1 WLR 20, 23.

[97] It is also difficult to see how it would have been possible, in a proprietary sense, to avoid the initial loan. If avoidance had been sought before the mortgagee sale then the sale itself (and hence the claim to the traceable proceeds of the sale) as a "mortgagee" could not occur. If avoidance had been sought after the mortgagee sale it is difficult to see what transaction Halifax could rescind. For upon the mortgagee sale the loan would have wholly ceased to exist. The same conceptual difficulty raised by this fiction of rescission vesting the ownership of the property *as if* it has always been in the claimant arises where the property has passed to a *bona fide* purchaser so that the transaction *itself* cannot be rescinded but the claimant wants to claim the traceable proceeds of the sale: See S Worthington *Proprietary Interests in Commercial Transactions* (Clarendon Press Oxford 1996) 166.

[98] *Attorney General* v. *Blake* [2001] 1 AC 268 (HL) 288.

[99] [1990] FSR 11.

[100] *Potton* above note 99, 18.

coherent principled approach) except to show how an analysis and understanding of its application should be seen in the context of the different restitutionary and disgorgement measures in the law of wrongs.

The reference to adequacy of a personal remedy is a reference to whether the personal award can achieve the purposes for which it is given. So the reference to adequacy in the context of allowing specific performance instead of compensatory damages is usually because the personal award is inadequate *to compensate*. This will, however, mean that these proprietary awards are far less commonly available than is usually thought. Lord Millett has made this observation. Even in the traditional (very limited) area where proprietary specific performance is ordered because compensatory damages are inadequate, courts are increasingly developing compensatory damages so that they *are* adequate to compensate.[101] And in cases of modern land speculation, specific performance has been refused by the Supreme Court of Canada precisely because land no longer carries the same irreplaceable importance as it did in previous times, a money remedy measured by the value of *performance* was held to be adequate.[102]

(a) *Proprietary restitutionary awards*

A recent detailed consideration of proprietary restitutionary awards was made by Lord Millett, who considered the circumstances in which a proprietary restitutionary remedy should be available for unjust enrichment. The same conclusions should be true for a restitutionary proprietary award corresponding to restitutionary damages in the law of wrongs. Lord Millett thought that proprietary restitutionary remedies should be available in two circumstances. The first is instances of proprietary rescission which should be available where monetary rescission is inadequate:[103]

"the right [of rescission] to reconveyance is a form of specific performance (or 'specific unperformance') which equity makes available because a money judgment is an inadequate remedy. If this is right, then the remedy should be confined to cases of land or other property of special value to the transferor."

The claimant entitled to proprietary rescission should, like the claimant entitled to specific performance, also have an equitable property right conferring priority in insolvency.[104] In cases of specific performance, the remedy is ordered

---

[101] See for example the loss of amenity award designed to redress a loss of consumer surplus in *Ruxley Electronics and Construction Ltd* v. *Forsyth* [1996] AC 344 (HL).

[102] *Semelhago* v. *Paramadevan* [1996] 2 SCR 415. See ch. 5, text accompanying note 112. In England compare *Lord Napier and Ettrick* v. *R F Kershaw Ltd* [1993] AC 713 (HL) where compensatory damages were held to be an inadequate remedy to protect an insurer's implied contractual right to be subrogated to a settlement fund: Criticised in *Goff and Jones* 85–86.

[103] P Millett "Restitution and Constructive Trusts" in W Cornish et al *Restitution* 216. See also AJ Oakley "Restitution and Constructive Trusts: A Commentary" in W Cornish et al. *Restitution* 218, 230.

[104] *Swiss Bank Corporation* v. *Lloyds Bank Ltd* [1979] Ch 548, 566–567 (Browne-Wilkinson J). See also *Freevale Ltd* v. *Metrostore (Holdings) Ltd* [1984] Ch 199.

because compensatory damages are inadequate to compensate the claimant.[105] In cases of the award of proprietary rescission the analogy requires its award where restitutionary damages in the law of wrongs or restitution in the law of unjust enrichment cannot adequately reverse a transfer with a money award.

The second instance contemplated by Lord Millett, where proprietary restitution should be available, is where a claimant has a continuing beneficial interest under a resulting trust.[106] As mentioned above, this proprietary interest arises in cases in which two requirements are satisfied. First, there must have been a transfer of the claimant's property without her intention.[107] Second there must be a breach of trust or fiduciary duty. The first requirement might also be explained as an instance in which restitutionary damages (or, in the law of unjust enrichment, the award of restitution) would be inadequate. Where a claimant never intended to part with property, a money award might not adequately reverse the transaction. However, it is difficult to see why, in the law of wrongs, the award should be confined to cases of breach of trust and fiduciary duty and not other wrongs. For instance, statute now recognises that in a case of wrongful interference with goods an order can, "where appropriate", order the delivery up of the goods.[108] It would seem "appropriate" to make that order in circumstances in which restitutionary damages cannot adequately reverse the transaction.[109]

(b) *Proprietary disgorgement awards*

It is precisely the same reasoning (that a personal award is inadequate) which lead Lord Millett to advocate, and the Privy Council to accept, the disgorging proprietary award in *Attorney General for Hong Kong* v. *Reid*.[110] Lord Templeman, delivering the advice of the Privy Council, held that a proprietary disgorging remedy was necessary:[111]

> "the false fiduciary will receive a benefit from his breach of duty unless he is accountable not only for the original amount or value of the bribe but also for the increased value of the property representing the bribe . . . because he is not allowed by any means to make a profit out of a breach of duty."

The reason that Lord Templeman considered this to be the case was because, approving extra-judicial statements by Sir Peter Millett (as he then was), he considered that the personal award was limited to the first receipt.[112] Thus, "in the

---

[105] The classic statement to this effect is that of Lord Selborne LC "specific performance instead of damages only when it can by that means do more perfect and complete justice": *Wilson* v. *Northampton and Banbury Junction Railway Co* (1874) 9 Ch App 279, 284.

[106] P Millett "Restitution and Constructive Trusts" above note 103, 217.

[107] Delivering the advice of the Board, Lord Millett again enunciated this in *Air Jamaica Ltd* v. *Charlton* [1999] 1 WLR 1399 (PC) 1412.

[108] Torts (Interference with Goods) Act 1977 s. 3(2)(a).

[109] As noted in ch. 4, the term "damages" in the Torts (Interference with Goods) Act 1977 has been read broadly to encompass restitutionary damages: See ch. four, text accompanying note 39.

[110] [1994] 1 AC 324 (PC).

[111] *Reid* above note 110, 331.

[112] P Millett "Bribes and Secret Commissions" [1993] RLR 7, 17.

absence of such a [disgorging proprietary] remedy a fiduciary who receives a bribe and invests it at a profit will retain an advantage".[113] Some authors have argued, with Lord Templeman, that the maxim that "equity regards as done that which ought to be done" requires a proprietary remedy.[114] However, it was noted in chapter three that developed notions of remoteness of disgorgement damages should mean that a personal award of disgorgement damages could now be adequate to effect their purpose of deterrence of wrongdoing leaving the more extreme proprietary disgorgement award as unnecessary.[115]

Nevertheless, there will be circumstances in which disgorgement damages will not be adequate to effect deterrence and a proprietary disgorging award will be necessary. In *LAC Minerals Ltd* v. *International Corona Resources Ltd*[116] the defendants, LAC Minerals, acquired from the claimants confidential information about gold deposits on a piece of land during negotiations about a joint venture to exploit the great mineral potential of that land. After negotiations failed LAC Minerals cynically, and in breach of confidence, used the confidential information to make enormous profits from mining the land itself. A majority of the Supreme Court of Canada accepted that LAC Minerals held the land on constructive trust for the claimants. This is a case in which disgorgement damages might be inadequate fully to strip profits made from the breach, "having regard to the uniqueness of the . . . property, to the fact that but for LAC's breaches of duty, Corona would have acquired it, and recognising the virtual impossibility of valuing the property".[117]

Another example is *Korkontzilas* v. *Soulos*.[118] In that case, a real estate broker, negotiating the purchase of a property for a client, Mr Soulos, purchased it for his wife instead and subsequently transferred it to himself and his wife as joint tenants. The client brought an action for breach of fiduciary duty seeking only a proprietary remedy (a constructive trust) as the value of the property had since fallen. Delivering the majority judgment (with which La Forest, Gonthier, Cory and Major JJ agreed), McLachlin J gave two reasons why a proprietary award was necessary. The first reason justified the proprietary award because an award of compensatory damages would be inadequate to compensate. Mr Soulos showed a continuing desire to own the property. A nominal

---

[113] P Millett "Bribes" above note 112, 17.

[114] S Worthington *Proprietary Interests in Commercial Transactions* (Clarendon Press, Oxford 1996) 192–193.

[115] *Fyffes Group Ltd* v. *Templeman* [2000] 2 Lloyds Rep 643, 688; P Birks "Property in the Profits of Wrongdoing" (1994) 24 UWAL Rev 8, 12; L Smith *Tracing* 21; W Swadling "Property and Unjust Enrichment" in JW Harris (ed.), *Property Problems: From Genes to Pension Funds* (Kluwer Law International London 1997) 130, 142; R Goode "Ownership and Obligation in Commercial Transactions" (1987) 103 LQR 433, 442–445; P Birks "Obligations and Property in Equity: *Lister* v. *Stubbs* in the limelight" [1993] LMCLQ 30; D Crilley "A Case of Proprietary Overkill" [1994] RLR 57. An intermediate position is that *both* could be concurrently available: *Goff and Jones* 742; *United Pan-Europe Communications NV* v. *Deutsche Bank AG* [2000] 2 BCLC 461(CA).

[116] [1989] 2 SCR 574 (SCC).

[117] *LAC Minerals* above note 116, 52. See JD Davies "Duties of Confidence and Loyalty" [1990] LMCLQ 4, 5.

[118] [1997] 2 SCR 217 (SCC).

monetary compensation remedy (because the market value had fallen) would have been inadequate to compensate Mr Soulos.[119] Alternatively, it was held that as a proprietary award corresponding to disgorgement damages it should also have been available. The Supreme Court noted that any award of an account of profits would have been nominal because no monetary profit was made by the real estate agent on the transaction. But such a nominal disgorgement damages remedy would be inadequate:[120]

> "The message will be clear: real estate agents may breach their duties to their clients and the courts will do nothing about it, unless the client can show that the real estate agent made a profit. This will not do."

(c) *The developing principle*

In *Westdeutsche Landesbank Girozentrale* v. *Islington LBC*,[121] Lord Goff posed the hypothetical question: "why should the plaintiff bank be given the additional benefits which flow from a proprietary claim, for example the additional benefit of achieving priority in the event of the defendant's insolvency?" The answer to which English law seems to be moving is "because where the personal award would be inadequate to achieve its purpose a claimant will be entitled to a proprietary award." Priority in insolvency will simply be a *consequence* of fulfilling that purpose. Thus, in cases where compensatory damages are inadequate to compensate, specific performance is ordered and priority in insolvency is an accepted consequence. Where restitutionary damages are inadequate to reverse the transferred benefit from a defendant, a proprietary restitutionary remedy might also be ordered. And where disgorgement damages cannot properly effect deterrence, proprietary disgorgement might again be ordered.

Regardless of whether this approach comes to be accepted, a coherent understanding of these proprietary awards, like an understanding of rules of election between damages remedies, is only possible if the different nomenclature used to effect each type of gain-based damages are recognised as like responses and if restitutionary damages and disgorgement damages are separated and understood independently. Then, like awards will be treated alike and different awards treated differently.

---

[119] *Korkontzilas* above note 118, 242.
[120] *Korkontzilas* above note 118, 242–243.
[121] [1996] AC 669 (HL) 683–684.

Bibliography

A Abdullah and T Hang, "To Make the Remedy Fit the Wrong" (1999) 115 LQR 376

American Law Institute, *Restatement (Second) of Contracts* (American Law Institute Minnesota 1981)

——, *Restatement on Restitution* (American Law Institute Washington 1937)

——, *Restatement of the Law of Restitution and Unjust Enrichment: Discussion Draft* (American Law Institute Philadelphia 2000)

——, *Restatement (Second) of Torts* (American Law Institute Minnesota 1979)

J B Ames, "Assumpsit for Use and Occupation" (1889) 2 Harv Law Rev 377

——, "The History of Assumpsit" (1888) 2 Harv L R 1

——, "History of Trover" (1898) 11 Harv Law Rev 374

N Andrews, "Civil Disgorgement of Wrongdoers' Gains: The Temptation to do Justice" in P Birks (ed.) *Wrongs and Remedies in the Twenty-First Century* (Clarendon Press Oxford 1996) 155

Anon, "Moses v Macferlan—Is it Sound Law" (1915) 24 Yale LJ 246

P Atiyah, "Personal Injuries in the Twenty First Century: Thinking the Unthinkable" in P Birks (ed.) *Wrongs and Remedies in the Twenty-First Century* (Clarendon Press Oxford 1996) 1

J H Baker, *An Introduction to English Legal History* (3rd edn. Butterworths London 1990)

——, "The History of Quasi-Contract in English Law" in W Cornish et al. (eds) *Restitution: Past, Present & Future* (Hart Publishing Oxford 1998) 37

E Bant, " 'Ignorance' as a Ground of Restitution—Can it survive?" [1998] LMCLQ 18

K Barker, "Restitution of Passenger Fare: The Mikhail Lermontov" (1993) LMCLQ 291

H Beale, (Gen ed.) *Chitty on Contracts* (Sweet and Maxwell London 1999)

——, "Damages for Poor Service" (1996) 112 LQR 205

J Beatson and D Friedmann, (eds) *Good Faith and Fault in Contract Law* (Clarendon Press Oxford 1995)

J Beatson, "The Nature of Waiver of Tort" (1979) 17 Uni of Western Ont Law Rev 1

——, *The Use and Abuse of Unjust Enrichment: Essays on the Law of Restitution* (Clarendon Press Oxford 1991)

J Berryman, "The Case for Restitutionary Damages over Punitive Damages: Teaching the Wrongdoer that Tort does not Pay" [1994] Can Bar Rev 320

P Birks, "Accessory Liability" [1996] LMCLQ 1

——, *An Introduction to the Law of Restitution* (Revised edn. Clarendon Press Oxford 1989)

——, "At the Expense of the Claimant: Direct and Indirect Enrichment in English Law" (2000) Oxford U Comparative L Forum 1 at *ouclf.iuscomp.org*

——, "Failure of Consideration" in F Rose (ed.) *Consensus Ad Idem: Essays in the Law of Contract in Honour of Guenter Treitel* (Sweet & Maxwell London 1996) 195

——, "Inconsistency between Compensation and Restitution" (1996) 112 LQR 375

——, "Misnomer" in W Cornish et al. (eds) *Restitution: Past, Present & Future* (Hart Publishing Oxford 1998) 1.

P Birks, "Obligations and Property in Equity: *Lister* v. *Stubbs* in the limelight" [1993] LMCLQ 30
——, "Profits of Breach of Contract" (1993) 109 LQR 518
——, "Property and Unjust Enrichment" [1997] NZLR 623
——, "Property in the Profits of Wrongdoing" (1994) 24 UWAL Rev 8
——, "Restitution and Wrongs" (1982) 35 CLP 53
——, "Restitution for Wrongs" in E Schrage (ed.) *Unjust Enrichment: The Comparative Legal History of the Law of Restitution* (2nd edn. Duncker & Humblot Berlin 1999)
——, "Restitution without Counter-Restitution" [1990] LMCLQ 330
——, "Restitutionary Damages for Breach of Contract: *Snepp* and the fusion of law and equity" [1987] LMCLQ 421
——, *Restitution—The Future* (The Federation Press Sydney 1992)
——, "Rights, Wrongs and Remedies" (2000) 20 OJLS 1
——, "The Concept of a Civil Wrong" in D Owen (ed.) *Philosophical Foundations of Tort Law* (Clarendon Press Oxford 1995)
——, "The Law of Restitution at the End of an Epoch" (1999) 28(1) UWAL Rev 13
——, "The Role of Fault in the Law of Unjust Enrichment" in W Swadling and G Jones (eds) *The Search for Principle—Essays in Honour of Lord Goff of Chieveley* (OUP Oxford 1999) 235
——, "Unjust Enrichment and Wrongful Enrichment" (2001) 79 Texas Law Rev 1767
——, "Unjust Factors and Wrongs" [1997] RLR 76
—— (ed.), *Privacy and Loyalty* (OUP Oxford 1996)
——, *The Classification of Obligations* (Clarendon Press Oxford 1997)
——, *The Frontiers of Liability* (Vol 1 OUP Oxford 1994)
—— (ed.), *Wrongs and Remedies in the Twenty-First Century* (Clarendon Press Oxford 1996)
—— and NY Chin, "On the Nature of Undue Influence" in J Beatson and D Friedmann (eds) *Good Faith and Fault in Contract Law* (Clarendon Press Oxford 1995)
—— and F Rose (eds), *Lessons of the Swaps Litigation* (LLP London 2000)
—— and G McLeod, "The Implied Contract Theory of Quasi-Contract: Civilian Opinion Current in the Century Before Blackstone" (1986) 6(1) OJLS 46
R Bowker, *Copyright: Its History and Its Law* (Houghton Mifflin Boston 1912)
M Brazier, (Gen ed.) *Clerk & Lindsell on Tort* (17th edn. Sweet & Maxwell 1995)
J T Brennan, "Injunction Against Professional Athletes Breaching their Contracts" (1967) 34 Brooklyn L Rev 61
A Briggs, *Conflict of Laws* (OUP Oxford 2001)
——, "From Complexity to Anticlimax: Restitution and Choice of Law" [1996] RLR 88
D Brown, *Ashburner's Principles of Equity* (2nd edn. Butterworths London 1933)
A Burrows, "Contract, Tort and Restitution—A Satisfactory Division or Not" (1983) 99 LQR 217
——, "No Damages for a Third Party's Loss" [2001] 1 OUCLJ 107
——, "No Restitutionary Damages for Breach of Contract" [1993] LMCLQ 453.
——, "Quadrating Restitution and Unjust Enrichment: A Matter of Principle" [2000] RLR 257
——, *Remedies for Torts and Breach of Contract* (2nd edn. Butterworths London 1994)
——, "Solving the Problem of Concurrent Liability" [1995] CLP 103
——, *The Law of Restitution* (Butterworths London 1993)

P A Butler, "Viewing Restitution at the Level of a Secondary Remedial Obligation (1990) 16 Uni Q Law J 27

G Calabresi and AD Melamed, "Property Rules, Liability Rules and Inalienability: One View of the Cathedral" (1972) 85 Harv L Rev 1089

P Cane, "Exceptional Measures of Damages" in P Birks (ed.) *Wrongs and Remedies in the Twenty-First Century* (Clarendon Press Oxford 1996) 302

——, *The Anatomy of Tort Law* (Hart Publishing Oxford 1997)

——, *Tort Law and Economic Interests* (2nd edn. Clarendon Press Oxford 1996)

D Carroll, "Four Games and the Expectancy Theory" (1981) 54 S Cal L Rev 503

J Cartwright, "Taking Stock of O'Brien" [1999] RLR 1

R Chambers, *Resulting Trusts* (Clarendon Press Oxford 1997)

——, "Resulting Trusts and Equitable Compensation" (2001) 15 TLI 2

M Chen-Wishart, "Restitutionary Damages for Breach of Contract" (1998) 114 LQR 363

——, "Unjust Factors and the Restitutionary Response" (2000) 20 OJLS 557

N Chin, "Rescission: A Case for Rejecting the Classical Model" (1997) 27 UWAL Rev 66

R Coase, "The Problem of Social Cost" (1960) 3 Journ Law and Econs 1

J Coleman, *Risks and Wrongs* (CUP Cambridge 1992)

L Collins, (Gen Ed.) *Dicey and Morris on Conflict of Laws* (Sweet & Maxwell London 2000)

E Cooke, "Trespass, Mesne Profits and Restitution" (1994) 110 LQR 420

B Coote, "Contract Damages, *Ruxley*, and the Performance Interest" [1997] CLJ 537

——, "*Dunlop* v. *Lambert*: The Search for a Rationale" (1998) 13 JCL 91

——, "The Performance Interest, *Panatown* and the Problem of Loss" (2001) 117 LQR 81

A Corbin, "Waiver of Tort and Suit in Assumpsit" (1910) 19 Yale LJ 221

W Cornish, *Intellectual Property* (4th edn. Sweet & Maxwell London 1999)

——, R Nolan, J O'Sullivan and G Virgo *Restitution: Past, Present & Future* (Hart Publishing Oxford 1998)

D Crilley, "A Case of Proprietary Overkill" [1994] RLR 57.

I Davidson, "The Equitable Remedy of Compensation" (1982) 13 MULR 349

J D Davies, "Duties of Confidence and Loyalty" [1990] LMCLQ 4

J Dawson, "Restitution or Damages" (1959) 20 Ohio St Law Journ 175

——, *Unjust Enrichment* (Little Brown & Co Boston 1951)

S Doyle and D Wright, "Restitutionary Damages—The Unnecessary Remedy?" (2001) 25 Melb Uni LR 1

I N Duncan Wallace, "Third Party Damage: No Legal Black Hole?" (1999) 115 LQR 394

——, "Defects and Third Parties: No Peace for the Wicked" (1999) 15 Const LJ 245

R Dworkin, *Taking Rights Seriously* (Duckworth London 1978)

J Edelman, "Claims to Compound Interest Part II: Extending Compound Interest claims for Wrongdoing" (2000) 28 ABLR 115

——, "Claims to Profits in Actions for Trespass" (2000) 116 LQR 18

——, "Exemplary Damages for Breach of Contract (2001) 117 LQR 539

——, "Money Had and Received: Modern Pleading of an Old Count" [2000] RLR 547

——, "Remedial Certainty or Remedial Discretion in Estoppel after Giumelli" (1999) 15 JCL 179

——, "The Compensation Strait-Jacket and the Lost Opportunity to Bargain Fiction" [2001] RLR 104

——, "The New Doctrine of Partial Failure of Consideration" (1997) 15 Aust Bar Rev 229

J Edelman, "Unjust Enrichment, Restitution and Wrongs" [2001] Texas Law Rev 1869

S Elliott, "Compensation Claims Against Trustees" (D.Phil Thesis University of Oxford 2001)

——, "Restitutionary Compensatory Damages for a Breach of Fiduciary Duty" [1997] RLR 135

——, "Fiduciary Liability for Client Mortgage Fraud" (1999) 13 TLI 74

——, "Rethinking Interest on Withheld and Misapplied Trust Money" [2001] Conv 313.

E A Farnsworth, "Your Loss or My Gain? The Dilemma of the Disgorgement Principle in Breach of Contract" (1985) 94 Yale LJ 1339

P Finn, *Fiduciary Obligations* (Law Book Co Sydney 1977)

——, "The Fiduciary Principle" in T Youdan (ed.) *Equity, Fiduciaries and Trusts* (Carswell Toronto 1989)

D Fox, "The Transfer of Legal Title to Money" [1996] RLR 60

G Fridman, *Restitution* (2nd edn. Carswell Ontario 1992)

D Friedmann, "Restitution for Wrongs: The Basis for Liability" in W Cornish et al. *Restitution: Past, Present & Future* (Hart Publishing Oxford 1998)

——, "Restitution for Wrongs: The Measure of Recovery" [2001] Tex L Rev 1879

——, "Restitution of Benefits Obtained through the Appropriation of Property or the Commission of a Wrong" (1980) 80 Col LR 504

——, "The Efficient Breach Fallacy" (1989) 18 JLS 1

W Friedmann, "The Principle of Unjust Enrichment in English Law" (1938) 16 Can Bar Rev 243

L L Fuller and W R Perdue, "The Reliance Interest in Contract Damages" (1936) 46 Yale LJ 52

S Gardner, "Knowing Assistance and Knowing Receipt: Taking Stock" (1996)112 LQR 56

——, "Wives' Guarantees of their Husbands' Debts" (1999) 115 LQR 1

R Goode, "Ownership and Obligation in Commercial Transactions" (1987) 103 LQR 433

——, *Principles of Corporate Insolvency Law* (2nd edn. Sweet and Maxwell London 1997)

W Gordon, "Of Harms and Benefits: Torts, Restitution and Intellectual Property" (1992) 21 Journ LS 449

R Grantham and C Rickett, *Enrichment and Restitution in New Zealand* (Hart Publishing Oxford 2000)

—— ——, "Property and Unjust Enrichment: Categorical Truths or Unnecessary Complexity?" [1997] NZLR 668

W Gummow, *Change and Continuity: Statute Equity and Federalism* (OUP Oxford 1999) 49

——, "Unjust Enrichment, Restitution and Proprietary Remedies" in P Finn *Essays on Restitution* (Law Book Co Sydney 1990)

H C Gutteridge, R J A David, "The Doctrine of Unjustified Enrichment" [1934] CLJ 204

T H Haddan, *Outlines of the Administrative Jurisidiction of the Court of Chancery* (London W Maxwell 1862)

M Halliwell, "Profits from Wrongdoing: Private and Public Law Perspectives" (1999) 62 MLR 271

C Harpum, "Accessory Liability for Procuring or Assisting a Breach of Trust (1995) 111 LQR 545

J Harris (ed.), *Property Problems: From Genes to Pension Funds* (Kluwer Law International London 1997)

H Hart, *The Concept of Law* (2nd edn. Clarendon Press Oxford 1997)

P Hastie, "Restitution and Remedy in Intellectual Property Law" (1996) 14 ABR 6

D Hayton, (ed.) *Law's Future(s): British Legal Developments in the 21st Century* (Hart Publishing Oxford 2000)

S Hedley, "The Myth of Waiver of Tort" (1984) 100 LQR 653

P Hellwege, "The Scope of Application of Change of Position in the Law of Unjust Enrichment: A Comparative Study" [1999] RLR 92

R Heuston and R Buckley, *Salmond on the Law of Torts* (21st edn. Sweet & Maxwell London 1996)

J D Heydon, "Equitable Compensation for Undue Influence" (1997) 113 LQR 8

——, "The Negligent Fiduciary" (1995) 111 LQR 1

L Ho, "Undue Influence and Equitable Compensation" in P Birks and F Rose *Restitution and Equity (Vol 1): Resulting Trusts and Equitable Compensation* (LLP London 2000) 193.

J Hodder, "Profiting from Tortious Use of Property: A Reply to the Lost Bargain Theory" (1984) 42 U of T Fac Law Rev 105

W Holdsworth, *A History of the English Law* (4th edn. Methuen London 1927)

O W Holmes, *The Common Law* (Dover New York 1881)

——, "The Path of the Law" (1897) 10 Harv L Rev 457

V House, "Unjust Enrichment: The Applicable Statute of Limitations"(1950) 35 Corn L Q 797

D Ibbetson, *A Historical Introduction to the Law of Obligations* (OUP Oxford 1999)

——, "Sixteenth Century Contract Law: *Slade's Case* in Context" (1984) 4 OJLS 295

——, "Assumpsit and Debt in the Early Sixteenth Century: The Origins of the Indebitatus Count" [1982] CLJ 142

I Jackman, "Restitution for Wrongs" [1989] CLJ 302

R Jackson, *The History of Quasi-Contract* (CUP Cambridge 1936)

P Jaffey, "Disgorgement for Breach of Contract" [2000] RLR 578

——, "Restitutionary Damages and Disgorgement" [1994] RLR 30

——, *The Nature and Scope of Restitution* (Hart Publishing Oxford 2000)

G Jones, "Bribes and Bribers" [1989] CLJ 22

——, "The Recovery of Benefits Gained from a Breach of Contract" [1983] 99 LQR 443

——, "Unjust Enrichment and the Fiduciary's Duty of Loyalty" (1968) 84 LQR 477

——, (ed.) *Goff and Jones on Restitution* (5th edn. Sweet & Maxwell London 1998)

——, W Goodhart, *Specific Performance* (2nd edn. Butterworths London 1996)

W A Keener, "Waiver of Tort" (1892) 6 Harv L Rev 223

J Kondgen, "Immaterialschadenseratz, Gewinnabschöpfung oder Privatstrafen als Sanktionen für Vertragsbruch? Eine rechtsvergleichend-ökonomische Analyse" [1992] RabelsZ 696

A Kull, "Disgorgement for Breach, the 'Restitution Interest' and the Restatement of Contracts" [2001] 79 Tex Law Rev 2021

——, "Rationalising Restitution" (1995) 83 Cal L Rev 1191

——, "Restitution and the Non-Contractual Transfer" (1997) 11 JCL 93

Law Commission, *Aggravated, Exemplary and Restitutionary Damages* (Law Com No 247 1997)

Law Commission, *Aggravated, Exemplary and Restitutionary Damages* (Law Com Consultation Paper 132 1993)

——, *Breach of Confidence* (Law Comm No 110 1981)

Law Reform Commission Ireland, *A Law Reform Commission Consultation Paper on Aggravated, Exemplary and Restitutionary Damages* (Law Reform Commission Ireland 1998)

E Lawes, *Practical Treatise on Pleading in Assumpsit* (W Reed London 1810)

N MacCormick, "The Obligation of Reparation" in N MacCormick (ed.) *Legal Right and Social Democracy* (Clarendon Press Oxford 1982)

I R MacNeil, "Efficient Breach of Contract: Circles in the Sky" (1982) 68 Vir L Rev 947

P Maddaugh and J McCamus, *The Law of Restitution* (Canada Law Book Co Ontario 1990)

F W Maitland, *The Forms of Action at Common Law* (CUP Cambridge 1965)

B Markesinis, *The German Law of Obligations : Vol II The Law of Torts: A Comparative Introduction* (3rd edn. Clarendon Press Oxford 1997)

A Mason, "The Impact of Equitable Doctrine on the Law of Contract" (1998) 27 Anglo-American Law Review 1

——, "The Place of Equity and Equitable Remedies in the Contemporary Common Law World" (1994) 110 LQR 238

N McBride, "A Case for Awarding Punitive Damages in Response to Deliberate Breaches of Contract" [1995] Anglo-American LR 369

P McGrath, "Knowing Receipt and Dishonest Assistance: A Wrong Turn" [1999] LMCLQ 343

H McGregor, "Restitutionary Damages" in P Birks (ed.) *Wrongs and Remedies in the Twenty-First Century* (Clarendon Press Oxford 1996) 203

——, (ed.) *McGregor on Damages* (16th edn. Sweet & Maxwell London 1997)

M McInnes, "Disgorgement for Wrongs: An Experiment in Alignment" [2000] RLR 516.

——, "The Plaintiff's Expense in Restitution: Difficulties in the High Court" (1995) 23 Aust Busi Law Rev 472

E McKendrick, "Breach of Contract and the Meaning of Loss (1999) CLP 37

——, *Contract Law* (Macmillan London 2000)

——, "Total Failure of Consideration and Counter-Restitution: Two Issues or One?" in P Birks (ed.) *Laundering and Tracing* (Clarendon Press Oxford 1995) 217

G McMeel, "Complex Entitlements: The *Albazero* Principle and Restitution" [1999] RLR 20

——, *The Modern Law of Restitution* (Blackstone Press London 2000)

G Mead, "Restitution within Contract?" (1991) 11 Legal Studies 172

R Meagher, W Gummow, J Lehane *Equity Doctrines and Remedies* (3rd ed. Butterworths Sydney 1992)

P Michalik, "The availability of compensatory and exemplary damages in equity: A note on the Aquaculture decision" (1991) 21 VUWLR 391

P Millett, "Equity's Place in the Law of Commerce" (1998) 114 LQR 214

——, "Equity—The Road Ahead" (1995) TLI 35

——, "Restitution and Constructive Trusts" in W R Cornish et al. (eds) *Restitution Past, Present and Future* (Hart Publishing Oxford 1998) 199

——, "Tracing the Proceeds of Fraud" (1991) 107 LQR 71

C C Mitchell, "Civil Liability for Bribery" (2001) 117 LQR 207

——, "Mesne Profits and Restitutionary Damages" [1995] LMCLQ 343

——, "No Account of Profits for a Victim of Deceit" [1996] LMCLQ 314

C Mitchell, "Remedial Inadequacy in Contract and the Role of Restitutionary Damages" (1999) 15(2) JCL 133

G Muir, "Unjust Sacrifice and the Officious Intervener" in P Finn *Essays on Restitution* (Law Book Company Sydney 1990) 297

C Needham, "Recovering the Profits of Bribery" (1979) 95 LQR 536

B Nicholas, *Introduction to Roman Law* (Clarendon Press Oxford 1962)

Lord Nicholls, "Knowing Receipt: The Need for a New Landmark" in W Cornish et al. (eds) *Restitution: Past, Present & Future* (Hart Publishing Oxford 1998) 231

R Nolan, "How Knowing is Knowing Receipt" [2000] CLJ 447

A J Oakley, "Restitution and Constructive Trusts: A Commentary" in W Cornish et al. (eds) *Restitution: Past, Present & Future* (Hart Publishing Oxford 1998) 218

R O'Dair, "Restitutionary Damages for Breach of Contract and the Theory of Efficient Breach: Some Reflections" (1993) 46 CLP 113

——, "Remedies for Breach of Contract: A Wrong Turn" [1993] RLR 31

Ontario Law Reform Commission, *Report on Exemplary Damages* (Ontario Law Reform Commission Ontario 1991)

G Orwell, *The Road to Wigan Pier* (Penguin Harmondsworth 1937)

D Owen (ed.), *Philosophical Foundations of Tort Law* (Clarendon Press Oxford 1995)

D Paciocco, "The Remedial Constructive Trust: A Principled Basis for Priority over Creditors" (1989) 68 Can Bar Rev 315.

G Panagopoulos, *Restitution in Private International Law* (Hart Publishing Oxford 2000)

J Paterson, (ed.) *Kerr on Injunctions* (6th edn. Sweet and Maxwell London 1927)

G Pipe, "Exemplary Damages After Camelford" (1994) 57 MLR 91

R Posner, *Economic Analysis of Law* (5th edn. Aspen New York 1998)

F Reynolds, *Bowstead & Reynolds on Agency* (Sweet and Maxwell London 1996)

C Rickett, "Equitable Compensation: The Giant Stirs" (1996) 112 LQR 27

W Rogers (ed.), *Winfield & Jolowicz on Tort* (15th edn. Sweet & Maxwell London 1998)

F Rose, "Interest" in P Birks and F Rose (eds) *Lessons of the Swaps Litigation* (LLP London 2000) 291

——, "Lapse of Time: Limitation" in P Birks and F Rose (eds) *Lessons of the Swaps Litigation* (LLP London 2000) 348

——, (ed.), *Consensus ad Idem, Esssays in Honour of Guenter Trietel* (Lloyds London 1996)

——, (ed.) *Failure of contracts : Contractual, Restitutionary and Proprietary consequences* (Hart Publishing Oxford 1997)

K Rusch, "Restitutionary Damages for Breach of Contract—A Comparative Analysis of English and German Law" (2001) 118 Sth African L J 59

J W Salmond, "Observations on Trover and Conversion" (1907) 21 LQR 43

L Sealy, "The Director as Trustee" [1967] CLJ 83

E Schrage (ed.), *Unjust Enrichment: The Comparative Legal History of the Law of Restitution* (2nd edn. Duncker & Humblot Berlin 1999)

P Shaffer, *Amadeus: A Drama* (S French New York 1981)

R Sharpe and S Waddams, "Damages for lost opportunity to bargain" (1982) 2 OJLS 290

L Sheridan, *Fraud in Equity* (Pitman and Sons London 1956)

L Smith, "Constructive Trusts and Constructive Trustees" [1999] CLJ 294

——, "Disgorgement of the Profits of Breach of Contract: Property, Contract and "Efficient Breach"" (1995) 24 Can Bus LJ 121

L Smith, "Restitution: The Heart of Corrective Justice" (2001) 79 Texas Law Rev 2115
——, *The Law of Tracing* (OUP Oxford 1997)
——, "The Province of the Law of Restitution" (1992) 71 CBR 672
——, "Unjust Enrichment, Property, and the Structure of Trusts" (2000) 116 LQR 412
——, "W(h)ither Knowing Receipt" (1998) 114 LQR 394
S Smith, "Concurrent Liability in Contract and Unjust Enrichment: The Fundamental Breach Requirement" (1999) 115 LQR 245
——, "Contacting under Pressure: A Theory of Duress" [1997] CLJ 343
H Stephen *A treatise on the principles of pleading in civil actions* (4th edn. Saunders and Benning London 1838)
J Stevens, "Election between Alternative Remedies" [1996] RLR 117
S Stoljar, "The Transformations of Account" (1964) 80 LQR 203
——, "Unjust Enrichment and Unjust Sacrifice" (1987) 50 MLR 603
E Stone, "Infants, Lunatics and Married Women: Equitable Protection in *Garcia* v. *National Australia Bank*" (1999) 62 MLR 604
H Street, *Principles of the Law of Damages* (Sweet and Maxwell London 1962)
J Swanton, "The Convergence of Tort and Contract" (1989) 12 Syd LR 40
W Swadling, "A Claim in Restitution" [1996] LMCLQ 63
——, "Property and Unjust Enrichment" J W Harris (ed.), *Property Problems: From Genes to Pension Funds* (Kluwer Law International London 1997) 130
——, "The Myth of *Phillips* v. *Homfray*" in W Swadling and G Jones (eds) *The Search for Principle: Essays in Honour of Lord Goff of Chieveley* (Oxford University Press Oxford 1999)
——, "What's in a Name" (2002) 65 MLR (forthcoming)
—— and G Jones (eds), *The Search for Principle—Essays in Honour of Lord Goff of Chieveley* (OUP Oxford 1999)
A Tettenborn, "Bribery, Corruption and Restitution—The Strange case of Mr Mahesan" (1979) 95 LQR 68
——, "Damages in Conversion-The Exception or the Anomaly" [1993] CLJ 128
——, "Misnomer—A Response to Professor Birks" in W Cornish et al. (eds) *Restitution: Past, Present & Future* (Hart Publishing Oxford 1998) 31.
G Treitel, *The Law of Contract* (10th edn. Sweet & Maxwell London 1999)
G Virgo, "Clarifying Restitution for Wrongs (*Attorney General* v. *Blake)*" [1998] RLR 118
——, *The Principles of the Law of Restitution* (Clarendon Press Oxford 1999)
S Waddams, *The Law of Damages* (3rd edn. Law Book Company Canada 1997)
——, "Breach of Contract and the Concept of Wrongdoing" (2000) 12 SCLR (2d) 1.
P Watts, "Property and Unjust Enrichment: Cognate Conservators" [1998] NZLR 151
——, "Restitutionary Damages for Trespass" (1996) 112 LQR 39
E Weinrib, "Information and Property" (1988) 38 UTLJ 117
——, "Restitutionary Damages as Corrective Justice" (2000) 1 Theoretical Inquiries in Law 1.
——, *The Idea of Private Law* (Harvard Univ Press Mass 1995)
G Williams, Mistake in the Law of Theft" (1977) CLJ 62
——, "The Aims of the Law of Tort" (1951) 4 CLP 137
——, "Theft, Consent and Illegality" [1977] Crim LR 127
P Winfield, *Province of the Law of Tort* (CUP Cambridge 1931)
——, *The Law of Quasi-Contracts* (Sweet and Maxwell London 1952)

S Worthington, *Proprietary Interests in Commercial Transactions* (Clarendon Press, Oxford 1996)

——, "Reconsidering Disgorgement for Wrongs" (1999) 62 MLR 218

—— and R Goode, "Commercial Law: Confining the Remedial Boundaries" in D Hayton (ed.) *Law's Future(s): British Legal Developments in the 21st Century* (Hart Publishing Oxford 2000)

D Wright, "The Statutory Trust, the Remedial Constructive Trust and Remedial Flexibility" (1999) 14 JCL 221.

——, *The Remedial Constructive Trust* (Butterworths Sydney 1998)

Lord Wright, "Sinclair v. Brougham" [1938] CLJ 305

——, "United Australia Ltd v. Barclays Bank Ltd" (1941) 57 LQR 184

T Youdan (ed.), *Equity, Fiduciaries and Trusts* (Carswell Toronto 1989)

K Zweigert & H Kötz, *Introduction to Comparative Law* (3rd edn. Clarendon Press Oxford 1998)

Index

account of profits, 72–73
  see also disgorgement damages
anti-harm wrongs, 129–30

bargaining:
  loss of opportunity, 99–102, 128
  and unjust enrichment and contract, 51–52
Beatson, J, 94
Birks, P, 37, 68, 69, 71, 78, 93, 107, 108, 130
Blake case, 149, 150–52, 178–81, 188–89
breach of confidence:
  and disgorgement damages, 213–15
  as equitable wrong, 204-06
  and restitutionary damages, 209–11
breach of contract:
  and *Blake* case, 149, 150–52, 178–81, 199–89
  and failure of consideration, 185–87
  cynical, 154–55, 158
  and disgorgement damages:
    legitimate interest in performance, 153–54,
      155–58, 162–64
    and remoteness of damages, 160–62
    test proposed, 152–53
  and expense saved, 176
  conflation and gain-based damages, 91–3
  measuring contractual rights to monetary
    benefits, 178
  measuring contractual rights to non-
    monetary benefits, 177–78
  and money had and received, 143
  and performance damages, 182–85
  and restitutionary damages, 174–75 187–88
    legitimate interest, 173–74
  and skimped performance, 176
  value transferred, measurement, 66–8, 70,
    177–78
  and wrongful transfer of contractual rights,
    172–74
breach of fiduciary duty:
  and disgorgement damages, 212
  dishonest participation, 201–02
    and disgorgement damages, 213
    and restitutionary damages, 209
  as equitable wrong, 191–93
  dishonest assistance, 198–200
  dishonest receipt of property, in, 200–01
  and restitutionary damages, 207–08
  see also breach of trust
breach of trust:
  as equitable wrong, 26–32, 191–93

dishonest assistance, 194–95
dishonest receipt of property, in, 195–98
  see also breach of fiduciary duty
bribery, 141–3, 206
  and disgorgement damages, 216
Burrows, A, 36, 107, 108

Cane, P, 78
Carter, J, 36
causation, 103–06
  in disgorgement damages, 104
  in restitutionary damages, 103–04
Chambers, R, 256
change of position defence, 96–97, 202
civil wrongs:
  common categories, 30–32
  and criminal wrongs, 32
  see also wrongs
coal, unlawful removal, 137–8
commercial uncertainty, and contract, 170–71
commissions, *see* secret commissions
compensatory damages, 5–6, 116
  and disgorgement damages, election
    between, 248
  and restitutationary dammages, election
    between, 249–50
  and equity, 27–29
  and exemplary damages, 7
  and loss of bargaining opportunity, 99–102,
    128–29
  and restitutionary damages for torts, 129
  where claimant would obtain less than
    market value, 101
  where claimant would obtain more than
    market value, 100
  where no bargain would have been made,
    101
compound interest:
  awards, 88–91
  and disgorgement damages, 136–37
confidence, breach of, *see* breach of confidence
consideration failure of, 185–87
contract:
  and commercial uncertainty, 170–71
  efficient breach of, 162–64
conversion:
  and disgorgement damages, 139–40
  and money had and received, 140–41
copyright infringement:
  and disgorgement damages, 234–46